D0435782

ALSO BY KATHLEEN BRADY

Ida Tarbell: Portrait of a Muckraker
Inside Out

LUCILLE

LUCILLE

The Life of Lucille Ball

Kathleen Brady

HYPERION

NEW YORK

Various photographs courtesy of Personality Photos, Inc., P.O. Box 50, Midwood Station, Brooklyn, N.Y. 11230.

MGM Collection still used by permission of Turner Entertainment Corporation.

Library of Congress Cataloging-in-Publication Data
Brady, Kathleen.
    Lucille: the life of Lucille Ball / by Kathleen Brady.
        p.   cm.
        Includes index.
        ISBN 0-7868-6007-3
        1. Ball, Lucille, 1911–1989. 2. Entertainers—United States—
Biography. I. Title.
PN2287.B16B63   1994
791.45′028′092—dc20
        [B]   94-13275
                                                                    CIP

Design By Gloria Adelson/Lulu Graphics

FIRST EDITION

10 9 8 7 6 5 4 3 2 1

For Larry, Debbie, Benjamin, and David Brady

Acknowledgments

Writing is supposed to be a solitary business, but when I look back on the effort of doing this book and consider all the people I met and all who helped me, I see that in this effort I was never alone. Rick Kot of Hyperion is in every way the editor all writers dream of having. Bob Miller, my publisher, was always available to me and a true supporter. My thanks also to Lauren Marino, David Cashion, Carol Smith, Victor Weaver, Gloria Adelson, Trent Duffy, Victoria Mathews, Angela Palmisono, and Debby Manette of Hyperion, who unfailingly moved this book forward.

Thanks also to my agent, Ginger Barber, and her staff—Alison Becker, Jennifer Rudolph Walsh, and Jimmy Vines.

I interviewed more than 150 people, including Lucille Ball herself. Most are mentioned in the text and notes, and their help made this book possible. Bart Andrews, a true Lucy scholar, was generous with his time and friendship. His having written *The "I Love Lucy" Book* would have been aid enough, but he offered insight, advice, and friendship, and I bless him for it. I wish to cite these others for particular help: the Biography Seminar at New York University, Kathy Aaronson, Patricia Bosworth, Dr. A. H. Brady, Hattie Caldwell, Cathy Cashman, Daphne Davis, Chuck Ferraro, Barbara Fowler, Sue Lane and Reece France, Louise J. Kaplan, Ronnie Kasorla, George and Louise McGann, Jerry Mayro, Tom Mohler, Donna Munker, Richard Natale, Stephen M. Silverman, Bob Thomas, Toni Vesotski, Mary Anne Walk, and Jane Wilson.

The role of librarians in preserving American history and culture is often overlooked. I thank them all, particularly Ned Comstock of the University of Southern California, Cinema-Television Library and Archives of Performing Arts, and Leith Adams of the Warner Brothers Collection there; Brigetta Kueppers of the University of California at Los Angeles Theater Arts Library; Lyn Olsson of Special Collections, San Diego State University; the staff of the Margaret Herrick Library of the Academy of Motion Picture Arts and Sciences, Beverly Hills; and the New York Public Library, particularly those in its Interlibrary Loan service and theater collection.

Also, Rosemary Harris of the Library of Congress, Motion Picture, Broadcasting and Recorded Sound Division; Alfreda Irwin of the Chautauqua Institution; and the staffs of the following institutions: U.S. Department of Justice, for sending me Federal Bureau of Investigation files, per the Freedom of Information Act; Franklin D. Roosevelt Library, Hyde Park, New York; Harry S. Truman Library, Independence, Missouri; Dwight D. Eisenhower Library, Abilene, Kansas; Ronald Reagan Library in Simi Valley, California; the American Film Institute, Los Angeles; Fenton Historical Society, Jamestown, New York; the Wisconsin Center for Film and Theater Research in Madison; the Screen Actors Guild; the Actors Guild and Actors Equity and Larry and John Gassman of SPERDVAC (Society to Preserve and Encourage Radio Drama, Variety and Comedy) in Los Angeles.

Introduction

In the years since she captured the American imagination, much has been written about Lucille Ball. While some accounts portray her life as a romp, others portray her as chronically miserable, tense, and unhappy. None of the many books devoted to her or to *I Love Lucy* has explained *who* she was, her contradictions and the source of her ambition.

At her peak, her comedic mastery seemed effortless, but in fact, in the films Lucille Ball made in the thirties and forties with The Three Stooges, The Marx Brothers, Edgar Bergen, and Harold Lloyd, she was wooden. She appears to have been no more aware than her co-stars of her natural gifts. How did so apparently ordinary a performer discover her great genius? How did she later remain so seemingly humble in the face of her hold on the American public? Lucille Ball is one of the greatest performing artists America has produced and probably the most familiar by virtue of the reach of television. Her work is on a par with that of Chaplin or Keaton, but because her shows are rerun every day—several times in some markets, and even more often on cable systems—her virtuosity may have become too accessible to achieve the mystique of art. Admittedly, she did not write and direct her own material as Chaplin and Keaton did, and although her greatest character, Lucy Ricardo, is a brilliant creation, she cannot be judged profound. While Chaplin's Little Tramp outwits his betters, and Keaton stoically bungles into success, both of these classic clowns remain poignant and heroic strugglers against life and fate.

Lucy Ricardo, in contrast, rebels the way most people rebel—without intending to abandon what is comfortable about her life. That she is doomed to fail in show business is not a thing of tragedy, for her talent lies in the realm of havoc and tricks. A blend of incompetence and cunning, she inspires laughter with her subversion of the conventional, and her exaggerated way with the commonplace. In sum, Lucy Ricardo defies the imperatives that mold lesser souls—reason and judgment, propriety and the prudent course—and proclaims that one dogged individual can prevail on her own illogical terms.

Biographers seldom have an opportunity to meet their subjects, but on the last day of June 1986, I met Lucille Ball. Had I never spent time with her, I doubt I could have understood what a puzzle she presented. Each of her changing moods had a force and intensity that she herself did not entirely command.

I went to see her on assignment for *Working Woman* magazine. When her maid answered the door in Beverly Hills, the theme of *I Love Lucy* was playing in the house, as if my ringing the bell had cued the waiting band. I sat expectantly on a green armchair in her citrus-colored den until I heard, "Kathleen! I'm late! Don't shake my hand, my nails are wet. Shake my elbow!" Wearing a pink jogging suit, she strutted in, elbow first. She was a few months shy of her seventy-fifth birthday, a fact she could not deny because for three decades her age was a published fact, but she tried to obscure the obvious signs of time by wearing large glasses tinted as blue as her eyes were supposed to be. She had dropped the curtain on the exaggerated expressions that delighted her audience, but still cultivated her trademark carrot-colored curls.

She had, she informed me, just been chatting on the phone with Desi Arnaz, her ex-husband for a quarter century, whom she continued to credit with 90 percent of her business success. She had done her hair and nails while watching *I Love Lucy*, which explained why I heard the theme. When the small talk was over, she seemed to brace herself for questions by putting her hands on her knees. Dealing with this Scheherazade of a thousand interviews proved to be exhausting, a matter of lugging her over subjects she didn't want to talk about, and then easing the tension with well-worn questions—was William Frawley really as irascible as Fred Mertz?

Topics I thought would upset her did not; comments I thought innocuous unnerved her. She grew belligerent when I observed that people said she was tough. By then, most powerful women had come to accept that quality as potentially positive, but not Lucille Ball. "Who says I'm tough? I want to know exactly who told you that! I want their names!" she demanded, and stood up to full height to glare at me. I mollified her by turning the conversation to Edward Sedgwick: "Thank you for mentioning the name of my great mentor," she said softly. "No one knows who he is anymore."

I asked about things a later generation of women thought they had invented—marrying younger men, giving birth for the first time at the age of thirty-nine, and running her own company. What had made her such a trailblazer? "Happenstance! Happenstance!" she shouted. "I was trying to do things like everyone else!" Her statements, I would later learn, were not entirely to be trusted. I asked if it was true that the gossip columnist Hedda Hopper had bequeathed her a Rolls-Royce. Eyes wide with what I thought was respect for my research, she confirmed that it was so. Years later, checking Hopper's will in the basement of the Los Angeles Courthouse, I learned that Lucille's husband Gary had purchased the car from Hopper's estate. Since my story was better than that fact, she certified it.

For all her fame, she was quite ordinary. Her den was no more remarkable than that of any middle class home except that it was larger and sunnier, and decorated with pictures of Lucille Ball. Her handbag, which rested on a straight-backed chair near the door, was shaped like a workman's lunch pail.

She snapped at me and laughed with me, then instructed me to turn off my tape recorder, at which time she counseled me on how to lighten my hair and decide on a husband. I was a stranger, but while she had me with her, she was determined to put my life on track.

Although the interview was scheduled for forty-five minutes, she let me stay two and a half hours, until it was time for her dental appointment. Later I realized she encouraged me to linger because she simply had not wanted to be left alone.

When I was a child, in the 1950s, I wanted to be Lucy Ricardo. I wanted to stun my family with extraordinary pranks and to experience the kind of improbable adventures that were everyday events for Lucy. When I was an adolescent, I wanted to be Lucille Ball. Like her, I wanted to be the master of extraordinary talents, to have total control of my life, to be able to rectify all my mistakes while having everyone honor and love me.

When I grew older, I knew there was more to her story than so apparently effortless a mastery of circumstance, that surely she had to work at life to make things turn out so well for herself. As a biographer, I intended to learn how much of what I thought I knew about her was true, and how much was the creation of her own showmanship.

LUCILLE

1

AROUND HER, people rocked with laughter. The skinny fourteen-year-old girl with chestnut hair and vibrant blue eyes was less aware of the performer in front of her than she was of the extreme effect he was having on the people in the theater. Her name was Lucille Ball and she sat motionless, no longer caught up like the others, but simply trying to figure out how the man was able to so delight them.

On a stage bare except for a single chair, a table, and a glass, Julius Tannen—tall, dour, and dressed in a business suit—stood in the stark spotlight and delivered a monologue that at first convulsed, then sobered, the people of Jamestown, New York. Firing off observations on matrimony, politics, and life in the mid-1920s, he delayed his punch lines just long enough for the sense of human folly to possess his audience.

Exactly what Tannen said that day she would never quite remember, but his usual routine was to become several characters, women as well as men, each speaking a different dialect and uttering a

3

different plaint. Although his humor did not survive vaudeville, in his day Tannen was considered brilliant and became known for such signature lines as "Pardon me for being late—I squeezed out too much toothpaste and couldn't get it back" and "I sent my collars out to the laundry to be sharpened." He also had the gift for ad-libbing in the demands of the moment. Once, in New York City, when a loud noise boomed from backstage and interrupted his monologue, he shouted "Sneak thieves!" Another time a theater's mouse catcher wandered out in the middle of his performance and Tannen hissed it away, saying "This is a monologue, not a *cat*alogue."

As he talked he drew together all the disparate types in the Jamestown audience—the president of the furniture company, the Swedish lathe turner, the Italian grape picker, and the straitlaced Protestant matron—and united them in a single wave of happiness. Lucille knew at once that she wanted to move people as this man did, to lift them from their daily concerns and transport them from tears to laughter and back again with just a strong voice and a deep belief in every action.

By the 1920s, Jamestown, in western New York State, was a manufacturing town that provided a bare living for Lucille's family. It was both a business hub and smoke-covered factory town with a population of 43,000 people and an air of bustle heightened by the clangor of its many red trolley cars. For a century the area's pine forests and the water power of the Chadakoin River had made it a center for furniture manufacturing, where immigrant cabinetmakers joined native-born workers to turn out tables and chests. Expansion into the production of metal furniture and mechanized voting booths provided an economic boost, but at the dawn of the flapper era, the town and its family-run businesses were losing out to the cheap labor and newer factories in the South.

Lucille came from a line of working people who had come to America in the middle of the seventeenth century. By the time of the Civil War, her Ball ancestors had worked their way west as far as the Great Lakes. Then, in 1865, her great-grandfather Clinton Ball was visited by luck. Oil was discovered near his property in Pithole, Pennsylvania. He quickly sold his farm for three quarters of a million dollars, abandoning the filthy, unpredictable business of rigs and derricks to gamblers and roustabouts. His prudence was canny, for the boomtown busted within the year. Clinton Ball took his Pithole windfall and bought four hundred acres of clay-rich soil in the "grape belt" along Lake Erie, where Dr. Thomas Branwell Welch founded America's concord grape juice industry. Along with his fellow wealthy growers, Clinton built a handsome house in nearby Fredonia, a beautiful, enterprising village that had been gas-lit as early as the 1820s, when natural gas was discovered there.

Perhaps to show his gratitude to the Lord, perhaps to keep true to the straight and narrow path that had led to earthly wealth, Clinton heaped donations on local Protestant churches, closely tested itinerant ministers on fine points of Scripture, and so fiercely disapproved of dancing that he forbade his children to skip a step to music.

But one of his sons rebelled. Lucille's grandfather, Jasper, known as Jap, the third of Clinton's six children, chafed against righteousness. He sold land he was supposed to pass down to his children and invested their heritage first in butter manufacture and then in the telephone. In the mid-1890s, like other entrepreneurs around the nation, Jap took advantage of the expiration of Alexander Graham Bell's patents and started his own telephone exchange in rural Busti, New York. This venture floundered, but he remained confident that he could make money in new technologies pioneered by Bell and Thomas Edison. After settling his wife and five children in Jamestown, Jap traveled to Missoula, Montana, where he became manager of the Securities Home Telephone Company.

His younger son, Henry Durrell Ball, nicknamed Had, followed him there and became an electrician for a telephone company. Had was slim to the point of gauntness with big blue eyes, physical traits his only daughter would inherit. Had's face was almost like a Plains Indian's, with a stoic expression that seemed ready to accept life's difficulties. He returned to Jamestown in early 1910 to see his mother and sisters, and there he fell in love. On September 1, 1910, at the age of twenty-four, Had married eighteen-year-old Desire Hunt, who had already softened the implications of her given name by changing it to Desirée. His new wife had narrow eyes that constantly assessed what she saw and a mouth that was firm but full, features that could be considered harsh or sensuous depending upon how she turned her face or where she stood in the light. Their wedding, with 140 guests presided over by a Baptist minister, was held at the home of the bride's parents and reported in detail on the local society page. Fred and Flora Hunt were a woodworker for a local furniture company and a midwife who had raised her orphaned siblings. A year earlier they had lost their only son, Harold, to tuberculosis. For their elder daughter they decorated their home in yellow and white and filled it with autumn sunflowers in what was perhaps a deliberate act of faith in the future.

The newlyweds headed to Montana, but returned to Jamestown eleven months later so that Flora could help deliver their first child. On Sunday, August 6, 1911, at five in the afternoon, Desirée gave birth to a daughter in her parents' two-story gabled home at what is now 60 Stewart Avenue. The couple apparently deliberated a few days before deciding to call her Lucille Desirée, because they did not include the name in the newspaper notice that ran a few days later, nor was it entered on the baby's birth certificate.

Lucille spent her first few years in Montana and in Wyandotte, Michigan, outside Detroit, where Had worked as a lineman with the Michigan Bell Company. She was lively, talkative, and fearless. When she was three and a half and Desirée was pregnant with a second child, Had was stricken with typhoid fever. So that she could nurse her husband while the child played outside, Desirée tied a rope around Lucille's waist and attached it to a metal runner on the wire clothesline. As long as she heard the metal riding along the wire, Desirée was confident of her system, but when the traveling gadget fell silent she ran anxiously downstairs only to find her daughter outside talking the milkman into setting her free. "Mister, help me. I got caught up in this silly clothesline. Can you help me out?" Lucille was asking. Exasperation surely battled amusement in her heart, but over the years Desirée would recount the story as an example of her daughter's precocity.

Had died of his illness and Lucille was left without a single recollection of what he was like, or how he lifted her up, or whether he had played with her at all. With his absence he left a psychic impression of loss so indelible that Lucille came to register February 28, 1915, the date of her father's death, as her first memory: "I do remember everything that happened . . . hanging out the window, begging to play with the kids next door who had measles . . . the doctor coming, my mother weeping. I remember a bird that flew in the window, a picture that fell off the wall." That bird became a haunting reminder of loss so deep that the sight of bird motifs forever after caused her to panic in anger. Psychologists call such a fetish a "screen memory," an image to hold in place of one that is far worse, such as the death throes of her father and the grief of her mother. Lucille's antipathy to birds remained so vehement that decades later stagehands on the *I Love Lucy* show learned never to place porcelain parrots on the set, and her favorite florist in Beverly Hills, having suffered her outrage over finding a tiny artificial robin lurking in her bouquet, instructed his staff never again to garnish any of her floral arrangements in such fashion.

While Desirée and her brother-in-law made arrangements to ship Had's body to Jamestown, a grocer named Mr. Flower took little Lucille to his store and sat her on its counter with an empty jar. Sympathetic neighbors filled it with coins as she recited nursery rhymes and told the story of a frog that went "harrummph" as it jumped up and down. "Although she didn't know what she was doing at that age, I guess you could say it was the first money she ever earned acting," Desirée later said.

At the beginning of March, when the winter landscape of western New York is at its bleakest, Desirée took Had's body home. She moved in with her parents and eighteen-year-old sister, Lola; then, a month before Lucille's fourth birthday, she gave birth to a son, whom she named Fred after her father.

Aside from a few cousins, Lucille and her brother had little contact with the Ball family. According to family legend, Jap Ball, whose business ventures failed, rustled cattle for a time. If so, he carried the gene for the bold and dramatic and passed it down for better and greater manifestation in his celebrated granddaughter. However, his only probable influence on her life was as a legend of squandered resources and neglected obligations.

Desirée took a job in a factory after America entered World War I in April 1917, and there she met Ed Peterson, a tall, strapping man with a mobile face and eyebrows that punctuated his forehead with quick dashes. Ed, whom Lucille later described as "ugly/handsome," was, like many of the townspeople, a second-generation American, the son of Swedish immigrants. At thirty-one, Ed was devoted to enjoyment, and in light of the sorrows of her own past, his ebullience appealed to Desirée. She married him on September 17, 1918, in Jamestown, when she was twenty-six, after three years of widowhood. She joked that she wed him because he wore nice hats.

Although Lucille and Fred, now seven and three, were delighted to have a father, by all accounts Ed did not like children and refused to let them call him "Daddy." Soon after the wedding he took Desirée to Detroit, where he had a job that was supposed to last six months. Desirée entrusted Lucille, now in first grade, to Ed's parents and left Fred with her own.

The fatherless Lucille now had for her temporary mother a punitive figure worthy of a Grimm's fairy tale. Sophia Peterson was stern and forbidding with the long winter of Sweden in her soul, and such was her shadow that it seemed to subsume her husband. At the age of sixty, intending that Lucille become a God-fearing woman without conceit, "Grandma" ridiculed the way the child looked, spoke, and walked. With her long legs, oversized feet, crooked teeth, and high shrill voice, Lucille was easy to mock. Grandma Peterson saw fit to put her in dresses long enough for her to grow into and shoes so hard they squeaked. She parted Lucille's mousy brown hair in dead center and pulled it back so tightly that the girl had a look of perpetual shock. As mirrors encouraged vanity, Sophia banned them, except for one in the bathroom, where once she found Lucille staring at her face. Punished for her self-importance, the girl nevertheless found a way to study her face and the range of her various expressions. In the reflecting windows of the trolley car that carried her to her Hunt grandparents, she widened her eyes and moved her mouth to see the effect, exaggerate, and judge it.

This sad, inventive child created the imaginary friend Sassafrassa with whom to share secrets and phantom adventures. Sassafrassa made her existence known to Grandma Peterson the day she walked in and found Lucille wide-eyed with arms flailing as she talked to an apparently empty chair.

Grandma assigned a schedule of chores, which ranged from Lucille's least favorites, rolling the edges of linen towels for stitching and darning heavy hosiery, on to her favorite, crocheting. Nightly she stood on a box at the kitchen sink and washed dishes by the light of a little gas jet so dim that her work was sloppy and often needed to be redone.

Money was so scarce that Lucille did not have a pencil in school, a shame so searing that even in her forties she continued to hoard pencils that were meant for her employees to use. When an executive asked her where they were going, she took him to her closet and opened the door, revealing a cache of unopened packages. "If when you were a little boy you didn't have a pencil in school, the way I didn't, you would understand," she said, and surrendered them only after he convinced her that she owned all the company's pencils, no matter who used them, and that she was stealing only from herself.

On Lucille's ninth birthday, when she was getting ready to visit the Hunts for the day, Grandma Peterson, who regarded any pleasure as "devil's bait," warned her to prepare for a surprise party and thus turned what should have been a treat into an obligation. "I made crazy faces all the way to the party, trying to think of ways to look surprised," Lucille said.

The energy and activity of her mother's family seemed blessed, and she longed for its warmth. Fred and Flora Hunt's house was crowded with people, which is probably why Lucille, the elder, was farmed out and only her brother allowed to stay there. Lola, who had married a handsome Greek immigrant named George Mandicos, had returned home to give birth to her daughter, Cleo. Lucille was told she should be grateful to Grandma Peterson, and she truly was, counterbalancing any harsh memories by acknowledging ways she had benefited under her rule: Her grades had been above average, she had been made self-reliant, and she learned to live in her imagination while outwardly doing what she was told. However she may have missed her mother and her true grandparents, Lucille clung to the one thing she admired in the woman who raised her from her eighth to her twelfth years. Behind her narrow little house, Grandma cultivated a flower garden with daisies, lilies, and daffodils, and her rich green grass was comforting to bare feet that even in summer had to pad indoors at sundown while other children played outside.

Lucille responded to a love that meant well and to the older woman's attention, for it was all she knew. Implacable as Grandma Peterson may have been, she was the one who sent her off to school with a lunch bag and felt her clammy forehead when she was sick. Grandma Peterson was a presence in the child's life when her parents were a distant memory. To Lucille, Grandpa Peterson was a shadow without voice or substance who demonstrated no affection until he broke down and wept the day Desirée finally came to take her back for good.

Lucille left the Petersons unable to ever bear to be alone. To her privacy was never a joy, for her solitude had been abject. She lacked a sense that a loving person waited beyond a closed door or kept her in mind when she was out of sight. Her need for companionship was desperate and only in her childhood was she able to mask that fact. Over the course of her life she reenacted the harsh treatment she had received in dramas of fire and flood that those who experienced never forgot. Fiercely she would scold friends as to how they should behave or how they should live, and then after her hot outburst she would dissolve into helpless tears.

When Desirée returned from Detroit with Ed in mid-1922, she took Lucille to Celeron, a village ten minutes from Jamestown on the trolley line, a spot so unprepossessing that vaudevillians who played Jamestown learned that just mentioning the place guaranteed a laugh. Fred and Flora Hunt had bought a house there because it was a less expensive place in which to meet expanding responsibilities for their tribe. Flora, who was in her midfifties, was suffering from cancer of the uterus, and it was the failure of her costly medical treatments in Buffalo that brought Desirée home to take care of her mother and to reunite her young children. The Celeron house still accommodated Lola, who had separated from her husband, and her tiny daughter Cleo, who called Desirée "DeDe," the name she finally liked and that she used forever afterward.

Lucille came "home" to a family strained and in shock. Whatever relief she may have felt at being back with her own blood was frustrated by the illness of Flora Hunt, who died shortly after the girl reached Celeron. Yet Lucille would remember that house on Eighth

Street (later renamed Lucy Lane) as Eden, her Oz, her place of perfect childhood.

It was a boxy two-story white dwelling with a small front porch surrounded by lilac bushes whose heady fragrance would forever return Lucille in memory to this place. Inside the front door, just past the foyer, was a staircase where Lucille performed songs and dances for whoever took the time to watch. This makeshift stage looked into the living room, closed off by a curtain that was by turns Lucille's prop or the means of privacy for those who were ailing. There was also a downstairs bedroom and a dining room where the family congregated, a kitchen with a huge iron sink, and a half bath. Upstairs were the full bathroom and the bedrooms, including Lucille's, which to her delight gave her a view of the chickens in their yard.

Her grandfather Fred Hunt was the presiding spirit of the establishment, wielding a pipe of Prince Albert tobacco and wearing an old cardigan sweater and a wide-brimmed hat at a tilt. In his prime he had the full fleshy look of a salesman sure to meet his quotas, but as the years passed his features wrinkled and sagged, as if time were depriving his face of hope. He sang naughty songs at the piano and liked to exasperate his wife by claiming the first Hunt in America was a horse thief. Actually, that man was Thomas Hunt, an indentured servant to the governor of the Colony of New Haven when he arrived in 1639. Four years later Hunt and his wife were banished to Stamford for befriending, particularly on the Sabbath, a "lewd and disorderly" person. Whether Fred Hunt knew the truth about his distant ancestor or not, he certainly was aware that his grandfather Elvin Hunt, one of the area's early settlers, had been renowned as "an excellent worker in wood, having great natural mechanical genius. So great was the reputation of Hunt's goods that they always commanded the highest prices," according to a local history.

Fred himself was a woodworker, a craftsman who wanted to be his own boss but was snared in the Machine Age and relegated to performing mechanical tasks at a succession of local furniture factories. Fred was a union man and, to the probable annoyance of his bosses, an ardent proponent of the ideas of the Socialist leader Eugene V. Debs.

Fred's authority was not questioned by Ed Peterson, who did not either feel the need or see the opportunity to be head of his own household. He did not interfere in the running of family affairs, nor was he willing to help DeDe's children. Himself raised by Sophia Peterson's principles, he had a passivity Lucille could never acquire, even when she attempted to. "My stepfather was a dud. He did no damage, no good," Fred Ball said.

His outlet, according to neighbors, was drink. "Lucille's stepfather made good money. Weekends he overindulged. Her mother was happy to have a husband and although she had a strict upbringing, she became loud and joined in imbibing with Ed," said Pauline Lopus, who lived next door.

Of necessity and by inclination, the Hunt household was a hard-working one. At least part of the time Fred ran a grocery and studied chiropractic. Lucille's aunt Lola, with her niece often underfoot and wanting her hair done, operated a beauty shop in part of the house. DeDe was a saleswoman at a Jamestown dress shop, and Ed worked in local factories.

The children also had their tasks. Cleo dusted, Freddie made the beds, and all three took turns doing dishes and setting the table. As the oldest, Lucille was in charge when the adults were away, and she started the children at their whole day's tasks only in early evening when they heard the bell of DeDe's trolley as it reached Celeron. "Domesticity was not Lucy's thing. You didn't find her beating up a cake in the kitchen," Cleo recalled.

To Grandpa the children were Lucyball, Fritzi Boy, and Cleo Baby. Despite a difference in their ages—when Lucille was twelve, Fred and Cleo were eight and four—they formed so tight a bond that Lucille and Fred called Cleo their sister. The trio was often on its own, a situation that intrigued their friends and scandalized the neighbors. "We were taught from the beginning to take care of ourselves. That was probably the attribute that caused Lucille to be successful," said Fred. They also had to stand up for themselves among themselves. "The most important thing I learned from the family was to put problems on the table, right up front. The idea was: Don't harbor. If you've got a comment, complaint, criticism, put it on the table. I can't remember when we ever had an extensive argument. Discussions, yes, but no catastrophic differences of opinion."

The Hunt-Ball-Peterson-Mandicos family life was like a topsy-turvy doll: rich and beautiful if you looked at it one way, as they themselves saw it all their lives; or rough and neglectful if like some acquaintances you stood it on its head. A hardy independence was called for, and although Lucille was strong enough to thrive under this regimen, she also perceived its severity. A neighboring family of nine whose business was training seals and police dogs made her wistful: "I had a crush on the whole Strassel family. They were beautiful in the way they looked and the way they lived. Togetherness described their life."

Lucille developed a personality shared by many who have had a traumatic childhood: a need to be in control, a sense of responsibility for others (particularly DeDe), and an inability to relax. She was also profoundly claustrophobic, a condition that has been associated with a longing for the mother. She would not submit to her own hurt feelings, whether they were over her father's death or the cruelty of Grandma Peterson, but she could hardly bear it when, however mistakenly, she saw another's need. "She had almost a fetish to help people and tell them what to do. When a train derailed, Lucille ran over with two pails of water because she thought that a tramp might be caught in the wreck and would need water. Most kids stare at a blind man. Lucille would try to help him, probably more than he wished," Pauline said. Above all, Lucille savored attention. "If someone was interested in her, she clung to them."

The Hunt house was a skipping stone from Lake Chautauqua, surrounded by pastures and animals, a street away from Celeron Park, whose midway and Ferris wheel came to life in summer and turned the small town into a magnet for the whole area.

People from as far away as Pittsburgh came to ride the Phoenix Wheel that was some four stories high, to skip along with Sousa's marching band and applaud bears, seals, dancers, actors, and jokers who stretched themselves into bizarre shapes for strangers who loved them in those moments when they made them laugh. The appeal of Celeron Park was to appetite and aspiration, something like the rush of falling in love. Visitors came by steamer across the lake or by a double-deck trolley that ended on the dock. They alighted to the *pop-pop* of air guns on the midway and the screams of people dipping and reeling on the roller coaster. The aroma of hot popcorn and frying treats tempted those parading past the theater with its mock Palladian portico and pilasters painted to look like stone. So festive was the place in summer that Celeron picnics with sack races and tables heaped with ham, potato salad, and watermelon would be the model for Desilu company picnics and even for Lucille's own memorial gathering.

"When Lucille arrived in Celeron, things began to bustle," Pauline recalled. The girls played dress-up in their mothers' old clothes, which they stored in DeDe's bottom drawer, and attended movies that were shown for free in Celeron Park. A projection booth set high up on a pole in the middle of the park played one-reelers and advertising slides even during rainstorms while concession booths stayed open in hopes of business. Since the picture was shown against a building wall, the projectionist learned to pull the lamp back to get the sharpest possible image at the center while the edges blurred into haze. Lucille and Pauline saw Charles Chaplin and Buster Keaton, as well as Pearl White in *The Perils of Pauline*, but their favorites were the Western adventures *Riders of the Purple Sage* and *Under the Light of Western Stars*, which they reenacted on broomstick horses for weeks afterward. Knowing she had once lived out West may have heightened Lucille's enthusiasm, but both girls were so caught up in these tales that they looked into DeDe's copies of the Zane Grey novels, which had inspired them, and felt betrayed when they realized that Hollywood had substituted automobiles for the more authentic buckboards.

Unlike Lucille's family, Pauline's parents had a car, and Lucille was thrilled when they took the girls to the nearby Seneca Indian reservation and bought sassafras bark, which seemed a sign from her old imaginary friend. Lucille began calling Pauline Sassafrassa, and if Pauline didn't sign her notes that way when she passed them in class, Lucille asked if she was angry with her.

Lucille involved the well-behaved Pauline in her stunts. The day Pauline wore a new black store-bought dress with a scarf tied down in front to school, Lucille sent her a note saying she wanted to try it on, and asked to meet her in the basement lavatory. In the girls' room, Lucille slipped out of the cream-colored smock and aqua dress DeDe had made her and donned Pauline's, which was tight because Lucille was taller and broader. After admiring herself before the mirror, Lucille walked upstairs, leaving Pauline with no choice but to put on Lucille's clothes and follow her. Their classmates snickered as they caught on, but the teacher was mystified as to what had happened.

As a student, Lucille was good but erratic. She was alert and absorbed information, but did not bother to study now that she was no longer under Grandma Peterson's sway. The one person who could make her obey was her elementary school teacher Lillian Appleby, who was old enough to have a daughter in college. Pauline, who later became a teacher and guidance counselor herself, said, "When Mrs. Appleby would say, 'Lucille, don't do that,' she stopped whatever it was. Lucille wanted more discipline than she had at home. She needed someone to clamp her down and give her security." The truth of that statement was underscored by Lucille's own enthusiastic description of Mrs. Appleby, given when Lucille was in her sixties: "She was wonderful. She used to slap our hands." The year of her death, Lucille reminisced, "Lillian Appleby was like a second mother to me and she worried about what I was doing at home as well as in school."

In that era, when radio was just aborning, and people learned only from the printed page, Mrs. Appleby introduced a few mispronunciations into her geography classes, including "Yose-mite" Valley. When Lucille moved to California in her twenties, she corrected a person who pronounced the word "Yo-se-mi-te" and was persuaded that Mrs. Appleby erred only after checking with half a dozen people.

Her craving for attention found a natural outlet in performing. As an angel in a school play, Lucille flapped her arms to move her wings and kicked the cherub in front of her, who was shy about going on stage. "Lucille said, 'Get going!' and pushed me out," said her classmate Cecilia Ditonto Welch. Later she faked the songs in school operettas and stole the show because she was comical and moved her mouth with great expression. "She didn't know how funny she was and she didn't always mean to be," said Ernestine Young Klomp, who played piano for the musicals.

Lucille chose Cecilia to be her wardrobe mistress at recess when, having brought a bundle of clothes from home, she announced, "I'll perform today. Everybody come watch me!" She made up her own act, arranged her clothes on a bush, and went behind it to change with Cecilia's help. Wearing a big hat with a huge rose on the side, she would dance, tell jokes, and sing. Lucille did not have much of a voice, but had some familiarity with an e-flat alto saxophone and the piano. Friends describe her keyboard chords as questionable. Her piano teacher insisted she learn "To a Wild Rose," but because Lucille did not think the tune would entertain anyone, she didn't bother to practice it.

Pauline remembered them performing to music on a boat on Lake Chautauqua while other children gathered around. "The kids asked 'How did you learn that?' Lucille simply said, 'We're actresses.' "

She was self-assured and fearless in stating what she wanted. When she was twelve Lucille found a job at George Barker's concession stand selling hamburgers and hot dogs. Her sales pitch was simple and effective. When potential customers came toward her, she fixed her gaze on them and yelled "Stop!"

When she saw a neighbor's bicycle, which her family could not afford, she immediately asked to borrow it, and at her grandfather's company picnic, she marched up to the harpist in the band and inquired, "When you die, will you leave that to me?" If asking failed, she improvised a substitute. Wanting makeup, she and Pauline dipped crepe paper in water and rubbed the color on their cheeks, then used burnt matches to darken their eyebrows.

Approaching adolescence, Lucille wanted to improve her bright blue eyes by darkening her light lashes, coloring her wide mouth with lipstick, and experimenting with the part of her straight brown hair. She was thin, and during those rare moments when her face was in repose, she had the serious stoic look of her lost father.

Inevitably she became interested in boys. The first sign was that she stooped down to be as short as the ones she liked, but she soon abandoned subtlety and wrote Cecilia's brother a note declaring "I love you so much."

"My mother found it and told him, 'I'll go after you with a broomstick and if I don't catch you, I'll catch her!' " Cecilia said. Lucille moved on to others, most of whom "liked" her in the way of adolescents because she was fun and happy-go-lucky.

During her freshman year of high school in Celeron she organized the Dramatics Club, composed of herself, Pauline, and Alice and Katharine Osbourne. The teachers told her they were too busy to supervise a new school organization, but Lucille persuaded the principal to approve it after she promised they would practice only after school and would donate the admission price they charged to their productions to the freshman class.

She wrote a play, closely following the lines of the popular story of mistaken identity and pranks *Charley's Aunt*, casting herself as the hero, and, of course, directed it. "Lucille would get cross if we didn't know our lines, but she would be so busy helping us she wouldn't know her own, so she'd ad-lib. I scowled through our entire performance because I was worrying about what she would say next," Pauline recalled. DeDe, perhaps to make up for her earlier absence, had involved herself at Lucille's school. She was then president of the PTA and was given a copy of the script so she could prompt them quietly, but she laughed so hard that everybody could hear her and follow her cues.

DeDe was a woman of great zest who did not so much juggle the rival claims of husband, children, and job as step up to bat and swing at every pitch. By day she worked in the Marcus Dress Shop, Jamestown's toniest store, which offered her the chance and obligation to look her best and be apprised of current fashion. At night DeDe took her father to task for instigating union activity and warned him he would be fired, then dealt with her children and her husband, who by all accounts continued to resent the needs of youngsters who were not his own. The same year she was president of the PTA she was active in the Home Bureau, a woman's organization that sponsored activities for children. Ed made her quit.

"Lucille's mother was a nice woman who wanted fun," said Lucille's friend Irene DeVita Roselli. "When the Marcuses came to town, they'd have terrific parties in speakeasies. Lots of people figured Lucille wasn't brought up properly, but her grandfather shut them up."

DeDe heeded the counsel of her heart at the expense of propriety.

To her niece Cleo she was a special and natural pal. "I got along better with her than with my mother because she was less strict," Cleo recalled. "She was the one I ran to. I could always cry on her shoulder if I felt I had been unfairly treated."

DeDe was as indulgent as she could afford to be. When Lucille coveted a black-and-white leather hat she saw at Marcus Dress Shop, she begged DeDe for it, promising to do extra chores if only she could have that hat. "Finally she got it," said Pauline. "One day I went over to her house and she was washing dishes wearing it. Years later when a friend and I watched the 'I Love Lucy' episode where Lucy slept in her new mink coat, my friend said, 'That's silly. Who would do that?' I said 'Lucille would.'"

Inevitably, Lucille's love of attention and drama nettled her mother. Breaking into vaudeville in New York City seemed imperative, and on more than one occasion Lucille took little Cleo's hand in hers and walked down the road in the general direction of Broadway until they were apprehended by exasperated relatives. Once DeDe cut short one of her daughter's trips by packing her a lunch and placing it with an umbrella on the front porch. "I think you'll need this," she wrote on a note. Lucille took to her bed in a huff.

She arrived late and in tears at the Osbourne house the day the sisters invited some classmates to their home to play the game Cootie. They now called Lucille "Bobby," for when she was around thirteen she was the first to cut her hair in the new and daring "boy bob." When she finally arrived at the party, she was holding a bandaged hand and whimpering. "You know how Ed puts his razor on top of the Hoosier cabinet instead of taking it up to the bathroom?" she asked her sympathetic friends. "Well, just what my mother said would happen finally did. After I washed the dishes I shut the door, and the razor came down and cut my face and hand."

They fussed over her, patted her shoulder, and brought her lemonade. When Lucille began picking at the bandage, Pauline protested, but Lucille kept playing with it and finally ripped it away, revealing no cut. She had made the whole thing up and delivered her first believable performance of a household misadventure.

2

LUCILLE'S BOLDNESS and her insistence on being noticed tried people's patience when she was a child, but as she grew into her teens and discovered men, neighbors found a new word for Lucille. She was wild.

She and her girlfriends adored the school principal, Bernard Drake. When he and the coach led the class on a five-mile hike, Lucille and Pauline Lopus went ahead with the two men in the rain to set up a cookout at their destination, an old house on Lake Chautauqua. The four were drenched by the time they arrived. As Drake built the fire, he told the girls to go upstairs where they would find old clothes to change into while their sweaters dried. Lucille put on a moth-eaten bathing suit that dated from the Cleveland administration, stuffed it with crepe paper, and clowned for the class while Pauline served hot dogs in an Indian blanket bathrobe. The class left at three in the afternoon, and by the time Pauline reached home, her mother was demanding an explanation of what had gone on in that house. "She had a phone call saying we were at a wild party and Lucille was going

19

around naked," Pauline said. "The next thing I knew, Lucille came over to ask if my mom had had a phone call because hers had. My mother trusted me, but she didn't trust Lucille. That party was like the Baron Munchausen show on the radio. His line was 'Vas you there, Charlie?' That's what I thought of whenever I heard that party mentioned. Everybody knew about it, but they weren't there. We finally figured out that the story started with a sickly fellow who had a crush on Lucille and was jealous over her."

People thought they had a pretty good idea of what Lucille was up to. She was a girl with a reputation not only because she bobbed her hair, but because in 1925, at the age of fourteen, she had started to go around with a local hoodlum named Johnny DeVita, who was twenty-one. As he was the most lawless boy in the area and she was at his side, she quickly became known as the wildest girl.

The Romantic Hero is both myth and point of view. Scornful and rebellious, and thus fundamentally antisocial, his archetype is Byron and in various times his standard-bearer has been Valentino, James Dean, and Elvis Presley. For Lucille Ball on the shores of Lake Chautauqua in the 1920s, this champion was Johnny DeVita, dark, husky, mustachioed but short, with a hairline even less dependable than he was himself. As Pauline recalled, "He wasn't well educated and he lacked finesse. He tried to make up for it all by dressing well. Lucille gloried in being seen with him, and his family thought she was wonderful.

"People envied him because he got away with so much. He wasn't a gangster. The police may not have thought he was as important as he thought himself." Johnny was, however, a gambler. Living as he did relatively close to the Canadian border during Prohibition, he engaged in rum-running as well, although it was several years before his arrest in Buffalo for possessing and transporting bootleg whiskey and carrying a gun without a permit. Lucille and Johnny met at Celeron Park, where his sisters introduced them, according to his sister Irene, who had first played basketball with her and had a standing invitation to change into her bathing suit at Lucille's house before going to the lake. "Lucille and Johnny were crazy about each other. He was so proud of her because she was so beautiful," Irene said. Lucille made a special pet of their sister Florence, who was about twelve. Far from shunning a younger child, she paraded her everywhere and even entered her in a children's beauty contest, which Florence won. Perpetual big sister and organizer of others, Lucille no longer had many friends her own age. The inner storms and surges of adolescence lift up childhood attachments and set them down in new places, often hopelessly askew. After she started going around with Johnny, Pauline faded from her life. "My folks clamped down on my being with her," Pauline explained. "Older people didn't understand. They imagined the things she did were worse than they were." Irene acknowledged, "My brother being her friend made it difficult for her."

Lucille relished driving around the lake in Johnny's car and sometimes rode on the hood to show off. He brought her home to meet his mother in Jamestown. "Lucille was always in and out of our house," Irene said. "She came in like a bolt from the sky crying 'Mom, I'm here!' She'd be a tornado and rush past us. 'Where's Ma?' Once she found her, Lucille would say hello to the rest of us." If Lucille loved John's mother, Anna, who by all accounts liked and enjoyed the girl's enthusiasm and exaggerated stories, in Johnny she found something of a father figure. At twenty-one, he was very much the older man who was able to look out for a fourteen-year-old. Johnny's own father, Louis, had emigrated from Italy before the turn of the century and made a prosperous living through insurance and Italian produce businesses. He employed John as a driver and was rumored to use him in less legal business interests as well. But Louis was generous to those who needed help. According to Irene, when Lucille came to visit the DeVitas he would not let her go home until she had taken vegetables and pasta for her family.

Johnny took Lucille to movies and to live performances in Jamestown. Irene's boyfriend and future husband Frank Roselli recalled, "Lucille used to love to go to the five acts of vaudeville at Shea's and the Palace." The shows opened with acrobats or a musician, a wire walker or cyclist, always followed by a "dumb" act without dialogue that could not be disrupted by latecomers shuffling into their seats. Then, while the audience was still settling down, a song-and-dance team or a singer performed in front of the curtain while the next scene was set up backstage. This was a "sketch" or "flash act"—such as performing women ("14 English Daisies—24 Dancing Legs" read one curious bill, which seemed to leave the dancing daisies four legs short)—that was followed by a juggler or dancer to keep up momentum. All this preceded a headliner known to the audience. Ralph Bellamy, Fifi D'Orsay, and Dolly Dawn are among the acts Lucille's contemporaries remembered having seen in Jamestown during this period.

Sitting in the audience, Lucille longed to get up on stage herself, and her supporters believed that was where she belonged. Some of her teachers, including the adored principal Mr. Drake, thought Lucille was so gifted an actress that she should have professional training. The Robert Minton–John Murray Anderson School of Drama in Manhattan was famous for nurturing young talent, and it was there that Lucille wanted to go.

Around the time she turned fifteen, and possibly because her family thought she should get away from Johnny, Lucille was granted her wish to leave home for drama school. Although the school was expensive, DeDe found the money to pay the first part of the tuition and to board Lucille with friends in New York City. Given the strains on family finances at the time, Johnny may have helped to give Lucille her big chance.

Many neighbors were appalled that the girl was being sent away to take up so dubious a career. "It was shocking to the neighbors, no doubt about that," said Cleo. "DeDe was greatly criticized. The general idea was Don't Let Your Daughter Go on Stage, but DeDe understood that Lucy was a determined, willful teenager. Nothing would have stopped her. If DeDe hadn't sent her, she would have run away." Lucille's friends believe it was too late for DeDe to turn into a disciplinarian.

In the autumn of 1926, making what would prove to be a false start on her ultimate path, Lucille Ball departed Jamestown with $50 sewn into her underwear. At the Minton-Anderson School she watched other girls audition as the "high-hat" Juliet, possibly reciting Shakespeare's balcony scene. Lucille, in contrast, won admittance by delivering one of Julius Tannen's tart monologues.

Robert Minton and John Murray Anderson were well-regarded professionals. Minton was frequently called America's preeminent stage director, having done *He Who Gets Slapped, Outward Bound,* and *The Dark Angel* on Broadway. Anderson was a leading producer who originated *The Greenwich Village Follies* and Irving Berlin's *Music Box Review.* They had attracted a board of advisers for their drama school that included Otis Skinner, Jerome Kern, and Efrem Zimbalist.

The building itself was in a four-story Italianate structure on East Fifty-eighth Street between Park and Lexington avenues. Through its open-work iron gate Lucille entered the world of "thay-ah-ter." Frightened and homesick but eager to learn the arts of performing, she was suitably hushed by the gleaming parquet floors and stately antique wing chairs arranged as if on a stage. The Minton-Anderson catalog for 1927–28 described its program as "a modern school for the training and development of such pupils as show evidence of real talent and who are willing to apply themselves seriously." It advised that the administration might drop a student at any time and return the fee, which was $350 dollars for a five-month term. Courses were ten hours a week of technical work with equal time for diction and voice, dramatic interpretation, fencing, and makeup. That year Character and Interpretative Dance were taught by Martha Graham, a struggling choreographer at the beginning of her own distinguished career.

The star student of the Robert Minton–John Murray Anderson School of Drama was a young New Englander named Bette Davis, then eighteen, a remote presence intimidating to Lucille. According to Davis's memoirs, beginning pupils were informed every morning that they were embarking on the toughest, least glamorous life possible and one that offered them only sweat, jealousy, competition, disillusionment, and insecurity. One by one all but true thespians dedicated to their art fell from the ranks. Davis, who started in a group of seventy and ended in a class of twelve, recalled making a two-reeler movie the season she was there and acting in a play a week. "We were constantly at work, rehearsing and memorizing while we forged ahead in our studies."

The overwhelmed girl from Jamestown faltered rather than forged. Lucille suffered through a vocal drill designed to warm her sharp voice and alter the broad vowels of western New York, which rendered "water" as "worter" and "horses" as "hasses." She was too unnerved to crank up her courage or twist her face into the features that usually guaranteed a supportive laugh. "The more I was put down, the more I shrank. I don't improve under that kind of tutelage. The more embarrassed I get, the quieter I get," she recalled. After television made her America's foremost performer, Lucille mocked the training and her trauma, claiming instructors taught her the live-and-suffer method and useless techniques for turning herself into spaghetti by relaxing into a boneless heap and slithering fluidly from her chair onto the floor.

Lucille's brief career at this institution is the familiar story of the brightest girl in Smalltown, U.S.A., coming to the big city and encountering peers from Everywhere Else. In Celeron she had created opportunities to perform and display her talents, while in New York, where she had an opportunity to perform, she was too terrified to speak, a failure that she laid at the Dickensian door of Grandma Peterson.

Intimidated, Lucille could not find a source within herself from which to draw courage. She was lonely and distracted by thoughts of home, for she missed her mother terribly. By nature she was as eager as quick sparks, but she had yet to learn to tend the slow and steady burn of determination. Criticism, even when it was meant to be constructive, diminished her. She envied the self-confidence of Bette Davis. She may have been in the audience the night Davis appeared in an examination play and won the scholarship for six months' free tuition, only to turn it down a week later because she was offered a real professional engagement. Davis's final assessment of the program was: "I knew at least the rudiments of my chosen profession . . . I had acquired at least a kind of technical security on stage—impossible without any training." In contrast, Lucille Ball claimed, "All I learned in drama school was how to be frightened." John Murray Anderson wrote DeDe that she was wasting her money. Abashed but relieved, after about a month in New York Lucille went back home.

Saying little to her friends about the experience, she just resumed high school life. Immersion in the theater must have had some effect, however, because once back in Jamestown Lucille began writing poetry—June-moon verse that she said she played with for the sake of the rhyme, a foreshadowing of the love of word games that obsessed her in her late years.

By the summer Lucille turned sixteen she had graduated from red crepe paper dye to real rouge. The manager of Celeron Park asked Lucille to do the makeup when Norma Smallwood, Miss America of 1927, made an appearance there. Lucille had no thought of entering the beauty contest herself because she thought she was too skinny.

That summer was a tragic, horrible period for the family, leading to what its members called "the Breakup" and the loss of their home. For his twelfth birthday over the Fourth of July holiday, Fred Ball received an expensive .22-caliber rifle, which all the kids in the neighborhood wanted to see. When Lucille invited Fred's friend Joanna Ottinger, who was visiting relatives in Celeron, to come over to shoot at a target on Sunday morning, the girl brought along her eight-year-old cousin Warner Erickson.

Given the privilege of trying it out for herself, Joanna lifted the weapon to her shoulder, pulled the trigger, and saw her cousin fall bleeding on the ground. The bullet had passed through his neck and lodged in his left lung. Warner's legs, back, and arms were paralyzed for the rest of his short life.

The horror and grief following the accident can only be inferred from brief legal documents filed soon after. Cleo had been sitting on the ground beside Warner when the shot was fired, and Lucille was the one who had to run to his parents to tell them that their son was shot. Fred Hunt followed after her, carrying the boy, who whispered, "Mama, I am dying." Lucille stood in horror on the Ericksons' staircase as the ambulance raced in from Jamestown and took him away.

Fred Hunt was cited as the man who had placed the rifle in Joanna's hands, although some say it was really one of the youngsters. Because he was responsible for the children by virtue of being grandparent and owner of the house, Fred Hunt was accused of negligence and sued for $5,000, plus court costs, to cover the boy's medical care.

Celeron was sympathetic to the Ericksons and without pity for Fred Hunt and his brood. Without money, his only asset was his house. Attempting to save it, he transferred the deed to his daughters, who could not keep up the payments. The couple that held the mortgage then sued Fred and his daughters, as well as Warner and his father,

Einer Erickson, for the money due them. A year after the shooting, Fred was jailed briefly and then declared bankruptcy. In July his mortgage was foreclosed and his home was lost.

Bernice Faulkner, who with her husband, Zuhr, bought the house, said they found Fred's abandoned chiropractic books in the attic, and she figured out which room had been Lucille's. "She wrote on the walls. There were pictures of bodies and scribbling." Lucille and her family were forced to leave Celeron, and because of circumstances and finances they would never all be under the same roof again. She felt cast adrift as she had in the days of Grandma Peterson.

While Lucille's aunt Lola studied nursing at Gowanda Hospital, forty miles away, Cleo was sent to live with her father. Lucille, her mother, brother, and stepfather moved to a cramped two-bedroom apartment in a redbrick building on East Fifth Street in Jamestown. Situated on the ground floor, they heard not only the street noises but the reverberating sounds of their neighbors as they slammed the front door or trudged up the stairs. Fred Hunt stayed with them sometimes as he eked out a living doing odd jobs in the area.

Soon after the family home was lost, Lucille made the first of several short-lived trips back to New York. Her fears and tension only heightened the family difficulties, and she herself wavered between hope of a career and homesickness, between flight from the family's problems and determination to help out. Between the ages of sixteen and eighteen, Lucille would submit to being a schoolgirl until, unable to stand that tedium any longer, she would catch a ride to New York, sometimes with Johnny, to renew her efforts at getting into show business.

The exact chronology of her comings and goings is impossible to track, but it is clear that on her first trip back to Manhattan after a few unhappy months at Jamestown High, Lucille decided to set aside the diffidence that had made her a failure at the Minton-Anderson School and attempt to remake herself. She took on the name Diane Belmont (after the nearby racetrack) and claimed to be from colorful Butte, Montana. Wearing her aunt's wedding outfit, which may have been the best dress the family could provide, she tried out as a showgirl on various musical reviews. One audition was for Earl Carroll, whose "Vanities" ranked with Ziegfeld's productions. Carroll, a lean bald man of about forty, had a domed forehead and the nick-name Bathtub Man, as a result of having hosted a scandalous party featuring a naked chorus girl splashing in a tub of champagne.

When Lucille stood before him, he pulled the fabric of her baggy bodice tight around her figure and decided she would do, but let her go a few weeks later, as producers invariably did. "I was the only girl fired each time and I finally figured out why: I was so frightened I never opened my mouth. The other 'paraders' were cliquey anyway, and nobody noticed an outsider like me," she recalled.

Flo Ziegfeld's corpulent right-hand man, Stanley Sharpe, hired her for the third road company of *Rio Rita* and urged "Get in there and open your mouth!" but she stayed mute and gawky. After a few weeks he gave up, saying, "It's no use, Montana. You're not meant for show business." Her boyish figure lent nothing to the abbreviated costumes of Carroll's or Ziegfeld's chorus lines—Iron Boobs was the nickname she gave herself. She was also sensitive, unable to stand up to the calculated rivalry of professional showgirls who criticized her inexperience and her lack of curves. Since she was never paid for the time she spent in rehearsals, she scraped up money by jerking sodas at a Broadway drugstore and, according to legend, got so involved in the creation of one saccharine construction that she omitted the banana from an elaborate banana split and was fired. She stayed at a boardinghouse where she made tomato soup from ketchup and hot water and sometimes took meals at lunch counters where a doughnut came with a nickel cup of coffee. She slid onto the stools of prosperous departing patrons who left their doughnuts uneaten, snatched up their nickel tips, ordered "more coffee" in their cups while munching on their abandoned pastries, and then when she was finished, re-placed the nickels they had left.

In hope and desperation she answered an ad for showroom coat models and found that for once her figure was an asset. This led to a few assignments with commercial photographers and a job with Hat-tie Carnegie, a top dress designer who saw great potential in Lucille's resemblance to Constance Bennett, the svelte blonde movie goddess with big round eyes who was earning $30,000 a week in Hollywood. Lucille's blue eyes, fair skin, and reed slimness were Bennett's, but her full dark eyebrows and light-brown bob obscured the similarity until Lucille obliged by washing her hair in peroxide.

Like other American stylists, Hattie borrowed freely from the French, but she alone dared put her own name on the labels of her clothes. In business she was a natural and entirely self-made. Born Henrietta Kanengeiser in Vienna in 1889, she changed her name to that of the Pittsburgh steelmaker Andrew Carnegie partly in tribute and partly in hope of emulating his success.

Petite, particularly when dieting, Hattie was groomed to invincible attractiveness down to the roots of her red-gold hair. A writer for *The New Yorker* observed: "She can reduce the strongest man to a pulp in less time than it takes to tell it; the storm subsides as suddenly as it struck, and she will return to her conversation, unruffled, detached, and vague as a saber-tooth tiger after the kill."

Discipline and professional ministrations kept her looking thirtyish, but she was around forty, an avid backgammon player, and a bride for the third time when she met Lucille. Her voice was deep, a touch metallic, and her nearsighted eyes narrowed to questioning slits as she sized up people and situations.

Lucille found Carnegie's other models to be a tough, haughty, and jealous lot. After she was hired, Carnegie's competitive and disdainful mannequins froze out this threatening but undeveloped girl by talking gibberish they pretended they could understand. On the day they asked her opinion of their conversation, Lucille replied that her comments would not matter. With that, they accepted but did not befriend her.

She was now finding it possible to support herself, but she was so lonely and frightened that she gave up her job and returned home on the Erie Railroad to enroll as a bleached blonde sophomore at Jamestown High School and catch up for the time she had missed. Slowly and obviously, her chestnut hair grew back in.

Although Lucille's treasured Celeron was a town with few pretensions, the city of Jamestown had a heritage of Founding Fathers and a pecking order with the right streets to live on and the right work to do. On this grid, the Hunt-Ball-Petersons counted for nothing.

One of Lucille's deepest recollections of this inhospitable Jamestown was an incident in which she was physically attacked, knocked down by a man who beat her head against a rock. When she returned to the city in 1956 to help publicize her movie *Forever Darling*, she stood on a downtown street corner with her public relations man, Charles Pomerantz, and told him, "This is where I was attacked. That's the rock he hit my head against. He kept hitting my head against that rock." More than thirty years later, she gave her friend Jim Brochu a different version in which a teenage friend of Ed followed her home from the movies, tried to start up a conversation, and then put his arm around her. When she squirmed away, he threw her on the ground. In that telling, she recalled the object she bumped into as her stepfather's shoe. She said that Ed scared away the boy, who was never seen again, and walked her home without their ever saying any more about it. Brochu asked if she didn't think Ed's presence a strange coincidence, but she said she never wondered about it until Jim brought it up.

Irene and other friends said they never heard the story, nor could they give it much credence because no one would have dared attack Johnny's girl. It is hard to understand why Lucille, who had earlier turned a warning about the placement of a shaving razor into a skit complete with tears and bandages, would not have maximized the dramatic possibilities of a real attack, unless she was afraid Johnny would react violently. Whatever the truth of the matter, her differing accounts suggest a sense of an injury for which she was never properly consoled or comforted.

She did find one true friend at Jamestown High School. A beautiful, placid brunette named Marion Strong was going to class one day when she saw a girl coming down the central staircase running so fast that her dark green dirndl skirt swirled around her long legs when she stopped at the landing. Marion recognized her as the girl who sold hot dogs at the amusement park and was drawn to her animated personality, just as Lucille was drawn to Marion's serenity and support. "I was slow and precise. Lucille was neither. You never knew when she was acting and when she was natural. You either loved her or you hated her," Marion admitted. "Many people couldn't stand her."

The two girls became best friends and flappers, Jamestown style. Lucille acquired a blue ukulele, an opossum coat dyed to mimic raccoon, and high unbuckled galoshes. "The more noise the buckles made, the better they flapped, that's why we were called flappers,"

Marion recalled. These sophisticates smoked cigarettes and drank nickel Cokes at Harvey Carey's Drug Store until it was time for Lucille to go to one of her part-time jobs—jerking sodas at Walgreens, running the elevator at Lerner's Department Store, or selling cosmetics at Bigelow's. A friend remembered that she looked demure and innocent as she coaxed women to try new creams and lotions, while wearing a straw sailor hat that she speared with a big white daisy.

Johnny still was very much in Lucille's life during this period, which saw Lucille drop out of school altogether. According to his sister Irene, when DeDe's employers would come to town from New York, they would all go to a speakeasy, possibly the "club" Ed was managing out on Dutch Hollow Road. "My brother bought her pretty things from the store where her mother worked. When he bought for her, he also bought for me. I'm sure my brother saw to it that she had change in her purse. Her blue eyes got so big whenever you did anything for her."

For all his largesse, Lucille kept Johnny off balance. She was vexed that he was shorter than she, so when Guy Lombardo, Cab Calloway, or Duke Ellington brought their big bands to the Celeron Pier Ballroom, she sought out taller boys to dance with. "Give Johnny the slip," she would tell Marion.

He also had to keep careful track of his roadster. When she was eighteen, Lucille saw fox terrier puppies advertised in the local paper, then picked up Marion and drove his new car twenty-five miles to claim a pet. "Johnny thought she had a license. She knew how to drive, although she hadn't passed her test. Whenever I told her 'Don't go fast,' she'd go faster. We went eighty miles an hour down Hunt Road, which I think was named for her family," said Marion.

After they arrived at their destination and Lucille saw the puppies, she chose the runt of the litter and planned to name it Sparky, but Marion convinced her that Whoopee, the title of Eddie Cantor's new movie, was better because it meant fun. Marion recalled, "She brought the puppy home to Mrs. Peterson, who said in her Swedish accent 'Voopee? Vat kind of a name is that?' Mrs. Peterson ended up keeping him, and my son and I raised Whoopee's grandson."

Johnny also had to patch things up between the girls when Lucille went too far. After she angered Marion into saying she never wanted to see her again, Lucille dispatched Johnny to bring her around. "I told her she did things just to provoke talk, and she gave me a look that said she knew it, but she didn't care," Marion said. "People didn't approve of Johnny, and I didn't either, but I chose her to be my friend."

Marion and Lucille stood side by side with tears running down their faces the Saturday afternoon in June 1930 when the Celeron Pier Ballroom caught fire. A cigarette butt had apparently smoldered against the old timbers until they began to blaze into a conflagration that consumed seven concession stands and the ticket booth, all scenes of their childhoods, in the space of an hour. Fire departments came from all around the area, and as people from Jamestown saw the smoke they came in autos and trolley cars to see what was going on. After the haze cleared, the Pier Ballroom was a mound of charred wood and twisted metal on a few concrete pylons. Rebuilding began immediately and Lucille's generation was able to dance to the music of Rudy Vallee a few months later at a Spanish castle on that very spot, but for them the one true Celeron Park had vanished.

Lucille was still open to advice from anyone claiming to know how to help her get on the stage. A stranger attending the Shriners annual production at Jamestown's Little Theater convinced her he could help her if she would let him take some photographs. Like many an aspiring actress, Lucille may have been duped into revealing poses, but whatever happened, she certainly felt the photographer deceived her: "I even bounced up the stage of the Palace Theater in Jamestown once to allow myself to be made a fool of by some traveling shyster who had fallen heir to an old camera and some bad film," she said of her gullibility. At least one topless photo of her does survive, but the likelihood is that it was taken in New York when she was struggling to earn money for food and rent. An important opportunity did present itself in her hometown, however.

Jamestown had a theater group called the Players' Club, which was generally limited to members, but the sisters who founded the group heard Lucille was talented and had been to drama school. They were casting *Within the Law*, which involved a salesgirl's being wrongly sent to prison for theft and then attempting to take revenge by marrying her accuser's son. The wife of the assistant district attorney was given the lead and Lucille, whose relationship with Johnny may not have been known to the thespians, was cast as Agnes Lynch, a budding criminal who with a male confederate cheated unsuspecting people of their money.

Lucille and Marion decided that Art demanded that she once again enliven her wholesome chestnut hair. "We bought Golden Glint shampoo. It was terrible, it came out half orange and pink, so we washed in Bright Auburn over and over until it came out right," Marion said.

In the midst of the hubbub of rehearsals and the unreliability of hair tints, Lucille decided that one of the other actresses could use her help and told her so. Her bluntness was appreciated. Margaret Blossom recalled, "She was four or five years younger than I was, but she saw I enjoyed chocolate and had pimples. She offered to give me a facial if I'd go buy the products. She was meticulous. She listed each item and its price carefully in clear handwriting so I couldn't make a mistake. I think that showed a number of qualities—her ability to organize, plan and be specific, and a real feeling for other people."

Within the Law had its premiere on June 24, 1930, in the auditorium of the Nordic Temple, a four-story commercial building that housed the Swedish lodge. On opening night, Marion sat in the audience worrying for her friend. She knew Lucille to be unable to remember popular song lyrics or even the names of their former classmates, but as the play went on and she delivered every line perfectly, Marion relaxed into a comfortable pity for the lead actress who was clearly being eclipsed.

After one performance, the play moved to the Chautauqua Institution, an educational summer resort twenty miles from Jamestown. Chautauqua had begun as a religious summer camp in the nineteenth century and had since evolved into a picturesque lakeside village of gingerbread cottages with pointed gables and mansard roofs. By the turn of the century its summer programs in science, history, and literature helped spur the development of the adult education movement.

When *Within the Law* opened there, a thousand people filled Norton Auditorium, an Arte Moderne concrete structure with bas-relief panels that contrasted markedly with the rest of Chautauqua. For some reason, the Players' Club had no dress rehearsal, but Lucille again stole the show. "They couldn't put that in the review because the leading lady was prominent in town, but those of us in the show knew it," Margaret Blossom recalled. A role that engaged her, plus sensitive and supportive direction, had nurtured the talent that until then had not been fully expressed.

The Jamestown Morning Post, after taking due note of the star, reported, "Miss Lucille Ball, as Agnes Lynch, a particularly hard-boiled little crook, who is undergoing a process of refinement . . . was also admirable. Miss Ball's acting furnished the comedy relief so necessary in the play of the intensity of *Within the Law*."

The Chautauqua Daily acknowledged in a long account:

Miss Ball gave one of the most impressive portrayals of the evening; she lived the part of the underworld girl with as much realism as if it were her regular existence. It was her sparkling action and lines that brought continued applause from her audience at her first exit of the [second] act and again in the last act. . . . The high spot of *Within the Law* was undoubtedly the start of the last scene with the interview of Agnes Lynch and Inspector Burke. Lucille Ball played with even more enthusiasm than before and put her part across to the audience in the best manner of the evening. In a role that required action, and a good deal of it, she exhibited remarkable maturity and poise.

On the night of her triumph, Lucille was stranded at the theater, for Johnny and her family had not made the twenty-mile trip to Chautauqua. Lucille stood alone backstage until two of the prop men offered her a ride. It may have been on the drive home that they told her about an upcoming revue called *Capers* that would benefit the Jamestown hospital, for she appeared in the production in a dance number with the two of them. She added to the choreography by falling down in the middle of it. "This brought amusement from the audience and a lot of applause," said Margaret Blossom. "I think she did it deliberately to liven things up."

She had overcome the stage fright that had immobilized her in New York City, but more important, she had the satisfaction of moving an audience to laughter and appreciation, just as her hero Julius Tannen had done. She again believed there was a place for her in show business, and so she returned to New York where Hattie Carnegie once more gave her a job that financed another round of auditions.

3

DISASTER ALWAYS FOLLOWED TRIUMPH in the life of the young Lucille Ball. She had no sooner escaped Grandma Peterson and gone back to live with DeDe than Flora Hunt, her true grandmother, died. She found Johnny, then her family lost its home. And finally, a few weeks after she was back at Hattie Carnegie's in New York and was still encouraged by her success in *Within the Law*, her aunt Lola suddenly died at the age of thirty-two.

Lola Mandicos was felled by acute peritonitis in the middle of August 1930, while she was completing her nursing training at King's Park Hospital on Long Island. Pauline, who had not seen Lucille for a long time, went to the services in Jamestown and was upset to find her so unnerved. "I didn't see Lucille until she came out of the funeral home. She looked awful, as if she had been sick."

Lucille grieved for Cleo, who would now be fully in her father's custody. "I'll never see my cousin again!" she cried to Marion. She herself was unable to come to terms with the reality of death, her aunt's or that of her grandmother eight years before. Having experi-

34

enced the vulnerability of the women around her, she feared for her mother's life and coped with her emotions by living as she pleased.

Now nineteen, Lucille moved into an apartment in Jamestown, which most people believed Johnny subsidized. The two went everywhere together, and the drama of their relationship was expressed in fights with vituperative shouting on the street, fisticuffs, and an occasional black eye for Lucille. Lucille later told close friends in Hollywood that she had had an abortion during this period. Marion would say only, "A true friend would not say whether she did or not" and "In reaction to Lola's death, Lucille did things she shouldn't have."

After she became famous as a movie actress, Lucille's own account of her late adolescence was that she was bedridden in Jamestown, cut off from any social life, paralyzed but valiantly struggling to regain the use of her limbs. "My mother said she could hear me thumping around upstairs nights getting out of bed trying to balance myself," she said. She began telling reporters about this ordeal after she played a tragically bedridden character named Gloria, the role of which she was most proud, in *The Big Street* in 1942. By the 1980s she would recall: "When something happens to you at seventeen—seventeen!—and I'd been working for a couple years—and you're bedridden until you're nineteen and a half—you appreciate your health. You miss proms and dates, you *really* miss them because you don't make them up."

Lucille would at times explain that her "condition" was the result of an automobile accident in Central Park that left her buried for hours in a snowbank, but closer to the truth was a version of the story in which she was stricken with rheumatic fever or rheumatoid arthritis—she claimed she was never sure which—while working at Hattie Carnegie's. She recalled being exhausted from working day and night as a mannequin and suffering lingering effects of a bout with pneumonia until the afternoon she dropped down before Hattie's clients felled by searing pain in both legs. "Hattie took me to her doctor, who was just around the corner. I had no money and he knew it, so he sent me to a clinic. I was very lucky. They said I might not walk for many years, if ever, but I walked in less than two and I was not left with a heart murmur."

Certainly her health broke down in New York from overwork and undernourishment, but it strains credulity that she could never find out the exact nature of her illness, even after she became wealthy and well connected. Rheumatoid arthritis is a persistent condition and would not have vanished forever, as she claimed her malady did. Possibly she had rheumatic fever and was cured by a sulfa drug, a relatively new treatment at the time.

An ailment did require her to wear therapeutic shoes to build up her muscles, but her closest friends and relatives know little more about her paralysis than what they subsequently read or heard about it. As Fred recalled, "When she was in New York City, she had problems. I'm not sure what it was. She was incapacitated." Pauline said, "I've never been able to track down the rumor that she had rheumatic fever. She didn't want to discuss the idea that she couldn't walk." Marion stated, "She's responsible for a lot of this erroneous stuff. Lucille wasn't paralyzed. She came home one fall wearing heavy shoes with insets."

Following Lola's death, DeDe went to Washington, D.C., and worked in a department store while Ed stayed behind with his mother. With her mother gone, Lucille left Jamestown and Johnny to return to modeling. Depressed about her aunt, she could not summon the energy for auditions and so decided that earning a living was more essential to her than performing. As a model she was called upon not to do but simply to look her part. She enjoyed the designers, seamstresses, and retailers, all the people in the clothing business, some of them unpolished, but most with passion and heart.

In the 1930s, and for decades afterward, clothing manufacturing was the largest industry in New York. It employed more skilled workers than any other and was the strongest force in a city that led the nation in printing, banking, finance, shipping, publishing, and insurance. Like show people, those in the garment trade were temperamental, creative, jealous, and schooled in the anxieties of presenting their work and seeing it hit or flop.

The vast hard-angled city itself, with its might and possibilities, did not inspire Lucille but intimidated her. She was able to see the Empire State Building as it neared completion and watched as tenements were bulldozed across from St. Patrick's Cathedral to make way for Rockefeller Center. That New York was home to the world's titans of finance, its most influential citizens, and its most stupendous edifices was irrelevant—indeed was a reproach—when she had to weigh her every penny.

Lucille was fortunate to be supporting herself at a time when the deepening Depression buffeted most New Yorkers. Cars were parked undisturbed for months at a time as their owners were unable to afford gasoline to move them. Everywhere there were empty storefronts, former shops that had been turned into cheap diners, and lines of silent men accepting handouts of coffee and doughnuts from trucks owned by William Randolph Hearst.

In contrast, Lucille had the relative luxury of a comfortable seat before the mirror in the models' dressing room. There she frequently powdered her nose and shoulders before slipping on Hattie's most expensive organdy dresses in preparation for the arrival of Constance Bennett. Bennett had been front-page news since her career began in the silent era. She was uninhibited, twice divorced, and titled, having just married Gloria Swanson's ex-husband, the Marquis de la Falaise.

Typically Bennett entered Hattie's shop at 42 East Forty-ninth Street, just off Park Avenue, a clutch bag under her elegant arm. Disdaining racks of ready-made dresses, costume jewelry, and beaded purses, she ascended the gray-carpeted stairway to the second floor, where her personal saleswoman, and possibly Hattie herself, received her in the gilded salon. At a signal, Lucille glided in, her derriere angled in a fashionable slouch. Bennett noted the costumes that interested her, consulted over the selection of fabric, and scheduled a minimal number of fittings because, like other very good customers, she had a dress form sculpted to her measurements in the workrooms upstairs.

In letters home under her "stage" name of Diane Belmont, Lucille proudly described parading before the star of *This Thing Called Love* and *Sin Takes a Holiday*. As time went by, Lucille's tart good sense eclipsed her excitement. "If you want to be a dress model, you better know how to sell," she observed. "You walk out in that dress and if the buyer doesn't buy, you're a punk model. It wouldn't occur to the boss that there's anything wrong with the dress. So what do you do? You wave your hips."

Hattie was a kind if demanding employer who lent dresses to models and saleswomen for special events and permitted stockroom girls to wear inexpensive but faithful copies of the best styles, which sometimes startled customers who thought they were buying exclusivity. With her sabbaticals to Jamestown in this period, Lucille was an intermittent but regular employee whom Hattie nevertheless fired at least once. On that occasion, a raw October morning in 1930, Lucille was en route from the Kimberly Hotel on Seventy-fourth and Broadway, a popular address for young women in show business where she had a tiny room, to Hattie's salon when she came across a crowd of people and learned they were standing on tiptoe and craning their necks for a glimpse of Clara Bow. The "It" girl was in the city filming exterior shots for *No Limit*, a tale of the adventures of an innocent girl caught up in a world of fast gamblers. The *New York Times* reporter who trailed Bow wrote: "Bystanders trooped around her as she rested between scenes. It was like a monster game of hide and seek with most of New York's idle doing the chasing." Lucille herself was so engrossed with Bow that she lost track of time and arrived so late for work that Hattie did not take her back for months.

In the meantime she worked for other fashion houses and stores, including Bergdorf Goodman's. Lucille McDonald Carroll, who modeled with her at shows held at the Central Park Casino, remembered that in the frantic atmosphere of the models' room Lucille stood out as a perfectionist and managed to make them laugh. "People used to confuse us because we had the same first name, but she was *the* Lucille. The two things I remember about her most are that you always knew when she was around and she was homesick a lot."

Lucille's work for designers and retailers, plus posing for commercial photographers and illustrators, led to a social life that ranged from speakeasies to hunt and polo clubs. On one visit home, she wore her own riding regalia and borrowed a friend's horse and, with Marion watching, rode it out of the field and on to the street. Something went wrong and the horse fell on her. "She just remounted," Marion remembered. "She couldn't stand it if someone else could do something she couldn't. She had bought boots and jodhpurs in Macy's, so then when she was here she had to find a horse."

Although Lucille continued to care for Johnny, the romance had by now run its course. Instead of an air of excitement, he carried the taint of malevolence. In late September 1930, just before Lucille encountered Clara Bow, Johnny had a nearly fatal auto collision in Buffalo, which led to charges of possessing and transporting bootleg whiskey. In mid-December he was charged with carrying a gun without a permit and on February 17 was arrested for disorderly conduct and interfering with the police. Johnny and another young man were described as guarding a room where ten men gambled illegally amid gaming tables and blackboards chalked with racing results. Johnny's father, Louis, was among them. Four days later Louis was gunned down near his home and left lying facedown in a pool of his own blood with his discharged revolver lying under him. An unknown foreigner in a brown overcoat whom he had argued with was sought in connection with the killing, but was never found.

In New York, Lucille was increasingly able to meet types of men she would never have found back home. They were attracted to her naturalness and her anything-for-laughs sense of fun. She was uninhibited and quick to tell stories about herself, exaggerating their details, no matter how significant or trivial. Hugh Sinclair, a British actor then working in New York theater, recalled, "She disarmed you. You saw this wonderful glamorous creature and in five minutes she had you roaring with laughter."

Two of the more socially prominent men she remembered dating were Sailing Baruch, Jr., a nephew of the well-known financier, and Pat di Cicco, a public relations man who later successively married Thelma Todd and Gloria Vanderbilt. Such men were probably not attracted to models for their finishing school manners, nor did they find them in Lucille. "When I was a clumsy kid from the country, this nice man took me to a beautiful country club and led me up to a table of his friends. Before he could even introduce me I reached out and squashed a mosquito on the forehead of one of the girls—I almost knocked her out, and they all thought I was crazy," she said.

Several of her closest friends aided her professionally, particularly Roger Furse, a tall, dark, bearded British photographer and commercial artist in his midtwenties. Furse was descended from both the

Kemble and Siddons theatrical families and later achieved artistic fame designing sets and costumes for Laurence Olivier's film and stage productions. When Lucille knew him he was a provocative, exotic artist with big absorbing eyes, a type that young girls find irresistible. His distinction was that he also made a good and useful friend.

Another helpful photographer was Arthur O'Neill, a cousin to the Vanderbilts who took up portraiture in Paris in the 1920s and worked for Paris *Vogue*. Sandy-haired and mustachioed, he let it be known that he had a trust fund that yielded him $125 per month, of which $100 went toward rent for his home and studio, the rest to gardenias and gin. In the spring of 1931, during one of her periodic returns to Jamestown, Lucille dramatically and falsely described O'Neill to Marion as a terrible person, an ogre, whose face was so ugly that its sides didn't match. It was with such tales of the city and its people that she persuaded Marion, who unlike Lucille had graduated from high school, to come along and see it for herself.

As they made their plans, Lucille advised that two necessities in Manhattan were sensible shoes and slacks. "Lucille told me, 'If we go, I won't listen to the story of your sore feet. Get decent shoes. Charge them to my mother's account.' I told her she just wanted me to have ugly shoes like she did, but we went to the store and she told the salesman, 'You fit her right so I don't have to listen to her complain.' " Men's pajamas were the closest approximation to women's slacks that they could find in their small town, so they ordered some from a catalog and became the first females to wear trousers on the streets of Jamestown.

When Lucille announced they were ready to depart, Marion pointed out that they had no money. "Lucille said 'I'll win twenty dollars this Saturday in a poker game with Ed's friends.' She did."

A newspaperman from Cleveland gave them a ride to New York, a trip of some ten hours. They immediately called on Roger, who hired Lucille to model for a Yardley soap poster, and then borrowed cots so they could stay with him. The three proceeded to Colombo's Restaurant on Third Avenue, a hangout with red-checked tablecloths. There Lucille gave a particularly enthusiastic greeting to a glamorous fellow who intrigued Marion. "That's Arthur," Lucille told her. "You *can't* think he's good-looking." The elegant O'Neill criticized Lucille's blue satin pajamas, then asked Marion for a date. Lucille was so jealous she let her temper fly after they left the restaurant and for a few days afterward. Her friend's triumph with a man Lucille was attracted to remained a sore spot long after they lost track of him. If Marion dared to bring up Arthur, even decades later at Lucille's Beverly Hills home, Lucille would bristle.

Marion quickly found a job as a secretary to an antiques dealer who was an acquaintance of Arthur. Lucille earned $40 a week modeling and Marion made $20 at the shop, which was not paltry during the Depression. Still, they kept to strict budgets. They paid $18.75 a week for room 712 at the Kimberly Hotel and allocated 25¢ a day for breakfast, except on Sundays when they splurged on corned beef. They depended on their many dates to provide their supper. "We would go to speakeasies where a slit would open in the door and you'd say your name," Marion recalled. At El Morocco and other nightspots they slowly sipped their drinks and managed to make a meal of French canapés and anchovies.

They were delighted by what was new and enchanting to them— garden courtyards hidden like oases behind certain brownstones, servings of noodles and rice instead of the potatoes that were Jamestown's standard fare, and, most of all, sidewalk stalls of colorful spring flowers. In the fashionable cloche hats and waisted dresses of the 1930s, they strolled to the Schwab Mansion, a turreted French chateau with landscaped grounds near their hotel. Inevitably, Lucille kept a pace or two ahead, "running like a streak." "You'll be killed here if you don't hurry!" she warned Marion as they sprinted one day across broad Park Avenue.

Marion celebrated her twentieth birthday in New York City. "Lucille and I had a spat the night before. I don't remember what it was about, but we weren't speaking. When I came home from my job she was out modeling, but she had filled one of the water glasses with daffodils and made a sign—I don't know where she found the crayon—that said Happy Birthday, Scrap Iron!"

However exhilarating this time was for Lucille, she often worried about her family, particularly Fred Hunt, who was supporting himself with various jobs in Celeron, some of which offered board. "When

Lucille found out her grandfather had only strawberries to eat during the Depression she screamed, 'Some day I'll see to it that he has enough to eat!' " Marion recalled.

After a few months the two returned to Jamestown, where Marion decided to marry her high school sweetheart, but by now Lucille knew her life was in New York and went back. Roger came to be so important to her that one night in the middle of a party they decided to elope. Halfway to a friendly upstate judge, they thought better of it and turned their car around.

Furse, Lucille, and Hugh Sinclair and his wife, Valerie Taylor, were perennially broke, but they blew occasional windfalls at their favorite club in Harlem listening to the pianist and dancing until dawn in candlelight. Whether it was the trick of being able to read lips or an instinct developed during her time with Johnny, Lucille had a knack for knowing when there was going to be trouble. Furse nicknamed her "Two Gun," possibly because she claimed a stray bullet drained her bathwater onto the floor one night at the Kimberly Hotel. One evening while dancing with Sinclair she spied a man standing on the edge of the floor and suddenly announced, "I think it's time we got out of here." A minute after they left, a patron was shot dead.

Sinclair suspected she had a rich admirer because when she finally rented her own apartment, she did not invite her friends to see it. Lucille also seemed able to come up with money when anyone needed it: "She was always willing to lend someone a hundred dollars, and if she hadn't it right there she'd go out and get it." But at times Lucille had her family with her. Her brother attended high school for a time while he worked at the Waldorf-Astoria Hotel. At another point DeDe came to stay and worked at Stern's department store, where Lucille modeled.

Furse thought she had the flair and talent for the theater, but Lucille would not be coaxed back to auditions or acting lessons. As well as her disappointing experiences as a chorus girl, she had been given several screen tests, a common practice for models at this time, and failed each so decisively that she again convinced herself she had outgrown her childhood ambitions.

Ironically, it was her very success as a model that presented the opportunity that led to her true career. On a scorching afternoon in mid-July 1933, Lucille was on her way to buy underwear on sale at an expensive shop when she ran into an agent named Sylvia Hahlo just outside the famed Palace Theater. Lucille had recently been chosen as a Chesterfield Cigarette Girl, posing in a blue chiffon dress and matching picture hat with two Russian wolfhounds, so Sylvia now offered her the chance to leave Manhattan's steamy heat: There was a call for poster girls to go to Hollywood to appear in an Eddie Cantor movie called *Roman Scandals*. One question in Lucille's mind was money. By working two jobs, she was earning $100 a week in New York. The Goldwyn assignment paid three times that much, with overtime, but only for the six-week shooting schedule.

Realizing that California presented a chance to escape the uncomfortable work of modeling high-necked fall woolen suits and broadtail coats in the middle of summer, Lucille decided the assignment would be a pleasant vacation. She ascended the back stairs of the Palace Theater and found Sam Goldwyn's right-hand man, Jim Mulvey, cooling himself in the labored draft of an electric fan. He looked over the skinny model with peroxide blonde hair, a girl without singing, dancing, or acting credentials, but only the momentary status of being a Chesterfield girl, and accepted her. She solved his problem and enabled him to get on with other things. "They were desperate. If I'd been tested I probably would never have gotten it, because I wasn't beautiful, zaftig, or any of the things these girls were," she recalled. Lucille was in fact a backup, the thirteenth girl chosen when the company only needed twelve.

4

EVEN DURING THE GREAT DEPRESSION, money could cost a girl too much. So thought one protective mother who forbade her child to travel to Hollywood and there become a Goldwyn Girl. On a Wednesday afternoon in July 1933, this unknown young woman dropped out of the chorus of *Roman Scandals*, leaving her place to Lucille Ball.

A few days later, Lucille, twenty-one years old, was among the dozen excited beauties who boarded the train at Grand Central Station for a journey to the coast. Lucille considered it a paid holiday, a chance to see something of the world before returning to New York that autumn. The girls stopped in Chicago long enough to make a promotional appearance at the World's Fair with the popular radio star Ben Bernie, then traveled on through desert and mountains in the luxury of air-conditioned cars.

Although her colleagues had all learned how to parade and pose in Shubert and Ziegfeld stage productions, the inexperienced Lucille got along with them well. As the girls wound their pin curls and applied their creams in preparation for arrival in Los Angeles, she clowned and let down her guard. Lucille, representing the Constance Bennett type among them, became particularly close to Barbara Pepper, who was selected for her resemblance to Jean Harlow. Barbara's congenial sexuality had a hint of Mae West, which her mother, who was traveling along as group chaperone, kept in check. Barbara was the first of many women Lucille would befriend throughout her life because of their close bonds with their mothers.

On their arrival in Los Angeles, Goldwyn representatives greeted them at the station and escorted them to their lodgings, a series of rooms scattered in little houses along Hollywood's North Formosa Street near the studio. Lucille was delighted to learn she would have kitchen privileges, which would allow her to save even more of her salary. While some of the other girls bought furs and cars, Lucille biked to work, happy to be building a bank account for her family and herself.

Goldwyn Studios was a Spanish colonial citadel with a bell tower on Santa Monica Boulevard. Although Samuel Goldwyn had moved there as an independent producer four years before, oldtimers referred to the location as "Doug and Mary's" because it was the former Fairbanks–Pickford United Artists studio. Lucille was part of a wave of fresh faces surging onto his lot to replace a generation of silent stars. Screen deities like Fairbanks, Pickford, and Charlie Chaplin were fading at the box office and even the "It" girl was in eclipse. Clara Bow was so traumatized when she heard her Brooklyn accent in the talkies that anxiety over her career reinforced her craving for drugs. "Now that the talkies had taken hold, the charm and insouciance of Hollywood were gone," Chaplin lamented. "Overnight it had become a cold and serious industry." Finance and technology, not theatrical artistry, were now driving the business. The lingering effects of the Wall Street crash in 1929 increased the need for the participation of bankers and financial experts, even as the coming of sound made engineers and technicians crucial.

The best thing Lucille could do now was to be noticed. According to her own account (possibly inspired by her high school stunt of packing crepe paper into a moth-eaten swimsuit), when she learned that Samuel Goldwyn himself was going to inspect the new arrivals, she decided to amuse him by mocking her lack of fleshly assets. She stuffed toilet paper, gloves, and socks into the top of her swimsuit and lined up with others in front of barnlike Stage 3. By the time Goldwyn appeared, some of her wadding was dangling in view. "He noticed me," she said.

In his early fifties, Sam Goldwyn was tall, broad-shouldered, and almost bald. He could be loud and was known for malapropisms ("In two words—im possible!") yet for twenty years he had been making successful films, by 1933 no more than two or three a year, because he strove for quality. His imagination was captured by the legendary Ziegfeld chorus, so when he brought the Broadway musical *Whoopee!* to the screen in 1930 he established the Goldwyn Girls. His pro forma attempts at seducing them were an open joke, but he was always serious about their caliber, which he felt would rank with Ziegfeld's group. Professing that they needed to have more than shapely legs and pretty faces, he said his standards were intelligence, coordination, stamina, and an ability to perform intricate routines, plus a radiant, scrubbed cleanliness that ruled out artificiality. His choreographer Busby Berkeley claimed, "I could tell a lot about them by their eyes, something few people are willing to believe."

After looking over the girls for *Roman Scandals* in person, Goldwyn evaluated their screen tests and announced that two—Barbara Pepper and Lucille Ball—were not up to his standard; however, Berkeley saw something promising in them and intervened, prevailing upon Goldwyn to let them stay.

Berkeley also intended to circumvent the film industry's moralists in the making of this picture. Although the Hays office, which enforced the Motion Picture Production Code, and the Catholic Legion of Decency were by now scrupulously studying every script and piece of footage for any hint of sex, Berkeley envisioned a scene in which the "scrubbed" Goldwyn Girls would look as if they had just emerged from a bathtub, naked. In a slave market scene shot at night on a closed set, he filmed them clad only in flesh-colored body stockings with long blonde wigs draped over their censorable parts.

Lucille collected overtime for the night shooting and then a few days later again made a point of capturing the attention of Sam Goldwyn. A designer named John Harkrider, who had worked for

Florenz Ziegfeld himself, had decided to try to impress Goldwyn with a dramatic presentation of his work. He arranged the producer and other key studio people on several rows of folding chairs before a bilious green curtain, then sounded a large Chinese gong. The curtain parted, and in came the undulating Goldwyn Girls swathed in Harkrider's togas. The pomposity of the staging irritated executives, according to screenwriter Nat Perrin: "One girl thought the whole thing was ridiculous and she started bumping into the other girls and pulling at their wigs while the others played it straight. It was Lucille. At the end Harkrider turned to Goldwyn and asked what he thought. In his high adenoidal accent, Goldwyn said, 'The show was great, but the costumes stink.' That was when people started noticing Lucille."

In New York City she had been too lonely and overwhelmed to express the brasher aspects of her personality before strangers, particularly when she needed to assert herself, but Goldwyn Studios was a self-contained community where the lines, all of which led to Goldwyn himself, were clear. Being on the lot every day, Lucille could see how things worked, learn whom she needed to know, and stay underfoot until she was able to meet them. New York auditions were quick in-and-out interviews. Here she had more time to take a person's measure and work up her confidence so as to feign assurance and competence. What made it easier, in the beginning, was that she thought it was only a six-week experiment.

"My stick-to-itness came out here," she recalled. "Suddenly I was in show business. It interested me because I was learning, and because I was learning I never complained. Whatever they asked, I did. I did one line, two lines, with animals, in mud packs, seltzer in the face. Eddie Cantor noticed it first at Goldwyn. He'd say 'Give it to that girl, she doesn't mind.' I took it all as a learning time."

She lacked innate glamour but had the gumption of a trouper. In a scene set in the harem's beauty salon, Cantor and Berkeley wanted to try a sight gag where Eddie, pretending to be an Ethiopian beauty doctor, bent over and missed a flying glob of mud pack that hit one of the girls full in the face. Knowing that slapstick was not what the beauties were hired for, they asked if anyone wanted to do the bit. Lucille volunteered. That gag and one where she claimed she was "gummed" by a crocodile were cut, but she did show up in mud pack.

When the other girls warned her, "Nobody will know who you are," she retorted, "Nobody knows who I am anyway," and covered her face in gook.

In truth, Lucille is not always easy to spot in *Roman Scandals*, but in some scenes one catches mannerisms of the star-to-be. A lanky belly dancer at the slave market has the loping swagger of Lucy Ricardo emoting at Ricky's nightclub; a mud-packed slave girl reporting that a man is loose in the harem offers the innocent bobbing nod of the meddling housewife.

As the weeks passed, Lucille stepped up her campaign. She pestered Perrin and his partner Arthur Sheekman to give her just one line to say. In the end, it may have been that she divided them and conquered, for she ended up with two separate pieces of dialogue. In one scene, a young Lucille Ball in marceled hair with a sharp quivering voice takes up the phrase: "He says the city put us here and we should live here." And at the end of the film she hops through the crowd shouting: "Eddie's coming! Eddie's coming!" She was not granted any lingering close-ups, for her teeth were too crooked for an enticing smile, but those two lines made her the Goldwyn beauty with something to say.

"She was far from unbeautiful," Nat Perrin said, "but the others were more attractive. Some of us wondered how she stayed so thin. She was hoydenish, anything for laughs."

The social life of Hollywood's aspiring newcomers centered around hangouts such as the Clover Club, a nightclub that offered gambling, and Ciro's and Mocambo, all of which were new establishments supplanting orange groves along Sunset Strip. Lucille was one of the liveliest in any group. She got the greatest reaction from recounting things she had done that day, complete with gestures for emphasis and overstatement. She was never just hungry, she was so famished that she could chew on the wall; she was never just surprised, she was so shocked that she would not have batted an eye if President Roosevelt waited on their table. She would call her early years in Hollywood her "hey hey" period when she had a new beau every night, went to all the clubs, and loved to dance.

"The only way I remember that I got any laughs was when I related stories on myself," she explained. "I've always had the ability to laugh at myself, and see the ridiculous side, and I enjoy telling stories on myself more than on anyone else." Lucille's sense of her absurdity began with Grandma Peterson's criticisms of her. She had always felt she had to extend herself to make people like her, and that strategy was finally beginning to bear fruit.

One day a heavyset Texan named Ed Sedgwick observed Lucille in conversation in front of one of the sound stages, relating a story with great animation. Sedgwick had started in show business in his family's vaudeville act a half century before and was reputed to have discovered Tom Mix and Hoot Gibson. More recently he had directed the Keystone Kops and Buster Keaton. He first noticed Lucille because she was pretty, but then he watched raptly as her face turned to rubber, her eyes swelled, and her lips wavered in a figure eight. He had seen Mabel Normand work to create such effects in her close-ups. He walked over and told Lucille, "Young lady, if you play your cards right, you could be the greatest comedienne in show business." Having a set reaction to fat men over the age of forty, Lucille gave him a disdainful look that so amused him he was convinced he was right. But Sedgwick's influence in Hollywood went no further than two-reelers and physical comedy. Knowing that neither Lucille nor producers would listen to him, he simply walked away.

Like most young actresses, Lucille had reason to suspect that men in Hollywood usually had ulterior motives. While she wanted those in power to notice her, she was not calculating in matters of the casting couch. George Murphy, the actor and dancer who became a U.S. Senator, recalled a conversation with her one day on the set, " 'I got a note from an old guy who wants me to come up to his office. What do you suppose he wants me to come up to his office for?' And I said, 'Lucille, I'd rather not think about it.' She said, 'Don't, because I'm not going.' "

Still, she was rumored to have had many brief attachments, including ones with the writer S. N. Behrman, who had just written *Queen Christina* for Garbo, and with Goldwyn's assistant Fred Kohlmar. Sam Goldwyn himself was said to have propositioned her, as he did others. "When she first arrived, Goldwyn tried to attack her in his office. She told us the story at the time and it was hilarious," recalled Nat Perrin. "He started to chase her around the office and she ran downstairs and out on Formosa to Santa Monica Boulevard. She told us she was still running when she said, 'What the hell am I running for? He can't attack me here.' Later I doubt she would have run so much."

Roman Scandals was expected to be a hit, thanks largely to the proven box office appeal of its star, Eddie Cantor, whom Lucille described as "a father—with a gleam in his eye." He had been a major film presence since 1930, when he strutted to popularity playing the good-hearted innocent with infectious charm in *Whoopee!*, Goldwyn's adaptation of the successful Broadway show.

When Cantor came to Hollywood, he brought along the brilliant choreographer Busby Berkeley. Cantor proved to be a shrewd judge of talent, for in *Whoopee!* Berkeley took his first steps in establishing film as a medium for musical extravaganza and himself as the master of the genre. He recognized that while a line of thirty-two high-stepping chorus girls was exciting in the theater, it would shrink to insignificance if he tried to shoot it straight on for a movie. Berkeley's innovation was to make the camera lens seem to wink. He filmed the Goldwyn Girls from overhead as they formed a series of kaleidoscopic patterns and also presented them in sequential close-ups, amplifying the effect of a single pretty face by fanning it out in a succession of others.

If Lucille Ball expected to see herself in a feature with the impact of Berkeley's *Whoopee!*, she was disappointed. In *Roman Scandals* he did not innovate new filming techniques or drill the dancers in precision choreography. In the slave market scene, for example, the girls were out of step and muddled in their movements, a raggedness perhaps excusable in the frenzy of the slaves' plight.

Everyone on the lot believed that Berkeley had been distracted by drink. "We just sat around waiting for Busby Berkeley to come in off a binge, literally," Lucille said. She and the other Goldwyn Girls saw the amount of their paycheck swell from the guaranteed $300 to $600 and $700 per week, thanks to the nights and weekends they worked overtime, while the six weeks of their contract stretched into months of work and Lucille happily renewed her contract. In fact, the production bogged down, not because Berkeley was carousing but because he was working double shifts. He siphoned his ideas for new dance sequences to a rival studio that, unlike Goldwyn, was willing to put him on a long-term contract. Berkeley had signed with Warner Brothers, where he spent his nights choreographing *Footlight Parade*.

Roman Scandals emerged from single-minded hopes and divided loyalties to combine comedy with telling social comment and beautiful girls. Eddie Cantor plays a generous ne'er-do-well who exposes a corrupt philanthropist for building museums and jails—homes for statues and criminals—while putting people on the street.

The film eventually made millions for Goldwyn, despite legal wrangles with Berkeley and the writers, Robert Sherwood and George S. Kaufman. The suits delayed for months the start of the next Cantor picture. Lucille told friends that, to make sure she kept working during this time, she waited outside the studio gates each morning and hitched rides inside with delivery men, so she would be on hand when extras were needed. In this way she was hired by Darryl F. Zanuck, whose new Twentieth Century Company was renting studio space and equipment, even desks and filing cabinets, from Goldwyn.

Lucille had a bit part in *Broadway thru a Keyhole*, based on a story by the New York newspaper columnist Walter Winchell, who spent some time on the set and gave her a small plug in his column. In Zanuck's *Blood Money* she played a gun moll at the races. Both these crime dramas were released before *Scandals*. Neither offered her a chance to do bits of dialogue as *Scandals* had, but they certified that she had talent and convinced her that if she worked at it, she could make a place for herself in Hollywood.

Also on the Goldwyn lot was George Raft, who was making *The Bowery* for Zanuck. Raft, then in his late thirties, was born in New York's notorious Hell's Kitchen. Although some of his boyhood pals grew up to be mobsters, he took his dark Italian good looks and dancing talent to Broadway, where he became a tango king before going into pictures. Raft's sidekick and assistant, Mack Grey, was one of Lucille's boyfriends at this time. Known then and for years after as a gofer, first for Raft and later for Dean Martin, Grey had been an aspiring fight manager named Maxie Greenberg in New York in the 1920s. After moving to California, he ran into Raft one Friday night at the fights at Hollywood Legion Stadium. Raft cherished him as a kindred soul who shared his background and knew his old pals from New York. With Grey, Raft dropped the pose of self-confident star to the extent that when his mother died, a distraught Raft had Grey make all the funeral arrangements. As Raft's assistant, Grey shared his penthouse apartment at the El Royale on elegant Rossmore Avenue. The pair went to fights, races, and ball games together and even had cosmetic surgery at the same time—when Raft had a boxing scar removed from his ear, he treated Grey to a nose job.

During the period that Grey and Lucille were seeing each other, Raft himself was involved with Carole Lombard, who was divorcing William Powell. She and Raft were co-starring in *Bolero*, a musical that became a great hit and also marked the film debut of a stocky forty-six-year-old vaudevillian named William Frawley, who endured as a contract player for years until he went to television as Fred Mertz.

Raft, a man rarely at ease, was comfortable with Lombard's blend of glamour and bawdiness, and Lucille was in awe of her. The most uninhibited comedienne of her day, Lombard had supported herself and her mother as a child actress, then as a Mack Sennett bathing beauty. Her classic features would have rendered her coldly perfect had she not had the language and gusto of a sailor on leave, as well as an irreverent sense of humor. When Grey had a hernia operation, Lombard found out that the Yiddish word for the affliction was *killa* and gave Grey the nickname of "Killer," going so far as to send extras toting toy pistols to stand guard outside his hospital room.

Lombard approved of what she saw in Lucille and tried to help her, as she did other extras. Clothes were an important point of discussion. Lucille preferred sporty, spectator outfits to the dressier styles the studio's designer suggested for her. Carole advised Lucille on how to dress economically and how to accessorize what clothes she did have. When the demoralized Lucille felt forever condemned to bit parts, Carole Lombard came up to her on the set and said, "What are they doing to you? Tell the so-and-sos to give you a break. You've got something. Tell them I said they're missing the boat again."

Lucille clung to this encouragement, but her resemblance to Constance Bennett was of more immediate benefit. She doubled for Bennett in dance numbers of *Moulin Rouge* and had a bit part in her star vehicle, *The Affairs of Cellini.* To Lucille's humiliation, Bennett had no recollection of having met her at Hattie Carnegie's.

Goldwyn loaned Lucille out to Zanuck again in late 1933 where she had small parts in *Hold That Girl* and in *Bottoms Up.* The latter was a spoof of the movie business in which a Goldwyn-like producer garbled words of more than two syllables, appropriated all credit for successful films, and blamed others for the flops. Spencer Tracy starred in it, and one supporting player was Thelma Todd, the beautiful blonde heroine of many two-reel silent comedies as well as of the Marx Brothers' *Monkey Business* and *Horse Feathers.* Todd was about to complete her divorce from Pat di Cicco, whom Lucille had dated in his bachelor days in New York. The shooting schedule on the film was so tight that Zanuck, a thirty-two-year-old wunderkind, forbade his day players to fall ill. He mandated that whoever had a sniffle was to alternate a cold capsule with an aspirin each hour until well. The remedy must have worked for Lucille because a few decades later, when she owned her own studio, she urged this remedy on her own sniffling employees.

In the autumn of 1933, after *Roman Scandals* had finished shooting, Goldwyn gave Lucille a small role as a chorus girl in *Nana;* this could be taken as a sign of favor, for he was determined that this adaptation of Zola's classic novel about a French courtesan would make a Garbo of Anna Sten, a beautiful Ukrainian actress who spoke not a word of English. A month into the shooting, seeing that the picture was not working, Goldwyn scrapped thousands of dollars worth of footage and started over, calling in Dorothy Arzner to rescue it. Having distinguished herself as the director of the highly regarded *Christopher Strong* with Katharine Hepburn, Arzner decided her best tack was to keep Sten's lines to a minimum and let the other actors carry the story. These efforts were to no avail; *Nana* proved to be a great embarrassment to Goldwyn.

Of the dozen girls who had come to California in July 1933, Lucille was one of four still working for Goldwyn the following spring. She had not yet stepped out of the chorus line, but she was proving herself to be a dependable bit player on loan-outs to Zanuck. Her prize indulgence was a fox terrier she named Toy. Acquiring a pet and signing a six-month contract with the studio convinced her that the

West Coast would be her home. Hollywood seemed magical and she wanted her friends to share it. Lucille wrote Mildred Schroeder, a showgirl she knew from Broadway, that she must come out and get into pictures. But Mildred was preoccupied with romance. She stayed in New York and married the actor Bert Lahr.

Above all, Lucille was determined to bring her family, particularly her mother, to California. Instinctively, she felt that if her mother were finally and reliably in one nearby spot, any challenge could be faced. Lucille had sufficient cash, supplemented by a $100 loan from George Raft, to rent a small white three-bedroom house a dozen blocks away from the studio at 1344 N. Ogden Drive, north of Sunset Boulevard. However much she had come to love Southern California, she had never been drawn to its signature Spanish colonial architecture, with its thick plaster walls and red-tiled roofs. Instead, for her family home she chose a more familiar style in a neighborhood of neo-Georgian bungalows whose gables, columns, and pediments made them look as if eastern mansions had been miniaturized and shipped west to Hollywood.

Her brother, Fred, was the first to join her on Ogden Drive and added his savings to the family reunion fund. "When I came out to California, our objective was to get the family back together," he explained. Lucille had determined that she would set them up in the best manner possible. She and her new friend Ann Sothern, who had already appeared in several films and Broadway musicals, fixed up the place by laying down linoleum, scrubbing floors, and "laughing like loons" over their efforts and mishaps. "Lucille never quit," recalled Fred, who did the heavier work. "It was an old house and she had ideas of how to paint it. There was no way she would settle for anything less than the best."

Before beginning the next Eddie Cantor film, *Kid Millions*, she went home to Jamestown. Goldwyn and his studio must have been trying to promote her, and may in fact have paid her plane ticket to New York City, as they had her make two Vitaphone short subjects and do some radio interviews in Manhattan. She reached Jamestown late in June 1934, just as the lilacs were fading, and there she set about to untie the knots that held her there. She saw Johnny, but each knew that short of his moving to California, there was no way for them to be together again. She stayed with Grandma Peterson, who had been widowed for many years, and friends say that Lucille was concerned that she had enough money for food and clothes. Ed, often in ill health, possibly because of drink, was the only one living with his mother now. DeDe was still working in a store in Washington, D.C., and had left him for good. Fred Hunt remained in the area, and Lucille undoubtedly worked to persuade him to move to the coast, as Cleo had already agreed to do once she graduated from high school in Buffalo.

Before leaving, Lucille gave her first newspaper interview. The local press requested it, possibly after a United Artists press agent wired an advisory: "Jamestown has a right to be proud of this beauteous girl who has become internationally famous as foremost of the Goldwyn Girls, the cream of American pulchritude." Wearing silk pajamas with a gold braid that captivated her interviewer, Lucille exhibited an attractive blend of Hollywood panache and hometown coziness, promoting her image while playing herself down. She casually said that she was flying back to California via New York City, rather than nearby Buffalo, so that she could bring her dog, and claimed that she had been in three Broadway shows, which she boasted had given her the presence that only the New York stage can give. Her scampering dog, Toy, nipped at the reporter's hat and gnawed his pencil while he stared at the brilliant red toenails peeking through Lucille's silver sandals. He was impressed that she had someone else (a cousin) packing her bag under her supervision, but noted that Lucille was more interested in having him see her dog do tricks than in hearing herself praised. At the end of his story this anonymous reporter became the first of a long line of journalists to note that despite her success she remained down to earth: "Her rise in the cinema world has not made her assume any of the airs and graces usually assumed by successful actresses."

By the time shooting began on *Kid Millions*, Lucille was at home at Goldwyn Studios. She heartily greeted by name everyone on the set, from the grips to executives, and felt she had learned how to adapt to the dozens of people she encountered each day, each with a different temperament and problem and hangover. While she was again cast as an extra—what she called "atmospheric background"—

Ann Sothern was featured as an ingénue, a fact that Lucille surely recognized as a sign that she herself was not getting ahead at Goldwyn Studios. However, she now had more faith in her ability. George Murphy, who made his film debut in *Kid Millions,* observed, "Lucille had a great deal of self-confidence, a great sense of humor. She had a quality that was unique and she knew it."

Lucille was still irrepressibly bent on making herself known, although she had already been on the lot for more than a year. Murphy recalled her behavior during the ten-minute cigarette breaks from shooting. "Ben Silvie, the assistant director, would call, 'All right, girls, all back on the set.' Then you'd count to ten and he would say, 'Miss Ball! Miss Ball on the set, please!' So I said to her, 'Lucille, you keep doing that, and one day they'll be calling someone else's name.' And she said, 'Maybe, but at least they'll know who I am.'"

In *Kid Millions* Cantor inherits $77 million from an archeologist father he never knew. To claim it he travels to Egypt, with a pack of rascals (including Ethel Merman) in pursuit. For the finale, "Ice Cream Fantasy," Goldwyn decided to incorporate the new three-strip Technicolor process. Goldwyn and Technicolor's co-inventor Herbert T. Kalmus were so obsessed with getting the spumoni spectrum of the scene right that only when Goldwyn smacked his lips in the screening room was he convinced they had succeeded. The joke at the time was that he was more concerned with the performance of the strawberry than with that of his stars.

The quip did not amuse Cantor, who felt his pictures were overloaded with gimmicks, dancers, and subplots, to the detriment of his character, who was never allowed a love interest. In fact, the featured romance of *Kid Millions* was between Ann Sothern and George Murphy. To appease Cantor, Goldwyn plucked Doris Davenport from the newest crop of Goldwyn Girls to play his girl back home. Recognizing that newer starlets were receiving preferential treatment may have helped to convince Lucille that she would have to leave Goldwyn if her career was to advance.

The writers Arthur Sheekman and Nat Perrin provided her with the means of taking that step as the result of an encounter with their agent, Bill Perlberg, on the stairs of Goldwyn's main building. "He told us he wasn't going to be our agent any more as he was going to

Columbia as head of casting," Perrin recalled. "He asked if we knew someone with talent that he should talk to. Simultaneously we said 'Lucille Ball.' We didn't mention her as an actress because we knew her as a personality. We told him she was funny and amusing. He gave her a contract at Columbia at seventy-five dollars a week."

When she worked as a Goldwyn Girl, rather than on loan, her pay was much greater, but her contract was about to expire and Lucille asked out, explaining, "I didn't want to be a showgirl any more. I wanted to get on with it and I had a chance to be a contract player at Columbia, although I was making a lot less money than I did as a showgirl."

When Lucille arrived at Columbia in the fall of 1934, the kingdom of Harry Cohn was known for dispensing quickie films on such a low budget that it was nicknamed "Poverty Row" and "Columbia, the Germ of the Ocean." Located a few miles east of Goldwyn Studios on Sunset Boulevard, it comprised a dozen or more shacks clustered around an inner courtyard. In an area MGM would consider sufficient for only a single stage, Columbia squeezed in three, plus a row of shops, parking places for trucks, and, in one corner, cutting rooms, film vaults, and projection rooms stacked up one on top of another like boxes and accessible only by a steep, exterior iron staircase.

Cohn's legendary—and cultivated—toughness was already manifest. He routinely bawled out contract players for infractions such as drinking coffee, smoking, or wasting electricity. To those directly responsible for box office success or failure, he gave free creative rein, which meant that he fired those who did not make money for him and left alone the ones who did. It was that freedom that encouraged Frank Capra, the talented director who was slowly earning Columbia respect with such films as *The Bitter Tea of General Yen* and *Lady for a Day*, to remain with Cohn rather than signing on with classier, more meddlesome producers.

While Carole Lombard was shooting *Twentieth Century* on the lot with John Barrymore, Lucille appeared in several shorts, including *Three Little Pigskins* with the Three Stooges. No inventor, scientist, or social reformer worked with greater zeal than this heat-seeking trio in their pursuit of laughs. Although they were then renowned for their comic timing, which was planned and rehearsed to a certainty and augmented by percussive sound effects, they demonstrated little of it in this performance. Despite her role as a gangster's girlfriend, Lucille looks angelically pretty, tall and very slim. Her big scene comes when the Stooges appear in flouncy women's lingerie and shoot her with a bottle of seltzer. Often asked what she learned from the Stooges, she said they taught her that seltzer is painful if squirted up one's nose.

She had bits in several full-length features, including Capra's *Broadway Bill*. This racing picture about a long shot was a disappointment to the director because its leading man, Warner Baxter, was afraid of the leading horse, which did not make for good screen chemistry. Lucille, however, was animated and natural as a telephone operator who relays a tip. She also forged lifetime bonds with some of her fellow bit players on *Broadway Bill*, including Charles Lane, who played a crook, and Irving Bacon, who played a hot dog stand owner. Both actors later appeared regularly on *I Love Lucy*. Most memorably, Lane was the clock-watching clerk who finally granted Lucy Ricardo her passport; Bacon was an innkeeper hoping to protect Lucy from Ricky's "improper" advances after she is led to believe they were never legally married. Lane was even cast as a banker, a precursor to Gale Gordon, in Lucille's first post–*I Love Lucy* series.

The young actress was pleased with her progress at the studio and happily expecting the arrival of her mother and grandfather at Ogden Drive when her Columbia family was broken up and she suddenly found she was off the payroll: "One day at six o'clock they fired about fifteen of us. We were out lock, stock, and barrel. We were on the street. We just stood there. What happened? Nobody knew."

Dazed, she went out to dinner with Dick Green, whose brother Johnny composed "Body and Soul" and "I Cover the Waterfront." Green told her that RKO was doing a picture set in a Paris fashion house and had put out a call for girls with modeling experience. "I don't want to be a showgirl!" she protested. "Well, you don't want to be out of work either," he replied. Grudgingly, she went to the audition that night and impressed the casting director with the fact that she had modeled at Bergdorf Goodman's and could carry clothes like a professional mannequin. She was one of five models hired for *Roberta*, starring Irene Dunne and the new dance team of Ginger Rogers and Fred Astaire. She was happy to be earning $75 a week.

She liked to say later that when she lost her job, she called her family back East and said, "Don't take the train! Take the bus!" but this was an example of her making a good story even better, according to relatives. She was in fact able to pick up DeDe at the train station in George Raft's limousine and take her out for a lavish dinner on money he lent her. Lucille would be one of Raft's few debtors who at least tried to repay him for his generosity. Six years later, when she presented him with the sum she had borrowed, he was surprised that she was attempting to honor a debt he had completely forgotten.

After DeDe and Lucille's celebratory dinner, Lucille showed her mother the home she had made for them, the living room and three bedrooms all in pastels with the dark woodwork painted over. "This is how you live in California, with oranges and avocados growing in the yard!" Lucille announced. Cleo, who soon joined the others, said, "We saw palm trees for the first time and thought it was paradise."

"That was the point when Lucille assumed responsibility for the family," she recalled. "Her support made it all possible. It was important for her to have us all together, and wherever she went, it was 'Mama, come with me.' Lucy needed that." In bringing her loved ones to live with her, Lucille dispelled the curse of separation that came upon them when Warner Erickson died. She established a home at last because she had finally taken charge.

5

THE STUDIO that Lucille signed with in late 1934 was a major player in the film industry, but it operated under absentee ownership. Whereas the others had a strong individual leading them, a mogul like Goldwyn with his self-glorifying expansiveness or Louis B. Mayer with his iron-fisted sentimentality, RKO Pictures was under the sway of a changing cast of executives whose hegemony depended on decisions and alliances having little to do with making movies. It was not that RKO's leaders were faceless; they simply changed with such speed that their features were a blur to those who stayed in Hollywood to make pictures year after year.

RKO was the only studio formed specifically to make talkies. It began in 1928 with the union of David Sarnoff's Radio Corporation, purveyor of sound equipment to Hollywood; Joseph P. Kennedy's small movie lot called the Film Booking Office; and the Keith-Albee Orpheum circuit of theaters located in the Northeast. By the time Lucille Ball entered its Spanish colonial gateway at 780 Gower Street off Melrose, Kennedy had returned to Wall Street and Sarnoff's role was that of major stockholder. RKO's parent company, Radio-Keith-Orpheum, was suffering from bad business decisions, especially the financial burdens of overexpansion, compounded by the Depression. It had committed itself to building too many theaters, including Radio City Music Hall and the RKO Roxy in New York, where it had leased an excess of expensive office space in the new Rockefeller Center.

Without a central creative authority, RKO was turning out a series of offbeat and unusual films that ranged from *King Kong* to *Little Women*. The studio's leading female star, Katharine Hepburn, wore pants and went for walks, evincing a New England athleticism that prompted more than one person who thought himself authoritative to describe her as a "nut."

Roberta was planned as a splashy musical, a genre the studio had only recently begun to attempt. Producer Pandro S. Berman had acquired the property, a Broadway hit with a book by Otto Harbach and music by Jerome Kern. The cast was led by Broadway dancer Fred Astaire and a rising starlet named Ginger Rogers, in their third film together, and the popular actress Irene Dunne, in her first important musical. Dunne played a dispossessed Russian princess who excelled as a Paris couturiere, Rogers a bogus Polish countess, and Astaire the man who knows she is really an American singer in disguise.

Lucille, as one of the Parisian mannequins, was on the set just before the New Year's holiday, then again for another six days in January 1935. She was supposed to have a line of dialogue, but the French accent the role required proved beyond her power, as dialect of any kind generally would. Her sentence was cut in the finished film, and she appears only in the finale fashion parade wearing an ostrich-plume jacket over a slinky silk evening gown. In contrast to the covert, midnight glamour of the other mannequins, Lucille is a luminous American sweetheart who has mistakenly wandered into a nightclub on her way to the prom.

She used her forty hours on the set of *Roberta* to advantage, however, by carefully observing Irene Dunne. At thirty-six, Dunne was thirteen years older than Lucille, a well-loved star who played gracious, well-bred heroines and was also an accomplished soprano. Watching from the sidelines, Lucille saw Dunne do take after take, the same scene fifteen or twenty times, and each run-through surprised her, because Dunne acted each different from the time before. Studying Dunne's technique led Lucille to begin to think about the different ways of reading and delivering lines.

Lucille had also managed to get on the set of a Hepburn movie, and saw that this star telegraphed whenever she was about to be funny and played a scene the same way over and over, no matter how often it was done. Earlier, Lombard impressed Lucille by managing to believe with consummate faith everything she said or did before the cameras so that she seemed ever fresh in her line readings. Lucille decided she would do best to follow Lombard's technique, yet Dunne's resourcefulness continued to amaze her.

In the experimental, all-for-laughs atmosphere of the Cantor pictures, Lucille had shown her moxie, but her bravado failed her before the patrician Dunne. She could not bring herself to compliment or question her. So awed was Lucille by Dunne that, years later, when she herself was renowned and found herself in an elevator with the older actress, she started to ask about her method, but still could not work up the courage to broach the subject. After Lucille confessed this to a seminar at the American Film Institute in 1974, author James Harvey went to Dunne herself, who was pleased to hear this praise from a woman she called "the top comedienne of all time." Dunne speculated that if she had varied her takes, it was because she thought the director expected her to improve.

Perhaps due in part to management's loose control over the studio, RKO in Lucille's early days there had an easy family feeling. Management changed too fast to have time to fire disfavored employees, so writers would sit in their windows and watch presidents go and come secure that they would outlast them, but wondering if any new executive might have time to help their career at all. Since everyone knew one another, no one needed to lunch alone in the commissary, which was a plain affair with tables and a long counter along one wall. The sets were always open, except for Katharine Hepburn's—either because she allowed few visitors or because her presence itself was so forbidding.

Betty Furness was then another RKO newcomer, five years younger than Lucille and, like her, a former model from New York.

Unlike her, she was brought up on Park Avenue, attended junior college, and was now working because her father insisted she must "do something useful" at a time when many were starving. Betty encountered Lucille in the makeup room and liked her enormously. "I thought Lucille was swell from the word go. She was the most no-nonsense woman I ever met. She took her work seriously, but never took herself seriously. She was always direct and to the point and said what she thought, which was not what you caught from every actress at RKO," she said.

One day Lucille surprised her by volunteering the name of her dressmaker. "That was typical of her," said Betty. "She never had any notions that you would want to keep something good to yourself. Her dressmaker made me a navy taffeta evening coat for $18."

Lucille had the tall, lanky frame of the 1930s, but not its face. She was not regarded as especially pretty, lacking as she did the sculpted planes and brooding lips that were the decade's hallmarks of glamour. Although makeup artists did their tricks, plucking her eyebrows and raising her hairline to open her features and make them more photogenic, they could not make her look chic in close-ups, which she knew was a deficit. She continued to hoof in the background or have small character parts, happy to be part of the business if she could not yet be a star.

In February 1935, Lucille saw her name on the screen for the first time, billed as The Nurse in *Carnival*, her last film for Columbia. Heartened by this credit, she applied herself with renewed energy. "I've always been a family person, and I adopted RKO as my studio family," she said. "I talked to everyone I met from office boys to executives—possibly because of that urgent need I'd always had to make people like me."

Al Gerston, then an aspiring RKO director, recalled, "She would get so involved in a project! I was casting a play we were doing on the lot and telling her about my difficulties with Actors Equity. The conversation continued as we went into the contract players' dressing room and she walked into the bathroom and sat down on the toilet. I followed her. When we realized what had happened, we were hysterical with laughter."

She became especially good friends with Bernard Newman, who

had designed the opulent costumes for *Roberta* and had been the house designer at Bergdorf Goodman's in her New York days. They went to industry functions together, and Newman gave her extra publicity when he named her the studio's best-dressed young player.

Lucille was cast next in *Top Hat*, the fourth Fred Astaire and Ginger Rogers vehicle. As a florist's assistant who was to say "What can you do?" and "Really?" in a Cockney accent, she kept muffing her lines. The director, Mark Sandrich, tried to help her, but the robust pronunciation of London's East End eluded her. Finally, rather than drop her and call in someone else, Sandrich settled for an accent that was softly English. She was so grateful for his kindness that twenty years later, a young man fresh from the army found it surprisingly easy to get a job as the second assistant director on the *I Love Lucy* show. He wondered why Lucy, who by then could be sharp with people around her, was always considerate toward him, until the day Lucy told him that she never forgot his father's generosity. Jay Sandrich, who was thirteen when his father died and considered landing his first television job a fluke, went on to direct *The Mary Tyler Moore Show*, *Soap*, and *The Cosby Show*.

Lucille was still considered to be Mack Grey's girlfriend and was often seen with him, but they remained basically no more than friends. In 1935, it was an open secret that the powerful—and married—Pandro S. Berman had taken an interest in Lucille and had been meeting with her at his hideaway apartment near the studio.

At thirty, Berman was both boy wonder and grand old man of RKO. He had been on the lot since 1923, when his father, the general manager of Joseph Kennedy's Film Booking Office, got him a job as a script clerk. Berman briskly moved ahead to become an assistant director and film editor and was now the functioning head of the studio. Motion pictures encompassed every aspect of his life; he had even married the daughter of a Kansas City film exhibitor. Sleeping and eating, even his weekly card game, meant less to Berman than talking about the fine points of a script or the preferred way to cut a scene.

Film production had now become so complex that it made the moviemaking that had gone before it seem like a simple matter of aiming the lens. Producers now exercised the authority that had once belonged to such directors as Griffith or Chaplin. Berman himself was responsible for the Astaire-Rogers films and those of Katharine Hepburn, and although he preferred to supervise individual features, he was then overseeing the RKO studio while his boss, the forty-year-old Merian C. Cooper, recuperated from a heart attack.

Unlike Sam Goldwyn, Pandro Berman was definitely Lucille's type—dark, broad, and fleshy. Like Johnny, he was energetic, forceful, and loved gambling, but Berman had no need for self-aggrandizement. He loved people, especially the "average" ones with whom Lucille herself was most comfortable, and was never grand, despite his position. He lunched with cutters and technicians at a small café across from the studio, and when he wanted to see someone, he simply walked into the fountained courtyard the executives shared and called to the man through the office window.

"Pandro Berman was crazy about Lucille Ball," her cousin Cleo Smith recalled. "He was good to her and did all he could for her on the RKO lot. She respected his successes. He was so taken with her. Smitten is the word. I don't think she found the situation awkward. She was a savvy lady and had wonderful instincts and chutzpah. She was made of strong stuff." At twenty-four, Lucille was in fact quite independent and too experienced to have romantic dreams about men. She loved to play flirtatious games, but these were more to gratify her own ego than to manipulate others. She was more of a pal than a vamp. "Lucille was one of the guys. She liked men. There was none of the threat of the war between the sexes, no guard so men would feel challenged or defensive," said the actor Arnold Stang, who later worked with her.

However much Berman may have wished to help Lucille, he wisely did not give her parts beyond her capabilities. Had she been cast in a featured role and flopped, as a newcomer she would have been branded a box office failure. Worse, she would have harmed a film for which he was responsible. One does not know how much of this entered into his calculations, but certainly romance is overrated as a career builder, for it is at the box office and not on the casting couch where one ultimately succeeds. Sex whispers, but money talks.

Because of her relationship with Berman, directors and other key people did feel it politic to aid her when they could. She had access to scripts scheduled for production and she would read each one to see if it had a part for her. Berman later said of Lucille, "She was very talented and very determined. She was ambitious, and she had to make it. It would have killed her if she hadn't."

One of several films Berman cast her in was *I Dream Too Much,* which he hoped would be the vehicle to launch the French soprano Lily Pons in Hollywood. Unlike most divas, Pons was a gamine and thus a potential rival to Grace Moore, the American opera star who had become popular in Columbia films. Lucille replaced Betty Grable, an eighteen-year-old stock player who had also been on the Goldwyn lot, in the minor role of Gwendolyn Diddey, a bleached-blonde gum-chewer visiting Paris with her parents and little brother. Her one line was: "Culture is making my feet hurt," a gem that she delivered with conviction. Lucille was funny in her small part. She exaggerated her character, as did everyone else in the cast, except perhaps Henry Fonda as the composer who is Pons's struggling husband.

Lucille then made *Sew and Sew,* a short with Billy Gilbert, the character actor who made a career of being a fat and flustered stooge. She is not memorable except in a scene where her body signals its longing to do physical comedy. When Gilbert kisses her hand, her face shows surprise, but her elbow shudders with amazement.

In *Chatterbox,* starring Anne Shirley and Phillips Holmes and filmed in November 1935, Lucille played a cynical actress. She is introduced as the camera follows her from behind striding into a village theater ready to battle her director. Most of the supporting players talk at one another in long speeches that slow the pace. Lucille's lines were short and snappy, but again her character did not quite come to life.

She often discussed her career over lunch in the commissary with Margaret Hamilton, who played the film's landlady. Hamilton was thirty-three, but her hatchet nose and unrelieved plainness gave her the older, worn look she would use to advantage as the Wicked Witch of the West in *The Wizard of Oz.* As they ate, Lucille would ask hopelessly: "Am I ever going to succeed? I have financial responsibility for my mother and I need to make money." So heartfelt was Lucille's distress that in the late 1950s, when the two ran into each other on that same lot and had a quick lunch in that familiar commissary, Hamilton was drawn back to those days and asked with real concern about her mother and how things were going. "Margaret, Margaret," Lucille replied, her eyes widening. "I bought the studio!"

Over Christmas 1935, Lucille filmed her scenes in *Follow the Fleet*, starring Astaire and Rogers as former dance partners who tap around each other to such songs as Irving Berlin's "Let Yourself Go" and "I'm Putting All My Eggs in One Basket." She was one of the gorgeous women gliding through "Let's Face the Music and Dance" and had a small role as a been-around dancer who pretties up Ginger's mousy sister, played by Harriet Hilliard, the future Harriet Nelson of *Ozzie and Harriet*.

As a contract player, Lucille had to be available between shootings for publicity photos ("I posed for every cheesecake picture they asked for"), be drilled in how to conduct herself on interviews, meet directors, and, she would later claim, learn to be quiet. The atmosphere stimulated her even as she hoped for greater things, and the person who drilled her to develop her talent for them was Ginger Rogers's mother.

Lela Rogers was a formidable woman in her middle forties with hair bleached blonde like her daughter's and features that were similar, but more sharply drawn. Through several marriages, Lela doted on her only child, taking time away from her only during World War I when she became one of the nation's few female marines. When Ginger became the Charleston champion of Texas at the age of fourteen, Lela put her on the vaudeville circuit, directed her routines, and dutifully refined the act in response to the occasional bad review. Lela was so single-minded that one afternoon in Memphis when she heard that the stage manager planned to cancel Ginger's act, she whisked the girl off to a Chinese restaurant so he couldn't fire her before Lela coached her to improvement. "Leelee," as "Geegee" called her, was the guiding light of her talented daughter's life. "My mother went through hellfire and damnation to take care of me," said Ginger Rogers. Her drive and managerial skills piloted her child on to Broadway and thence to Hollywood. RKO executives found that Lela Rogers was an unreconstructed Republican in the age of the New Deal and a ramrod Christian Scientist who once claimed that Ginger ended an attack of appendicitis by throwing up the inflamed organ. More irksome still, she objected when they bleached her child's chestnut curls and exercised their prerogative to decide which costumes she would wear.

Lela's ability to cultivate budding talent was proven, however, so in order to keep her occupied, RKO executives asked her to open a workshop for contract players on the lot. This she did with characteristic verve. Betty Furness remembered her as the den mother of all the players at the studio. "She was very bright, very quick and energetic, and wanted to be in on a lot of things. And she was."

Lela studied with several coaches and would return from her classes to pass on what she had just learned to the young RKO company. She staged plays, many of them written by her friends—*Breakfast for Vanora* would be one Lucille remembered best—and charged a quarter admission. She instructed her charges to read classics and encouraged them to improve in every way they could. In response, Lucille bought a copy of Samuel Pepys's diary and dipped into his seventeenth-century adventures as she sat around on the set. Knowing she had much to learn, Lucille was delighted to be under this energetic lady's wing. "Lucy picked Lela's brains and spent time with her. Lela knew Lucy had talent. I don't know whether or not she recognized her timing, but she probably did. She was astute," said Cleo, who became a contract player herself.

Lela's niece, Phyllis Fraser Cerf Wagner, was also a young hopeful, and recalled that Lucille was enrolled as a dancer in Lela's workshop. "Lela took a great shine to Lucille and thought she was a natural comedienne." One of Lela's ancestors had been a Ball, and she suspected they were both related to George Washington's mother, Martha Ball. Without bothering to check the lineage, Ginger, Phyllis, and Lucille blithely told people they were cousins and became a trio.

"Lucille would come up to Ginger's house off Schuyler Road and we'd sit around the pool. People worked too hard to have much time for friendship. We were just three females together. We didn't talk about men, at least I didn't. They were probably more interested in talking about work," Phyllis said.

As the singular Katharine Hepburn had temporarily lost favor with the public and was being labeled "box office poison," Ginger had become RKO's reigning female star, and work consumed her life. Because the Ginger-Lucille friendship could not be between equals, Lucille was especially appreciative. "Ginger and her mother were wonderful to me. They helped me more than I have ever been helped," she said.

One night when Ginger went out with Jimmy Stewart, she fixed Lucille up with his roommate, Henry Fonda. The evening began in Brentwood, where Fonda cooked dinner. Lucille did the dishes while Ginger instructed the men in the new carioca dance steps in the living room. Then the foursome proceeded to the Cocoanut Grove, danced for hours, then stopped off for breakfast at Barney's Beanery. Dawn found them on the sidewalk, where the sun's first rays revealed the dissolving remains of the actresses' heavily applied rouge and mascara. Ever a man of few but telling words, Fonda looked at Lucille and exclaimed "Yuk!" Thus ended any possible romance. Years later he lamented with more humor than regret: "If I'd behaved myself, they might have named that studio Henrylu."

Although Lucille may have compared herself unfavorably to Ginger and Ann Sothern, her own mother was mindful that no other girl from Jamestown had access to George Raft's limousine or was dangling her toes in Ginger Rogers's swimming pool. As Ginger had "Leelee," Lucille had DeDe, who was not a stage mother but whose presence did provide an anchor in Hollywood's choppy seas. "Lucille's mother was charming. I recall she had a lean figure and was jovial and sweet," said Ginger Rogers. DeDe planted herself to stay in Hollywood, whose climate, excitement, and stars appealed to her as much as they did to her daughter.

By now Lucille had moved to her own apartment and hired a maid for DeDe, whose job was to look after her ailing father. Fred Hunt, now seventy-one, had suffered a stroke, and to add to the difficulties of age and illness, he resented having been uprooted. He was also impatient with people who were more intrigued with the doings of Clark Gable than the Socialist Norman Thomas. Most at home in the living room, where he kept his pipe and tobacco and took the occasional nip, he read *The Daily Worker*, which carped that Roosevelt was the worst of leaders because his "pseudo-reforms," such as the

Civilian Conservation Corps, blocked real revolutionary change.

His interest in politics inspired him to make Fred Ball, DeDe, and Lucille promise to vote as members of the Communist Party. On March 19, 1936, Lucille obliged him by going to downtown Los Angeles and registering for the primary. "I remember feeling quite foxy about the thing, because I registered. We had a very bad feeling we had done that. I always felt I would be all right if I didn't vote it," she would say years later. On June 12, after they met the residency requirements, Fred Hunt, DeDe, and Fred Ball followed suit.

Lucille was now filming *Bunker Bean,* a comedy about an efficient male stenographer who believes himself to be the reincarnation of Napoleon Bonaparte. Lucille, startlingly thin in a dark business dress, played the part of an oblivious receptionist well. The only other cast members whose names endure had even smaller roles—the future columnist Hedda Hopper, who played a social-climbing mother, and the comedienne Joan Davis as a telephone operator.

At home, Fred Hunt put his deeply held social convictions into practice in ways that varied from the eccentric to the dangerous. When Lucille hired cleaning women and nurses to watch over him, he told them their jobs were beneath the dignity of workers and their pay less than a living wage. Several believed him and decamped. One story has him going so far as to attempt to organize the prostitutes who worked on nearby Selma Avenue into a union.

Looking out the window, where he brooded on his own, Fred was annoyed by a tree that obstructed his view and shed too many leaves in his yard, so he decided it had to come down. DeDe warned him that it was city property, but he managed to saw away at its roots over the course of a wet winter. On the night it finally toppled over, it crushed Lucille's new dark-blue Plymouth convertible. As the family examined the cut roots and crumpled metal, Fred feigned amazement, but DeDe snarled that she knew better: "Don't tell me you don't know about this!"

Lucille's grandfather also hosted an introductory meeting for party members on Ogden Drive. A woman who was there recalled that before the class began, "an elderly man" proudly said they were all the guests of Lucille Ball, the actress, showed them her pictures and scrapbooks, and said she was happy to loan her home to the Communist party.

Fred was a socialist by temperament, and his troubled life had made him passionate in his concern for the common man. That this fervor was directed against a tree or the hiring of a cleaning woman made him seem a crusty and comic character to those who met him. His family had learned to humor him whenever possible, so when he handed Lucille some petitions, she simply scribbled her name and went on with more practical concerns.

On Election Day in 1936, when Roosevelt was reelected in a landslide, Lucille was too busy making a second Lily Pons film to cast her vote. The public had spurned *I Dream Too Much*, so Pandro Berman decided its story might have been too highbrow. In *That Girl from Paris*, he cast Pons as a soprano who attaches herself to a swing band and steals the heart of the boyish bandleader, played by Gene Raymond. Lucille, as Raymond's girlfriend, was again cast in what was supposed to be an important film for the studio, but it failed critically. Pons was such a strong emphatic presence that she seemed conniving rather than cute, and the audience hardly cared when she won Lucille's screen beau—and probably suspected Gene Raymond was making a mistake.

The film provided opportunities for Lucille to demonstrate her gift for knockabout comedy, but her technique here seemed accidental. In a key scene where she was to do pratfalls on a dance floor, the prop man soaped her shoes and waxed the floor so thoroughly that she had no more control on the highly polished surface than the character she played. Some of her painful tumbles were real. Had she been more experienced, she would have protected herself physically and artistically by checking the floor and her soles before the cameras rolled. As it was, she could only be bruised and annoyed.

RKO's publicity department, in contrast, was inspired by the incident and sent out a press release boasting that in *That Girl from Paris* Lucille Ball had had to fall down thirty-six times in one day. This news appeared as a caption under a color drawing of her that ran in Sunday comic sections around the country.

She and others would later characterize herself in those early days as a performer who never made demands. However, Lucille acknowledged that her temperament did flare in two memorable incidents. In a film shot in the San Fernando Valley (possibly *The Three Musketeers*), she fainted from the heat and insisted on being driven home.

When the casting director asked her why she had walked off, she announced she would no longer go on hot locations, and supposedly he acquiesced.

The other episode had far more dramatic consequences. RKO's prestigious photographer Ernest Bachrach had postponed taking important publicity shots of Lucille until she had her teeth straightened, a process that took a year and required having porcelain caps made for nine of her teeth at a cost of $1,300. Bachrach usually delegated photographing stock players to his assistants, but he lived up to his promise and told her he would work her in between other shootings. On the morning they agreed upon, she went early into the makeup room, but after having her hair done she discovered that the only available makeup man was Mel Burns, who headed the department and was assigned that day to Katharine Hepburn. He nevertheless applied foundation to Lucille's face and was beginning work on her eyes when Katharine Hepburn appeared. Summarily he shooed out Lucille, locking the door behind her. Lucille was in the hallway, her face half done and late for Bachrach, when she realized her caps, which were crucial to her photo session, were locked inside. She lifted up the wooden panel of the pass-through window to ask Burns to give her the box, but he ignored her. Enraged, Lucille picked up a cup of coffee and hurled it at him, but her aim faltered. The cup hit the back of the makeup chair and rained down, not on Burns, but on Hepburn. Looking on aghast through the frame of the window, Lucille saw the star rise, furious and dripping, and depart, thus ending production for the morning.

Executives immediately called Lucille to the front office and demanded to know her version of the story, which she presented in tears. Fearing she had lost her choice opportunity with Bachrach, and possibly her job, Lucille retreated to the commissary to find sympathetic listeners. News of the occurrence had already reverberated through the studio, and both Ginger (who was not only Lucille's friend but Hepburn's rival) and Lela let it be known that they thought Hepburn had overreacted and that they did not want Lucille fired. By lunchtime a large group had assembled around Lucille to hear her account for themselves. In the midst of one of her woeful retellings, Hepburn herself strode in and apologized. "Lucille was a friend of mine," Hepburn recalled a half century later. "I think if she was reckless it was because she was reckless by nature." In the aftermath, some suggested that Lucille believed she could vent her rage at Burns because she had Pandro Berman behind her. Others said her job was saved only because of Berman's clout. Ginger Rogers insisted simply that her mother preserved Lucille's job.

Fortunately, however, her star was on the rise after her whole-hearted tumbles in *That Girl from Paris*. Two weeks after it wrapped, she spent a few days shooting *Don't Tell the Wife*, a slow-moving short about swindlers who set up a phony mine stock deal. Now brunette rather than platinum blonde, Lucille is present mostly as a voice over an intercom, but on camera she gives a self-assured performance as the con men's confederate.

More important, during the course of the production she was also preparing for a part in a play that was expected to make its way to Broadway. This was an important step for her, because in this period success on the stage gave an actress status and legitimacy in films, as it allowed her to prove that she had something more meaningful to offer than looks alone.

Berman had tried earlier to secure her a part in *Stage Door*, a Broadway play by George S. Kaufman and Edna Ferber about young actresses rooming together in a boardinghouse. Kaufman's agent, Leland Hayward, had flippantly and adamantly rejected her, so Berman and Lela Rogers came up with another vehicle with a similar setting. *Hey Diddle Diddle* was a comic satire of the film industry and the hopeful young women trying to storm it. This was not one of Lela Rogers's student workshops, but a professional production. Anne Nichols, the author of the enduring *Abie's Irish Rose*, which ran five years on Broadway and earned her a personal fortune, was producing and directing it.

Lucille played Julie Tucker, one of three roommates coping with neurotic directors, confused executives, and grasping stars who interfere with the girls' ability to get ahead. Although in films she had been constantly cast as secretaries, actresses, or gun molls—something that was both a reflection of roles that were available and an indication of the impression she conveyed—Lucille was the standout in *Hey Diddle Diddle*, just as in her Jamestown hit *Within the Law*. Needing connection, Lucille came alive in response to a live audience in a way she did not before impersonal cameras and technicians.

Hey Diddle Diddle opened in Princeton, New Jersey, on January 22, 1937, to a welcoming audience and appreciative reviews. Two weeks later, a performance in Washington, D.C., was even more warmly received. A *Washington Post* reviewer wrote: "If there is one young person who is going to add to her professional stature in *Hey Diddle Diddle* it is Lucille Ball, just about the slickest trick you ever saw in slacks."

The response to Lucille was exactly what she, Berman, and Lela Rogers had hoped for; however, it did not get her to Broadway. The play was beset by problems, chiefly with its star Conway Tearle, who played the director and was in poor health. The playwright wanted to replace him, but Anne Nichols said the fault lay with the character and insisted that the part needed to be reshaped and rewritten.

The two could not agree, so in mid-February, a week after *Hey Diddle Diddle* opened in Washington, the producer closed it, thwarting Lucille's hopes. Anne Nichols, however, had clearly been impressed by her. A few months later, Nichols told an interviewer that she hoped to revive the play, but that the only one of the originals she would ask to return was Lucille Ball.

However, on that day in February, Lucille's new plateau revealed not new vistas of success but valleys into which one could fall. It was no longer enough merely to get a part, keep it, and please an audience. Lucille saw that if she was to succeed, every aspect of a production, from script to cast to director and producer, had to be top notch. She could not transcend a bad production, but she could take a good part and make it superb. She saw that she would be able to reach only as high as the people she depended on could grasp.

6

HOWEVER FRUSTRATING HER EXPERIENCE with the stillborn *Hey Diddle Diddle*, her success in it enabled Pandro Berman to cast Lucille in his film version of *Stage Door*. The heavy-handed theme of the Broadway play was that Hollywood's crassness destroys art, but this notion obviously could not be carried over to the screen. Berman's *Stage Door*, rather, was a clash and interplay of character, its theme that struggle is necessary for achievement and that hard work, decency, and strength can sometimes prevail over easier routes.

The concept of a group of aspiring actresses living under the same roof while trying to break into the theater offered roles for several young contract players, including Eve Arden and Ann Miller, but the film was intended as much more than just a showcase for new talent. Like a gambler rattling dice in a cup, Berman also threw together two proven talents who seemed to have run out of luck. Gregory La Cava had directed *My Man Godfrey* for Universal with Carole Lombard the year before, but because of his belligerent refusal to be super-

75

vised, he remained a free agent without a permanent home in any studio. Katharine Hepburn, whose recent films *Sylvia Scarlett* and *Mary of Scotland* had failed utterly at the box office, now had to prove that she was not a jinx unable to draw fans. The only guaranteed winner in the cast of *Stage Door* was Ginger Rogers, who was given top billing and was expected to draw the audience.

Show business requires faith, if not in the Transcendent, then in assorted egotistical and terrified ingénues, matinee idols, bit players, and character actors. As the saint sees an angel is a vagrant, so the seasoned motion picture executive must discern Elizabeth the Great in an actress reaching for her lipstick and find Dr. Jekyll in an actor straightening his tie. Pandro Berman had great faith in Hepburn, La Cava, Rogers, and Lucille Ball. Undoubtedly he believed in the others in the picture—Adolphe Menjou, Ann Miller, Eve Arden, and Andrea Leeds, who would be nominated for an Oscar as Best Supporting Actress, and in Gail Patrick, who played stone-hearted beauties and later went on to co-produce the *Perry Mason* television series. His confidence in *Stage Door* and its participants would prove to be justified, but as production got under way, his seemed to be the faith of martyrs. Although normally Berman was intensely involved with each project, in the case of *Stage Door* he gave La Cava the free rein the director insisted upon. Age forty-five with dark eyes and receding gray hair, La Cava was a grizzled, vigorous man with abundant humor and a fierce integrity. He derived some of his unorthodox methods from the silent era, including "cuff shooting," in which the director made up a story and dialogue as he went along. This was to prove to be his technique on *Stage Door*. Thus, when rehearsals began on June 2, 1937, there was no script, and La Cava informed Lucille and the other players that they were to create their roles as the filming went along.

La Cava was a devoted student of psychology, and he intended to base each character on the actress playing her. He preferred that the women wear their own clothes before the cameras to reflect their tastes. Each morning at nine, he had them rehearse a scene and play it as they wished. He eavesdropped on their conversations during breaks, studied their reactions to one another, and developed a sense of how they would behave if they were in fact struggling neophytes living at the Footlights Club in New York.

The cast, however, was not a sorority of guileless aspirants but a collection of Hollywood stars and starlets each trying to measure out her own turf. While method actresses of later years might have delighted in this challenge, these performers were simply appalled. "I thought, the hell make it up as I go along! If I could do that I wouldn't be here," Hepburn recalled. Lucille, who sought direction and instruction to take her to Hepburn's level of accomplishment, felt the same. Ginger pointed out that none of them knew people who were not successful, only the ones who were. In addition, she and Hepburn had been rivals for years and bristled in each other's presence.

The group bonded briefly on June 7, the day shooting started, when they heard that Jean Harlow had died at the age of twenty-seven. They gathered around while Ginger and Eve Arden read newspaper accounts of William Powell's bedside vigil as the young star succumbed to uremic poisoning. Ann Miller, who was fourteen and had won her role only after Ginger and Lucille assured the producers that she *had* to be eighteen (the minimum age for compliance with the labor laws), tapped her feet in a time step and smacked her gum, murmuring "Oh, my gawd, poor Jean Harlow" to the click of her dance shoes. La Cava used this behavior in a close-up of Miller grinding away at her gum and in a scene where the gang beat time as Miller dances to her own repetition of sentences.

La Cava's "script" by now consisted of index cards and a loose-leaf notebook containing the life stories of all the characters. At the end of each day he and the writers, Morrie Ryskind and Anthony Veiller, would decide on upcoming scenes. According to the screenwriter and director George Seaton, who was then one of his young aides, La Cava was so desperate to appear brilliant that he actually worked with uncredited writers late at night. Then during the day on the set he could disappear into his office and quickly emerge with pages of dialogue that seemed all the stronger and insightful for having apparently been produced on the spot.

Lucille, a contract player billed below Rogers, Hepburn, and Menjou, was awed by Hepburn, whose Bryn Mawr diction was a chisel etching her every word in stone. "The very way she talked was terrifying for me," said Lucille. "She didn't talk to me directly, so it didn't matter, but I was riveted to her. So was everyone else. She was beautiful and not standoffish. She just ignored the whole set."

In fact, Hepburn was paying attention and finding that she floated around the edges of scenes instead of dominating them. When she took her puzzlement to the top, her friend Pandro Berman dismissed her with the advice that, given the state of her career, she would have been fortunate to have the sixth part in a successful picture. She then asked La Cava to explain her role, but he confessed, "I'm damned if I know, Kate." Her character, Terry Randall, was a debutante with a can-do approach to life and talent that was developed only through personal devastation, so La Cava devastated Hepburn. For her climactic moment in the film, he appropriated her key scene from *The Lake*, the Broadway play that prompted Dorothy Parker's famous remark that the actress "ran the gamut of emotions from A to B." Forcing Hepburn to confront her own inadequacies may in fact have been good for her, for she was able to deliver the line "The calla lilies are in bloom again. Such a strange flower, suitable for any occasion" in such a way that it had meaning and poignancy.

The star, who doubtless knew Berman was looking out for Lucille, noticed her more than she realized. Hepburn recalled, "I don't think Lucille in any way thought she was beautiful, and at the beginning of her career, no one else did. She had 'it.' She was always an amusing creature and she was funny on her own. She had a lot of spunk."

This spunk was reflected in Judy Canfield, the character La Cava developed for Lucille. She had had a bit part in his *Affairs of Cellini* on Goldwyn's lot a few years earlier, but La Cava formed his impression of her only on the *Stage Door* set, and it was that of a girl who dresses well but did not have the talent or determination to make it.

Lucille wears sporty jackets and trousers elegantly. In her beautifully manicured fingers she constantly holds a cigarette, but when she puffs at it, she draws her fist to her face, like a bettor at the track. The sardonic Judy always has a date, thanks to a steady supply of boors that keeps arriving from her hometown of Seattle. She finds the best in them because, as Lucille and Marion had in New York City, Judy relies on them to provide her meals, and she is eager to fix up her friends so they can share the windfalls. Her housemates like and trust her and heartily agree when she announces that she prefers "Amos 'n' Andy" to Shakespeare. The basic realities of life, personified by food, friendship, and a good man's love, are what truly matter to

Judy. They constitute her existence as well, for she has not worked in more than a year. As Lucille plays her, Judy is wise and wary, as if she knows better than even to bother trying.

Judy is still very involved with her family. Receiving mail full of their woe, she announces ruefully, "There's nothing like a cheerful letter from home . . . lots of love and can you spare fifty dollars?" She ultimately sees she is not getting anywhere and chucks the theater for marriage and a dependable life in the Northwest. As she departs the boardinghouse, Rogers and Hepburn muse that she will have kids and all they will have is scrapbooks no one will want to see. In a house full of young women in a 1937 film, one actress had to counterbalance rampant female ambition, but it is intriguing that of the many talented members of the company, La Cava picked Lucille to play the unaffected clear-eyed realist. She goes home not because she longs for domesticity, but because she recognizes the limits of her talents and opportunities.

Through his confusing and precarious cuff shooting, La Cava produced a film classic in two months. The actresses are astonishingly natural and fresh as they interrupt and walk in front of one another, just as if they were real people instead of actresses on screen. Aside from the performance of Constance Collier, the British grand dame who played a deliberately theatrical coach, the acting is without apparent artifice. The film was universally regarded as superior to the stage version, and Kaufman himself good-naturedly referred to it as "Screen Door." *Stage Door* was the most honored RKO picture of 1937 and a commercial success. The New York film critics named La Cava outstanding director, and the Academy of Motion Picture Arts and Sciences nominated it for four Oscars: Best Picture, Best Director, Best Supporting Actress, and even Best Screenplay. Hepburn was redeemed. Audience surveys indicated they thought that it was the best picture she ever made.

Lucille personally received little attention for her performance, the one that gave her the highest billing she had had to date. Andrea Leeds was considered the film's discovery. Perhaps in a fit of pique, Lucille billed the studio for the use of her clothes. RKO did not pay.

Just before *Stage Door* was released, Lucille began filming *Having Wonderful Time*, a story of young Jews from the Bronx who meet and fall in complicated love at a summer resort in the Catskill Mountains. Arthur Kober's play was a hit on the stage, and Hollywood quickly optioned it, but at the insistence of the Hays office, its naughtiness was gelded and its ethnic flavor thinned. The leads of the Borscht Belt drama went to the indisputably gentile Ginger Rogers and Douglas Fairbanks, Jr., while Lucille played Miriam, who pursues with single-minded assertiveness the camp's Lothario, played by the eelish Lee Bowman.

Lucille and her co-star Eve Arden attempted Bronx accents, but Lucille's was the better with her pronunciation of "gawjus" for "gorgeous." The only standout in the misconceived ensemble was Red Skelton, making his film debut as the resort's lively social director.

The cast and crew were bused to Big Bear Lake in the San Bernardino Mountains so they could film exterior scenes, and, except for the fact that everyone was expected to rise at dawn, a holiday atmosphere prevailed. When excess drink claimed the fourth assistant director, a handsome extra named Robert Parrish was quickly promoted to his job. Since he was constantly encountering the studio's bankers and lawyers at Big Bear, Parrish believed the film was made partly to allow them to meet the beautiful models who played extras.

One day Lucille invited Parrish to lunch and demanded, "What the hell are you doing with me when all these beautiful girls are around? I'll tell you why! All these other girls are taken by bankers and lawyers."

"Lucille, I'm eating with you because you asked me," he protested.

Parrish, who later became an Oscar-winning film editor and a director, was assigned to go to the private cabins and awaken the groggy players at four in the morning. "One of the first ones I had to wake up was Lucille Ball. I knocked on her door and a gruff man's voice said, 'Who's there?' I said, 'It's the fourth assistant director.'

" 'Whaddya want?'

" 'I want to wake up Miss Ball.'

" 'Come in here.' "

Parrish took a deep breath, entered, and found Lucille alone. He asked where her friend was. She said, " 'There's no one else here. That was me. I answer all my early calls like this. Come have coffee.' And we sat down and had a cup together. Lucille was not a phony.

She said what she thought. She was always active and talking to people. You felt she was in control of herself and those around her."

Douglas Fairbanks, Jr., concurred. "She was obviously gifted, charming to work with. Everybody assumed she had a fine future. She worked hard and seriously developing her technique and cooperated with everyone."

Like most other actresses in Hollywood in the late 1930s, Lucille was swept up in David O. Selznick's quest for the perfect Scarlett O'Hara for *Gone with the Wind.* With everyone from Carole Lombard and Bette Davis to contract players being tested, Lucille was well aware that the search for Scarlett had become a publicity stunt. Knowing that this stunt would pay off for someone, RKO instructed Lucille and several other of its young players to prepare three scenes of Scarlett at sixteen, eighteen, and twenty-one with the help of a Southern voice coach. Lucille did not show up on the day she was to be tested because she had no expectations of success, but then Selznick himself summoned her to come to his office at Culver Studios to read for the role.

She drove there in her open convertible on a day marked by one of Los Angeles's winter cloudbursts. By the time she arrived in Selznick's office she was drenched, shivering, late, and completely unrecognizable to Selznick's assistant, Marcella Rabwin. Marcella asked how she could help her. "Get me out of here" came Lucille's reply. Selznick had gone out, but had asked that Lucille wait, so Marcella gave her brandy and a sweater and placed her by the fire in Selznick's inner office. Lucille was sitting on the floor by the fire, empty brandy glass in hand, when Selznick arrived. From her vantage point, he appeared eight feet tall. "Shall we begin?" he said. "Begin what?" she asked, feeling the effects of the brandy. Later she realized she had played all three scenes on her knees.

Still a contract player, although now earning more than $1,000 a week, in January 1938 Lucille made *The Joy of Living*, where she was cast as Irene Dunne's grasping and dependent younger sister, and in February, she did *Go Chase Yourself*, a slapstick comedy featuring Joe Penner, a radio comedian with a soup-bowl haircut. Penner played a pea-brained bank clerk and accidental kidnapper, and Lucille his exasperated but supportive wife. It is hard to believe that these two would converse, much less marry each other, which may be why Lucille surpassed mediocrity in only one scene. In that, she lands in jail and with shuddering animation assesses in turn every bar that holds her.

At this time her name was linked romantically in the columns with that of Gene Markey, a screenwriter who had been married to Constance Bennett's sister Joan, and with the actors Paul Douglas and Broderick Crawford. Crawford was the burly son of Helen Broderick, the matronly figure in many Astaire-Rogers films. When the publicity department announced that Lucille was engaged to him, some claimed the story was a cover for her relationship with Berman.

Milton Berle, another RKO contract player who was then filming *New Faces of 1937*, recalled dating Lucille a few times: "I saw this beautiful girl walking down the lot. It was the first time I saw a girl with completely white slacks. I took her to Trocadero, found out she was from Jamestown, and we became friends. In those days if I went out with a girl more than a few times, my mother broke it up."

Her romance with Pandro Berman had run its course, possibly because he and his wife now had a baby son, and Lucille was increasingly uncomfortable being the other woman. In late 1937, when she was twenty-six, she began a long relationship with Alexander Hall, a forty-three-year-old, twice-divorced director. *Here Comes Mr. Jordan* (1941) would become his most famous film, but at this time he was most identified with Shirley Temple's *Little Miss Marker*, which made the tot a star and secured his place as a director at Paramount.

Hall's slicked-back hair and his pouchy eyes gave him the face of a disengaged owl. Women saw his charm, but men were less convinced, particularly young men closer to Lucille's age, some of whom initially distrusted Lucille for going out with him. Garson Kanin, then beginning to direct, recalled him as a competent comedy director but a rough-and-tumble person. He said, "Al Hall was the one thing about Lucy I never understood. I adored her. I thought she was a peach, but he was a beast." At Hall's request, Kanin read a script Hall was directing in which one black man spit in another's face. Kanin questioned its taste and thought the scene offensive, but Hall retorted, "What do you mean? It's nigger to nigger, isn't it?" Kanin said, "That was Al Hall. Well, she was an ambitious girl and he was a contract director."

They were at different studios, and if Hall ever found parts for her, RKO was unwilling to release her for them. Those who knew them as a couple describe the relationship as more practical than passionate, yet given Lucille's nature, the romance was not without volatility. One story regarding the pair was that during one argument, Lucille took an ax to Hall's door.

Once she began to win featured roles, Lucille disciplined herself to conserve her energy and her looks by keeping weeknight dates to a minimum, but she and Al did go to Hollywood hangouts and industry functions together and enjoyed weekend junkets on gambling boats that anchored outside the three-mile territorial limit. Above all, Hall introduced her to a group that treated her as a young girl to be helped, petted, and enjoyed, a role she had never really been allowed. Undoubtedly, part of Al's appeal for her was that he had been in vaudeville as a child and introduced her to many of the vaudeville greats. Jack Haley, the spindly, diffident actor who later was the Tin Man in *The Wizard of Oz*, and his wife, Flo, threw her a family party each year she was with Al. Her birthday, August 6, was four days before Jack's, so Flo dubbed them "The Augustonians" and honored them with a double celebration on August 10.

Flo Haley recalled that Lucille impressed Al Hall's other vaudevillian friends not only because she was very funny but because she was supporting her grandfather. Often when Al was busy in Hollywood, Lucille traveled to San Francisco with the Haleys to see friends perform. On the drives up the coast, Lucille sat in the backseat wearing her customary slacks and tailored jacket. She entertained her hosts by reading aloud from the influential gossip columns of Louella Parsons and Hedda Hopper, asking Jack if he knew the people being written about and then speculating herself on what effect the items would have on their careers. She also read reviews of films and nightclub acts, sometimes delivering them with great pontification, other times being hilariously snippy. "If you introduced Lucille to someone who put on an air, she would wait until their back was turned and throw back her head as if she had smelled an odor," said Flo Haley. Al Hall was not always amused by her cutting up. "Al was older than she and didn't get gags the way she did. He was on the serious side," she remembered.

Besides the Haleys, Al's circle included Arthur Treacher, George

Burns and Gracie Allen, the Fred Allens, and the actor Charles Ruggles and his wife. Most important, Hall reintroduced Lucille to Ed Sedgwick, the Texan who had directed the Keystone Kops and Buster Keaton, and who had told Lucille in her Goldwyn days that she had great comedic gifts. His wife, Ebba, was a large, heavyset woman who had been born in Sweden, like so many people Lucille knew in Jamestown. The Sedgwicks became her surrogate parents, and Ed gave her the informed encouragement she would have liked from a father.

Lucille basked in Ed's attention and praise but was not ready to focus strictly on comedy as her vehicle to stardom. She knew she did not have the delivery of such reigning comediennes as Lombard, Dunne, or even Hepburn. Line readings probably did not matter much to Sedgwick, who saw that she had the talent of a Mabel Normand, whose wit was in her eyes and body, and of Keaton and Chaplin and other greats, whose gifts were physical but who faded with the coming of sound.

Another couple Al and Lucille were friends with was Al's doctor, Marcus Rabwin, and his wife, Marcella, who had rescued Lucille on the day of her ill-fated meeting with Selznick. Marc was closer to Al's age, Marcella closer to Lucille's. The four spent Sundays at Al's new seventy-five-acre turkey ranch in Simi Valley northwest of Los Angeles, where they barbecued pullets. Marcella recalled Lucille's genuine affection for Al's friends, especially Dr. Rabwin. "She and I became particularly close because of her love for my husband, who became a replacement father for her. She was always looking for a father. She did like Al. He was a quiet and decent man, and when she first met him, he was a bigshot in her eyes."

According to Marcella, Al and Lucille lived together for a while, an arrangement that was cozy enough that DeDe, who was just a few years older than Al, also took up residence. "Her mother moved in with them largely because Lucille was desolate without her. She loved her, she depended on her. DeDe was a dictatorial, petulant sort of woman, very forceful in her speech. She would tell everybody what to do, and you very well better do it too, but Lucille just adored her."

Like Judy Canfield in *Stage Door*, Lucille was diligent about keeping strong ties to her family and friends. She advised her brother to continue his education. As Fred Ball recalled, "She offered to put me through college when she hardly had the money. She said we could do it, but I was making so much money, I couldn't afford it." She also wrote to Pauline Lopus that it was time for her to get out of Jamestown.

"When Lucille started to be famous, she got concerned about me because I stayed home. She thought I was wasting my life," Pauline said. One night when Lucille was on a promotional tour, she wrote her old friend a fifteen-page letter on hotel stationery informing Pauline where she had gone wrong. "My mother was ill at the time and I had a job and a contract with the school board. I never let anyone see the letter, I burned it. I knew she meant it kindly."

In 1938, Lucille began work on a string of films that would earn her the unofficial title of "Queen of the Bs" at RKO, which had a more varied B schedule than any of the other major studios. A "B film" was a low-budget production, with a predictable plot or one that was simply lifted from an earlier hit. Its cast, directors, and writers were drawn from the ranks of staff less experienced, and hence lower paid, than those who made A films. The B unit was the domain not only of the up and coming, but also the territory of stars and directors whose time had clearly passed.

As the 1930s wore on, B pictures were increasingly in demand because audiences had to be coaxed to part with their money. The novelty of talkies had passed as the Depression set in, so filmgoers expected their money's worth with a bill of two features, plus newsreel, cartoons, previews of coming attractions, and even the occasional free plate or cup. Only the most luxurious movie palaces in major cities could present a single A feature headlined by reigning film stars.

Like MGM, Twentieth Century–Fox, Warner Brothers, and Paramount, RKO controlled every aspect of production, from the creation of films to marketing and distributing them in its theater chain. Since RKO's own theaters demanded a constant supply of new features, it was cost-effective for the studio to keep its stock company and directors busy supplying them.

As a contract player who had to justify her salary, Lucille Ball was turning out so many pictures so quickly that the costume department was usually stitching up two or three wardrobes for her simultaneously. Edward Stevenson had so distinguished himself with the costumes in *That Girl from Paris* that he had succeeded Lucille's friend Bernard Newman as head of the wardrobe department, and he was as considerate of her as Newman had been. He read every script, even the Bs, so he could understand the characters whose clothes he was creating, and he refused to go along when the studio suggested, for reasons of time and money, that he simply buy Lucille's clothes off the rack. This mark of respect for her work and the integrity with which he approached his own job impressed Lucille. Like so many others Lucille met during this period, Stevenson would one day see her reward his selfless friendship and professionalism by putting him to work on *I Love Lucy.*

Fortunately for her, especially at this stage of her career, she alternated playing the third or fourth lead in A films, which were intended to enhance her stature, with B pictures that reminded executives that she was earning her salary, which was now $2,000 a week. In such Bs as *Don't Tell the Wife* and *Go Chase Yourself*, she played types, not characters. "I started as a model because I looked like a model, and 'the other woman' or 'the career girl' because I have a deep aggressive voice that has no softness or romance to it," she said.

Such types populated her next eleven pictures, filmed between May 1938 and December 1939. In two *Annabel* films (*The Affairs of Annabel* and *Annabel Takes a Tour*), she plays the eponymous heroine, a ditsy actress who ricochets like a pinball though a series of publicity stunts that lead her into housecleaning and even a jail term. The pesky porcelain caps that had gotten her into trouble with Hepburn again caused problems. In the first Annabel film, she literally spat out one line: "I'm Annabel Allison, you fool!" enunciating like Elmer Fudd and ejecting her caps into the grass, where some were lost forever.

In *Annabel Takes a Tour*, she demonstrates her gift for physical comedy as she rises from a three-point landing on elbows and nose. She has total conviction in her role and plays it without a trace of farce. At her best in scenes calling for exasperation, she otherwise shows a limited range, although Frank Nugent of *The New York*

Times did note that she was rapidly becoming one of the country's brightest comediennes. Lee Marcus, who supervised the B pictures, planned the Annabels as a B comedy series, but scrapped it when Lucille's co-star, the puckish rogue Jack Oakie, who played her press agent, demanded too much money to continue.

Lucille then took a crack at screwball comedy. *The Next Time I Marry* was one of an explosion of such features inspired by Frank Capra's 1934 success with Clark Gable and Claudette Colbert in *It Happened One Night*. The basic format for this genre involved a wealthy vixen's being tamed by a handsome working man. In *The Next Time I Marry*, Lucille is a rich girl who marries a ditchdigger from the WPA to subvert the terms of her father's will. In her funniest scene, she sets fire to the trailer in which her husband, played by James Ellison, has locked her.

The New York Times pronounced it one of the best B comedies of a banner crop. "And of course there is Miss Ball—the former lanky and glass-eyed comedienne—who has prettied herself up, put her eyebrows in the wrong place and everything. No student of the motion picture in its more thoughtfully budgeted branches can afford to miss it."

The film's director, Garson Kanin, recalled, "She was extremely inventive to the point I was surprised she didn't want to write. Like most good actresses, she did not like to be directed. She didn't need to be. She was her own self. It has to be carefully remembered that there are stars and there are actresses. Movies are just interested in great personalities. I think Lucy was a great, great personality. She was an individual, and that's what got her going at the time."

Beyond personality, the studio knew she had something that no one could quite define. Like a flint that inexplicably refuses to catch, however, her talent resisted most efforts to make it ignite. RKO cast her as a beautician who turns a successful wrinkle cream into a cosmetics empire in the melodrama *Beauty for the Asking*. Lucille's character nobly teaches her ex-boyfriend's socialite wife how to hold him and suffers bravely up to the happy ending. By now movie reviewers were beginning to complain about the hackneyed and patched plots to which Lucille was subjected and called on the studio to make better use of her. The *New York Times* review was typical:

"She is one of the more promising young players on the RKO contract list but she will be a long time getting anywhere unless the stories improve."

The studio gave her opportunities to show what she could do and to earn her salary. In the hard-boiled crime picture *Twelve Crowded Hours,* she was the sister of a petty hood sent to jail by her boyfriend, a newspaperman played by Richard Dix. Still thin, but plumper than when she arrived in Hollywood, she was a beautiful brunette with her hair falling from a center part. She has few lines to say in the film, but emotes effectively through her eyes and hands, particularly when she and Dix are captured by a mobster.

In *Panama Flo,* a remake of RKO's own 1932 film *Panama Lady,* she plays a persecuted dancer named Lucy who tries to earn passage home from Central America and ends up accused of murder. Her resilience was beginning to fail her and production had to shut down several times because she was ill. Her only recollection of making the picture involved an accident that endangered her life. She was on the set ensconced in what was supposed to be a seaplane when she saw a shower of sparks descend from the ceiling to the flammable wing cover. She jumped into a pool of water four feet deep to escape. That mishap was cut, and critics abhorred what they did see.

Five Came Back, a suspense adventure in which she played a gold-hearted floozy, was better received. The plot was predictable, except for the identities of the ultimate survivors, but Lucille would seldom be privileged to have more distinguished talent behind the camera. The film was directed by John Farrow and based on a screenplay by the writers Dalton Trumbo and Nathanael West.

Next came *That's Right—You're Wrong,* a good-natured spoof of Hollywood image making. Folksy bandleader Kay Kaiser plays himself and Lucille is an affected glamour girl who helps him with his screen test. Then in November 1939, two months after England and France declared war against Germany, she made *The Marines Fly High* with past co-stars Richard Dix and Chester Morris.

But the hallmark of this period of her professional life was *Room Service,* in which Lucille Ball, future Queen of Comedy, was teamed with the Marx Brothers and they produced a dud.

With the participation of the famous wild men and a play like *Room*

Service—a madcap hit on Broadway for which Berman spent a record $300,000—RKO believed it had as much of a sure thing as anything could be in pictures. But creatively the brothers were at a low ebb, and indeed their best films, such as *A Night at the Opera* and *A Day at the Races*, were behind them. They now lacked a mentor, for the great friend and guide of their glory days at MGM, Irving Thalberg, had died in 1936. Thalberg had nurtured and honed their demented artistry by allowing them time to develop their material and to test it on the road before committing it to film. Instead of being given months to prepare *Room Service*, however, the brothers had five weeks to shoot. The plot that evolved basically came down to Groucho's attempt to raise money to meet their hotel bill by producing a Broadway show, with Lucille and Ann Miller around to provide some hope of romance. But because the project was not originated for the brothers, it was not a true Marx film. The fact that they were cavorting to others' specifications shows, and their anarchism burst through only off camera. Miffed to hear one day that visitors were on the set that they had requested be kept closed, they plotted revenge. In the scene scheduled for that day, Lucille was to run into a room, shut the door, and keep going, chased by the Marxes. The brothers stripped, burst through the door, and pursued her completely naked, which stunned the spectators, who happened to be priests and nuns.

Lucille did not enjoy the short but grueling shooting schedule or the Marx Brothers themselves, except for Harpo. She found him less manic than the others and was impressed that he spent time quietly reading by himself. She was Harpo's date at a dinner at Sam Goldwyn's palatial home, where she sat in opulent rose-colored surroundings at a long table for twenty, waited on by liveried servants. Already intimidated, she was flummoxed by the sight of her first artichoke and started to attack it with knife and fork, but Harpo moved quickly to save her from humiliation and showed her how to pull its tough petals apart. Harpo, and Harpo alone, appeared on *I Love Lucy* in the classic episode that introduced the brothers to a generation that knew only of Groucho and his duck.

Groucho never truly warmed to her and claimed that he saw no sign of her potential when they worked together because she was not really a comedienne, but an actress. "I've never found Lucille Ball to be funny on her own. She's always needed a script," he told his biographer, Hector Arce.

Although Lucille stayed mum on the subject of Groucho, she was uncharacteristically impolitic in making no secret of her anger at Zeppo, who she felt cheated her of work and money. At the time Zeppo was launching a career as an agent and had negotiated for his brothers a lucrative $250,000 contract for *Room Service*. He claimed his bargaining chip was the threat that if RKO didn't pay what he demanded, he would return to the act. Zeppo told Lucille he would serve as her agent if she would let him know when she heard of parts that might interest her. When other actresses won the roles Lucille told him about, she felt that he used her information to get jobs for other people.

Lucille was leaden in *Room Service* and added little to it beyond her looks. Why could she not catch fire in pictures? Poor scripts were not completely to blame. She outdid herself in radio in February 1938, when she began appearing with Jack Haley on his weekly CBS show sponsored by Wonder Bread. With the five-foot-seven Lucille, jauntily leaning her elbow on Haley's shoulder, the two did the vaudeville routines Jack had performed with Flo before she retired to raise their children. As Flo recalled, "She didn't know she could do comedy as well as she could, and she got over her fear around Jack, because when a comedian gets with comedians, they start to let loose." Then the radio personality Phil Baker invited her on his radio show. She was such a standout that *Variety* observed, "Her material was only so-so, but her timing and knock 'em dead emphasis on the tags italicized the humor. Her withering style of always belittlin' was particularly well suited to go with Baker's fooling."

Why did radio inspire her in ways that films did not? One reason, which she herself later recognized, lay in the laughter of the studio's live audience. In films, the immediate spectators were preoccupied cameramen and technicians, and the joy of a moment's performance was lost in fretting over its long-term impact on a career. Her makeup was so heavy that she had to be careful lest she ruin it by moving her face, and the standard routine of takes and retakes only made her more anxious. "In pictures, by the time they get around to the close-up, the comedy is gone," she told Hedda Hopper.

As an actress, Lucille did not have the gift of pretended fragility that Lombard had, the willing suspension of strength of Rogers, or even the ultimate tamability of Hepburn. She seemed able to take care of herself and unwilling to accept interference, even in Hollywood fantasies. In life she needed no assistance, for she was successfully supporting not only herself but her mother and her grandfather. One of Lucille's liabilities was that she was a strong person who lacked the ability to persuade an audience that she was anything else.

7

WITHIN A FEW WEEKS of Lucille's arrival in Hollywood and her success as the cut-up slave girl in *Roman Scandals*, revolution swept away the world of a pampered sixteen-year-old Cuban named Desi Arnaz. Those weeks of August 1933 were one of the many times when the currents of their lives, so potent when they coursed together, flowed in opposite directions. Later Lucille would turn to astrology to explain this phenomenon: Desi was a Pisces, whose glyph was a pair of fish. According to her, he feared success and in him each fish thrashed at the other so as to sink to the bottom first, while she, the Sun-blessed Leo, reigned and roared.

Desiderio Alberto Arnaz y de Acha III was born by the sea on March 2, 1917, in the historic city Santiago de Cuba, on the southeastern shore of the island. As Lucille's Jamestown was paced by the factory whistle, Santiago was set in motion by a massive cathedral bell. Its peals reverberated over pastel houses worn soft with age in the torrid sun, across the town plaza and its open stalls and the fortress with its fifteenth-century ramparts, up past the modern hos-

92

pital, and then echoed to silence toward the mountains of Oriente Province. The mantilla, high comb, and scarlet sash of nineteenth-century Spain were still in evidence on the town's cobbled streets, along with men who boasted they had ridden up nearby San Juan Hill with Teddy Roosevelt's Rough Riders in 1898.

However uncomplicated the lives of the 45,000 souls in Santiago seemed to be, the family of Desi Arnaz controlled or participated in everything that happened to them. Unlike Lucille, whose family was inconsequential in her town's social scale, Desi Arnaz was acknowledged as someone who would one day attain prominence. His father, Desiderio, was Santiago's mayor and his uncle its chief of police. His mother, Dolores de Acha, called Lolita, was considered the most beautiful woman of her day, and was the daughter of an executive of the Bacardi Rum corporation. Desi's grandfather, a doctor who had also been Santiago's mayor, had cared for the Rough Riders after their assault on San Juan Hill.

Desi was dark and contemplative with liquid brown eyes and the flexible thumbs and flat feet of his mother's family. After he outgrew his toddler's Buster Brown haircut, he was given a boat that he and his friends used to row out over the sunken hull of an old American vessel to fish for snapper, bass, and yellowtail. On land he devoted himself to music. Most Cuban homes, huts and haciendas alike, had an assortment of percussion instruments, including a set of maracas made from the hollowed-out fruits of the calabash tree, sticks of polished hardwood called *claves*, and the *vina*, a seed instrument that shook African sounds into Cuban music. But Desi's special love was the guitar, and his joy was to woo and serenade his grandmother, who as matriarch would summon all her grandchildren and their parents to her house one afternoon each week to correct or encourage them and to enjoin them to keep all problems and discord within the family.

Desi had six aunts and uncles on his father's side and eleven on his mother's, but he himself was that rare Cuban, an only child. His father, who had learned pharmacology in Atlanta, mapped out his son's future, which he hoped would involve a legal career and studies at Notre Dame in the United States.

Whatever he learned of piety and righteousness as the only son of his devout and adoring mother, Desi came to see quite clearly that the men in his family led secret double lives. For each, there was the professed realm of propriety and respect for women, and then there was the more interesting, obvious, but unmentioned life of *la casa chica*, "the little house" where one kept one's mistress and illegitimate brood. Desi's grandfather divided his time between the progeny of each of his establishments, but would force his mistress to hide in the barn whenever his wife paid a surprise visit to his mistress's domain. In this regulated world Desi was convinced that both women were content. "I am sure Grandma must have known, but she never said a word, and the mistress never got upset about having to get out and hide. As long as he continued to love each of them, and cared for their children equally, they were satisfied."

His mother, Lolita, was a sheltered, privileged Spanish gentlewoman serene in the knowledge that the perfidy of men made women all the more angelic and consequently too elevated even to acknowledge betrayal. Once in a burst of temper young Desi told his mother that she was to blame for his father's faults, because she treated him like a king. Her response, which impressed him all his life, was that treating her husband like a king enabled her to be a queen. With Desiderio's political and personal interests often keeping him away from home, Lolita devoted her being to her son. Cosseted and cherished, given all and thus expected to return all, Desi's unconscious reaction was to make certain that no one woman could have such power over him again.

From his adolescence Desi had a strong interest in women, an interest that was more often than not mutual. When he was fifteen, his uncle arranged for him to enter the world of men by taking him to Santiago's finest brothel for an evening's education. Having learned everything about women, Desi still remained intrigued by girls. By his own account, romantic interests sabotaged his studies at the Jesuit high school in his crucial third year, but he was spared academic disgrace by personal disaster. As Lucille's fate had been to see successive homes collapse, Desi's was to have what seemed an immutable structure destroyed. Political uprising ended his days of privilege and led him into an exile that would force him to make for himself the sort of life he had expected to be bestowed.

One summer afternoon in his sixteenth year, instinct impelled him to break off a card game and hurry home. He arrived in time to receive a frantic telephone call warning him to find Lolita and flee—his father's patron, Gerardo Machado, the president of Cuba, had been overthrown by dissidents. Over the next few days, as the Arnazes hid at an uncle's house, every possession they owned in Santiago, at three ranches, and at an island beach house was burned or looted. Desi saw charred bits of his clothes wafting in the wind, the melted neck of his guitar, and, more harrowing, men dragged behind horses through the streets to the cemetery, where they were executed and buried.

Desi and his mother, cousin, and uncle disguised themselves as revolutionaries and drove five hundred miles to Havana over mountains, thick forests, sugar plantations, and open plains. Whenever they came to a town or saw a gathering crowd, Desi and his cousin would jump on the running board and shout *"Viva la revolución!"*

His father was jailed for six months and then fled to Miami, where Desi joined him in 1935 while Lolita remained in Cuba. The city's rainbow-colored buildings, fantastic robber-baron estates, and tufted palms reminded them of home, but they lived first in a rooming house and later in a corner of a rat-ridden warehouse while the elder Arnaz tried to make a business of importing building tiles. To learn English and earn his high school diploma, Desi enrolled part-time at St. Patrick's High School in Miami Beach, where his best friend was the son of the mobster Al Capone. "Sonny" used to bring him home for lunch and lemonade in his walled and guarded mansion.

Miami, a city of 350,000 people, was slowly recovering from the collapse of its land values and a devastating hurricane in 1926 that had claimed lives and property and, for a while, ruined the lucrative tourist industry. Nonetheless, it had long been a haven for Latin Americans who had profited, often excessively and illegally, from close ties to politicians at home. Some prominent friends of Desi's father, fearing that a coup would occur, had banked their money in Florida and established homes there against the day when they had to flee Cuba. Through these old connections, Desi was able to find two jobs that appalled Desiderio—he cleaned birdcages for a man selling canaries on consignment, and he sang with a Latin band.

Destiny reclaimed him as its child the night he stood on the bandstand and strapped on a conical Afro-Cuban drum to drown out the cacophony of an everything-but-Latin band. The primeval beat and Desi's energy set his audience wild. He was a popular draw in Miami and by 1938, Desi was featured with the "Rhumba King," Xavier Cugat, at the new Starlight Roof of the Waldorf Hotel and at a club called La Conga in New York. Although he could not read music and had only a passable singing voice, Desi's enthusiasm and the vogue for Latin music made him a compelling entertainer, especially when he beat out the native follow-the-leader dance called the conga. At twenty-two, Desi was dazzled by Manhattan and his success, and was overly gallant with even the boldest woman, but when he strapped on his drum, he shouted like a tribal chieftain. "At these moments," said the young and influential reporter Dorothy Kilgallen in September 1939, "the night club becomes a wild temple dedicated to delirium." Perhaps because the columnist Walter Winchell called this line dance of three short steps and a leap "the Desi Chain," Desi came to boast that he himself had introduced the conga to the United States. In fact, he had only helped popularize the craze.

The conga's accented and syncopated two-four beat was easy to dance but difficult to play. Desi performed it so well that he drew to La Conga such demanding nightclubbers as Brenda Frazier, the celebrated debutante, and Polly Adler, the renowned madam. They and other women in the audience were wild for him, with his full sculpted mouth, avid eyes, and sense of sweet, naughty fun.

La Conga also featured a young Puerto Rican dancer named Diosa Costello whose trademark was that she could swish her derriere at warp speed. George Abbott, the wizard of Broadway, had directed or produced dozens of hits, including *Twentieth Century* and *Room Service*. He was taken with Diosa and wanted to feature her and the conga in his next show, a college musical called *Too Many Girls*. Fifty-two years later, by which time most of his ingénues had died in old age, the centenarian Abbott recalled, "I was crazy about Cuban dancing and I would see Desi when I'd go dancing with Diosa Costello at La Conga. I wanted a Latin quality for my new play, so I wrote a part for her and for him. Turned out the part I wrote for him was better than the one for her."

Thus Desi was cast in a Broadway show before he ever saw one and set audiences howling with comical lines he did not even comprehend. *Too Many Girls*, a romp about girl-mad Ivy League football players, featured music by Richard Rodgers and Lorenz Hart, who contributed the classics "I Didn't Know What Time It Was" and "I Like to Recognize the Tune" to the project. Desi, who played an Argentine football hero, was sufficiently self-assured to advise America's foremost musical comedy writing team to rephrase "Harvard Look Out" for the conga and showed them how to do it.

Each evening after performing in *Too Many Girls*, Desi and Diosa would hurry six blocks up Broadway from the Imperial Theater to La Conga on West Fifty-first and put on a few more shows. Such was Desi's youth and vitality that he thrived. "Desi was outgoing and gregarious. He *loved* everybody, especially women," said Eddie Bracken, who made his musical comedy debut in *Too Many Girls*. One afternoon Desi introduced Bracken to the treacheries of horseracing at Jamaica Park. There the neophyte struggled to understand his racing form, was emboldened to up his wager to $5, and picked a winner. Frustrated, Desi, who had lost every bet, decided to make up his losses by placing several hundred dollars on two horses in the same race. The young men watched in excitement, then horror, as the outside horse veered in, forcing both of Desi's horses to the rail while Bracken's pick came in first. Wild with fury, Desi kicked chairs and hurled them about, bellowing that everybody hated him because he was Cuban.

Squandering several hundred dollars must have been particularly galling since Desi now had total responsibility for his mother, who had joined her husband and son in America soon after they left the warehouse. As a struggling immigrant in Miami, Desiderio was forced to live in unaccustomed close domesticity with Lolita until his son's success offered him escape. Pursuing happiness in the way of his new country, the elder Arnaz soon initiated divorce proceedings. Now forty-five, he moved in with another woman and her daughter and put a public notice in the newspaper declaring that he did not know the whereabouts of his wife. Lolita, a graying forty-three, maintained proud serenity in the face of abandonment and wore her wedding ring until her death.

Desi was choleric when he learned what his father had done. The divorce of his mother was unthinkable, and when Desiderio called offering excuses, his son slammed down the phone. Lolita soon took up residence in Desi's bachelor duplex apartment on Central Park and sat at a front table every night at La Conga, where she suggested he play pretty songs instead of sweating over his guitar. Her presence chilled the heated life he had enjoyed as a twenty-two-year-old male with access to women ranging from Polly Adler's girls to Betty Grable. He hid his annoyance from his mother, but not his anger at his father. Lolita persuaded her son to mend the breach, and eventually Desi came to blame his parents' problems not on their characters but on the revolution that had shamed his father and driven him from his wife.

As if to check his mother's influence, or at least better regulate his life, Desi decided to get married. He came to an understanding with Renée de Marco, a dancer who was six years older than himself, dark-haired and petite, with a vaguely Catholic background. She and her older husband, Tony, were a popular inventive ballroom dance team, but their marriage was stormy by the time she met Desi. The love and vitality of the handsome younger Cuban gave her an incentive to seek a divorce from the man who was her livelihood. Certainly she asked little of Desi, who valued her as a woman who loved and understood him and ignored his obvious affairs with other women. Although he might never acknowledge it, Renée was much like his mother.

When Abbott went to Hollywood to make the movie version of *Too Many Girls*, he invited Desi and Bracken to go along. They were the only leads from the Broadway production chosen for the film, and it is unlikely that Desi would have had the opportunity had there been other young Latin actors with more intelligible English to choose from.

Desi arranged for Lolita and his fiancée to follow later, and for his own journey from New York to Hollywood, he purchased a silver-gray Buick Roadmaster convertible, hired a driver, and found him a uniform. After they crossed the country and reached Pasadena, they got lost and took four muddled hours to figure out the ten-mile route to RKO. At first they mistook the ornate gates of a Jewish cemetery for the portals of the studio, but Desi eventually did manage to make a grand and arrogant entrance. The RKO guards found him so authoritative that they dropped the chain and let him pass, even though only company vice presidents and major stars were allowed to drive on the lot. Those who saw him park in front of the Little Theater thought that the Latin was either the next Valentino or a total fool.

When Desi arrived at RKO in June 1940, Lucille was in the midst of a lucky streak. She had started off the year with a role as a dowdy housewife who impersonates an Argentine adventuress in *You Can't Fool Your Wife*. The film's improbable plot was weakened further by the Hays office, which insisted that RKO reduce a tale of adultery to one of flirtation. Lucille was believably pathetic as the mother-ridden wife and enticing as the playful bare-shouldered spitfire. This B picture, however, led to one of her best roles, that of a burlesque queen named Tiger Lily in *Dance, Girl, Dance*.

This opportunity came at the very time RKO was in turmoil. Majority stockholders, led by the Rockefeller interests, had recently installed George Schaefer as president. Through the years, Pandro Berman had been able to serve as a buffer between the businessmen and those who actually made the pictures, but when Schaefer demanded final say on all films and brought in producers to work independently of Berman, Berman decamped to Metro-Goldwyn-Mayer.

Schaefer decided RKO would thrive by concentrating on quality films. He deemphasized B production and manic comedies and went so far as to put under contract young Orson Welles, the theatrical director who had just caused havoc with his broadcast of H.G. Wells's "War of the Worlds," which persuaded terrified radio listeners that Martians had actually landed in America.

Another member of Schaefer's quality team was the German producer Erich Pommer, who quickly went to work on *Dance, Girl, Dance*. Wiry and gray-haired, with a nervousness accented by relentless consumption of cigarettes that he was trying to give up, Pommer cast Maureen O'Hara, a hit in his *Jamaica Inn* and *The Hunchback of Notre Dame*, as the Good Girl and Lucille as the Bad. Pommer, who had seen promise in a minor actress named Marlene Dietrich and put her in *The Blue Angel*, claimed that Lucille combined the traits of Jean Harlow and Mae West while remaining herself, and he was intrigued by her potential. Ralph Bellamy and Louis Hayward played the love interests, and the great stage actress Maria Ouspenskaya was the girl's noble ballet mistress. For verisimilitude the Russian dressed in the very clothes she had worn as a drama student in Moscow after the revolution.

Aside from Pommer, *Dance, Girl, Dance* was conceived and directed by women. Tess Slesinger wrote the script, based on a story by Vicki Baum, author of *Grand Hotel,* and Dorothy Arzner directed it. Short and stocky with cropped hair and a brusque manner, Arzner began her career as a stenographer at Paramount, worked up to being script girl for Alla Nazimova and film cutter of Valentino's bullfighting scene in *Blood and Sand,* and finally began to direct pictures herself. After the failure of Goldwyn's *Nana* with Anna Sten, she directed Rosalind Russell in the sentimental *Craig's Wife,* which increased Arzner's reputation for ability to deftly handle emotional material.

Dance, Girl, Dance is the story of two dancers struggling to earn a living. One is determined to serve art as a ballerina, the other turns to burlesque to get money from men. In the 1970s, it became a feminist cult film, for its sympathetic portrayal of two women loyally helping each other even as they compete, and film students discerned in it a deeper, mythic strain in which O'Hara's character had to pass heroic trials, many at the hands of Lucille's Tiger Lily, to become a true artist. At the time it was made, however, one critic called *Dance, Girl, Dance* cliché-ridden and garbled, while saying "It is Miss Ball who brings an occasional zest into the film, especially that appearance in the burlesque temple where she stripteases the Hays office."

For her role, Lucille bleached her auburn hair blonde as a contrast to O'Hara's red curls and set about to experience the milieu her character inhabited. She and Al Hall went to South Main Street in downtown Los Angeles, taking along a newspaper reporter for publicity. Amid honky-tonk Philippine dance halls, saloons, and gypsy astrologers, they found the Follies Theater and took their seats. As the lights went down and the suggestive music began, Lucille's anticipation gave way to careful study. She noted that some strippers shed their clothes to a slow march while others preferred a quick step, but the gusto of one performance made her gasp. She decided to make her own movements brisk, and turning to the reporter, promised that hers would be a dance of the seven veils multiplied.

She felt confident that she understood the theory of burlesque, but its practice was more arduous. The Hungarian-born choreographer Ernst Matray drilled her in the fine points of suggestive bumps, grinds, and thigh slaps until she collapsed from exhaustion. Thanks to the skill of her strutting, only the most astute viewer would discern that she was in fact emulating a striptease, as the single piece of clothing she takes off is her coat.

Lucille kept her hair and makeup in repair with the help of a mirrored makeup stand on wheels, possibly made by Fred Hunt, and she also acquired the services of a personal maid. One Saturday morning she tuned in to a radio call-in show for job seekers and heard a young black woman named Harriet McCain announce that her mother worked for Jack Benny's wife and that she too wanted to be a lady's maid. Lucille phoned the station and said the girl was hired.

Harriet was tall, plump, and pleasant with a moon face that was deceptively sweet. As a teenager in the 1920s, she had briefly tried show business herself, dancing in black clubs in Los Angeles. She had a fund of stories and reserves of patience for her new boss. When Lucille's emotions flared, she threw her hairbrushes at Harriet, who at first picked them up quietly. Over the next forty years, however, the balance of power altered. By the late 1940s, Harriet would get exasperated, shout at her boss, "You can't tell me what to do!" then decamp to San Francisco to visit a friend until both she and Lucille cooled down.

Later, when Lucille had become the top star in television, she settled into the makeup chair one day at CBS Studios and called for a drink of water. Someone handed a glass to Harriet, who passed it on to her employer. Lucille took it and saw it contained ice, which she had proscribed. Furious, she tossed it in Harriet's face. The maid sped out for more water, rushed back to the makeup room, paused, then hurled it in Lucille's face. Saying nothing, Lucille calmly called for a towel.

Harriet was the first of Lucille's closest aides who would stay with her for decades. Like Lucille, members of her staff typically had a sturdy humanity that was the product of having weathered hard times. They understood and overlooked Lucille's flashes of belligerence because they knew that, if necessary, she would defend them with the same fierceness with which she occasionally attacked. "The lady was a democrat with a small d," said one assistant, explaining what inspired his loyalty.

Like the characters they played, Lucille and Maureen each protected her own turf. "We were competitive," said Maureen O'Hara, "but in a friendly way." For all the care and preparation that went into *Dance, Girl, Dance,* the two stars had to scramble to come up with a decent pair of black stockings between them for their dance scenes. "It used to be a battle to see who would get the stockings without runs," she recalled. "I don't know why the Wardrobe Department couldn't help us, but I'd show up and say, 'Give me the ones with no runs in them.' She'd say, 'No, give me the stockings with no runs.' The loser would accept it and swear to get there earlier the next day."

Dorothy Arzner had the trick of whispering on her sets and thus established a mood where electricians, actors, and camera crews were hushed and serious too. Absent were the bawdy jokes that normally punctuated filmmaking. On this picture with Lucille simulating a striptease, it was probably just as well, except that O'Hara and Ball declined to be dignified about their fight scene.

They charged admission the day of the filming and donated the money to charity. "Anyone who wanted to watch us beat each other up had to pay, and we battled like tomcats," said Maureen. When the battle broke, the combatants left the arena together to have lunch. It was while standing in the commissary with her hair falling forward over a black eye, the vision of a "two-dollar whore beaten by her pimp," that Lucille met Desi Arnaz.

The young Cuban seemed to have come from a dustup himself. He was dressed in the dirty old pants and green leather jacket he wore in the football skirmishes of *Too Many Girls.* Most probably, he had been rolling on the ground feigning a tackle when they broke for lunch. In sum, when Lucille Ball and Desi Arnaz first caught sight of each other, they looked like trash.

Those present noted a change in the atmosphere and believed the two were instantly smitten. "It was like Wow! A bolt of lightning!

Lucille fell like a ton of bricks," said Maureen O'Hara. Abbott claimed, "They hit it off right away. It was love at first sight."

The two were scheduled to work together because Lucille had been cast in *Too Many Girls*. Despite the impression their meeting left on others, after a few pleasantries Desi went off with Abbott and advised him to fire her, stating she was too tough and common for the role of ingénue. The Broadway players of *Too Many Girls* felt some resentment toward Hollywood actors such as Richard Carlson, Ann Miller, and Frances Langford, who had usurped their friends' places. Under the circumstances, they might well have expected Lucille to be even more beautiful and delicate than Marcy Westcott, the stage ingénue she was replacing.

Lucille always believed that she made so poor a first impression that people did not like her unless she worked at charming them. In this most important meeting of her life, her fears were somewhat justified, but she was drawn without reservation to Desi. He was her height, and although she usually preferred tall men, by virtue of being foreign, Desi had something of the renegade air of Johnny DeVita, and his dark hair and strong cheekbones were reminiscent of a younger, slimmer Pandro Berman.

Desi claimed he saw her appeal only later that day when a beautiful blue-eyed blonde in tight-fitting beige slacks and a yellow sweater showed up for a reading of the script. He asked someone for her name and was stunned to learn she was Lucille Ball, the bedraggled tart he had met that morning.

That afternoon they engaged in the cunning flirtation of two people nonchalantly signaling their interest. She called him Dizzy, then Daisy. He offered rhumba lessons and took her to El Zarape, a Mexican restaurant over a market near the Los Angeles business district. George Abbott, director and rhumba master, and the rest of the cast joined them there, but Lucille and Desi sat apart from the others at a table by themselves.

A few days later, Desi's fiancée, Renée, arrived. He took her to a party Eddie Bracken and his wife, Connie, threw for the cast at their Malibu beach house. Wearing a striped playsuit, Lucille caught sight of Desi, patted the sand, and said, "Sit down." He dropped to her side obediently, and by the end of the evening, Lucille's understanding with Al and Desi's engagement to Renée de Marco were finished.

Waking up beside Desi the next morning at her apartment on North Laurel Avenue, Lucille phoned Al Hall to tell him their romance was over. One story that subsequently made the studio rounds was that Hall as a parting gift sent her a trussed turkey from his farm.

8

WHEN WORD SPREAD that Lucille Ball, who had typically been involved with older, influential men, had cast off an established director for a twenty-three-year-old Cuban bongo player six years her junior, friends and studio executives expected the passion to flame out quickly. This strange involvement, in no way calculated to help her career, was a rare instance of her not putting her work first. On the contrary, as the infatuation intensified rather than faded, some tried to warn her that this Lothario was merely making use of her contacts and rising publicity value.

Lucille paid no attention to her critics because they said little that she herself did not suspect. She expected that Desi would jilt her—as he had others she knew about, including Renée de Marco and Betty Grable—and tried to prepare herself for it. She also knew she and Desi were hopelessly mismatched. She was practical, he daring. She banked on time and work, he on the lucky break. Nevertheless, the pain she expected from Desi was worth the pleasure of being with him and, in fact, made it more precious.

Desi Arnaz was a romantic and continued wooing her after she was already won. The evening after the first morning they woke up together, he called for her in a dinner jacket and squired her to Ciro's, the popular Hollywood club. The orchids he presented to her looked wrong with her flowing white evening gown, but rather than hurt his feelings, she compromised by pinning them to her evening bag and kept the blossoms hidden on her lap.

But far more important than romance, Desi offered hotheaded demanding involvement, a vital psychic bond that she had experienced with no one else who mattered to her, not even her mother when she was a child. His raw energy resonated with her own. The very excess of his emotions, his cataclysmic anger and his foreboding sulks, seemed to testify to his sincerity. Desi lived his life the way he drove his prized Roadmaster convertible: Rather than polishing its chrome or testing its oil gauge, he stamped his foot on its accelerator and drove it so hard that its parts shook loose and flew off. On a two-hour trip to Ventura, where he was taking Lucille to make a personal appearance, he kept the speedometer at one hundred on the lonely open road, swerved around obstructions, and slowed only when he was forced to stop. On the way back to Hollywood, he angled a cigarillo between his teeth in the style of FDR and sped into a dip so eagerly that he cast off a fender he did not bother to retrieve. Only when she whimpered "My mother wouldn't like this" did he slow down. Her own driving was reckless, but just as she had terrified Marion on their breakneck drive in pursuit of a new puppy, so Desi behind the wheel had the titillating power to frighten her out of her wits. She loved it, and explained away her screaming as an exercise recommended to deepen her voice.

The cast of *Too Many Girls*, particularly those who had observed Desi's amorous enthusiasm in New York, expected this combustive romance to end as quickly as it had begun. They made wagers on how long Lucille and Desi would last as a couple, and Eddie Bracken won the bet. "I had more faith in it than anyone," he recalled. "I said six months. They were both outgoing, but when they were quiet, they were two nice, calm people."

On the set, a backdrop college town built across two RKO sound stages, Desi displayed bravado, arrogance, and not a little incipient talent. Partly because it was his nature, partly to impress Lucille, he suggested how various scenes might be played and how some of the music should be phrased. Intrigued by the workings of the movie camera and why various shots were taken, he made note of how they were used to tell the story. Lucille pointed this out to his detractors as proof that he was not a vacuous glamour boy. She found him brilliant.

Whether her seven years of watching directors and technicians had made her an astute judge of talent, or whether passionate love had fired her to heights of prophecy, Lucille was the first to detect the brilliance that the television industry would much later acknowledge. Garson Kanin, who was working on *Too Many Girls* behind the camera that Desi fiddled with, was far less impressed: "Desi came on strong, bossy, and a pain in the ass." Kanin had been George Abbott's assistant on Broadway in the mid-1930s and was assigned to the picture to mediate between the studio's requirements and Abbott's better judgment. Abbott was mindful that RKO had debilitated his Broadway hit *Room Service* into a cinematic flop and was resigned when the studio still insisted on laying down conditions for the filming of *Too Many Girls*. Lee Marcus, who supervised RKO's B pictures, had wanted an actress other than Lucille to play the arrogant college girl, but Kanin suggested her to Abbott as so perfect a choice that she would not have to test. She was tested anyway and she won out because she projected the strength and sassy confidence the role required.

Under orders from the Hays office, the studio also insisted that the plot be sanitized. The conceit of the Broadway show was that the coeds wore beanies to proclaim they were virgins while the boys plotted to inspire them to throw away their hats. In the Hollywood version, the girls sported the beanies if they had never been kissed.

Abbott, who produced rather than directed the film, knew it would not be as good as the play had been, but he tried to be helpful when Lucille asked him for advice. He recalled her as "very down-to-earth, a straightforward woman. She was always asking, 'What do I do now?'" He told her to play her part as a self-absorbed rich girl, rather than as a young woman who wanted an education. Bracken's memory is that she was so heavily made up as a glamour girl in a freshman hat that she was unable to act spontaneously. "She didn't move because she might break."

From the end of June to the middle of August 1940, when *Too Many Girls* wrapped, Lucille and Desi were inseparable, but kept apart from everyone else. As Frances Langford recalled, "Lucy and Desi were so involved we didn't get to see too much of them." Their romance was helpful in promoting the picture as well as their careers, which made the RKO publicity department happy, but the many friends and executives who still regarded Desi as little more than a gigolo continued to warn Lucille she was making a mistake. Lucille abandoned her discipline of avoiding weeknight engagements, and each evening she left the studio and crossed Melrose Avenue to meet Desi at Lucey's Restaurant. From there they would go to El Zerape or Ciro's or to Grace Hayes' Lodge in the San Fernando Valley.

Weekends the two sped in the summer heat to Palm Springs with their suitcases filled with her frilly nightgowns and his silk pajamas and vivid Mandarin dressing gowns. Sunday nights ended with spats and pleadings. He would storm out of her apartment on North Laurel Avenue often feeling he needed to return home at a reasonable hour for Lolita's sake, and Lucille would follow, begging him not to go away. F. Scott Fitzgerald, who lived in Lucille's building, and his young girlfriend Sheilah Graham spied on their regularly repeated scene from his balcony and bet on which one would win the argument.

Each was jealous. When she goaded him to tell her about his past romances and grew suspicious of women to whom he was no more than polite, Desi said he was merely collaborating on research for an article titled "Latins Are Lousy Lovers." In turn, he brooded over the important men she had loved, such as Pandro Berman and Al Hall, and as if to wipe them from her history he decided to give her a name that would be his alone. He and he alone called her "Lucy."

Desi took her to meet his mother, for whom he had rented a house on Wilcox Avenue near the studio. As Lucille spoke no Spanish, and Lolita little English, Desi had to translate conversation over heaping plates of *arroz con pollo* he prepared.

According to Cleo, her family welcomed him at Ogden Drive. "Whatever she wanted was accepted by one and all. We knew why she liked him. He was adorable looking. Lucy was a mature person. I suppose DeDe was delighted she had fallen head over heels and was confident she could handle it."

Desi liked Lucille's mother, but he was more comfortable with Grandpa Hunt. Having lost everything in the revolution, Desi was not inclined to be sympathetic to the old man's Socialist theories, but he liked his crusty sincerity and rock-ribbed beliefs. When Desi saw *You Can't Take It with You*, the Kaufman-Hart play about an extended family of eccentrics including a Grand Duchess working as a waitress and a grandfather who collects snakes and ignores dunning letters from the Internal Revenue Service, it reminded him of Lucille's family; but they also exemplified the extensive and loyal blood relationships that he was familiar with from Cuba and that were relatively rare in Southern California.

On her twenty-ninth birthday, August 6, 1940, with an extravagance that then delighted her, Desi threw celebrations in her honor at the studio, at Lucey's, at Grace Hayes' Lodge, at Slapsy Maxie's nightclub, and at her mother's house, where he met Irene DeVita Roselli, who was visiting from Jamestown. Lucille blew out the candles of five cakes, inhaled the bouquets of special flowers at each location, and pinned on her first serious gift from him, a lapel watch in the shape of a heart.

The energy that surrounded the smitten couple is not evident in the film they were then finishing. Part of the problem with *Too Many Girls* was its miscasting. As Desi had rightly protested, Lucille was too mature and sophisticated to play even the haughtiest college student, and the same applied to the other Hollywood actors, although Langford's singing was a highlight. Only Eddie Bracken exuded the youth and enthusiasm of a football hero, and only he knew how to enunciate a broad Harvard "a," but none profited more from the project than a redheaded chorus boy named Van Johnson. His good looks and screen presence were so compelling that he was plucked from the band of extras and given a movie contract.

Reaction to Desi's performance was mixed. In the *New York Times* review, Bosley Crowther savaged him: "Mr. Arnaz is a noisy, blackhaired Latin whose face, unfortunately, lacks expression and whose performance is devoid of grace," while *Time* magazine described him as "a terpsichorean Rudolph Valentino." As for Lucille, *Variety* noted that she "continues her recent acceleration toward star standing with another display of fine talent as a comedienne."

When the film wrapped on August 15, Lucille and Desi had no reason to rejoice. He had to depart for Chicago immediately to do *Too Many Girls* onstage with Van Johnson, who now had the lead, and she left for San Francisco to promote her earlier picture *Dance, Girl, Dance* with Maureen O'Hara. Whenever they were in the Bay Area, she and Harriet, who was not only her maid but her gin rummy partner and confidante, visited Harriet's best friend, Dot. Knowing Lucille loved barbecue, Dot bought ribs, and they all sat in the kitchen eating them. "I kept staring at this beautiful lady eating messy ribs," said Dot's daughter Barbara, who was ten at the time. "Lucille loved children and she always treated me like a princess. She had her dressmaker make me pinafores and she sent socks to match. My mother was afraid I would be spoiled rotten, and I was. Lucille made people feel important in her company, because if she liked you, she loved you."

The little girl delighted in seeing how silly Lucille and her aunt Harriet behaved together. "They tried on hats with feathers and veils and pranced about like college kids." Harriet and Dot reminisced about being dancers together, and Lucille chimed in with tales of her Goldwyn Girl days. "The three of them would have a couple of drinks, then push the furniture back and form a chorus line, laughing and giggling and dancing," Barbara recalled.

Two weeks after the San Francisco trip, on Labor Day weekend, Lucille visited Desi in Chicago, where they learned to battle in earnest. As Desi would later describe it, "From that day in Chicago to November 30, 1940, the obstacles, the problems, the fights we went through would have been enough to discourage anyone from getting married. We would love furiously and fight furiously."

During her visit, he became outraged when a waiter brought her a message from Charles Laughton, summoning her from their table at the Colony Club for a brief business chat. Erich Pommer planned to feature Lucille in a film with Laughton and his wife, Elsa Lanchester, but because the portly actor had decided to back out, he wanted to explain his decision to Lucille. Laughton's note broke the romantic spell that Desi had been casting, and when she returned to him thirty-five minutes later, she tried to cajole him into speaking to her, but he simply sulked. She lost patience and walked out again, this time in fury. Lucille was striding down the block toward her hotel when she heard a plaintive Cuban accent pleading for forgiveness from the back of a slowly approaching cab. Her pace slackened, she listened and decided he was indeed contrite, so she climbed in with him and they proceeded to the theater, where he managed to peel himself away from their farewell embrace only at the sound of his entrance cue.

When Lucille rejoined Maureen O'Hara for more stops on their promotional tour, her co-star advised her to marry Desi if she loved him that deeply. Lucille responded that she was uncertain, partly because she worried that her small breasts and inverted nipples meant she could never have children. Her agitation was such that when a fan in Little Rock asked Maureen to sign an autograph and spurned Lucille, Lucille burst into tears.

As their tour moved east, Lucille sent Marion a special delivery letter framed with one-cent stamps to announce she would be near Jamestown. Marion remembered the message as "Grab Grandma Peterson and come to Buffalo and meet me and Maureen O'Hara." During their subsequent reunion, Lucille confided that she had met a new man who was important to her, but said little more.

In late September 1940, she was back in Hollywood filming her fourth starring role of that year. *A Girl, a Guy, and a Gob* originated as a script called *Three Girls and a Gob* for Maureen O'Hara and Jack Carson, but Maureen passed on the project and recommended Lucille. Because switching from "girls" to "gobs" required extensive story revisions, shooting began with only a partial script, according to George Murphy. He played the "gob," or sailor, in a love triangle involving Lucille and Edmond O'Brien, the young hero of *The Hunchback of Notre Dame*. Murphy recalled sitting up late each night with the director, Richard Wallace, to write scenes to be filmed the next day. The role that finally evolved for Lucille in the film was that of a secretary with an oddball family who tries to be loyal to her sailor boyfriend while falling in love with her wealthy and vulnerable boss, played by O'Brien.

It may have been a mark of increasing status for Lucille that instead of being paid as a contract player, she received a flat rate of $12,500 for this picture—$1,000 more than O'Brien, her leading man, an unusual accomplishment in those days for most leading actresses. On *Dance, Girl, Dance*, for example, Lucille was budgeted as a stock player and Maureen O'Hara received $12,400, while the male lead, Louis Hayward, earned $20,000.

RKO's new management signed Harold Lloyd, the master of two-reel slapstick stunts famed for playing timorous bespectacled heroes, to produce *A Girl, a Guy, and a Gob*. Ironically, Lloyd, like the Three Stooges and the Marx Brothers before him, played no part in shaping Lucille Ball's comedic development. Her career was like a farce where disguised lovers run on and offstage opening and slamming doors, but rather than meet in a shock of mutual recognition, all the players scurry out and never come back, never identify each other and never bother to try. In these years, the male comic geniuses Lucille worked with were busy about their own routines and she was considered a glamour girl. Lloyd intervened on the set only once, to show Edmond O'Brien how to pick up a handkerchief to comic effect. Lucille had no such funny bits of business that interested him.

Throughout the shooting, she was distracted by thoughts of Desi: whom he might be with, the meaning of even his most trivial comments on the phone, and above all, whether their love affair could survive. Harriet was not impressed by Lucille's young Cuban and did not trust him. As she ironed and packed the bags or dealt out the cards for another round of gin rummy, she believed the actress's tragic explanations of why the affair was doomed, then found herself listening in surprise to Lucille plot strategies to make the studio send her to join him on the road.

RKO did give Lucille time for another quick trip to Chicago and then later arranged for Desi to return to Hollywood in early October for the premiere of *Too Many Girls*. His two-day visit stretched to two weeks. By day he was on her set, sometimes politicking with executives, and nearly every evening they were together.

One night, however, she was busy and so he took out his old flame Betty Grable. Grable was a lusty, petite, and curvy blonde who, as Desi had reason to know, "looked like a peach all over." They had first met in New York, just after her divorce from Jackie Coogan, while she was appearing in *DuBarry Was a Lady* at the theater next door to *Too Many Girls*. She had been a chorus girl at twelve, then a contract player at RKO and Paramount. Now, soon to turn twenty-four, a few months older than Desi, she was working for Twentieth Century–Fox. When Desi and she had an affair in the middle of his romance with Renée de Marco, Renée had been understanding, but in vivid contrast, Lucille was not prepared to be tolerant.

After she heard that Desi had been seen with Betty, she sped to his house on Wilcox. Lolita tried to turn her away at the door by explaining that her son was still in bed, but Lucille barged in anyway, burst into his bedroom, and berated him as a two-timer and a cheat. Even in the presence of Lolita, Lucille expressed a fury and jealousy that Mrs. Arnaz herself had never been able to summon during the trying times of her own marriage. Unlike the delicate Lolita, Lucille showed a willingness to take care of herself not just financially, but emotionally as well. Her behavior, as vituperative and coarse as it was, was an honest declaration of both vulnerability and resilience, qualities Desi appreciated. In later years, he said he should have known to break off with Lucille when she made his mother witness their sordid battle. In fact, at the time her outburst made him begin to think that Lucille Ball was the woman he should marry, and he set about to win her all over again.

When he flew back to New York for a solo engagement at the Versailles, an East Side nightclub more prestigious than La Conga, he wired her an adoring message—"DARLING JUST ARRIVING IN NEW YORK. I LOVED YOUR NOTE AND I ADORE YOU. LOADS AND LOADS OF KISSES"—and then resumed his unfettered womanizing, meanwhile regularly checking up on Lucille by phone. Although Lucille was too smitten to bother with anyone else, over the telephone she hinted to Desi that he had rivals everywhere. To annoy him, she would let her phone ring unanswered when she knew he was calling so that he would think she was not at home. The next evening, when she did answer, he would demand to know where she had been the night before, and she would reply vaguely: "Here and there." He would curse, and she would swear until one or the other hung up, then relented and called back to apologize. His wire followed:

DARLING IT WAS WONDERFUL TALKING TO YOU TONIGHT BUT AWFUL WHEN I HUNG UP AND WAS LEFT ALONE. I LOVE YOU DEAR AND MISS YOU SO VERY MUCH. TAKE CARE OF YOURSELF AND BE GOOD. LOADS OF KISSES.

The next day it would be her turn to try to locate him through the night. Just before a matinee performance, Desi came to the phone to hear her scream: "You Cuban sonofabitch, where were you all last night? What are you trying to do, lay every goddamned one of those chorus girls? No wonder they picked you for *Too Many Girls!*"

Throughout, no declaration of love went untested, no malediction was allowed to be the final break. Each exchange was a spectrum of colorfully hued emotions that had to be experienced before a cycle was complete. Lucille estimated that her weekly telephone bill was $100 and boasted that Desi's bill was double hers.

By the beginning of November 1940, Desi concluded that marriage was the solution to their misery. It now appeared that he too would have a movie career. He had made a favorable enough impression that RKO signed him to make three pictures in the following two years for $10,000 each. Since he would no longer be on the road and they could be together in Hollywood, he decided they would elope as soon as she arrived in New York. Although he was now appearing in five daily shows at the Roxy Theater, he calculated that they would have time to elope to Connecticut and return in time for his first show.

He did not tell her of his plans but wired:

SWEETHEART IT IS WONDERFUL TO KNOW EXACTLY WHAT ONE WANTS. THESE FEW WEEKS AWAY FROM YOU HAVE BEEN VERY SAD AND PAINFUL BUT THEY HAVE SHOWED ME THAT I WANT YOU AND YOU ALWAYS. SO MAYBE IT WAS WORTH IT. I LOVE YOU VERY MUCH AND I WANT TO SEE YOU VERY SOON.

A sign of the frenetic state of their relationship is that at the very time he was investigating places where they could marry without a waiting period, he had a long telephone conversation with Lucille in which he agreed with her that their separate family obligations made marriage impossible. They were clear about only one thing. As Desi noted, "I was madly in love with her, and I knew she was in love with me."

Lucille's trip to New York was postponed when the studio extended her one-day benefit appearance in Milwaukee to a week. Desi was convinced she had taken up with that city's mayor and steeped himself in convulsive jealousy that abated only when he met her at La Guardia Airport on a chilly Friday.

She stepped off the plane, a glamorous star of the forties in a three-quarter-length silver fox coat and matching hat. Beneath this was the black dress she had worn for the benefits in Milwaukee. After kisses and endearments, and smiles for waiting photographers, Desi went off to do his first show of the day while she checked into the Hotel Pierre to prepare for an interview the studio had arranged for her. As soon as his show ended, Desi rushed over to tell her he would make her his wife, but he found his intended talking to an interviewer for an article to be titled "Why I Will Always Be a Bachelor Girl."

As the reporter lingered on, Desi rushed back and forth to the Roxy. The winter afternoon light was already dimming outside her hotel window by the time they were finally able to be alone and he could tell her they would marry the next day. To his amazement, Lucille was not as eager as he had expected. She suggested that rather than take so serious a step, they might live together in Hollywood to test things out. He knew how Lolita would react to that, so he insisted on marriage, children, and a home, adding, "I love you very much too. So what the hell else is there?" She doubted the marriage would last six weeks, but wanting it to endure forever, she agreed.

Any romantic celebration in her plush suite had to be postponed, for Desi had to race off for his fourth show of the day, while Lucille met with George Schaefer, their boss at RKO. After Desi joined them, Lucille noticed that Schaefer was making furtive but insistent gestures at her fiancé whenever she turned her back. Catching on, she looked at Desi and realized that in his agitation to return to her he had neither zipped his fly nor bothered to don a pair of shorts. Lucille calmly told the head of RKO to relax. "Desi believes in advertising," she said.

Lucille Ball and Desi Arnaz were married the following noon on November 30, 1940, just over the state line in Greenwich, Connecticut. Their day began just before dawn when they left the Pierre with Desi's theatrical agent and business manager to act as witnesses. The bride was forced to set aside pessimism, the groom to give up unrealistic hopes. Lucille, wearing her fox coat and weary black dress, was concerned that Saturday was an unlucky day to marry, but banished this thought. Desi believed they could be married and back in Manhattan in time for his eleven o'clock show, but he had not planned on the blood test, nor the search for a ring that ended at Woolworth's. Then after they found their destination, the justice of the peace persuaded them that his office was not sufficiently romantic for such a sacred event. Lucille and the four men—groom, witnesses, and Judge John P. O'Brien—repaired to the Byram River Beagle Country Club, where a river flowed through picturesque snow-laden pines. Before a crackling fireplace they said their vows. Now husband and wife, they were both so emotional that they kissed their wedding license as often as they kissed each other and Lucille impressed her red lip print on the license as her official seal.

Teary, ecstatic, and late for Desi's show, the new Mr. and Mrs. Desiderio Alberto Arnaz y de Acha III sped down the parkway to the Roxy. By the time they reached Manhattan, weaving through weekend traffic and early Christmas shoppers, the management of the theater had explained to one audience why Desi was not coming and to another why he would be late, so when they finally did arrive, a crowd of romantics and fans had lined up on the sidewalk to receive them.

The Roxy Theater had a capacity of nearly seven thousand people. It was so vast that some artists were shocked out of their stage fright by their terror at being so small in such a huge place. On this stage in the largest theater in the world, Lucille Ball and Desi Arnaz walked out to a thunderous ovation. People stood at their seats and lined up in the aisles madly roaring as if they had some idea of what this couple would someday become. The newlyweds laughed and cried and threw kisses to the crowd whose thunderous cheers were then as unanticipated as they would later be taken for granted.

Like the ending of a screwball comedy, two sympathetic people of different temperaments and backgrounds fused in a union of opposites. Her dress was black, the ring was tin, and he, a Prince from the tropics, married a Cinderella from upstate. In the movies, love suffices for the debutante and the butler, but they have the advantage of a director who knows to yell cut before the real challenges begin.

9

THE NEW MR. AND MRS. Desi Arnaz stayed at the Hotel Pierre for a week while Desi completed his engagement at the Roxy. He was so protective of his bride that he would not let her travel unescorted in a taxicab through New York City, a precaution that made her feel rare and precious. In return, he expected her to minister to him unquestioningly. In the middle of their wedding night, he awakened feeling thirsty, slapped her on her derriere, and told her to bring him water. Obligingly she padded from their bed to the sink, prepared a glass of water with ice, served it, and went back to sleep. The next morning she was aghast that she had been so subservient, so he told her that the simple solution was for her to place a pitcher of ice water at his bedside each night. While their disagreement over appropriate room temperature (she: window open, he: heat on high) was an issue that could not be as easily resolved, both recognized that in the end he was to be treated as boss. As Lucille acknowledged, "I knew Latin men expected their wives to take a secondary role. *I was all for it*. I think one of the reasons Desi

117

wanted to marry me is that I felt this way about him. That's a hard thing for a man or woman to resist."

Sitting in bed reading the columns for news of their wedding, turning past headlines about Hitler's air attacks on Britain, she had to note that the reports were not without cynicism: "Lucille Ball and Desi Arnaz obliged the RKO publicity department by getting married Saturday, so now (we hope) there will be no further item on Desi being seen with this or that glamour girl."

The men in his band were no less skeptical of Desi's suitability as a husband, but Lucille personally won them over by doing exaggerated rhumbas to their music and trading quips, particularly with his boyhood friend from Santiago, Marco Rizo, who now played piano with Desi's band.

For the trip back to California on the Super Chief, Desi booked two sleeping compartments and combined them into a honeymoon suite that he filled with red and white carnations, her favorite flowers. Lucille was so anxious about pleasing him that when he sat in a corner strumming his guitar and singing to himself, she worried that he was bored with her until he serenaded her with a new song he had written: "When I looked into your eyes / And then you softly said 'I do' / I suddenly realized I had a new world / A world with you."

As they traveled over the Mississippi River and through the Rockies, Harriet supervised arrangements with the outside world. She still did not care much for Desi, and her reaction when Lucille had phoned to say she had eloped had been to ask: "Who did we marry?" Now, cigarette in hand, she told porters where to place the luggage and what refreshments to bring, stressing always the importance of her boss, the actress Lucille Ball. Harriet was offhand with Lucille because she loved her; she was offhand with Desi because she was not convinced that he would last. She knocked at their door at inconvenient moments to remind them to put their shoes outside their compartments if they wanted the porters to shine them by morning, warning: "Cinderella, get out of those shoes. It's gettin' near to midnight!"

Back on Ogden Drive, Lucille's family accepted the news of the wedding graciously, largely because she was obviously mad about Desi and partly because she would not have suffered any objections to her handsome, charming, younger husband. Still, after they spent a few weeks in Palm Springs at the end of their honeymoon, Fred Hunt took a close look at Desi, who was deeply tanned from the desert sun, and pulled his granddaughter aside to observe, "He seems like a nice fellow, but he doesn't speak so good and he's a little dark, isn't he?"

At first the couple took up residence in her apartment on North Laurel Avenue, where they had boisterous parties with Carmen Miranda and Constantin Bakaleinikoff, RKO's musical director, who would arrive with the orchestra's latest soloist and Russian vodka and caviar, but they deeply wanted their own home. They went out to the San Fernando Valley to visit friends such as the Richard Carlsons, even Al Hall at his turkey ranch, and Carole Lombard and her husband, Clark Gable, who stunned Lucille and Desi by giving them a champagne supper at Chasen's to honor their marriage. The Gables' delight in even the simplest things about their small ranch in the Valley made a strong impression on Lucille.

The country life suited both Lucille and Desi, for they were informal people by nature. Her favorite meal was hamburger smothered in onions, and she was happiest in casual tweeds, which she called station wagon clothes. A visit to the home of her *Annabel* co-star Jack Oakie in Chatsworth in the Valley finally led them to a ranch of their own. Chatsworth was about thirty miles from the studio, situated between the Santa Susana Mountains and the Simi Valley, and was an orange- and fig-growing community then sparsely settled. When they said how much they loved the area, Oakie introduced them to the developer, William Sesnon, who was in the process of dividing a large tract of land for homes.

In a late winter cloudburst they saw property near Oakie's at 19700 Devonshire Drive, five acres with two hundred seedling orange trees and a dark green ranch house and pool at the end of a winding road. The living and dining rooms blended into what seemed an enormous space lit by floor-to-ceiling windows. Lucille was enchanted by the sun porch and the master bedroom, which looked out on a vista of mountains and orange groves. Sentimentalists, both were particularly captivated by the white rail fence running around the land like a gift ribbon. Sesnon wanted $14,500 for the property, which they did not have, but since he also wanted prominent names to attract other buyers, he agreed to a $1,500 down payment and a ten-year mortgage.

They moved in as soon as the sale went through, and slowly, as they could afford it, stamped it with their personalities. Desi set about to add touches of a Cuban ranchito. He had a talent for design and constructed bamboo furniture for the sun porch and turned the pool into a natural lake surrounded by rocks with a nearby *bohío*, or thatched Cuban hut. Lucille, meanwhile, decorated the interior of the house to look like a Currier & Ives print. Early American antiques were beyond her budget, so she went to secondhand shops in the Valley where settlers from the Midwest had unloaded their Morris chairs, Victorian love seats, and wicker rockers in favor of more contemporary furniture. She bought a couch, two fireside chairs, a chaise longue, a dressing table, and oil lamps for atmosphere. She hung white ruffled organdy curtains at some windows, chintz at others, and did the living room with a red carpet and bold cabbage-rose wallpaper, finding the near clash of the red and pink invigorating.

The master bedroom was in her favorite colors of yellow and gray, with starched curtains at the windows. In time she added a wall of mirrored wardrobe closets, but the dominant touch was a custom-built, seven-foot-square bed they proudly brought visitors in to see.

Friends gave them chickens and two calves. When one of the calves died, they wrapped the other in blankets and nursed it through a fever. The sickly calf became a lovesick cow madly grateful to Desi to the point that this "Duchess of Devonshire" once broke through their bedroom window in an attempt to nuzzle Desi's face. They planted corn, artichokes, and potatoes, and Lucille cultivated a crop of Swiss chard, her favorite vegetable. "No one else ever heard of it, but God forbid if you did not eat it when you went to her house," said Marcella Rabwin. As mistress of her own house, she gave free rein to her superstitions and home remedies. No one was allowed to leave by a door other than the one through which he entered, and anyone who spilled a condiment was advised on how to treat the stain. Their ranch needed now only a name. Douglas Fairbanks and Mary Pickford had Pickfair, so after rejecting LuDes and Arball, they decided to call it Desilu.

While they took great pleasure in their newfound domesticity, the professional lives of Mr. and Mrs. Arnaz were less rewarding in 1941. Desi filmed *Four Jacks and a Jill* with Ray Bolger and Anne Shirley, a musical comedy in which he played a prince and cabdriver. It was misguided and soon forgotten. RKO then assigned him to *Father Takes a Wife,* a comeback vehicle for Gloria Swanson with Adolphe Menjou in which Desi played an egomaniacal singing stowaway. He won the part when an RKO executive heard him sing "Perfidia," but the film's producer conceived it as an operatic aria. This was beyond Desi's powers, so the song that won him the role was dubbed by an Italian tenor.

In an audience survey in which his photo was compared to those of other young actors, including Edmond O'Brien and Buddy Ebsen, Desi was judged the most appealing, but that opinion was not shared by RKO's new management. The fact that his status was greatly inferior to that of his wife was brought home to him the evening they attended a premiere at the RKO Pantages Theater in Hollywood. They were eager to make a striking appearance, so Desi spent the afternoon polishing and buffing his beloved Buick, and the two dressed themselves for the parts of movie stars. The aura lasted through the evening until, as they prepared to leave, the valet looked them over and called out, "Lucille Ball's car, please!"

To the public as well, Desi was just her escort. Driving home through the canyons, he announced that he was leaving Hollywood and taking his band on the road. Lucille urged him to be patient, as she had been when she was starting out. She snapped on the dashboard light to read a promotional release that RKO had sent out about him: "Desi Arnaz, the newcomer, may be just what the doctor ordered for the revival of the Latin craze following Valentino's success, the blade to carve out such a revival." Desi, who had so mastered English that he had an apt retort, said, "I guess I was a few years too late and obviously my blade was not sharp enough." He stressed, "There's no way I'm going to stay here and become Mr. Ball!"

Desi recognized that he was flailing professionally and feared that his leap from conga line to Broadway show, and then to Hollywood, was a series of lucky accidents, an anomaly of being appropriate for specific and atypical parts. He was conscious of the fact that he seemed to others to be a young Latin who had seized the chance to marry a somewhat older and much more established woman. He refused to be supported by his wife or to remain in a situation where he felt ridiculed.

Lucille knew that if he left Hollywood, their marriage was unlikely to endure. Even now when she was sitting beside him at a nightclub, waiters delivered notes from women, often stars at other tables, asking Desi to dance with them. She had thought she would simply come to tolerate her husband's appeal to other women, but she knew he was unlikely to decline an invitation to dance—or do anything else—if she was not present.

She was completely and obviously besotted with her new husband. When Desi went to the studio's barber, she supervised his haircut from a perch in the bootblack's chair. A writer from *Collier's* magazine noted an amazing phenomenon: "The procedure is this: you start interviewing Miss Lucille Ball and then Mr. Desi Arnaz enters and Miss Ball leaves. It is not that she leaves in person, she merely leaves in spirit. . . . Miss Lucille Ball looked at Mr. Desi Arnaz as if he were something that had floated down from above on a cloud."

Lucille, who for several years had made films at a breakneck clip, did not appear in a single picture in the early months of her marriage. She still expected to be cast in a film with Charles Laughton, who had emigrated from England to America to escape the war. In Hollywood, where box office appeal was crucial, the tortured character actor was proving difficult to cast because of his unconventional phlegmatic personality and the specialty he had made of playing unsympathetic characters, like Captain Bligh in *Mutiny on the Bounty.* Laughton had bowed out of one picture Erich Pommer wanted him to do with Lucille; now Pommer wanted them for *Mr. Pinkie* with Elsa Lanchester. Laughton would play a bartender posing as an English lord who transforms a Brooklyn dancer into a movie star and turns a prim governess into a romantic vagabond. One wonders what Pommer might have been able to do for Lucille's career if he had been able to master American film production as thoroughly as he had mastered Germany's. As it was, he was not able to act on his faith in her. Again the studio tested audience reaction and plans for *Mr. Pinkie* were scrapped.

Lucille desperately wanted to do *Ball of Fire*, a Goldwyn comedy about a nightclub dancer who hides from the mob by joining up with a septet of professors who are compiling an encyclopedia. Goldwyn offered the role to Ginger Rogers, Carole Lombard, Barbara Stanwyck, and Jean Arthur, all of whom turned him down. No one thought the script remarkable, not even Howard Hawks, who directed it, or Gary Cooper, who played the male lead, but Lucille knew the role of a brassy wisecracking showgirl converted by the very men she is trying to con was perfect for her and thought it had Academy Award potential. RKO was apparently willing to lend her out, for she was tested and hired, but then Stanwyck, who also made a specialty of tough girls, reconsidered, took it from her, and did indeed receive an Oscar nomination.

During this period Lucille's career was also buffeted by another round of RKO corporate upheavals. George Schaefer's focus on artistic productions had not improved the studio's fortunes, nor had his faith in Orson Welles, who made the experimental *Citizen Kane*, which failed at the box office, and *The Magnificent Ambersons*, which was finally taken out of his hands. Innovations such as overlapping dialogue and deep-focus photography emerged from Welles's work, but he could not make a profit. Schaefer was removed, and Charles Koerner, a shrewd manager who had run the RKO theater chain, was put in charge of the studio.

Now RKO's emphasis was "Showmanship Not Genius," and it set out to determine who and what would sell tickets. It commissioned opinion polls on its stars, its scripts, and its marketing techniques from the Audience Research Institute (ARI), and discovered, among other things, that Lucille Ball had virtually no identity with the public. Earlier RKO regimes had seen promise in her and had increased her salary until she was now making $3,500 a week, but it seemed she did not return the investment. A mere third of moviegoers could identify her photo. Asked to evaluate Lucille specifically, ARI discovered that only 58 percent of its sample even knew that Lucille Ball was the name of an actress. According to the report: "Although she is known to Hollywood and exhibitors, she needs more pictures and build-up before the public is aware of her." The most encouraging aspect of its survey was individual reactions to her, which ranged from "common," "cheap," "a hussy," "vulgar," and "coarse," to "a sweet dish." ARI explained that such comments were healthier in terms of box office potential than notions that an actress was high class. Another positive sign was her popularity with adolescents: "The most plausible reasons for this anomaly are that she looks younger than she is and that she is known to very frequent theatergoers who normally become aware of a new star before the bulk of the theater-going public gets around to noticing her." Still, ARI concluded the study revealed no marked promise of her success. In a separate report, she and Desi Arnaz led the list, alphabetically, of forty-five personalities who failed to show promise of ever becoming big marquee names. William Holden, Victor Mature, and Ann Miller were also on it, along with people who did indeed disappear.

RKO now decided that what the public really wanted to see was radio stars, and came up with *Look Who's Laughing*, starring Edgar Bergen and Charlie McCarthy, Fibber McGee and Molly, and The Great Gildersleeve. In hopes of making her better known, and hence worthy of her salary, in mid-May 1941, RKO sent Lucille before the cameras as Bergen's love interest and as straight woman to some of the greatest names in radio. The film was popular and profitable.

She was again free from July to late September, when she began *The Valley of the Sun*, a western co-starring James Craig, with Cedric Hardwicke and Dean Jagger. She did not like this picture, in which she played a restaurant owner trying to help civilize the town while fending off Jagger's attentions. She joked that her costume—a bone-ribbed corset, a bustle, six layers of petticoats, and a billowy dress—involved more clothes than she had worn in her previous three films combined. Desi joined her on location in Taos, where intense heat alternated with drenching rain. They toured adobe dwellings and mesas of the Navaho and Hopi Indians, but before the filming ended, he was off to promote his two films.

His ill-considered B pictures would probably have failed on their own, but by the time they were released, the country was incapable of being diverted by comedies featuring the comic mishaps of the idle rich. On December 7, 1941, a week after the Arnazes' first wedding anniversary, the Japanese bombed Pearl Harbor and America entered the war. The couple was in New York City when they heard the news and were certain that the Japanese would next attack the Pacific coast. They flew home to join their families and to do what they could to protect their ranch.

In the early months of the war, Lucille accepted the fact that Desi would be leaving her, but whether he would abandon her for the army or for far-flung nightclub engagements remained undecided. She interpreted the care he lavished on their home as proof that he loved her, but she knew this offered no guarantee that it would last.

As for Desi, marriage inevitably magnified the faults he had always recognized in Lucille. She was innately tactless, almost gauche, which annoyed when it did not appall him. She thought she was being loving when she showed a reporter a photo he had taken and said he was exceptional, even when he was mediocre. "That's my Desi. Tops in everything. There is the *dullest* picture ever taken by a citizen of this continent."

One night when he was preparing to sing for guests at Chatsworth, Lucille decided to heighten the romantic mood by setting votive candles around his chair and turning out all the lights, as if it were a cabaret. Desi was furious at what he considered phony theatricality, kicked aside the candles, and screamed, "Don't make me look like a fool!" Embarrassed guests departed early. Marcella Rabwin, who was close to them over the years, said this was the only time she knew of Desi's berating Lucille in public.

But making up was ardent and fulfilling and provided material for entertaining anecdotes. After one fight, Desi disappeared for three days. On the third morning, Lucille awoke at six to find he had returned, seeming to be as grateful as a combat veteran finally to be home. She found him outside drinking in the sight of their house and petting all five cocker spaniels at once.

On another occasion he was packing while Lucille paced in the living room where she came upon a cigarette lighter in the shape of an antique dueling pistol. As he got into his car, she rushed at him, leaned in the window, and fired. The lighter flared near his chest. He lit a cigarette, thanked her, and drove off, remembering that as one satisfying moment when he finally had the last word.

In April 1942, Desi joined the Hollywood Victory Caravan, a train-load of twenty-two major stars (among them were James Cagney,

Olivia de Havilland, and Bob Hope) plus eight starlets and a troop of musicians and technicians on a two-month national tour to benefit the Army and Navy Relief. Since the group lived in close quarters in their train compartments, gossip was inevitable. Word was that in contrast to that other well-known ladies' man, Mickey Rooney, who confined himself to well-known actresses, most notably Norma Shearer, Desi democratically and enthusiastically chased after any available female. Rejecting the example of his father and grandfather, who counseled that infidelity was unimportant if a man was discreet, Desi felt that as long as he truly loved Lucille alone, his blatant promiscuity in the presence of her colleagues was irrelevant. In fact, his fanatic infidelity damaged him more than it pained her. Even the practiced adulterers of Hollywood, some of whom rode on the Victory Caravan, disliked him for the wholesale compulsive bedding that seemed as much a matter of showing off as of getting laid.

While Desi was touring, Lucille accepted what she saw as a great career opportunity. The film was *The Big Street*, based on the Damon Runyon story "Little Pinks" about a busboy in love with a heartless showgirl. And in a suitable twist of fate, her great inspiration, Julius Tannen, made a brief appearance as the exacting judge of an eating contest.

But the studio feared the characters might be unappealing and the ending too unhappy and once again commissioned market research. The Runyon story, as it appeared in *Collier's*, rated exceptionally low with the public; moreover, audience polling indicated that as a result of her last two pictures, Lucille's box office appeal had improved by only a few points. But having decided to make the film, RKO acknowledged that she was right for the role, and they put her in the film and cast her in what may have been a make-or-break test.

The character of Gloria Lyons was so unsympathetic as to be detestable. "Her Highness" is a callous, self-absorbed conniver who becomes paralyzed when her jilted lover pushes her down a flight of stairs. Confined to a wheelchair, she proceeds to deplete the resources of the busboy who adores her and abuses his benighted friends who in pity try to help. There is no gift that she does not snatch up as her due before belittling it. The characters of the user and the busboy do wear thin—more than thirty years later Andy

Warhol would pronounce *The Big Street* "the sickest film ever made"—but Lucille was right in judging that Gloria was a promising role.

Knowing that an actress is ultimately perceived as being the same person as the character she plays, however, she asked Laughton for his opinion of the project. He agreed with her that Gloria was an exceptional creation and advised her to accept the challenge as an artist rather than surrender to the crowd-pleasing inclinations of the movie star: "If you are going to play a bitch, play the bitchiest bitch who ever lived or don't play the part at all."

His counsel clearly had an effect. In the film, when she weeps, she weeps from the soul, like someone trying not to cry, and she struggles, successfully, not to succumb to any tender feeling. Physically, Lucille had never been more stunning. Her arms and shoulders were displayed at their best. Her hair was gathered into a crop of curls, and her lips were painted to new fullness, the look that would become her signature.

Henry Fonda, on loan from Twentieth Century–Fox, was her co-star. Since they had filmed *I Dream Too Much* seven years before, he had been nominated for an Oscar for *The Grapes of Wrath*, while Lucille had managed to reach only the top rank of contract players. Nonetheless, she seemed to be stealing their film. She so excelled in one production number that the director turned it into a solo and released the chorus girls without paying them. Lucille, who remembered being fired from road companies without pay, sent each a $25 war bond to make it up to them. Although her solo did not make the final cut, the publicity department sent out news of her good deed and kept up a barrage of promotional nuggets.

Fonda was a man of few words and not inclined to be generous to his promising co-star. He spoke little to her, but when she prepared for her best scene, what he did say was telling. Lying ill in bed, Gloria hears conga music on the radio. Her shoulders sway as she listens, then her arms and her hips, but her features freeze on discovering that her legs will not move at all. The director, Irving Reis, was delighted with the way Lucille rehearsed it and hurried to capture it on film before she lost the mood. But Fonda, who had been watching her work from the sidelines, went over to her and asked, "You're *not* going to do it like that, are you?" She murmured that Reis had liked it, but Fonda shook his head and walked away. He left her deflated, but she still made it her best scene in the film.

In typical Runyon style, *The Big Street* combined treacly goodness with melodramatic male violence. It offered a sampler of performances by such durable players as Agnes Moorehead, Hans Conried, and even Ozzie Nelson and his orchestra. Ray Collins, who later played Lieutenant Tragg on television's *Perry Mason,* was so vigorous and engaging as a Broadway denizen that one wishes he might have found a part in a dramatization of Dickens.

Runyon, who produced it, was delighted with the picture. As he sat in the screening room in a dapper suit, watching the film over and over, he would lean down to fumble on the floor for an imagined object to hide the sentimental tears streaming down his stolid face.

Lucille awed critics as well. James Agee in *Time* magazine accorded Fonda "the dignity of a wax grape of wrath," but said "pretty Lucille Ball, who was born for the parts Ginger Rogers sweats over, tackles her 'emotional' role as if it were sirloin and she didn't care who was looking."

Lucille was in some ways a Runyon character—a flashy Broadway type with a flinty amalgam of gold and sulfur for a heart, as likely to sparkle as to smoke. *The Big Street,* which allowed her to be true to herself and to her art, was her favorite film, the only one she would mention as being important to her. She not only starred in it, but she was noticed and praised.

At the box office, however, the film was a dud and signaled that her days at RKO, which had been her home for seven years, were coming to an end. Although her abilities, and her high salary, warranted featured roles, she could not inspire the public to buy movie tickets, so Danny Winkler of RKO approached other studios about taking over her contract. As she had displayed fire and personality in *Dance, Girl, Dance* and *The Big Street,* both Paramount and MGM expressed interest in her. Preferring Metro-Goldwyn-Mayer, she volunteered to be a celebrity cigarette girl at a charity affair where she knew she would see Louis B. Mayer, the head of the studio. In an abbreviated costume that covered no more than a bathing suit would have, she loitered around the table where he sat with Vic Orsatti, an agent who had a near monopoly on representing MGM stars. After the dinner, at two in the morning, she knew her self-promotion had worked when her phone rang in Chatsworth and she picked it up to hear Orsatti offering his services as agent in her negotiations with MGM.

Lucille had one final picture to make at RKO, *Seven Days' Leave*, a musical with Victor Mature. Filming started in mid-June 1942, four days after she finished *The Big Street*. The soundstage doors were opened and fans turned on to disperse the heat, yet the players—particularly the men in woolen uniforms—were so wet from perspiration that they had to keep changing costumes. Mature, who was on loan from Twentieth Century–Fox, was supposed to have approval of his leading lady, and made no secret of his anger that he was not working with Rita Hayworth, with whom he was having a passionate affair, but whom Harry Cohn would not loan out from Columbia.

Mature was twenty-six and handsome with dark hooded eyes. Raffishly certain of himself, he set about to punish Lucille for being in the picture. In their love scenes, he gathered her in his arms, held her close, and assaulted her with obscene movements and gestures. "She would either scream at him or go to her dressing room and cry," recalled Arnold Stang, who played his buddy. Stang said that when she wasn't incensed by Mature, she was lovesick over Desi, who visited from the set of *The Navy Comes Through* in a tropical-weight uniform. "She couldn't wait to get him alone. She would practically tear his uniform off. She was under great pressure from these situations."

Because Stang was underage, his mother left him in the care of his good friend Victor, who promptly installed him at Rita Hayworth's house. "Lucille knew I was spending time with Victor, but that didn't affect her feelings for me. She'd come in each morning from the ranch and greet me with a happy, full hello. I didn't recognize her because she hadn't been to Makeup yet and I thought she was the charlady getting ready to leave, until I saw the blue eyes. That was proof that she lacked pretension. Her makeup, the boobs, and eyelashes were her working outfit. How she looked was how she looked," Stang said.

In *Seven Days' Leave* she was given a chance to leap on chairs and evade sword thrusts with the great agility that would later be familiar to millions, but the story, in which Mature has to meet and marry her in order to claim an inheritance, is basically a slapdash screwball plot, with good songs by the celebrated team of Frank Loesser and Jimmy McHugh.

As soon as the film was completed, she prepared to leave for MGM, the Tiffany, the Harvard, the gold standard of Hollywood. Audiences so expected excellence from this institution that they even applauded the lion whose roar heralded every MGM picture. To be one of its players was an honor and an opportunity, but Lucille realized she would have rather stayed at RKO, where she knew the seamstresses and cameramen by name and remembered the colors every wall had been painted over the previous seven years. When she stepped outside its gates for the last time on a torrid summer day, she felt not the disdain of one who is bound for better things but the desolation of one who has been cast out.

10

LUCILLE BALL ARRIVED at MGM in August 1942, just when she turned thirty-one. Partly because of her age and partly because of MGM's reputation as a star-maker, Lucille was aware that if she was ever going to reach the first rank of motion picture actresses, that time was now. While the public might consider anyone in pictures notable, those in the business judged the true stars to be those whose names alone attracted audiences to whatever picture they appeared in. Louis B. Mayer, the autocratic chief of MGM, liked to think he would do anything for his players, and he would, unless they failed to prove themselves.

By 1942 Norma Shearer, Jeanette MacDonald, Greta Garbo, and Joan Crawford, who had all been synonymous with the studio in the 1930s, had departed. Lucille came in on a new wave of talent that included Greer Garson and Katharine Hepburn. Mayer typed Garson as the noble lady, Hepburn as the modern woman, and Lucille Ball as a bold adventuress, the flamboyant actress type. At RKO Lucille's greatest roles had been Bubbles the burlesque queen and Gloria the golddigger; but the grandeur of MGM was such that she was cast not just as any loose woman but as Madame Du Barry, celebrated courtesan and mistress of King Louis XV of France.

Mayer chose *Du Barry Was a Lady* as the vehicle for Lucille's Metro debut. It was a film version of Cole Porter's Broadway musical, which had starred Ethel Merman and had been produced at the same time that Desi was appearing in *Too Many Girls*. The studio intended it to launch both her and Red Skelton, though neither was particularly musical, because the public wanted musicals, and MGM excelled in them through the production unit of Arthur Freed, the driving songwriter-turned-producer who had guided *The Wizard of Oz* and *Babes in Arms*.

The studio, set on 172 acres in Culver City, five miles southwest of Hollywood, boasted permanent exteriors of the major cities of the world, plus Carvel, Ohio, home of the Andy Hardy family; a zoo with trained elephants, water buffalos, and monkeys; a school for child actors; a roster of 4,000 employees, including a police department of 75; and a power plant that could have fueled a small city.

From a vast office with white leather walls, Mayer ruled over this territory as patriarch, deploying producers and stars and disbursing princely sums from a white desk that arced around him. Six times a day he rose to enter a special soundproof telephone booth in the corner of the room so he could communicate with MGM's money managers in New York.

In these surroundings Lucille felt that she had landed not in Oz (which was in fact on the MGM lot), or even the court of Louis XV, but back at the Minton–Anderson school. Self-conscious and tense as she went through what she called "the glamour treatment" given every new Metro star, she surrendered to the adamant ministrations of strangers behind unfamiliar doors, most of whom did indeed know what was best for her. The costume designer Irene advised her to gain ten pounds so she would look more voluptuous, encouraged her to wear bright blues, pinks, and reds, and then proscribed the tailored look RKO approved in favor of dressmaker suits, clingy dresses, and strapless gowns to show off Lucille's exquisite shoulders.

Far less pleasant was the matter of changing her hair. The famed

Sydney Guilaroff, charged with making mousy hair roar, experimented with her bangs for forty-five minutes. His intense concentration brought on her claustrophobia, as the more he studied her face and snipped at her hair, the more he seemed to lean and breathe against her. "When she arrived at MGM, her hair was medium brown. I would not say that it was dull, but it was not interesting. I thought there were enough successful blondes, so why not a redhead?" Guilaroff said of the idea that launched the most distinctive hair color in the world. He dispatched Lucille to the colorists at the House of Westmore on Sunset Boulevard, which was entrusted with all of MGM's star tresses, but their proven formulas must have reacted with other chemicals she had used because when they finished, her hair was green.

"They worked hours to make it come out red. She was upset, so when it finally got to be a good color, she said enough and left," recalled a young stylist named Irma Kusely, who was watching from the wig department in the mezzanine. Later she would do Lucille's hair for *I Love Lucy* and for every other important appearance, and when they traveled she oversaw the transportation of Lucille's red wigs. For security reasons, she then had dog carriers purposely refitted for them with false bottoms and screens.

Soon after her day at Westmore, makeup artists assessed Lucille, her bold blue eyes and cool white skin. They chose orange-toned coral lipstick to match her hair, affixed a spray of spidery false lashes, and sketched more abundant eyebrows than the pencil lines she had been given at RKO. Thus the "Lucy Look" was born.

Next, this MGM version of Lucille Ball went to the Stills department, where glamorous photos were taken to accompany articles placed in such studio-fed periodicals as *Modern Screen* and *Photoplay*. The studio also commissioned *Esquire* magazine's illustrator Howard Baer to do a series of drawings of her as Du Barry.

Finally the studio acknowledged her stardom by awarding her the portable dressing room with sea-green velvet walls that Norma Shearer had used when she made *Marie Antoinette*. In contrast to this, and to the sophisticated tastes of other stars, Lucille made her permanent dressing room homey and comfortable, and felt no need to have it look impressive.

In *Du Barry*, Lucille played a glamorous nightclub singer and Skelton a checkroom attendant who falls in love with her. After he drinks a Mickey Finn, he dreams he is Louis XV, and their story is transported to eighteenth-century Versailles, where Lucille is Madame Du Barry and Gene Kelly a dashing firebrand trying to free the people from the royalist yoke. Lana Turner did a walk-on as herself, and bit players included Ava Gardner and Hugh Beaumont, who was later Beaver Cleaver's television dad.

Lucille was terrified during the weeks of rehearsals. Chuck Walters, who had choreographed *Seven Days Leave* at RKO and had played the Black Arrow, Kelly's part, on Broadway, was brought in to choreograph at Kelly's request. Walters was eager to prove himself and was concerned that they make each other look good, so when Lucille wailed, "I can't sing! I can't dance!" Walters told her, "You *can*, now just stop wasting time saying you can't and get it done."

The filming methods were as new to her as the studio itself. Lucille's singing was ultimately dubbed by Martha Mears, but syncing was an acting technique to be mastered in itself. Lucille was given a record of her songs to work with at home so she could practice her silent mouthing cued to clicks inserted between each phrase. She was coached not just to act as if she were singing, but in ways of putting over her songs visually with gestures and expressions that might have been impossible had she actually been making sounds.

Du Barry was her first Technicolor picture, and the lights, which were brighter and hotter than anything she had experienced at RKO, added to her tension. Overseeing photography, the play of shadows on her face, and the tints of backdrop colors was Karl Freund, a pioneer in the art of cinematography. Regarded as an innovative lighting genius, he had worked with such greats of German cinema as Erich Pommer and Fritz Lang and had created the first moving camera by placing a fixed one on a dolly for a film called *The Last Laugh*. Freund, credited with suggesting the forceful ending for *All Quiet on the Western Front*, had also photographed much of *Camille* and *The Good Earth*. Since Mayer decreed that all actresses be filmed through fine gauze to hide any unflattering expression lines, and because Lucille was in the title role of *Du Barry*, Freund took extra pains to enhance her appearance. Although Roy Del Ruth directed the production, Freund had command of the cameras. Under his guidance, assistants focused and checked the equipment, a still photographer shot promotional photos, and a gaffer, or chief electrician, adjusted the spotlights and arcs. Using stand-ins, Freund worked out detailed plans for camera positions and angles, and then during rehearsals scrutinized the set for unwanted reflections from chandeliers and crystal. These were the tasks of any top cinematographer, but Lucille was so impressed with Freund's knowledge and the results he achieved that her respect was obvious even to starlets.

She did pay a price for "the glamour treatment," however, for by the time her hair, makeup, and lighting were ready for the cameras, naturalness had been drained from her performance. Lucille was stiff in the production except when she was cavorting. Only action relaxed her. She seems to have fun in the finale, in which she, Skelton, Kelly, and Virginia O'Brien sing "Friendship" with hi-de-ho élan, but Lucille is at her best when strutting with Skelton through "Madame, I Love Your Crepes Suzettes." Munching on celery and wearing a twenty-seven-pound headdress, she joins him in a minuet that culminates on a trampoline bed. Walters had drilled her in bouncing from her rear back on her feet, and when they had it right, MGM invited in photographers from *Life* to document the feat. The story, entitled "Lucille Ball . . . winning her first chance as a big time star," noted the improbability of her shocking carrot hair. It pictured her dancing the solo that had been cut from *The Big Street* and bounce-dancing on the trampoline. *Life* reported that *The Big Street* had taught Hollywood that she could really act and observed: "Lucille herself is almost a true Runyon character. She is ambitious, hard, flamboyant and luxury-loving. Yet paradoxically, she is generous, funny and extremely sensitive and a crack poker player who often sends presents the next day to the losers."

Her vermilion hair gave the press something to focus on. Hedda Hopper noted: "Lucille Ball hates the color of her hair, too, and says 'I should wear a sign on my chest saying I hate it, but Technicolor demands it.' " As subsequent dye jobs made it even brighter, Lucille told journalists to call the color Tango Red.

MGM's methodical buildup worked. The public appreciated Lucille's beauty in both the sumptuous costumes of eighteenth-century

France and the glamorous gowns of 1940s Hollywood. The studio had made the most of its Technicolor investment by designing costumes and scenery in sherbet hues and forest tones, so *Du Barry*'s luxuriousness, its music, and its humor distracted Americans from wartime fears and rationing, and the film became a tremendous hit. MGM spent $1,239,222.56 to make it and took in $3,496,000 at the box office.

Studio executives were pleased with the project and concluded that they had typed Lucille successfully, but one forgotten employee on the MGM payroll believed there were better uses for her. Buster Keaton was a great star of the 1920s who conceived, produced, and directed his own films. The indomitable character he created stoically outwitted life's traps, such as the building façade that collapsed around him, and tangled triumphantly over formidable machinery, including a steamship in *The Navigator* and a locomotive in *The General*. Called the "Great Stone Face," he was a master of stunts and chases, and his 1928 film *The Cameraman* was used to train comics under MGM contract. In need of a paying job, Keaton was hired along with Ed Sedgwick to assist the studio with bits—but only bits—of comedy. From a corner of the set, Keaton watched appreciatively as Lucille transformed herself from a beauty to a clown with a well-trained bite of a celery stalk. He urged Mayer to take advantage of her unique gift, but the mogul insisted that beautiful women, not funny ones, sold tickets.

Now that she was the star of a successful MGM film, it seemed that Lucille had only to follow Mayer's formula. She attributed part of her good fortune to something Carole Lombard's mother had told her about numerology: The "A-R" combination of letters brought luck. Now that her name was Arnaz, she found that her career was indeed improving, but Desi's did not. He was grateful to land a spot in Ken Murray's "Blackouts," a popular show at the El Capitan Theater in Hollywood, and as he worked late nights and she had early calls, they rendezvoused at dawn or dusk at a spot in Coldwater Canyon Drive before heading in opposite directions to divergent lives. Hoping Mayer would find a picture for Desi so that he would have MGM status too, she let word of her distress circulate. One night "Papa" Mayer, who encouraged his players to bring him their personal problems, went to see Desi's act and promptly put him under contract.

Mayer told Desi he reminded him of his racehorse: "Busher looks very common when he's around the barn, but when they put a saddle on him, and he goes out onto the track, you know he's a champion. The same thing happens to you when they hang that drum around your shoulder. Up to that point you're just another Mexican." Desi eventually managed to persuade Mayer to pay him $650 a week instead of the $500 he offered.

The part Mayer gave him was a good one, the role of a doomed soldier in *Bataan*, a tale of duty and heroism with Robert Taylor, George Murphy, Thomas Mitchell, and Robert Walker. In later eras it would have been filmed in an actual jungle with special effects departments splattering the screen with exploding viscera, but except for its opening shots, *Bataan* was made on a soundstage. It has all the more authority for the lack of technical embellishment. Desi persuaded the director to let him say his dying "Pater Noster" in Latin as the Jesuits taught Catholic boys. He had the added satisfaction of winning the *Photoplay* award for the best performance of the month, but MGM let him know they had no other roles coming up for him soon.

Uncomfortable lounging around aimlessly, Desi used his free time to build chicken coops, a stone barbecue big enough to resemble a cathedral altar, and a guest or "rumpus" house at Desilu that he told everyone was the place where he slept instead of driving off when he and Lucille had a fight. The couple prized everything they acquired, everything they built. They seemed to be not only putting together their own home but re-creating homes they had cherished and lost.

Lucille was fiercely domestic, a woman her grandmother Flora would have valued. She made candles in milk carton molds, painted decorative designs on old bottles and jugs, and collected Meissen, Dresden, and bone china. She hung plates on the wall, organized her closets, and fastened each skirt to a metal hanger with clothespins, a hint she shared with the public via fan magazines.

She helped with the outside chores, fed the livestock on weekends, and cleaned house to the extent of throwing out all Desi's old moth-eaten clothes, which he had worn to reshingle the roof. When he found these treasures gone he erupted in a stream of vitriolic Spanish that Lucille did not understand, but which she hoped not to hear again.

Desi believed they could see their entire family through wartime meat shortages by raising animals for food. Besides their pampered calf, they acquired a piglet and two chicken incubators with 200 hatching eggs. Lucille's passion for their five dogs and madly reproducing cats did not enter into his plans for living off the land. During wartime winters she moved the chicks inside their den and had the calf warmed by hot water bottles in the pool house. The pig grew to 400 pounds and died of natural causes. None of these creatures contributed to the war effort, but lived out their natural lives as pets.

With some self-mocking, Desi and Lucille cast themselves as lord and lady of a vast estate while DeDe operated their motion picture camera. They strode through their grounds arm in arm, he in plaid bathrobe with top hat and cane, she in sky-blue pajamas, quilted jacket, and matching bonnet, a parody of Scarlett O'Hara at Tara. With their backs held straight and their steps magisterial, they inspected their crops of strawberries and Swiss chard, acknowledged the clucking of their pampered chickens, and surveyed the extent of their swimming pool.

Just as Lucille pasted valued press clippings and paper souvenirs into her scrapbook, so private affectionate moments like these were fixed on film. "I love you, I love you," Lucille mouthed, puckering and kissing at Desi behind the camera, her hair in a kerchief whose ends pointed out. They pedaled past the camera on bicycles, filmed their new red convertible by itself as a mammoth still life, and captured the parade of the whole group of relatives—DeDe, Fred Hunt, Cleo, Fred Ball, and Lolita, whose dignity and limited English kept her on the fringe of things—in an honor guard of family processing around the property.

Colorful costumes, splashy Bermuda shorts, and Hawaiian playsuits were all encouraged at Desilu, as well as expressive hats—Texan Ed Sedgwick boasted a Stetson and shy Lolita hid in a small straw sombrero. The conga was the official beat of Devonshire Street, particularly when Desi's New York club friends came to call, but Lucille wanted to have square dances, for which Desi had no patience. In contrast to primal, sultry Cuban movements, square dancing with its insistent callers and obedient steppers seemed mechanistic, and he endeavored to phase it out of their Chatsworth program.

Lucille encouraged games of Monopoly, Scrabble, or poker, and cards were a serious matter. "Lucille conned me into playing canasta one Sunday, and somewhere I made a horrible mistake," Maxine of the Andrews Sisters remembered. "She reamed me out. I think I cried all the way home. She acted things out funny, I thought at first it was a joke, but she was serious."

Virginia O'Brien, a talented singer and actress at MGM whose trademark was her beautiful but deadpan face, and her husband, Kirk Alyn, the original Superman, were often guests at the ranch. She recalled that Lucille's most popular hors d'oeuvre was strawberry jam and cottage cheese on Saltines, an unlikely but compelling combination of sweet, sour, and salty tastes.

Marcella Rabwin said: "It was such a long bad road to Devonshire that most people wouldn't go out there except when they gave a party, and boy, when they did, everyone came, because it was so much fun." Desi prepared Cuban chicken, black beans, and rice, a dish that new guests approached gingerly because it looked vile, but old friends begged for because they knew it tasted so good. "The only trouble with the barbecue was that we never ate until ten o'clock, which I think was the Cuban system. Everybody in California eats dinner at six or seven, and we would all be dying because they didn't serve hors d'oeuvres first. After dinner when the evening got damp, we'd go in the house and we'd play games. Lucille loved gag games, crazy things that made you laugh and made you uncomfortable at the same time. In one, she set up a broom between two chairs and the goal was to sit on it. Then, after a while, we played what we called 'The Game'—charades—and she was always terrific at that."

On many Sundays the solitary Clark Gable roared up their driveway on his Harley Davidson. Carole Lombard had been killed in a plane crash during a bond tour the first month of the war, and Gable always knew Lucille would be willing to talk about her. He rode the bike so recklessly that Lucille felt he was trying to kill himself, so on those frequent occasions when he said he wanted to visit Lionel Barrymore, who also lived in the Valley, Lucille drove him in her car. Barrymore had persuaded Gable to go into films when the young actor had wanted nothing but the stage. Their bond intensified as arthritis confined the older man to a wheelchair and Gable mourned the death of his wife. Lucille listened to the two sad men talk into the evening hours while Desi stayed home and fumed, certain that she was sleeping with Gable.

An outward change came over Lucille during these early years of her marriage. Before this time, friends summed up her vivaciousness by saying "You always knew she was there," but those who met her afterward remarked on how quiet she was. Although she still insisted that guests eat her favorite foods and play her favorite games, it was Desi with his warmth and charm who took center stage, impressing everyone with the ebullient way he did things, even merely entering a room.

After *Du Barry*, MGM assigned Lucille to take the place of the pregnant Lana Turner in *Best Foot Forward*. In this adaptation of a Broadway show, she was Lucille Ball herself attending a military school dance as a publicity stunt. Keaton could take satisfaction in some of her funny scenes, although they were hardly slapstick. In the course of the film, she has her dress ripped off and is forced to hide in a succession of dorm closets, while newcomers like Nancy Walker, Gloria DeHaven, and June Allyson dance to the music of Harry James. It was another hit. Made for $1,125,502, it grossed more than twice that sum.

Soon after she finished it, Lucille's renewed fear that Desi would go on the road was succeeded by a greater worry: that he would be sent overseas into a war zone. As he expected, he was drafted in May 1943, soon after he became a U.S. citizen. He was accepted in the air force, but the day before he was to leave for bombardier school, he tore the cartilage in his knee while playing baseball. Doctors mistakenly put his leg in a cast and, when it was removed and the knee would not bend, they recommended surgery. Desi dissuaded them by arguing that their treatment was contrary to what New York specialists had recommended for his other knee, which had been bothering him since he injured it playing soccer as a youth.

Lucille was now due on the set of *Meet the People*, a musical co-starring Dick Powell, but during deliberations over Desi's treatment, she phoned the studio to say she had severe laryngitis. She explained she would be out for a few days and was with a doctor, but the physician by her side was probably her husband's. The studio was forced to suspend production until she returned.

Finally, simple exercise was sufficient to restore Desi's knee, and he was reassigned to noncombat duty in the army teaching English to illiterate inductees. In addition, he was so successful at bringing performers like Lucille, Ann Sheridan, and Mickey Rooney to his base that he was put in charge of entertainment for the troops at Birmingham Hospital in the Valley, which received casualties from the South Pacific. Now a staff sergeant, he organized a musical called *G I'm Happy*, and with Lucille's help, lined up Eddie Cantor, Bing Crosby, Betty Hutton, and Martha Raye for various parts. They performed it within a hundred-mile radius of Los Angeles, including at secret camps in San Diego whose mission was to repel invasion. *Life* was now proclaiming Lucille as "Technicolor Tessie" because *Du Barry* was so popular with audiences while Desi was out of the limelight entertaining wounded troops. Although she had risked her career to be with him when he was hospitalized, Desi rarely came home on weekend passes, even when he was only a few miles from their ranch.

As in the days of their courtship, they used the telephone to miscommunicate on themes of jealousy and fidelity, then suffered and reconciled. Sometimes after hanging up, still hungry for each other's presence, they put their thoughts on paper. He wrote: "Lucy, sweetheart, you have no idea how happy you've made me—really and fully happy. You're a wonderful baby and I adore you. I don't mistrust you, baby, but I am jealous. I can't deny that."

Another time she wrote: "My baby, you called about an hour or so ago. I'm kind of lonesome tonight. Kind of lost again. Desi, darling, please don't worry about me. Believe me, I wouldn't do anything to make you unhappy. If you are going to do the right thing as conscientiously as I am we have nothing to worry about. Please believe that. All my love forever, Lucy."

Lucille, who hated to be alone, spent her evenings in Chatsworth with Harriet for company. DeDe frequently visited, checking closets and advising her on improvements. She was not always helpful. Toilet paper was scarce because of the war, and when she saw that Lucille had obtained a rare cache from Schwab's Drugstore, DeDe called its proprietor to demand "What do you have to be, a goddam movie star to get toilet paper? You gave Lucy a carton of toilet paper."

Still, it was to her mother and her cousin Cleo that Lucille confided her misery about her marriage and Desi's indifference. "I'm so unhappy, Mother," she admitted, weeping. Trying to come up with a way to comfort her daughter, but unwilling to say anything against her son-in-law because she thought they would resolve their differences, DeDe resorted to homilies. "DeDe always had a platitude that would be of no help: 'Everything turns out for the best.' 'It's always darkest before the dawn'—something like that," Cleo recalled.

With DeDe, Lucille returned to wintry Jamestown in January 1944 to bury Fred Hunt, who had died in California after a stroke at the age of seventy-eight. Dressed in mourning, warmed by a black fur jacket, she stood in the cemetery where her father, her grandmother, her aunt, and generations of her kin were buried and saw Fred Hunt laid to his rest.

The city was busier than she remembered, with new façades on old, familiar stores like the ones where DeDe sold dresses and Lucille demonstrated beauty creams. Ed Peterson had died the previous April, so Lucille urged Grandma Peterson, unsuccessfully, to come to live with them in California. She went over to Celeron and stood in front of her old house long enough to be noticed by the woman who now owned it, but either because she was afraid of an uncordial welcome or bad memories, Lucille did not seek to go inside. She walked over to Mrs. Appleby's house, only to learn that her old teacher had moved away, but she did visit Johnny DeVita, his mother, and the rest of his family.

MGM sent a publicity man along on the trip to make certain the populace knew she was back. A crowd, particularly adolescent boys, loitered around the lobby of the Hotel Jamestown to get a look at her and were dumbstruck when her old friend Cecilia Ditonto went to the great star's room with her little daughter Frances by the hand. Lucille, who had been the scandal of the county when she was with Johnny, seemed a rarefied being to those who met her now. Frances recalled how impressed she had been: "She had a frilly blue bed jacket and said she wasn't feeling well because she had been up late the night before. I remember her pushing up the sleeves of her jacket and seeing how beautifully manicured her nails were."

Ten years earlier, when she was interviewed by the local press as a Goldwyn Girl, she had exaggerated her Broadway career and her success in Hollywood. Now she no longer needed to, and Lucille was obviously touched by her welcome. Talking to a reporter from the *Jamestown Post-Journal*, she was generous with gratitude to as many people as she could think of. She cited Mrs. Appleby: "She was a wonderful woman and I always loved her although she came near to whaling me many times!" She credited the Jamestown's Players Club for giving her her start and described her rise as the opposite of meteoric. She now admitted that when she first went to New York she had tramped around unsuccessfully on sore feet with an empty stomach.

Lucille seemed more interested in telling people that Marion Strong's brother, who had gone to Hollywood, was doing well there and in crediting Sydney Guilaroff for inspiring her hair color than she was in talking about herself. She ended by asking the reporter to invite all the people she knew to call on her at the hotel. But no matter how interested she was in her old friends, she was in fundamental ways now alien to them. As a public person, she was attuned to a vast invisible audience. No matter how tired Lucille was, or how puffy her face in the morning, when a camera showed up at the local defense plant or the trade show at the Furniture Exposition, or at the bond rally at the high school, she glowed with vibrant energy. Her eyes shone, her smile sparkled. She was a movie star.

So great was the impression Jamestown's former daughter made that when she and DeDe boarded the train for Philadelphia, where she was to sell war bonds, police had to hold back the hundreds of people who showed up to see her off. She stood on the platform in a silver fox coat, waving good-bye to friends and fans over the labored clang of the departing train, leaving the place that was for her such a tangle of misery and love that she would never be able to unravel it.

As the months of 1944 wore on, Lucille was hoping to become pregnant. Although she had suffered a miscarriage in the first year of her marriage, she was confident that she and Desi could yet have babies. Desi, however, continued to avoid spending his weekend leaves at home. Instead, she went to see him at the base, where they were surrounded by performers who appeared in his shows and by the military doctors, nurses, and patients they entertained. By September she became convinced that he was having affairs with the starlets she had sent out to cheer the troops at Birmingham Hospital.

Lucille finally took action that would at worst end her marriage and at best convince her husband that he had to change. She hired a lawyer who phoned a dumbstruck Desi to inform him that his wife was divorcing him. The morning of the day Lucille began filming *Without Love* with Katharine Hepburn and Spencer Tracy, she went to Domestic Relations Court in Santa Monica and filed for divorce, charging mental cruelty. She said only that Desi would disappear for days, and otherwise refused to make a scandal or harm him in the press. To the columnist Louella Parsons she loyally assumed a share of responsibility and attributed their problems to a clash of temperaments—"I'm just as much to blame as Desi. We both have tempers and we're both difficult when we are battling."

Desi was unwilling to believe he had really gone too far, but he was sufficiently upset that he reached out to his childhood friend Marco Rizo, who was stationed in Memphis. "He called me and said, 'Guess what? Lucy wants a divorce.' He was surprised," Marco remembered. "I expressed my condolences, and he said, 'Well, you know how I am. I don't think it will be permanent.'"

In contrast, Lucille feared that it might well be. "The divorce for her was a sense of failure. She was devastated by the deterioration of her marriage. She loved him so much, and he loved her," Cleo said.

Lucille turned to Marion Strong, who was now living in the Hollywood Hills. After she was left a widow with a young son to raise, she joined her brother John, who was a contract player at RKO. Lucille, who hated to go anywhere alone, picked Marion up in her red convertible and took her along to fittings or sessions with her accountants. She loved playing tour guide, pointing out the Farmers Market, the great department stores on Wilshire Boulevard, and her local drugstore, Schwab's, which was allegedly the place where Lana Turner was discovered. Lucille and Marion regularly ended their day at Brown's ice cream parlor, where they slathered sundaes in hot fudge from small individual pitchers.

When Marion mentioned that she had joined a great books discussion group, Lucille saw an opportunity to make up some of her interrupted education. She asked Marion to enroll her under a pseudonym. "Well, of course they recognized her and that was the end of literary discussion—they wanted to know about her and the movies," Marion said. "After a few meetings, Lucille told me it wasn't working out like she had hoped and said she was going to quit. I told her it wouldn't be as much fun without her, so I left too."

Some evenings Lucille phoned Marion to ask if she was making Swedish rye bread, hinting that she wanted to smell "the heavenly aroma of fresh bread." Lucille soon arrived at Marion's, fussed over her fox terrier Nipper (grandson of Whoopee, the dog they found after their wild ride to Westfield), then closed her eyes and inhaled the yeasty aroma that brought back the smell of Jamestown's Swedish kitchens, especially Grandma Peterson's. "Food fit for the gods!" Lucille declared. She gave Marion butter, precious in wartime, that Richard Carlson's wife had churned on their ranch, then asked for an extra loaf to take home to Chatsworth.

The stress Lucille was under was evident the night she took Marion to an informal screening at MGM and fainted. As Marion remembered: "I tried to open the top of her blouse to get her air. When she came to, she was startled and couldn't figure out what I was doing. She waved me away and said it was nothing I should worry about." The spell may well have been due to an arrhythmia that was a legacy of her adolescent heart problem.

In late November 1944, on the eve of her fourth wedding anniversary, Lucille was preparing to pick up the decree that would end her marriage when she won her game of psychological one-upmanship on her final move. Desi had allowed her to file for divorce, then to testify against him. Finally, just before it was too late, he phoned and asked to see her. Over dinner in Beverly Hills, they held a postmortem on their marriage. They agreed that each would surely marry again and that they would certainly not make the same mistakes they had with each other. Next time she would not deliver ultimatums, threaten divorce, or fail to make adjustments. Next time, Desi said, he would sleep with the windows open and jump around like a fool at square dances, if that was what his second wife wanted. Reflecting on what perfect spouses they could now become, they decided that if anyone was going to profit from their mistakes, it might as well be they themselves.

They sealed their pact in bed at a nearby apartment, but the next morning, when Desi awoke in the chill of the window opened for her comfort, he found her dressing up to go to court. She told him the press expected her to be divorced that day and she wanted to show off the new suit and hat she had purchased for the occasion. With a good-bye kiss, she promised to return as soon as possible. Emerging from the courthouse with her provisional interlocutory decree, she was a content and radiant divorcée. Later, snuggled in bed, their divorce voided by their cohabitation, they read about themselves in the afternoon papers under photos of a well-dressed and dewy-eyed Lucille. Their stunt amused them until the legal bills arrived.

For all that they made a joke of their "divorce," it forced them to establish new, if unspoken, terms in their relationship. The problems of their marriage, the infidelity and anger and jealousy, could not be allowed to reach so destructive a state again. In going back to Desi Lucille acknowledged that she needed him enough to accept his "peccadillos," and she began to denigrate pride as a useless vanity. "On a cold night, who can warm her feet on the back of pride!" became a frequent comment to friends and journalists.

Like many other women, Lucille Ball believed she was neither complete nor socially viable without a man, but however crucial Desi was to her, she accepted that he would be no more accountable than a family pet who was liable to spend the night at the neighbors' and bark and growl at inconvenient times. Lucille wanted Desi to be faithful to her, so for her marriage to survive she had to believe that he was not responsible for his infidelities. The actress Janis Carter recalled, "Lucille used to complain about an actress who made off with Desi every chance she had. She would say 'That woman is blatant!' and I'd ask if her husband was at all to blame. Lucille said it was a weakness of the male and said that women shouldn't take advantage of it."

Desi too had a way of putting all the responsibility for their mutual happiness on Lucille—"Well then, quit the fucking film business and just be my wife!" He knew she could neither turn herself into his

At age three, around the time of her father's death. (Personality Photos)

In heavy shoes and the first pair of women's slacks seen in Jamestown, Lucille prepared to go to New York with Marion Strong. (Collection of Marion Strong Van Vlack)

Struggling to survive in New York City, Lucille posed topless. (Personality Photos)

Lucille and Marion in front of the Schwab Mansion, New York City, spring 1931. (Collection of Marion Strong Van Vlack)

As a starlet posing for a publicity still, Lucille kept her mouth closed to hide her crooked teeth. (Courtesy of the Academy of Motion Picture Arts and Sciences)

With *Follow the Fleet* starlets Harriet Hilliard (later, Harriet Nelson) and Betty Grable in 1936. (Personality Photos)

Pandro Berman, who produced the Astaire-Rogers films at RKO was, in the words of her cousin, "crazy about Lucille." (Courtesy of the Academy of Motion Picture Arts and Sciences)

After *Hey Diddle Diddle* closed in early 1937, Lucille visited Grandma Peterson in Jamestown. The little boy is Marion's son Bill Stubbs. (Collection of Marion Strong Van Vlack)

The offstage friendship of Ginger Rogers and Lucille was mirrored in the 1937 film *Stage Door*. (Personality Photos)

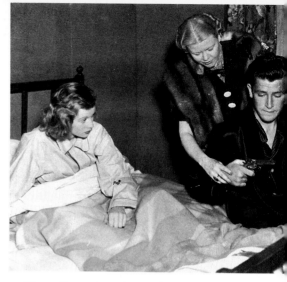

Ginger Rogers's mother, Lela, at center, was an early mentor to Lucille. She guided her and John Shelton in a workshop production at the Little Theater on the RKO lot. (Archive Photos)

When Lucille began dating the director Alexander Hall late in 1937, she was twenty-six; he was forty-three, twice divorced, and best known for his work with Shirley Temple in *Little Miss Marker*. (Archive Photos)

After a party Eddie Bracken (left) hosted for the cast of *Too Many Girls*, Lucille and Desi spent the night at her apartment. The next morning, he ended his engagement and she broke up with Al Hall. (Collection of Eddie Bracken)

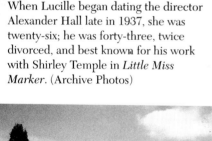

The bungalow Lucille rented for her family in Hollywood was styled after an Eastern mansion. (Kathleen Brady)

Desi missed a few performances of his five daily shows when he eloped with Lucille to Connecticut, but brought his bride back with him to the Roxy Theater, where fans greeted them with a standing ovation. (Personality Photos)

As an MGM star, Lucille regaled journalists with stories of the chickens she raised at Desilu, the Arnaz ranch at Chatsworth in the San Fernando Valley. (Personality Photos)

Gloria, a heartless, paralyzed showgirl in *The Big Street*, was the role of which Lucille was most proud. Based on a story by Damon Runyon (left) it co-starred Henry Fonda, who felt upstaged by her performance. (The Everett Collection)

Lucille and Desi reconciled the night before their divorce decree became final in 1944, but she picked it up anyway because reporters were waiting for her at the courthouse and she wanted to show off her new suit. (Bettman Archives)

Lucille was brilliant on the straw hat circuit in the show *Dream Girl*, but she was almost frantic with fear during rehearsals. She commended Herbert Kenwith (left) for pretending to ignore her outbursts. (Collection of Herbert Kenwith)

Her films for Columbia in the late 1940s, particularly *The Fuller Brush Girl*, were the first to reveal her unique gift for physical comedy. (Personality Photos)

DeDe helped make curtains for her daughter's home in Chatsworth. Lucille liked the effect of the clash of patterns. (Personality Photos)

In the radio show "My Favorite Husband," co-starring Richard Denning, Lucille played a wife who found herself in unlikely scrapes. (Archive Photos)

Network executives said audiences would reject an American girl married to a Cuban bandleader as the basis for a television series, so the Arnazes went on the road, where they delighted the public as a comedy team and proved the executives wrong. (Personality Photos)

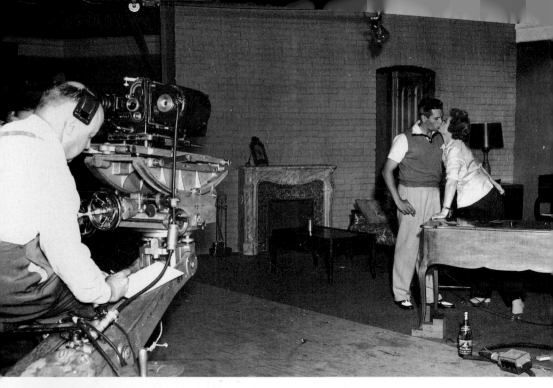

The Arnazes on the unfinished set of *I Love Lucy*, before the Ricardos' pictures were hung on the walls. (Archive Photos)

dependent nor give up the performing that she loved so much. Her professed reason for staying in pictures was that they needed to earn money to support Lolita and DeDe and to be able to afford the babies they would surely soon have. The divorce, however bogus, had in fact been good for them. Thereafter they spent as much time as possible together in Chatsworth. Desi now made the fifteen-minute trip home on weekends and evenings when he was not on duty.

By 1945 MGM succeeded in making the public more aware of Lucille Ball. The Audience Research Institute indicated that she had doubled her rating in the eighteen months she had been at the studio, although she had still not achieved the surpassing popularity the studio demanded.

In *Meet the People,* which she had filmed in the summer of 1943 when Desi had knee problems, she played an actress selling war bonds who ends up working at a shipyard to help the war effort. There was no chemistry between her and Dick Powell, who wears a straw hat at every opportunity and recites rather than acts out his lines. The most interesting aspect of the film was that its professed moral—that the people are the strength of a nation—was questioned by an increasingly influential group of anti-Communists who claimed social reformers, particularly those who were unionizing Hollywood actors, writers, and craftsmen, were in fact trying to undermine the government.

Lucille also appeared in some omnibus productions that brought out every player on MGM's roster. In *Thousands Cheer* (1943) she was one of many performers entertaining the troops. In *Abbott and Costello in Hollywood* (1945) she appeared as herself, accidentally sitting on the bungling Lou Costello. *Ziegfeld Follies,* an all-star revue, featured her elegantly cracking a whip while dressed in a mad pink outfit and seated upon the Lone Ranger's Silver, who was braided and duded up into a carousel horse. Her filming ended in early May 1944, but the picture was not released until the spring of 1946.

The producer Arthur Freed prepared *Ziegfeld Follies* with the care worthy of a general. Freed considered having Lucille do material by the British comedienne Bea Lillie, or teaming her either with Red

Skelton in a sketch called "Life with Junior" or with Greer Garson, Ann Sothern, and Nancy Walker in "If Men Did the Shopping." Among the other possibilities Freed planned but discarded was an unlikely pairing of Katharine Hepburn and Gene Kelly in a number called "Shakespeare in Tap Time."

"Meet the Ladies," Lucille's number, also starred Fred Astaire and Virginia O'Brien, and took director Vincente Minnelli ten days to rehearse and shoot. Ultimately the picture was several years in the making and more popular with audiences than critics. Extravagant rather than cohesive, it offers bits of film history—Errol Flynn in the chorus; Red Skelton in "When Television Comes" as a hilariously drunken announcer advertising "Guzzler's Gin," which prefigures Lucy Ricardo's "Vitameatavegamin"; and the character actor William Frawley playing a wary landlord to a crafty housewife played by Fanny Brice.

By now Lucille had starred in three MGM pictures, *Du Barry, Best Foot Forward,* and *Meet the People,* but the studio was concerned that she had still not excited sufficient enthusiasm in the public's mind. Part of her problem may have been that her private life was not fodder for the publicity machine. Fan magazines ran stories that stressed her preoccupation with her soldier husband, the pleasure she took in her flock of chickens, and her courtesy to the press. Other actresses were portrayed doing homespun activities in wartime, but Lucille, unlike a Lana Turner or a Myrna Loy, seemed to be truly ordinary. Except to adolescent boys, whom Audience Research showed to be devoted to her, she was not the stuff of fantasy. She herself knew that although she had achieved star billing, she was still just a performer. True stars had definable personalities that appealed to the public, and they seldom varied their personae from film to film. Rosalind Russell, for example, was the blithe executive female and Joan Crawford the struggling career woman with man problems. Lucille, who would make three pictures playing herself (*Best Foot Forward, Abbott and Costello in Hollywood,* and *A Woman of Distinction*), longed to be typed as something other than an actress in the public's mind.

She blamed some of her difficulties on her agents and on the contract system itself. After a dozen years in pictures, she looked back on the course of her career and compared herself to Olivia de Havilland, who brought suit against Warner Brothers in September 1943. The studio had suspended her when she refused parts she thought wrong for her and then would not terminate her contract on the specified date because it claimed the suspensions extended the term of the agreement. The court found in favor of de Havilland and criticized suspension practices as "virtual peonage for employees, even life bondage."

Recognizing that she too had to take more control of her career, Lucille telephoned de Havilland to discuss how she might get better professional representation. She said that Olivia's advice to her was "Watch. Ask. Find out when you're supposed to be paid." Lucille became more assertive with executives and allowed her brashness to cut like a dagger to the point. One day at the MGM commissary, which in contrast to the plain RKO facility had white tablecloths, Lucille casually joined a young actress named Irene Vernon and asked in greeting how things were going. The floodgates opened. Irene said she was frightened and miserable. First MGM had changed her hair and shaved her forehead, now Arthur Freed was chasing her. "Lucille immediately stood up and walked over to him and said, 'You leave this kid alone!' She saw I was sensitive and ambitious and I wanted to succeed," Irene recalled. "Women were so put down then, and it meant a lot to me that she was important and a woman and she had no ulterior motive for helping me." Irene soon moved over to Goldwyn's studios and ended up making a career in real estate.

In the autumn of 1944, the Audience Research Survey indicated that Lucille's popularity had dipped a few points and the studio relegated her to a supporting role in *Without Love*. This film has the questionable distinction of being the only flop Katharine Hepburn and Spencer Tracy ever made together, although Lucille and the rest of the cast, particularly Keenan Wynn, were praised.

With nothing else in mind for her, the studio next assigned her to make the brief supporting appearance in *Abbott and Costello in Hollywood*. Clearly MGM no longer considered her a property to be cultivated, nor did her agent, Arthur Lyons. She relied on him to keep her up to date on business matters, but her contract was expiring and neither he nor she had paid attention to the fact.

She challenged both MGM, which was not ready to let her go, and Lyons, whom she fired and eventually sued. While they tried to work out a solution and she tried to escape her agency contract, Lucille was free to make a suspense film at Twentieth Century–Fox titled *The Dark Corner*. Since its director, Henry Hathaway, believed that all great directors were cruel to actors, whenever Lucille muffed lines, he lambasted her. Hostility always rattled her, and with her status at MGM already in question, Hathaway's harshness reduced her to stuttering.

Lucille returned to MGM for *Easy to Wed*, a remake of the 1937 Spencer Tracy–Jean Harlow hit *Libeled Lady*, starring Van Johnson and Esther Williams. Lucille was again the second female lead, again a beautiful performer with upswept hair, but this time she was so determined to marry Keenan Wynn that she erupted into bravura mating calls. Her big moment was a drunken scene with Van Johnson. Eddie Buzzell, who had directed her in *Best Foot Forward*, told her to play it as she wished, probably the only advice to give an actor in that situation, as a drunken scene cannot be coaxed. An inebriated female is not a naturally appealing character, yet the drunker Lucille became, the more one cared about her. She oozed the sweet sexuality of the dumb girl who knows exactly how people perceive her and chooses to be a good sport about it. The scene was a specific and stunning piece of artistry, a performance that astonished everyone who saw the rushes.

Lucille's extraordinary work in *Easy to Wed* showed MGM she had a great deal of talent to offer, but the studio was not sure what to do with it. It signaled that it would renew her contract only at a decrease in pay. Ironically, it was Hattie Carnegie's husband, Major John Zanft, an MGM executive, who stopped by Lucille's dressing room to advise her as a friend not to seek the customary $500 raise. He informed her, correctly, that the studio was beginning to have financial troubles and was trimming its budget.

Infuriated, she allowed her agreement with MGM to lapse and stayed home the day after it ended. When the studio phoned her to ask why she wasn't in her dressing room, she related the story of the major's visit and made it clear she would not renew her contract under his terms. Lucille believed that Olivia de Havilland saved her from professional limbo by sending a man wearing a white suit to her door. "Lucille called me her knight in white because I was wearing a white *shirt* when I went to see her," explained Kurt Frings, who soon began representing her. "But Olivia de Havilland didn't send me. I heard Lucille was looking for a new agent and it was my idea."

In mid-1946 Lucille did a final picture for MGM, *Two Smart People* directed by Jules Dassin, at a reduced salary of $1,750. She was loaned out to other studios for several films, but both sides realized that the star buildup had not worked for her. "We knew she had talent, but not the quality expected of a big star," said Lucille Ryman Carroll, who headed the Talent Department and informed her that MGM was dropping her. "When I told her, she said, 'Oh, dear, what'll I do now? We won't have money and Desi will go out with the band.' Her life wasn't bound up in her work, it was bound up in Desi. He was the absolute focus of her life."

One summer day in 1946, Lucille drove home to Chatsworth with the news that she had been released. When she walked into the living room, she found Desi playing records of his songs for their neighbor Maxine Andrews. Maxine said, "In a matter-of-fact way, she said MGM had dropped her, then we made chitchat."

Now thirty-six, she was unlikely to be groomed as a star ever again. She had been demoted to the status of a freelance artist, one who would play supporting or B movie roles without the security of a steady paycheck. However calm her exterior, inwardly Lucille knew she had failed.

11

From July 1946, when *Easy to Wed* opened, to October 1951, when *I Love Lucy* was first broadcast, Lucille Ball recapitulated in her own career the history of American show business. She performed in the theater and on radio, honed her slapstick skills under the tutelage of Buster Keaton, and trouped on the remnants of the vaudeville circuit. While she believed that she was just simply managing to get work, she was in fact like an eagle circling one last time over familiar ground before soaring into new skies.

Money was one motivation for her dabbling in so many different media. When Desi left the army in November 1945, he was $30,000 in debt, much of it in back taxes. Lucille helped him meet his obligations, but Desi maintained his pride and sense of honor by treating the payment as a loan and keeping a strict account of the amount he owed her.

No longer on salary after she left MGM, Lucille hired a money manager who put her on a budget so strict that buying a coveted marabou peignoir seemed the height of indulgence. Virginia O'Brien recalled Lucille taking her into her bedroom at Chatsworth and showing it off, saying "Look what I treated myself to!"

Desi had expected Mayer to honor his contract once he was discharged from the service, but he discovered that a handsome, well-spoken, twenty-five-year-old Mexican named Ricardo Montalban now had first claim on roles for Latins. The cold welcome he received at MGM after having been away in the army for two and a half years convinced Desi that he had no future in the movie business. Early in 1946, when MGM was keeping Lucille under contract but loaning her out, Desi asked to be released from his contract so that he might return to what was for him a more dependable source of income, nightclubs. Latin music, particularly songs of Cuban origin, was still in vogue, so he assembled an orchestra with a sound that combined feisty Caribbean rhythms with a lush Continental smoothness. He and his band were soon a popular attraction at Ciro's, where Lucille spent many evenings as much to protect her marriage as to cheer him on. "His act was not the best, but he had a great close in 'Babalu.'" said George Schlatter, who managed the club. "Desi stayed on too long as so many do, so the waiters said 'Play "Babalu"!' as soon as he came out. Desi was not a musician or an actor. He was an entertainer."

When not in Hollywood, the band toured the country, often doing one-night engagements just to get a booking. Lucille's brother Fred was Desi's road manager, but his presence did not, as she certainly hoped, affect her husband's behavior. Not quite thirty, Desi was well able to stand up to the bacchanalian stresses to which he subjected himself and still be ready to do a show at night. He was as promiscuous as he had been before their "divorce" and was so dedicated a gambler that during a two-week engagement in Las Vegas, he lost the entire payroll at the tables. In other moods he was a different Desi, still entrepreneurial and willing to take a chance, but a man who relied on firm knowledge of business figures rather than the odds. While the wild man drew attention to himself with his profligacy, the efficient Desi knew where each penny was debited and how it had been earned. His innate abilities had been honed when he worked for Xavier Cugat and observed the Rhumba King's tight-fisted management of his own band. Like Cugat, Desi learned to present only what was commercial and focused on the appearance of his group, particularly dancers in rhumba shirts who stood before audiences continually rotating hips and mariachis and demonstrating how Latin dances were done. He developed a keen sense of the American audience, of which acts and presentations won them over and which fell flat. Often the relentless pace of touring wore away his bravado and revealed a lonely, sensitive man who longed for a rest. "He'd miss being able to use his boat because he loved the sea like all of us from Cuba do," said Marco Rizo, who was again in his band. Sometimes Desi would find Marco listening to classical music and would envy his friend's knowledge and the pleasure he could derive from it. "He'd say, 'What's that?' I'd say, 'Mozart' and he'd say, 'It sounds good.'"

Lucille was not capable of understanding, or even noticing, the gentler aspects of his nature, nor was he interested in revealing them to her. The man she knew was the one who caroused on the road and let her down. When she berated him over the telephone for transgressions real and imagined, Desi countered that he knew that she was going to nightclubs and industry functions and probably betraying him with her co-stars.

Whether she actually did repay him in kind for his infidelity or not, the only man he might have had reason to worry about was George Sanders, her co-star in *Lured*, a thriller released by United Artists in the summer of 1947. Sanders, at six foot three, was one of few men who towered over Lucille, who was five foot seven. He was forty, but nearly beautiful with light-brown hair, gray-green eyes, and the bored, impervious mien of an aesthete. He flattered women by listening to them attentively and delighted them with tales of his eccentric English family and their ties to old Russia. Sanders's father awaited the return of the czar, and with a rifle his uncle shot flies buzzing on his bedroom ceiling. Zsa Zsa Gabor described him as not knowing whether he wanted to be an English duke or a beachcomber. Lucille considered him the most sophisticated man she had ever met, far more interested in money than in acting, charming, handsome, brilliant, and "searching the world for his mother."

Although Lucille would deny it over the years, Zsa Zsa Gabor, who married Sanders a few years after her divorce from Conrad Hilton, was certain they had an affair. Zsa Zsa became suspicious when she picked up an extension phone at his home to hear Lucille demanding "What are you doing with that Hilton woman? You know that I love you. She's too young for you!"

Whatever her dalliances may have been, Desi remained Lucille's preoccupation and she was often his. They did laugh now over minor disagreements, such as whether bedroom windows should be open at night, but however she tried to rationalize his flagrant infidelities, she was not truly reconciled to them. This, and the predicament of her being so much more successful in her career, kept them from recognizing the still-deeper problem of fundamental conflicts in their personalities. She was unable to relax and surrendered totally to whatever mood was passing. When he was distant, annoyed, or impatient, she tried to wheedle, cajole, or seduce him into better humor, and when that failed, she quickly became shrill: "*Too Many Girls* is the story of your life!" or "It's *my* goddam money!" For his part, Desi professed a tropical sense that life was to be enjoyed and felt as blameless as a child. When people asked him why they fought, he said he didn't know because she wouldn't tell him.

Later, when he reflected back on their marriage, he observed: "I'm convinced that the reason we survived this constant arguing, fighting and accusation for so many years was because we had something extra-special going for us. We were very much in love with each other, and when we were able to be together, our sexual relationship was heavenly. Also, and perhaps even more important, we had a good sense of humor. We were able to laugh at ourselves and at our sometimes absurd and stupid arguments."

He described their reunions on the road as rare and tempestuous, occasions of either mad lovemaking or hellish fighting. Their quarrels were becoming standard filler items in the press, so that if columnists noted they were celebrating an anniversary, they predicted it would be their last. After Sheilah Graham reported that the couple had battled furiously in New York, Lucille phoned her, threatening revenge and demanding to know how Graham had heard this. Then, in an explosion of raw vulnerability that often followed such rages, she burst into tears. "You've got two children and you don't care. You say things like this about me and I will never have children!"

Increasingly frustrated by her own childlessness, Lucille doted on the offspring of others. By this time Barbara Bell, daughter of Harriet's friend Dot, had children of her own. Lucille met them in San Francisco and as Barbara recalled, "She wanted to hurry up and have kids so bad. When she met my son she loved him so much she kept stuffing money in his pockets. He was five or six and she thought it was a great game." Her desire for motherhood was such that even DeDe suggested they adopt a child if they wanted one so badly, but Lucille would sob, "I want Desi's baby."

That she did not get pregnant she continued to attribute to the fact that she and Desi had seldom been together in the mid-1940s. While he was on the road, her work in films, much of it on loan-outs to studios other than MGM, kept her close to Hollywood. Still, although MGM executives now warned her that the money and exposure were too little and the risk of failure too great, she seized the opportunity to go off on her own to return to the stage. After the war, the straw-hat summer stock theaters reopened, and she was offered *Dream Girl*, a romantic comedy by the Pulitzer Prize winner Elmer Rice being staged at Princeton, where she had so happily performed *Hey Diddle Diddle* ten years before. *Dream Girl* had been successful on Broadway, but the actresses who headed the casts in New York and on the road both fell ill and the runs were curtailed. Because it had been performed so rarely, Lucille thought she could put her own stamp on the role, that of a shy, repressed book shop manager who daydreams her way on to a confessional radio program, becomes the mother of twins fathered by her brother-in-law, is acquitted for a murder she did commit, and triumphs in the role of Shakespeare's Portia—all before she imagines she is a streetwalker who takes her own life.

The part was physically demanding, which may have accounted for the illnesses of its earlier stars, but Lucille coped with it by discharging stress in flashes of temperament. Herbert Kenwith, a compact combination of energy and discipline, who produced the play and persuaded her to do it, recalled her running to him in hysterics. "She was yelling, and I knew I couldn't outdo her, so I stood there quietly. Finally she stopped, burst into tears, and put her head in my lap. She said, 'Forgive me.' I asked what was wrong. She said, 'My dressing room. I don't like it.' "

Storm over, they resumed rehearsals, and at the end of the day she went to Herbert and said, "You did something marvelous and you must always remember it. Whenever someone is having an hysterical fit, say nothing." He did want her to be happy, so that night he and his assistants went to a department store in Trenton and bought fabrics and mirrors to fix up her dressing room. "When Lucille saw it the next morning, she was dumbstruck. She said she had never meant for us to go to such expense. We kept that room the way we fixed it for six years," he said.

Lucille had reason to be anxious about her part, because she was on stage for all but a few minutes of the production. Although she learned all her lines, she was terrified that she would rattle them off in the wrong scene. On opening night she ordered around her fellow performers, then made her entrance and went totally blank. With apparent calm, she turned to her co-star and asked, "Are you going to sit there and say nothing?" He began speaking, which jogged her memory and put her on track. It was only a momentary lapse and her performance was excellent. Elmer Rice commented in his autobiography: "I have seen other productions of this play, but the only actress whose performance really delighted me was Lucille Ball. She lacked . . . tender wistfulness, but her vivid personality and expert timing kept the play bright and alive."

By the time *Dream Girl* had toured regional theaters and opened in Los Angeles in January 1948, she was a seasoned trouper. She had played in large auditoriums and venues too small to accommodate the scenery and so cramped that rather than use real equipment, the crew had to spotlight her with flashlights. She learned to adjust her performance to each situation. Unfortunately, her stamina failed at the end of the run, and the Los Angeles engagement was cut short when she finally succumbed to the virus that had plagued the rest of the cast. Despite this, Edwin Schallert, who reviewed her for *The Los Angeles Times*, declared that she had been wasting her time in films: "She has efficiency as a comedienne. She can tinge a scene delicately with pathos. She has a special facility in dealing with sharp-edged repartee. She apparently never overdoes the sentimental side of a role, judged by her performance in the Elmer Rice play."

As soon as she was over her illness, Lucille resumed her movie career by freelancing at Paramount, where she made *Sorrowful Jones* with Bob Hope, and even briefly returned to RKO for *Easy Living* with Victor Mature and Lizabeth Scott. Although she was bouncing around, she boasted she was never out of work. Since leaving MGM, she had toned down her hair color from orange red to red gold. Relegated to black-and-white films, for a time she let her hair return to its natural brown and wore it in short curls, which gave her a matronly air. Lighting technicians were less careful with her than those at MGM had been, so sometimes the extra poundage MGM had urged on her made her look fleshy or blowzy.

As 1948 wore on, her career began to evolve in a new direction, one that might have seemed a stopgap to the irregularity of freelancing in the movies, but which actually was the final leg of the long journey that led her into television. Lucille became the star of her own radio show in a genre known as situation comedy.

Kurt Frings had an agent working in his office named Don Sharpe who had written and produced radio shows and was now carving out a new and important niche in broadcasting. He was thirty-six, short, dark, jowly, and vibrant when he met Lucille. His specialty was packaging movie personalities for the radio. Big radio names such as Jack Benny, Red Skelton, and Fred Allen were primarily comedians, but Sharpe brought popular actors, particularly those whose box office careers might have hit a slump, into ongoing radio dramas and sit-coms and set about to do the same for Lucille. The idea of putting together star, show, and sponsor and selling this "package" to a network was so new the word was written in quotes, but Sharpe made the idea work for Cary Grant, who did "Mr. Blandings Builds His Dream House," for Brian Donleavy with "Dangerous Assignment," and for Dick Powell with "Richard Diamond."

In the decade since she had made her debut on Jack Haley's variety radio show, Lucille had frequently appeared on the medium's come-dies and dramas, sometimes to publicize her movies. She enjoyed the work enormously because it brought her into contact with live audi-ences who egged her on to her best work and, she claimed, taught her to improve her timing and delivery. Sharpe approached Harry Acker-man, a vice president in charge of programming at CBS Radio, about giving her a show of her own. Together they came up with a show based on a little-known book titled *Mr. and Mrs. Cugat: The Record of a Happy Marriage* by Isabel Scott Rorick. Sharpe told Ackerman that he was so sure Lucille was right for the role of a ditsy society wife of a rising young banking executive that he would pay to record a sample broadcast of the show.

Since the network already had a successful light comedy hit in "The Adventures of Ozzie and Harriet" and billed the Nelsons as "America's Favorite Young Couple," Ackerman asked two of that show's writers to do a half-hour sample "Mr. and Mrs. Cugat," which aired in Los Angeles in July 1948 and co-starred Lucille and Lee Bowman. Although CBS did not find a sponsor, at the end of September it was so convinced of the potential of the formula that it was willing to "sustain" the show without one, as it did other programs it believed in. By the time it was scheduled, Bowman and the writers had other commitments. Richard Denning, an easygoing midwesterner popular in romantic film comedies, took over the male lead and the show was renamed "My Favorite Husband." The Cugats became Liz and George Cooper, and a new writing team was assigned. Madelyn Pugh and Bob Carroll, Jr., were both in their twenties and writing for Steve Allen, but they were so eager to have a crack at a network series that they paid Allen to write his own show one week so they could do Lucille's script. Bob had a pointed beard and keen sharp features that gave him the look of a devil or a seductive artist. Madelyn, a pretty brunette, was ladylike, at least until she sat down at the typewriter and maneuvered her characters into preposterous situations. She, somewhat more disciplined, excelled at outlining the story and at making it work. He supplied the jokes and dialogue. They had first met at CBS Radio, where all the young writers went bowling together once a week. Carroll, who had been plagued by an infected hip, did not bowl, but was essential to the outings because he was the only one with a car.

When they discovered their similarities, the two began dating and writing as partners. Both had written plays at the age of five, treasured the same books, grew up reading *The New Yorker*, and knew that whenever there was a school election or an editor to be chosen for the yearbook, they would always be the one to win.

They won the assignment of writing "My Favorite Husband" in September 1948, but Lucille was greatly displeased with their first efforts. In films, she was forced by Hollywood's factory system and the strictures of being a contract player to keep her critical judgment and temperament in check, but as the star of her own radio show, with producers and writers close at hand, she felt free to speak out tartly and directly. Her comments about one early script were so caustic that they reduced Madelyn to tears. "I wasn't afraid of her. I was awed. I think someone told her to come on strong and to run the show. She was trying to do that and it was terrifying at first," Madelyn recalled.

The two novices did need a seasoned hand, so Jess Oppenheimer, who had written for Fanny Brice's radio show "Baby Snooks" and done the voice of her little brother, was brought in as head writer and producer. Brice was a rare female star—homely, funny, and able to portray disparate characters from opera singers to evangelists with humanity and sensitivity. Since she was brusque and bluntly refused to perform material that did not meet her standards, dealing successfully with her gave Oppenheimer his stripes.

As a child he had been considered a genius; now at thirty-five, Oppenheimer seemed to radiate self-assurance, and most important, he knew how to mollify Lucille. "It began to work. She began to trust him," Madelyn said. "I think she'd had a hard time scrambling her way to the top, and it made her very wary. I guess she wasn't too sure that people would take care of her. All we wanted was to make her look good, and that hadn't happened to her before. She began to relax when she saw that if she did something funny on the show once, we'd use it again because it worked for her." Just before Christmas 1948, after CBS had sustained it a few months, General Foods agreed to sponsor "My Favorite Husband" to promote Jell-O.

A consequence of this was that Lucille had to do commercials. Lucille hated this, and to placate her, Jess had her perform them as characters from nursery rhymes. In portraying the confrontation of Little Miss Muffet and the spider, the contortions of her mouth and her comically foreboding gurgle so delighted the audience that the writers worked them into the show, noting "Spider" in the script as her cue. "Small Rabbit" and "Puddle" soon joined her repertoire of expressions that, at that time, only the studio audience could see.

To cement professional bonds, Bob and Madelyn invited Lucille out to dinner. As Carroll recalled: "She was skittish because she said that in motion pictures stars never talked to writers, only to producers and directors, but she went. She told us we should be writing for the movies because what we wrote was so physical." As she grew to trust the writers, she felt free to give them personal advice. When Bob shaved off his beard, Lucille looked at his naked jawline and said, "Grow it back, you son of a bitch!" She also decided they should marry, and told them so repeatedly.

Bob and Madelyn came to accept and sometimes use her tendency to overdramatize. When she announced, "Desi's been in a wreck!" everyone at the radio studio worried. "We thought he was in the hospital," Bob said, "but he showed up an hour later with only a little bruise." They quickly came to see that Lucille was a clown, a comic actress. When "My Favorite Husband" was broadcast to the country Monday nights, she and the rest of the cast dressed in evening clothes, but when the script called for it, she might add a black wig or a man's hat or wrap herself in an old shawl to milk the greatest laughs from the studio audience. Until then, Lucille had not felt any of her roles was truly hers, not the conniving Bubbles of *Dance, Girl, Dance,* nor the grasping Gloria of *The Big Street,* or the hopeful Gladys of *Easy to Wed.* But in playing Liz Cooper, who thought she knew better than the husband she adored, Lucille felt that something new and strangely appropriate came into focus. Liz pursued her ends with the best of intentions, but somehow little things jumped out of her control and led to the funniest mishaps.

In March of 1949, two regulars were added to "My Favorite Husband." Gale Gordon, a tall, natty actor much in demand for his blustery voice and knack for pluperfect pomposity, and Bea Benaderet, a handsome blonde actress with the tightly waved perm of the period who specialized in wifely supporting roles, were both in their early forties and played George Cooper's boss and his wife. This second couple offered the story possibilities of wives conspiring against the husbands and gave the show a boost and a dimension that pleased the network. Lucille respected her co-stars as much as her writers and because she considered them essential to her success, she did not hesitate to give them pointers. As Gale Gordon recalled, "My first impression of Lucille was that she was very pretty, very vital and incisive. Once at rehearsal I read a line and she told me, 'You know, there's a laugh there.' The director said, 'Miss Ball, you don't have to worry that he'll talk though a laugh,' but she wasn't chiding me. I found her comment acceptable."

Ironically, radio brought Lucille a personal, intimate recognition she had never experienced before. When she had been introduced at movie premieres earlier in her career, she could see people in the crowd whispering "Who's that?" After a few months of being a radio star whom the public accepted in their homes, however, she became someone people really wanted to meet. "It was 'Lucille Ball, the gal who plays Liz Cooper on radio' wherever I went," she said, delighted.

Buster Keaton and Ed Sedgwick were now working at Columbia. They, along with Kurt Frings, told Harry Cohn that Lucille was the best comedienne in Hollywood and that he should put her under contract. Keaton and his young wife, Eleanor, a dancer at MGM, and the Sedgwicks were frequent guests at Chatsworth. Since Fred Hunt's death, Ed, whom Keaton called "Junior," had taken over as Lucille's father figure. If Sedgwick had considered Al Hall wrong for Lucille, he was openly skeptical of Desi, partly because Cubans were not highly regarded in his native Texas, but mostly because he saw for himself how Desi hurt Lucille. The friendship Keaton bore her was much more straightforward. He admired her talent and told his wife that Lucille was a modern Constance Talmadge, the frisky and fun-loving comedienne of the silent era, who had once been his sister-in-law as well. Keaton and Sedgwick had the privilege of seeing Lucille relaxed in the company of friends. Unwary, she leapt about and triple-shook her hip in an exaggerated conga or embellished and acted out events of her life. If she tried to tell a joke, she was likely to go on interminably and then forget the punch line, but if she picked up an ashtray or other object she could use as a prop, she would effortlessly improvise a skit.

One Sunday afternoon she and Desi were members of a boating party at Balboa Beach that included Elliott Roosevelt, the late president's son. Lucille sat alone in the stern solemnly looking out to sea with Desi's battered fishing hat pulled down over her eyebrows and a tattered blue marabou negligee draped over her shoulders, an FDR parody magisterial in signature cape.

On another weekend she and Desi tied their small boat to a dock at Balboa and were frying catfish for dinner when a large yacht, horns blaring, steamed past with its crew saluting as they lowered its flag. Stunned by the spectacle and galvanized by the noise, she organized Sunday sailors to beat their saucepans while running their nautical flags up and down their slender poles.

The Sedgwicks and Keatons went to the ranch for poker games. "Lucille was semihyper," recalled Eleanor Keaton. "Washing dishes soothed her nerves." During one game, when Lucille folded her cards, she "sat out" the hand by taking down the draperies to have them cleaned. Oblivious, Desi simply raised his bids.

Manners were not Lucille's strength. Her well-intended praise was often left-handed and occasionally as pleasurable as a blow to the ear. Admiring a white crepe blouse of Eleanor's, she asked where it had come from and how much she paid. "I evaded telling her. She would try to pin you to the wall like a D.A., but she didn't mind if you sidestepped. She couldn't get her hair to grow, and she'd grab mine, pull it and say, 'Explain to me how you do that.' That was her way of complimenting me."

In early 1949 Keaton and Sedgwick's efforts on her behalf bore fruit and she signed a contract with Columbia. Harry Cohn's studio was by now a worthy competitor to the majors, a place quite different from the studio she was fired from fourteen years before. Cohn's respect for a dollar still prompted him to remind gaffers to turn off unnecessary lights, but now it also spurred him to spend top money for properties that were likely to be hits. Thus, Columbia had a blockbuster in *The Jolson Story* starring Larry Parks and enormous successes with both *A Song to Remember*, a life of Chopin starring Cornel Wilde, and the torrid *Gilda*, with Rita Hayworth. Lucille was not cast in any Columbia pictures in this class, but she did find an outlet for her particular gifts in an intriguing comedy unit. Along with Keaton and Sedgwick, it included Lloyd Bacon, who had acted with Chaplin and directed two-reelers for Mack Sennett, as well as *The Singing Fool* for Warner Brothers, the first motion picture with dialogue. Bacon's talents were in making innovative, difficult camera angles look natural and in his ability to energize dialogue. Lucille initially feared that going to Columbia for $25,000 a picture would reduce her value, according to Lucille Ryman Carroll, but Bacon and his young producer, S. Sylvan Simon, gave her the opportunity to do the full-out slapstick comedy she loved.

Sedgwick and Keaton shared an office near the commissary that they called "the Boors Nest" and where they welcomed anyone who was hiding from executives or simply had nothing to do. Studio writers were habitués, as was the Columbia representative of the Hays office whose standard exit line was "I have to go tuck in the tits." Lucille joined the group between takes and wardrobe fittings and later presented them with a large picture of herself autographed "From Your Favorite Madame," which they hung on the wall.

The jokes, reminiscences, and reenactment of well-loved movie bits that filled the Boors Nest were more than nostalgia. For the aging men, they kept the withering muscles of their comedy in shape. For Lucille, they provided informal professional training. Keaton was a master of props and sight gags, an amateur inventor who built replicas of the Golden Gate Bridge and a miniature railroad trestle that won first prize at a hobby show. In his films, his classic put-upon sad sack relentlessly battled motorcycles, trains, steamships, and other developments of the modern age. Up in the Boors Nest Keaton taught Lucille how to command props and how to throw herself into physical maneuvers without hurting herself. Speedy, rambunctious Lucille learned to slow down and refine action. Keaton drilled her in the mantra that was the foundation of her fabled comic timing: Listen, React, then Act. She learned to hear whatever another character said or did, respond to it, and then perform an appropriate action. If, as often happened in her comedy, a boat or barrel sprung a leak, she discovered it, gasped, and plugged the spouting hole, sometimes by sitting on it. Keaton watched her from corners of the set while she was filming and later made suggestions on how she might improve.

Miss Grant Takes Richmond, her first film under her new Columbia agreement, showed that his belief in her was justified. Lucille played a public-spirited secretary, a character so ditsy that watching her is like standing before a photographer's developing tray and seeing a photograph of Lucy Ricardo gradually emerge. Lucille takes a job in a bookie joint that she thinks is a realtor's office and, in the course of making it all come right, is caught in a mudslide, takes a jackhammer to building foundations, and threatens a criminal with the handle of a pencil sharpener.

Between takes, however, Lucille gave little indication that her career mattered much to her. As Janis Carter, who played her rival for William Holden but was a good pal on the set, commented, "Lucille's ambitions weren't about her career. They centered on Desi, on having a home and children. She said she'd take anything the studio threw at her so long as they gave her money. She also was one to poke fun at herself."

She recalled, "We both had a pet hate. Neither of us would admit to the other who it was, but I persuaded her to at least imitate the person. It was as though the other person emerged from her. Lucille had all her mannerisms down perfectly. I said, 'You hate her too! We're friends for life.'"

Miss Grant was quickly followed by *The Fuller Brush Girl*, a spinoff of Red Skelton's successful *Fuller Brush Man* that was tailored to her physical talents. Whatever she may have said to others about her professional aspirations, before the cameras her actions revealed her total dedication. As her co-star Eddie Albert observed, "Lucille was more devoted to her career and talent than anyone else I ever met. She thought only of being an entertainer. The ego of it was amazing! She sought out opportunities to do stunts and kept asking 'Can I do it?' She'd roll barrels and bowling balls and get blown up in the stunts. She was in smoke and fire. She was so stalwart. I was glad it was her and not me."

In this, her first breakneck comedy, Lucille was at last able to free herself creatively. Where once her face was merely expressive, now her features flare. She cross-hatches her body over a clothesline, disguises herself as a burlesque queen in gypsy makeup, and ends up on a stage where, with the help of gangsters lurking in the wings, she does a striptease.

As many vaudeville and silent screen bits were thrown into *Fuller Brush Girl* as running time allowed—a smokestack puts her in blackface, she tries to staunch a leaky wine vat by covering the hole with her mouth, and she even slips on a banana peel. One critic noted,

"When the gag bag was opened, it was opened all the way. The routines are milked for all they are worth and prove that many of them still have life." *Variety* said, "If there were ever any doubts as to Miss Ball's forte, *Fuller Brush Girl* dispels them. She is an excellent comedienne and in this rowdy incoherent yarn, with its Keystone Kop overtones, she garners major laurels."

With her new film commitments, Lucille was now intensely busy. Arising before six, she was in bed by eight-thirty at night and spent Sundays rehearsing for her Monday evening radio show. After work, when she arrived at Chatsworth, she did not unwind immediately, but embarked on her personal beauty routine—creaming her face until all the studio makeup disappeared, rubbing on surgeon's cream that she thought made the best moisturizer, steaming her complexion, and then taking a hot shower, followed by a cold one. To refresh herself, she did what she called her three-in-one treatment—she dangled her head over one side of her bed while propping her feet up on pillows, all the while vigorously brushing her hair.

Hair, her own and that of others, was her avocation. Friends who stopped by on weekends often found themselves under her scissors or submitting to permanent waves. She shampooed her own tresses every morning, changing products often to try out scents, then rinsed away the suds with vinegar or Burgundy wine. Pincurls in place, she sat under a hair dryer she bought from a beauty shop. On days off, she tied a colorful scarf around her curlers, put on a housecoat and ballet slippers, and cleaned her house alongside her help. Rest was unwelcome to her. She described naps as "deadening."

Desi was with her only sporadically. When Lucille did *Dream Girl* in the latter half of 1947, he was traveling from Detroit to New York, from Amarillo to Omaha, and then to San Francisco for a three-month engagement at the Palace Hotel, where they did a radio broadcast every night. Later Lucille joined him on weekends when she could, and she was suspicious, usually with reason, of both those singers who stayed with him over a period of months and of those who arrived and departed between her visits. Their married life through the summer of 1949 took place on occasional weekends when they either battled furiously or ardently made love before resuming their separate existences.

As she was beginning *Fuller Brush Girl,* Columbia's *All the King's Men* won the Oscar as best picture of 1949 and Broderick Crawford took the award for Best Actor. Lucille dreamed that she would yet have a comparably great role that would win her recognition and believed she had found it when Cohn acquired the film rights to the Broadway hit *Born Yesterday,* the story of a kept woman with a heart of gold. Its premise was a virtual elaboration of Lucille's memorable and best scene in *Easy to Wed* when she played the knowing dumb girl stuck in a life that even she disapproves of. Columnists like Louella Parsons and Hedda Hopper said Lucille's fans were hoping she would land the role, and thereby signaled to Harry Cohn that they expected him to consider her. Cohn, however, was thinking of Barbara Stanwyck, Alice Faye, or Rita Hayworth, while the play's author, Garson Kanin, wanted only its Broadway star, Judy Holliday, who had been playing the role of Billie Dawn for four years on stage.

Everything seemed to break right for Judy Holliday, plump and endearing with reddish blonde hair, eleven years younger than Lucille. Whereas each of Lucille's standout performances seemed to lead nowhere, recognition of Judy Holliday's talents resulted relatively quickly in new and greater opportunities. Kanin had initially seen her singing in a New York cabaret, where Leonard Bernstein sometimes accompanied her, and he hired her to replace the ailing Jean Arthur in *Born Yesterday* just four days before its opening. To prove that Holliday could carry the film version, Kanin got her a part as a jealous, husband-stalking, candy-addicted wife in *Adam's Rib* with Katharine Hepburn and Spencer Tracy. Her performance convinced Cohn. Not only did Lucille lose out, but she watched S. Sylvan Simon, who was her producer at Columbia, oversee Holliday's film.

Lucille's only unqualified success as the 1940s ended was her radio show, but she seemed to come to that medium too late. Sponsors and personalities such as Ed Wynn, Jack Benny, and Burns and Allen were abandoning it because they saw television eclipsing radio as talkies had the silents. In 1947 the public bought 179,000 sets; by 1949 the number jumped to two million, and Sears, Roebuck added them to its catalog. Milton Berle, who had been on the fringes of vaudeville, radio, and films for years, became the most popular performer in the nation, everywhere known as "Uncle Miltie" and "Mr. Television" because of his *Texaco Star Theater* on NBC Tuesday nights. When CBS told Lucille they wanted to transfer "My Favorite Husband" to television, she saw a chance to work with Desi and said she wanted him as her co-star, but the network balked. The notion of Desi Arnaz playing a midwestern banker was ridiculous. "Who would believe a typical American redhead married to a Cuban bandleader?" was the scoffing question that ended the discussion.

She may have been relieved. Lucille by all accounts was at first not eager to move to the small black-and-white screen. Such a step would have ended her movie career, because the studios were so fearful of the medium that they forbade their stars to appear on it without special permission. In cities with even one television station, a mortal trend had begun to emerge: Movie attendance dropped by as much as 40 percent, sports fans deserted stadiums, nightclubs and restaurants lost patrons, and libraries reported decreased book circulation.

Lucille was free to go on television as a featured guest on other people's shows to promote "My Favorite Husband" and films. She appeared on *The Chesterfield Supper Club* in February 1949 and then on Peter Lind Hayes and Mary Healy's *Inside U.S.A. with Chevrolet* in early December. On Christmas Eve of that year, she and Desi appeared together on *The Ed Wynn Show*, a rare CBS network program that originated from Hollywood and was photographed on kinescope film from a television tube so it could later be broadcast to the East Coast. In one skit, created by her radio show writers, Lucille pretended to be a Ziegfeld Girl by walking around with a lampshade upside down on her head. During rehearsals, no one felt the bit had been working quite right, so a CBS director named Ralph Levy tried to show her how to improve her showgirl stroll. "I didn't know she had been a showgirl. Instead of telling me off, she simply played along with me. She was so professional and so good. She walked away with the whole show," Levy recalled. The chief impression television made on Lucille at this point was the enormity of the cameras crawling in front of the stage and blocking the view of the audience.

Desi was far more excited about its potential than she was, partly because he had no film career to forfeit. Largely with Lucille's help, he had been named the musical director of Bob Hope's radio show, but his accent made it impossible for him to do much speaking. Desi tried to convince Lucille that television, where his accent offered less of a liability, offered them a chance to work together so that he could stop traveling and they could raise the children they expected to have.

Lucille continued to believe they would co-star in films, even though Hollywood was also reeling from an even deadlier blow than television. In May 1948, two months before "My Favorite Husband" made its debut on CBS Radio, the U.S. Supreme Court had ruled that the major studios could no longer be allowed to both produce and exhibit motion pictures. Forced to divest themselves of their theaters, which left them with fewer outlets to show their films, studios slashed production schedules and canceled the contracts of employees from actors to lighting technicians. Partly for tax purposes, at this time Lucille and Desi formed a company called Desilu Productions to make films that Ed Sedgwick would direct. The first project they considered was *Blazing Beulah from Butte*, written by Sedgwick, about a Mexican who comes to America to marry a cultured woman and ends up with a rambunctious hussy. A few months later they came up with *That Townsend Girl* in which a woman opens a gambling den in Cuba. As these projects foundered, Lucille began to wonder whether television might not offer her a better future.

Although Lucille and Desi were committed to the concept of working as a team and were united in their hope for a family, these bonds did not end Desi's womanizing. This was apparent the New Year's Eve they decided to roast a pig and invited Maxine and Laverne Andrews and Laverne's husband to share it. When Lucille welcomed them, their host was nowhere to be seen. As the hours went on, Lucille delayed dinner, insisted Desi would arrive at any moment, and refused to let them leave. As Maxine recalled, "He finally came in at one in the morning. We kept trying to jolly up the party, and Laverne's husband was trying to jolly Desi up, but everything was strained. I felt for Lucille because she'd planned a nice fun quiet New Year's Eve and it did not work out that way." One Sunday afternoon Lucille invited Maxine to come over, and when she arrived, Lucille suggested they go for a drive around the Valley. "I think she was looking for Desi," Maxine said.

Keeping him nearby was her obsession. Visiting Lucille Ryman Carroll at her ranch, Lucille said she was seriously contemplating doing a television show because it would keep Desi at home. "She didn't know what to do because it would kill her in the movies, but she said, 'If he goes on the road, I'll either travel with him or I'll lose him.'"

Together the couple visited television studios in Hollywood. The night Virginia O'Brien appeared on Ed Wynn's show, she looked up at the balcony and saw Lucille and Desi intently staring down, studying her, the cameras, and the director, obviously trying to figure out how they could possibly put together a television show.

12

When Lucille decided people needed help, she took it upon herself to provide it, although the results were often the opposite of what she intended. She displayed rare wisdom and sensitivity, however, when her friend Marcella Rabwin suffered her second miscarriage. Marcella was lying in her hospital bed doubting she would ever have a child when the door opened and in came Lucille. "I was terribly depressed and barely able to talk," Marcella remembered. "She did not say a word, not even hello. She simply started humming burlesque music. She took off her hat, she took off her coat and did a striptease down to her underwear. She had me screaming and laughing, and then she put on her clothes and went home and never did say one word to me about the whole incident. I was a different person after that."

Lucille's uncharacteristic understanding that in such circumstances there was nothing to be said suggested the depths of her own prolonged aching for a child. Desi wanted a son to carry on the Arnaz name, and he and Lucille had been so confident that they would start

171

a family after the war ended, when it seemed the entire nation was giving birth, that for their sixth anniversary Desi bought her a gold pin in the shape of a key engraved "Nursery." But, as if it were an omen of misfortune, the gift was stolen from his car before he could give it to her.

The couple turned to science, to God, and even to nocturnal calisthenics to overcome their infertility. Doctors advised them to have intercourse at the most fertile point in Lucille's cycle, which she could determine by charting her temperature. So conscientious were they about this procedure that on one occasion when Lucille Ryman Carroll was with her at Chatsworth and Lucille's thermometer indicated the hour was propitious, she telephoned Desi in Hollywood. He then informed his orchestra that their rehearsal was canceled so that he could hurry home for an afternoon of procreative activity.

Lolita believed the marriage was barren because Lucille and Desi had not been married before a priest, and told her son so. Desi admitted to his wife that he had never in fact felt truly married, so in preparation for a Catholic ceremony Lucille took classes for non-Catholics marrying into the church. While she did not go so far as to convert, she agreed to raise their children in the faith and for good luck, this time she chose a Sunday for the ceremony. On June 19, 1949, they were married by a priest at Our Lady of the Valley, a small clapboard-covered church near their home. She wore a full-skirted blue dress and hat and he a white suit. Both were as teary eyed as they had been the day they eloped eight years before. Ed Sedgwick gave Lucille away, and Lolita served as matron of honor.

Even after eight years of rocky marriage, the force of their mutual attraction was obvious to friends. Later that summer when Desi came to visit her at Paramount on the set of *Fancy Pants*, which starred Bob Hope, they had a screaming fight the whole crew knew about. But after Desi headed off for a short fishing trip with a friend, he phoned her to say he had detoured instead to Del Mar, a beach community down the coast, to see the Rabwins. He said he had won $2,500 opening day at the racetrack and teased her by adding "We had nothing but winners. Poor you." Each night he would call with more details of the beautiful weather and the fun they were having at the track and in the evening as they watched the sun set in the Pacific.

Marcella now had a son, and one night Desi reported that the little boy had bitten Desi's fishing buddy and driven him off. Missing these simple antics made Lucille feel like a kid trapped after school. She was also getting knocked about—the actor Bruce Cabot trod on one of her feet with his cowboy boot and a horse stepped on the other.

When Hope was thrown from a rocking mechanical barrel and confined to bed for days, shooting stopped, and Lucille seized the opportunity to escape. As Marcella recalled, "Before he hit the floor, Lucille was out of there. She got into her car and drove directly to us. She wore my clothes until her maid sent hers down. She stayed until the picture recommenced."

That December, six months after their second wedding, Lucille finally did conceive. Lolita claimed that God was now working in their marriage, and the grateful Desi took care to drive carefully over every bump when Lucille was in the car. But one evening at Chatsworth, soon after their appearance on *The Ed Wynn Show*, Lucille started screaming to Desi that she was bleeding. The next morning at Cedars of Lebanon Hospital, she lost the baby she had so longed for. In her despair, she blamed herself, her devotion to her work, and her past carelessness, both real and imagined, for her failure as a woman and as a wife. Her doctor sought to assure her that far from being unhappy, she actually had reason to rejoice: He had discovered that in treating her after her miscarriage in the first year of her marriage, doctors had inadvertently closed a fallopian tube, which he had been able to mend. The doctor sent her home with a warning not to attempt pregnancy for another three months and a present not often given to a woman who just lost a baby, *Cheaper by the Dozen*, the classic by Frank Gilbreth, Jr., and Ernestine Gilbreth Carey about the large family of the world's first efficiency expert.

As Lucille recuperated, an amazing thing happened. Each mail brought hundreds of letters from strangers, mostly faithful radio listeners sending messages of affection and encouragement. They told her they were praying for her, that she must have hope, and many confessed that they too were trying desperately to have a baby. "I think they were real friends," Lucille said, and personally answered every one of the 2,867 letters, although it took her five months.

During this period, Lucille consulted Don Sharpe, who was busily transferring his radio shows to television. Sharpe was one of a breed who streak through the entertainment world blazing a trail that others follow, often with surer results. Even in its earliest stages, television was a high-pressure business, and Sharpe was under such strain from juggling so many deals that sometimes when he consulted his notes, his hands shook so much that he could not read them. His first step for Lucille was to develop a strategy to overcome CBS's objections to Desi, and so Sharpe arranged for him and Lucille to appear in a series of movie houses in the summer of 1950 as part of a latter-day vaudeville bill opening for first-run films. They produced their act through their own Desilu Productions, with the help of Jess, Madelyn, Bob, and Pepito, a celebrated Spanish clown who was a fishing buddy of Desi. Part of Pepito's act involved a cello and a row of horns set up like a xylophone, and he taught Lucille his routine over the course of two weeks with the couple at the Coronado Hotel, the large Victorian seaside resort in San Diego.

Buster Keaton worked with Lucille on how she should handle her cello, an instrument that appeared normal but opened to contain key elements of the whole act—the seat she perched on, a bow that she shot at Desi, and a toilet plunger that guaranteed a laugh. He advised her to treat it reverently, as a violinist would a Stradivarius. He told her that a prop was as important as a jewel case, that she must guard it more carefully than her pearls and entrust it to no one else, for on this equipment her entire performance hinged.

From these lessons with Pepito and Keaton, she emerged a clown worthy of the fright-red hair that had been her emblem for a decade. Wearing a battered fedora and baggy tie and tails, she ran through the auditorium while Desi and his orchestra were in the middle of a Latin number. With great hullabaloo, zigzagging down the aisle, she sought "Dizzy Arnazi" with gruff belligerence, demanding a job. When he asked to see her credentials, she feigned shock at what she construed as his insinuation, and crossed her hands over her breast until the laughs died down.

Then on stage with great self-satisfaction, she nimbly plucked four finger caps from one hand and pulled a yards-long glove from the other to the sound of a drum roll. From the cello, she extracted her bow and stool, played horribly, and for the finale, honked the horns like the seal from Celeron Amusement Park.

The act had its debut at the Paramount in Chicago, where Eddie Albert was in attendance. As he recalled, "I saw Pepito do the part with the cello in Spain, but she did it better." In Chicago, their hotel room was robbed of a forty-carat aquamarine ring Desi had given her and other sentimental jewelry, a reminder of the loss of the stolen nursery key. A week later, on June 9, they opened for two weeks at the Roxy in New York and threw a tenth anniversary party for themselves five months prematurely. Sharpe joined them there, and at their suite in the Warwick Hotel they planned how to translate this success into a television contract.

Despite her excitement Lucille found herself exhausted and nauseated. Desi insisted she was pregnant. She refused to believe him, but still consulted a doctor. The following Sunday afternoon, as she was resting between performances, she tuned in Walter Winchell's broadcast and listened as he announced that she was expecting. In another dressing room, Desi had also heard. Both screamed and ran out into the hallway laughing, jumping, and crying "If Winchell says it, it must be true!" Winchell was correct, apparently tipped off by a paid source at the medical lab.

The Arnazes cut back their tour from twelve weeks to six. Each day Lucille had morning sickness and ate crackers by the handful, but still rolled on the floor like a seal at show time, a trouper making few concessions to her condition. In Miami, Lucille channeled her full energy into righteous rage. When the manager of their hotel refused to let Desi and Harriet walk through the lobby of white people, Lucille became apoplectic. She said that if her husband and maid could not walk with her, there would be no show. As Harriet told her friends Dot and Barbara: "The manager had that redhead's temper, and the shit hit the fan."

All these exertions may indeed have been too much for her. Upon their return to Chatsworth, Lucille and Desi threw a costume party during which she felt an agonizing pain. Crying out, she put both hands on her stomach as if to hold the baby inside her. Desi phoned for an ambulance to take them to Cedars of Lebanon Hospital. As they raced thirty miles through the Valley toward Los Angeles, the door flew open and Desi had to hold on to the intern so he did not fly out. Lucille claimed that the attendants were in such a hurry that they forgot to fasten the door, but the rush was to no avail: Five days later she suffered a third miscarriage.

She did not surrender to her grief, but persevered as she did in her career. One afternoon she was stalled in traffic on Sunset Strip and stopped parallel to her friend Betty Garrett, a pretty young actress married to the actor Larry Parks. Both were in convertibles with their tops down, and they began to talk over the hum of the engines.

Lucille asked how Betty was and heard, "Pregnant."

"You lucky bum!" Lucille yelled. "We're trying."

Garrett called out, "Put your feet up against the wall afterward!" Before the light changed, as other drivers listened in, Lucille said they would take her advice.

As she and Desi worked to get a television contract, an opportunity came that indicated that she was not yet finished in films. Her stunts on *The Fuller Brush Girl* came to the attention of the legendary producer-director Cecil B. de Mille, who decided she was right for his next film. Known for lavish, sometimes lascivious, epics such as *King of Kings*, *Cleopatra*, and *Union Pacific*, he had now decided to explore the cinematic possibilities of circus life in *The Greatest Show on Earth* for Paramount. He wanted Lucille to join the all-star cast as Angel, the elephant girl who rides on the animal's back and allows herself to be curled up in his trunk. The derring-do required of the part would include permitting an elephant to hold its foot above her face.

Lucille was avid for this role and for training with the Ringling Brothers Circus, but the first obstacle was Harry Cohn, who did not want to release her from her Columbia contract on terms that would satisfy anyone but him. Other Hollywood moguls were disliked, but Cohn was reviled. If Mayer was regarded by most people in the business as an iron-fisted patriarch, Cohn was considered nothing less than a shiv-wielding predator. He enjoyed tormenting those who worked for him and trusted that his viciousness would guarantee his reputation as an ogre not to be crossed.

He had loaned Lucille to Paramount to make films with Bob Hope when Columbia had nothing else for her to do, but now, in an effort to save money by forcing her into breaking her contract, he refused to release her to the great de Mille. To humiliate her, he sent her the script for *The Magic Carpet*, a slapdash story in which she would play a scheming Arabian Nights princess. Cohn, however, underestimated her practicality and overestimated her pride. Lucille agreed to go through her paces as the sultan's villainous sister. The film was made in a week, but when cameras began to roll her usually inadequate bustline proved to be too voluptuous to fit into her scanty costume and its thin tissue had to be let out. She was, to her great joy, pregnant, and when she next saw Betty Garrett, she cheerfully announced the foot-on-the-wall technique worked.

Now doing de Mille's film would be impossible. Her pregnancy, however longed for, came at a cost. Desi went with her when she tearfully told de Mille that she would be unable to work for him after all. According to Desi, who loved to repeat the anecdote, de Mille said to him, "Congratulations, Mr. Arnaz. You are the only man who has ever screwed his wife, Cecil B. de Mille, Paramount Pictures, and Harry Cohn, all at the same time."

The dismal *Magic Carpet*, in which her belly swelled out over her harem pants, was an anticlimactic end to her movie career. Despite having been groomed by MGM and showcased in comedies at Columbia, Lucille had never ascended to the first ranks of stardom. Now thirty-nine, she had little left to risk by going into television, particularly if by doing so she could keep her husband at home. Desi was noting that trade papers such as *Variety* and *The Hollywood Reporter* were filled with stories of the money to be made in this new medium. "Moola over the Mountain" was how *Variety* trumpeted Kate Smith's daytime show, while such old pros as Fred Allen and George Burns said television had more impact than any other branch of show business. But what finally reassured Lucille, she claimed, was a dream in which Carole Lombard, smartly dressed in a suit, urged her, "Honey, go ahead. Give it a whirl."

With that, the genius, luck, and experience of dozens of people, plus the communication technologies of the twentieth century, combined to see that Lucille Ball at last met her destiny. Her assortment of talents—the expressiveness of a silent film star, the cultivated beauty of a movie goddess, and the heedlessness of a vaudeville pratfaller— could develop to their fullest and be truly appreciated only in television. To this was added a workaday humanity that made her as accessible as a houseshoe or a pot of coffee and as welcome in the average home.

After long deliberations over Desi and the relentless efforts of Don Sharpe, CBS decided it would put Lucille on television on what amounted to her terms. Its rival NBC had locked in audiences on Wednesday with its stellar *Kraft Television Theatre* and on Saturdays with Sid Caesar's comedy landmark *Your Show of Shows.* CBS decided to try to win a Monday night following by adapting its radio situation comedies *Life with Luigi, My Friend Irma, Our Miss Brooks,* and *My Favorite Husband.* The network's original plan was to alternate these four in the same time slot, so that each would appear once a month. In the meantime, possibly to distract Lucille from her demand that her husband work with her, CBS executives gave Desi his own radio show, nudging aside an engaging young emcee named Johnny Carson. Carson's planned "Win Your Vacation" became instead "Tropical Trip," a game show hosted by Desi and sustained without a sponsor by CBS.

Meanwhile, Lucille and Desi decided to produce the "audition" (what would later be termed a pilot) independently, in hopes of shopping it to NBC and improving their bargaining position with CBS. Since Jess, Madelyn, and Bob were under contract to the network, they hired other writers who presented a script about the trouble an actress and her bandleader husband have in finding time to be together. It was their true story, but they rejected it as too Hollywood for most Americans to identify with, so they abandoned the idea of producing the "audition" on their own and turned to Jess, who called Bob and Madelyn back from a European vacation to develop a concept. The three quickly and deftly put together an amalgam of their vaudeville act, including Desi's solos, the lampshade bit Lucille had done on *The Ed Wynn Show,* and a role for Pepito. They called this situation comedy/variety show *I Love Lucy.* Lucille and Desi were to play Lucy and Larry Lopez, but since there was a bandleader named Vincent Lopez, at the last minute they became Lucy and Ricky Ricardo, a name containing the lucky "A-R" combination that Carole Lombard's mother had recommended.

Lucille was six months pregnant, and tented in loose clothes to hide her bulging stomach, when they drove to the glass-and-concrete CBS Studios at Sunset and Gower. They went to Studio A, which recently had been renovated for television, and was now like a theater, with an orchestra pit, cameras, and seating for an audience that would react to the performers. Despite the challenges it posed, those responsible for Lucille Ball's television show held on to one guiding principle: She absolutely required the response of a live audience.

They shot their teleplay on March 2, 1951, Desi's thirty-fourth birthday. Even as Lucille donned voluminous men's pajamas for her opening bedroom scene, their contract was still unsigned because some details were in dispute. Hal Hudson, a CBS executive, told Desi the filming could not go forward without their signatures on the document as CBS had written it. Furious and still hopeful of owning the pilot, Desi said he would pay for the kinescope himself and that it would belong to them, not CBS. The executive backed down, but Desi remained so upset that when the overhead lights accidentally went out during their opening scene, he leapt from his stage bed in front of the audience and said, "That son of a bitch pulled the plug!" "Why?" Lucille asked in amazement. "Because I didn't sign their fucking contract!"

The Ricardos of the pilot live in an apartment with a terrace that overlooks New York's Plaza Hotel. In a voice-over an announcer sets the scene, including the information that Lucy's hair is very red. The Ricky of the pilot is so successful a bandleader that he is on the brink of his own television show, but Lucy seeks a contract too, although Ricky wants a wife who is just a wife. The audition made the most of Lucille's facial expressions and physical dexterity, despite the obviousness of her pregnancy. Watching him shave in the mirror, she follows his movements, stretching her lip and jutting out her chin. In this as in the vaudeville act, she flops about on the floor like a seal. The payoff is that it is she, not he, who gets a contract.

Barney McNulty, the inventor of the cue card, was then a stagehand working on the pilot, and one of his jobs was to reverse the backdrops so as to give the appearance of interior and exterior scenes. With rehearsals, the pilot took a week to do. "That was a lot of time in those days," recalled McNulty, "but I felt good about working on it. Lucy was pregnant, so we crossed our fingers, but she was a rare combination of nervousness and effectiveness. Because she had hundreds of hours of production, she knew how things were going and she knew when she'd done it right."

Desi, who broke up laughing over her goofiness in the middle of the filming, knew when she had succeeded too. Although he wanted to be at least as well-known a celebrity as his wife, he knew her talents were extraordinary and raved about her performance to their friends. "Wait until you see Lucille. She's *fantastic!*" he told Frances Langford when he ran into her on the street. To accompany the audition tape, Bob, Madelyn, and Jess outlined eight shows for potential sponsors, all the while believing that another series they had conceived, starring an actor who had played the father of Baby Snooks, was more likely to be their entry into television.

Indeed, *I Love Lucy* was not easy to sell. The vice president of CBS network programming, Hubbell Robinson, who said no one would find Desi believable, took it to every advertising agency in New York in search of a sponsor. He presented it along with Sharpe's asking price of $26,500 per episode, about half of what top shows received. The only interested party was Milton Biow, who convinced his client, the Philip Morris Tobacco Company, to pick it up for CBS at a cost of $23,500 per episode.

Philip Morris and CBS offered a number of suggestions on how to improve the show. They said the number of variety acts and guest stars had to be held to a strict minimum for cost purposes, and Desi's singing and drumming, which executives found egregious, had to be avoided at all costs, unless they were integral to the plot. Whatever about Desi offended them—whether it was the sight of his bare barrel chest in a bedroom scene or the way he dropped his gs—their plan was that if the public liked "the Cuban" as little as they did, his part would grow smaller and smaller until he eventually disappeared from the series entirely.

Sponsor and network also set production requirements for the series. Since a coaxial cable to link television broadcasting facilities on each coast was not yet in operation, they decided *I Love Lucy* had to be done live from New York for the clearest broadcast to the East Coast cities, where most of the stations and the largest audience were.

Lucille and Desi, however, had no intention of being forced from Chatsworth. Television shows were being filmed in Hollywood also, and Lucille and Desi expected to be part of it, particularly after CBS executives announced that the network was committed to producing television comedy from Los Angeles live and on film. Developments that made that possible were spurred by Ralph Edwards, who hosted *Truth or Consequences* first on radio and then on television. He, his technicians, and those at RCA refined video production by shooting on 35 millimeter film and then converting it for the 16 mm equipment installed in television studios. They shared their findings with the industry via press conferences and written reports, and then, to make television filming feasible in Hollywood, worked to persuade labor unions to give up their demands that television technicians, who worked only at night, receive the same night bonus that motion picture technicians did. *Truth or Consequences* became the first live show regularly filmed before an audience on 35 mm film.

Although Edwards's crew filmed the shows for rebroadcast, they used the method developed for live television—"Multicam," two or more cameras recording different shots of the same action simultaneously. This technique was refined in early 1951 when RCA perfected a device to synchronize "Multicam" film. Conveniently, Edwards's program was sponsored by Philip Morris and filmed at CBS, the same partnership involved with *I Love Lucy*. Desi would later recollect that he had pioneered the three-camera setup, but that credit belongs largely to Edwards.

Although Philip Morris was not confident that the new techniques had been tested sufficiently for comedy, and CBS did not have a contract with unions whose members shot on film, Sharpe was able to negotiate a compromise whereby Lucille and Desi could originate the show in Hollywood on film, provided the quality was at least equal to that of shows broadcast from New York. To finance the filming, which was twice the cost of a kinescope, the couple agreed to a $1,000 salary cut, meaning their combined pay would be $4,000 per weekly episode, plus half of the profits for the first thirty-nine episodes. Desi, who loved negotiations as much as he loved the track, made this agreement with the proviso that he and Lucille would own the negatives of all future shows. Martin Leeds, a cost-conscious lawyer in charge of CBS West Coast business affairs, refused to renegotiate a contract that had already been signed, so Sharpe flew to New York to press the Arnazes' case. Executives there were apparently distracted by more pressing corporate battles, because they gave the couple ownership of all the shows. In matters of the series, this put Desi on par with CBS executives and, for the moment, with Jess Oppenheimer, who produced it. Desi estimated that their out-of-pocket expense, after taxes, for acquiring this crucial additional 50 percent was about $5,000.

The new agreement also had a snare for Lucille and Desi, who were now obligated to produce the show by themselves in their own production facilities, rather than those of CBS, which still lacked a contract with the necessary unions for film work. Furthermore, they had to deliver the finished product to the network. Possibly CBS thought this would force them to move to New York, but in fact by obliging them to create their own facility, it accelerated factors that led to the dominance of Los Angeles as the television entertainment capital.

Although CBS had given up ownership, it was still active in making the show work, particularly through the intervention of Harry Ackerman, a Dartmouth graduate in his late thirties with dark eyes and thinning hair who had worked with Sharpe and hired Lucille for CBS radio. He was that rare corporate individual who believed that ushers were as worthy of his notice as executives. Perhaps his greatest contribution to *I Love Lucy* was to hire Ralph Edwards's production coordinator Al Simon, although it was actually Desi who approached Simon with the offer.

Lucille was staying at home monitoring the first stirrings and kicks of her baby, so Desi invited Simon and his wife to Chatsworth to meet her. "I liked her the first time I saw her," Simon said. "She was very warm. She was very much in love with Desi and really wanted him to succeed, and she did everything possible to make it happen." Over a delicious Cuban meal, Simon sketched out his plans. "I was going to hire a first cameraman, but Lucy said, 'I wish you'd try to get hold of Karl Freund. He did a beautiful job lighting me at MGM.' I didn't think lighting would be a problem, but I figured it was important that she feel comfortable."

Simon tracked Freund down in Washington, D.C., where he was doing research for the government. Now sixty-one, having been instrumental in the development of motion pictures, Freund was intrigued by the technical challenge of the new medium, but his eagerness faded when he got to the set and remembered to ask about his fee. Freund learned that not only would he, an Oscar winner and recognized genius, be paid minimum wage, but he would have to make tests of the film he shot as well.

"*Me?* Tests?" He snorted, but Simon told him that CBS was insistent. "We expected the lighting to be the same as for motion pictures," Simon said, "but when Freund saw the tests he made, he just shook his head. I told him, 'Do what you have to do to fix it, even if it's polka dots before the lens.' " They had anticipated that their major challenge would be filming to advantage a forty-year-old woman who would by then be recovering from pregnancy, but that was the least of it. The most serious technical obstacle was that although the three cameras they were using could be moved to shoot different angles, the lights remained stationary throughout filming. But each shot required its own specific lighting, if all were to match in intensity. Freund became preoccupied with this puzzle, even at scale wages.

Several weeks after the pilot was completed, Judy Holliday won the Oscar for the role Lucille had coveted in *Born Yesterday*. Lucille also did the final episodes of "My Favorite Husband" as well as a radio play with Marlene Dietrich. The night of the broadcast, Dietrich stood before the microphone, a figure of strength and beauty in her black sheath dress and jacket adorned only with her French Legion of Honor medal. Lucille with wild red hair was beside her indisputably pregnant in a flared top with ruffles. "When Marlene pulled out a cigarette, twelve people tried to light it and there stood Miss Lucy, obviously one of the girls," said Dorothy Aldworth, who worked on the show. "It did not bother Lucille in the least that everyone was fawning over Marlene, but the contrast between the two was unbelievable."

Meanwhile, the problem of finding a place to produce *I Love Lucy* was becoming acute. Although many of Hollywood's film studios were available, particularly since movie production was at low ebb in 1951, none of them had facilities to accommodate an audience. Earl Spicer, who did audio for *Truth or Consequences*, suggested that Simon look at General Service Studios on Las Palmas Avenue, in a neighborhood of light industry. The studios not only had room to set up bleachers for an audience and create a public entrance on a side street, but as Simon discovered, they offered enough space to construct three or four permanent sets side by side. Because the sets would not have to be moved or struck down to make way for other shows, they could also be of better quality.

But renovation of this space, including modifications to meet fire codes, required money Desi did not have, so he went to Martin Leeds and told him he needed a loan. The shrewd Leeds, who was as savvy about money as he was about points of law, reminded Desi that because he owned the show, financing was no longer the problem of CBS. Still, since he wanted the show to work, Leeds advanced him an additional $50,000 and threw in CBS lighting equipment as well. With this CBS system Freund solved his problem by designing "flat" lighting, a revolutionary setup that placed the source of illumination overhead. To approximate the artistic results he was used to achieving at MGM, Freund had stagehands enhance the lighting by painting and repainting the set walls in various shades of gray for each scene.

Freund himself, who lived near the Arnazes, brought Lucille a scale model of his new design one evening on his way home. Lucille was satisfied with the show's progress, and with her husband's part in it, until the night Desi came home in a fury and informed her they would not do *I Love Lucy* after all. He told her Jess Oppenheimer was claiming he owned 20 percent of the show because his agreement with CBS gave him that share of whatever series he produced for them. Desi so objected to this provision that he was willing to abandon the project entirely, although Lucille felt it would ruin both of them professionally. Her first concern was that such a decision would leave them looking like fools in Hollywood. She phoned Jess in tears, pleading "Everyone knows we're doing it. If we don't go through with it, they'll say we failed. My entire career is at stake." Oppenheimer was adamant about his rights and pointed out that it was not his fault if CBS had not informed them he had part ownership. Through his lawyers, Oppenheimer won his share from Desi and gave 5 percent of that to Madelyn and Bob. He had fought for what he considered his due, but his victory marked the beginning of a power struggle between the producer and Lucille's husband. Oppenheimer surely believed he had weighted the balance in his favor when his lawyers negotiated his contract with Desi and inserted the key clause that gave him "complete creative control," as was customary for producers. It stipulated, however, that if he and Desi were unable to settle a dispute, Lucille would cast the deciding vote.

The filming of *I Love Lucy* was scheduled to begin after their baby was born. As they waited, Desi decided to expand their house while Lucille set about to maintain its interior exactly as it had always been, refusing to release from her life any possession that entered it. When she saw that her organdy and dotted Swiss curtains were timeworn, she did not replace as much as duplicate them. The Arnaz furniture was still standing where she had first fixed it as a bride, and when she needed a rocker for the baby and some additional tables, she sought them in the familiar shops along Ventura Boulevard. She found that with the end of the war, homey Americana was in fashion and was as costly as antiques, but her compensation for the extra cost was the knowledge that the castoffs she had come to love had tripled in value.

The only real change she countenanced at Chatsworth was the creation of the nursery. She imagined herself, as if in a movie, stepping from her own gray and yellow dressing room into a space of matching color scheme to attend to her child. But when they learned that building codes proscribed an addition that had to be entered through a bathroom, Desi, who did much of the work himself, decided they would redesign it to include a separate kitchen so the nurse could more easily warm the baby's bottles. With its separate plumbing and wiring, the wing cost more than the original price of their house. Hammering and the barking of elderly cocker spaniels attended the final days of Lucille's pregnancy, along with increasing claustrophobia and sensitivity to smoke. Lucille, who had puffed two packs of Chesterfields a day, now waddled through her rooms sniffing at stale tobacco scents and recoiling from ashtrays.

At Lucille's request, Maxine Andrews hosted the baby shower. "I was thrilled," Maxine said. "My sisters and I had never been in one place long enough for me to do something like that. Lucille was the director. She knew the food, invitations, the kind of silver she wanted given to the baby and the color scheme—gray and yellow. I had the florist dye the flowers and set things up in the pool area of my farm. Desi came in with his movie camera and took the pictures. It was a beautiful summer day, not too warm in the Valley. I'm sure Lucille appreciated it, but she was never effervescent about things like that. If she enjoyed your work, she said, 'You're fine.' She said she loved the party. That was it. You took Lucille for Lucille."

The baby was already ten days overdue when she had a visit from John DeVita's sister Florence and her husband, Joseph. Both from Jamestown, they were now living in California. Lucille was edgy and insisted that only their two-year-old, and not their older children, see her in her condition. When Joseph touched her stomach, she said, "Go outside and talk to my husband!" Desi, as he poured them drinks, asked Joseph about Johnny.

On July 17, 1951, twenty days shy of her fortieth birthday, Lucille at last gave birth to a healthy child. Every loving parent strives for perfection, and certainly Lucille Ball, so fiercely and forcefully committed to those she loved, believed that in motherhood she would be her best and truest self. She who envisioned herself floating through gray and yellow decor with her infant in her arms surely imagined child care as a whirl of feeding, burping, and changing as joyous as a dance by Fred Astaire. Babies, however, do not respond to direction. Her delivery was two weeks late and complicated. She was much older than most first-time mothers, and as labor went on, doctors saw the baby was coming out feet first and quickly decided to perform a cesarean section.

On awakening from surgery aching from stitches and corseted in bandages, she, who had been told to expect a boy, learned she had a daughter. "Susan. I want to see Susan!" she said, as that was the name she and Desi had picked for a girl. The nurse said, "You mean Lucie." "*I'm* Lucy," Lucille said, and then learned that Desi had already written the name on the birth certificate, probably as a surprise to his wife. The nurse brought in Lucie wrapped in a blanket. Tearfully Lucille took her daughter and held her, counting fingers and toes. "This is our baby," she kept murmuring as the nurse departed. Lucie started to cry and, as the novice mother struggled to reach for the bottle while coping with the baby and the pain of her incision, the infant slid out of Lucy's arms and fell toward the headboard. Lucille would remember her first moments of motherhood as a comic shtick.

One of the first friends to see the baby was Marion, who visited Lucille while on her honeymoon. She had returned to Jamestown to spare her son the excesses of Hollywood High, but the move proved beneficial to her too, as she had found a handsome new husband, Norman Van Vlack, in her hometown. "Norman didn't know what to make of Lucille," Marion said. "There had been an earthquake, and Lucille bumped against her walls to show him how she had carried the baby through the experience. Then Desi burst in. He was excited because he had just finalized the contract for the television show, but the first thing he did was ask who was in his parking space—it turned out to be Norman."

Lucille settled into motherhood, feeding and changing her baby and hiring a nurse. After six weeks of this domesticity, she went back to work, ready to tackle the filming of *I Love Lucy*.

13

WHEN LUCILLE ARRIVED at General Service Studios on Monday morning, September 3, 1951, for the first reading of *I Love Lucy*, she was fully prepared to be the star—the star as whip hand, the ringmaster to lash her fellow players into shape. Those who had worked with her on "My Favorite Husband" were unfazed, but others who anticipated the MGM personage of the fiery tresses and abundant lips were stunned by the arrival of a frowzy woman in a babushka and outsize top covering her bandaged stomach, which was still sore from cesarean surgery seven weeks before. Her affectation was the dark glasses hiding her eyes. She marched onto the lot, trailed by her housekeeper, Willie Mae Barker, an ample black woman with a strong, kind face, who carried a large hamper from which Lucille intended to dispense her husband's lunch.

A new floor that would allow cameras to roll silently was being set in place in the studio, and already improvisations were necessary. Their four sets would not fit in the available space, so stagehands busily wallpapered Masonite walls to create a breakaway living room for the Ricardos' friends, the Mertzes. Since General Service Studios was in an uproar of makeshift jerrybuilding and the din of hammering and maneuvering of cameras prevented having the preliminary reading on stage, Jess set up the run-through meeting in Desi's simple office.

At thirty-four, Desi was fleshier than the blustering youth who filmed *Too Many Girls* and was already turning gray, but he was still strikingly handsome. He welcomed the group with easy graciousness, but his accent was so thick that Madelyn remembered having difficulty understanding what he was saying.

Lucille meanwhile sought to hide her fright by trying to tyrannize those around her, but it showed as her feet crawled in her shoes and tapped nervously in front of her chair. She had wanted her trusted radio colleagues Bea Benaderet and Gale Gordon to play the Ricardos' friends Fred and Ethel Mertz, but they had signed with other new television shows before *I Love Lucy* was launched. She then asked that James Gleason, an actor known for his comedic New York characters, play Fred, but Gleason was too busy with other projects. Finally Lucille accepted Bill Frawley, whom she had known as a character actor from Columbia and MGM. Frawley was sixty-four, bald and stocky with age and boozing. Born to a large Irish Catholic family in Iowa, Frawley had defied his strong-willed mother and abandoned a promising career as a railroad stenographer to become a song-and-dance man on Broadway, where he introduced the standards "Carolina in the Morning" and "Melancholy Baby." He married his vaudeville partner during the Wilson administration and was divorced by the coming of Herbert Hoover. By the time Frawley signed with *I Love Lucy*, his devotions were to liquor, the New York Yankees, and the defiance of those in authority. Emboldened by his quarrelsome drinking, he had irked directors so thoroughly that before he was hired for *I Love Lucy*, he was reduced to playing a hot dog vendor on a television variety show to earn a desperately needed fifty bucks.

Lucille trusted Frawley to abide by his promise of sober dependability, but she was wary of the unknown who would play Ethel Mertz. Vivian Vance, at thirty-nine a year younger than Lucille, was a robust blonde who had made her career in the theater. Unlike

Lucille, Desi, and Bill, each of whom relied on bluster to cover their anxieties, Vivian was committed to coming to terms with her demons. She had lived with the specter of mental illness since her teens, when she had gone on the road with a band and made an early, tragic marriage to a musician who suffered a mental breakdown. In high school in Albuquerque, she was so promising and popular that her theater group put on a benefit performance to send her to New York. There she carved out some success and married a fellow actor, Phil Ober, in 1941. Four years later she suffered a nervous collapse and publicly and often credited her recovery to psychoanalysis. She was back on stage playing a tenderhearted prostitute in *The Voice of the Turtle* at the La Jolla Playhouse when Marc Daniels, who had been chosen director of *I Love Lucy* and knew her from New York, brought Desi to see her six weeks before the show began. After some deliberation, Desi approved her casting as Ethel, but Daniels had to persuade Vivian to turn down a movie offer and take a chance on television.

On the day of the reading, Vivian was aware she would have to win over Lucille. She was dressed in her best clothes, in contrast to Lucille's housecoat, but it quickly became clear that Lucille had conceived of Ethel as an older woman, a onetime showgirl married to an old vaudevillian turned landlord.

"Meet Vivian Vance," Daniels said, as the two women came face to face for the first time.

"For what part?" Lucille demanded.

"Ethel Mertz," Daniels replied, growing wary.

"She doesn't look like a landlady."

"I can look different," Vivian promised, but Lucille protested that Ethel had to be dumpy. "I photograph dumpy," Vivian said brightly. Lucille was only slightly mollified: "I expected you to look like Bill."

The first episode was titled "Lucy Thinks Ricky Is Trying to Murder Her," a notion Lucy Ricardo derives from the mystery she is reading. The writers may at first have conceived of the character of Ethel as being a troublemaker, for it is she who eggs Lucy on to suspect the worst of her husband. During the run-through, Vivian read her part in full voice, as if she were performing and not just reading, an approach of which Lucille approved. For the next twenty years, and well into the age of sophisticated sound equipment, Lucille would demand that the actors speak up during rehearsals so that the audience, though not yet present, could hear.

As the reading went on, a line was changed and Lucille asked to hear it read back. Maury Thompson, the slim young script clerk, quickly complied.

"How come you're so fast?" she demanded to know.

"When I told her I took shorthand, she said, 'Who hired you? Aren't we in the top drawer!,' but you couldn't tell it was a compliment from the way she said it," Thompson recalled.

After a few hours of going over the script, Lucille and Desi began to munch on fried chicken from their enormous picnic hamper, which seemed to the hungry actors to be brimming with food. At one-thirty, three hours after the reading began, Bill Frawley could stand it no longer. He inquired, "When do the peons eat?"

Lucille was dumbstruck. "None of you has eaten?"

"We didn't have lunch at ten-fifteen," he retorted.

Bill and Viv trooped to the commissary with Maury and enjoyed their first conversation, carefully avoiding the obvious topic of their bosses.

Even as the date of the first filming approached, *I Love Lucy* became a war waged on two fronts: the staging of the show itself—the plots, lines, scripts, and acting—and the solution of its technical challenges, which were far more problematic, as Lucille well knew. She took the production manager, Al Simon, aside and said, "You don't know how much this means to me. Can you really do it?" Simon, standing in a tangle of camera cables, had his own worries about keeping the audience from wandering onto the set and the microphones from picking up the sound of the rolling cameras, but he assured her that everything was going to be fine. Lucille's nervous energy was such that at some point she persuaded Viv, who was trying to win her over, to get some Bon Ami and help her clean the bathrooms at the studio.

As the week wore on, Lucille practiced her stunts, often before the mirror. She truly could not grasp the story from the script, but as she worked with it and physically acted it out, she possessed it, and it possessed her. As the script required, she tied a skillet to her stomach as a shield and practiced dodging about to avert the bullets Lucy, influenced by her mystery, is sure Ricky will fire.

Unexpected technical delays forced postponement of the filming of the first episode from Friday to Saturday, September 8, 1951. Lucille allowed herself to be preoccupied with worrying over how the audience would react and whether they would sit still if the filming was too slow or if the cameras blocked their view. It occurred to no one that people might be interested in seeing how television was done. There was also concern that the audience would grow restless during costume changes between scenes, so Lucille, who was in every one of them, layered her clothes so that she could walk into the wings and quickly peel them off.

The night of the filming, the crew and executives were given red carnation boutonnieres for luck. As the audience trooped in through a special entrance cut on a side street and settled into the bleachers, Jess told Desi to go out and talk to them, to "warm them up" and win them over. Always ready to perform, Desi grabbed a hand mike and headed from the wings, unaware that the fly on his tuxedo pants was as open as it had been on the day he proposed to Lucille. After a stagehand stopped him and they madly worked to close his pants, he stepped out, welcomed the audience, and promised that the cameras wouldn't block their view at all. To prove it, he signaled the cameras to move in even closer than they actually would have to. Desi then introduced each of the players. Even Vivian, whom no one knew, got an encouraging hand. Then Desi finally announced, "And now, the star of the show, the mother of my child, the vice president of Desilu Productions—I am the president—my favorite redhead—Lucille Ball!"

Taking the stage, she bowed, immediately called out, "Are you there, Mom?," and introduced DeDe sitting in an honored place in the bleachers under the control booth next to Lolita and Bob's and Madelyn's parents. Florence and Joseph Conte from Jamestown were also there, holders of six reserved seats behind DeDe. The show began. Lucy sat down, avidly reading *The Mockingbird Murder Mystery.* By the end of the evening, she has eavesdropped on Ricky, rigged herself up in a bulletproof skillet, and feinted and danced like a Kabuki moving target with pan attached. She came on stage as Lucille Ball, but when she made her final bow, she had become forever Lucy, Lucy Ricardo, one of the greatest comic characters of all time.

The first episode was such a mismatch of close-ups and long shots that it took weeks to edit properly. Finally George Fox, whom CBS installed as film operations manager, built a special Moviola that held four, rather than one, reels of film. In action, it sounded like a sewing machine with a treadle, but "the four-headed monster" was a great technical advance in editing that won great respect for Desilu. Not trusting the positive reaction of the studio audience, Desi screened the actual film before two test groups, first one at the studio, then another a week later in Riverside, California. People liked it but were not overly enthusiastic.

It was weeks before Lucy learned her show was a hit, though the very fact that they had not failed was a great relief. Philip Morris did not cancel the show, although its president did not like it and asked what breaking their agreement would cost. The second episode filmed, "The Girls Want to Go to a Nightclub," was actually the first one to be broadcast on Monday night, October 15. Television critics found the plot inane, but the viewing audience was delighted by what it saw. If the people in the bleachers at General Service Studios inspired Lucy to her best work, the millions at home sitting in rooms darkened to improve the snowy picture on their new sets quickly developed a cumulative appreciation that would make her not only one of the greatest phenomena in show business, but one of the most beloved women in the land.

By November 5, 1951, nearly 14 million people—one in nine Americans—were tuning in, and by December 3 the number approached 16 million. Telephone calls and water use decreased at 9:00 P.M. Eastern time on Monday because so many people were tuning in to see what Lucy was up to. Her funny faces and pranks spiraling out of control were incomparable, but the show offered much more. It had great heart. *I Love Lucy* was a story not just of the war between the sexes, but of the love between friends. The Fred who denounces Lucy as a ditsy woman bristles when someone else dares to accuse her of being a crook (although for story purposes he is soon ready to call the police). The show employed basic and timeless dramatic devices—especially in its dependence on the opposition of the practical Cuban steadying the scatterbrained American—and it balanced temperaments in a way that harkened back to the "humors" of the Elizabethan stage: patient Ethel, volatile Ricky, stolid Fred, and flighty, airy Lucy—couple against couple, boys against the girls. Although one in four married women was in the labor force in 1951, the housewife became a stereotype of the 1950s, and Lucy's subservience to Ricky's mastery fit in with society's idea of a woman's proper place. For all that Lucy could be devious, petty, and jealous, she preserved the sanctity of home: The dishes were washed and the vacuum cleaner put away before she impersonated Carmen Miranda. Moreover, unless she was baking bread, Lucy Ricardo was portrayed as a very fine cook. While Desi Arnaz's chicken and rice were renowned in Hollywood, and his wife was allowed only to toss the salad in a large wooden bowl, when Ricky Ricardo was maneuvered into cooking, he covered Lucy's clean kitchen floor with a lava flow of rice. Still, the relationship between the two of them has remained dynamic through changing decades because it so vividly depicts the eternal struggle for power against authority.

As time went on, the Ricardos and Mertzes began to be characterized in increasingly subtle ways. Audiences saw Ricky's decency when, because he bet Lucy he would not lose his temper, he coolly negotiated an agent down to a very low fee. Realizing he had treated the man unfairly, he relented, explaining that he had not intended to cheat him and would of course pay scale. The Mertzes were likewise given more dimension. With what was surely a thrill of revelation, viewers discovered that even Fred and Ethel must snuggle up at times, because in one jump-to-conclusion, Fred believes he and Ethel have a baby on the way.

The show's apparent spontaneity was always the calibrated product of discipline and control. As dubious as Lucy could be about a given script when she read it during run-throughs, once it was set, it was inviolate. She never deviated from her lines or from directions written for her. Her improvising took place only in rehearsals, and if successful it was typed into the final script. Even Ricky's vituperative eruptions, such as "Miraquetienecosalamujeresta!" were timed and typed in correct Spanish by Jess's bilingual assistant, the casting director Mercedes Manzanares, so that Desi could not get carried away and throw off the pacing of the show.

With experience they learned certain filming tricks. Bill Frawley's hands shook noticeably, so Fred invariably kept his hands in his pockets or held on to something to disguise it. Although Lucy was happy to blacken her teeth and mess up her hair, for normal shots care was taken to show her to advantage. She looked best not in profile, but with both her eyes in the frame. She wore flat shoes, partly because heels aggravated foot injuries that she had sustained during the filming of *Fancy Pants* and partly because she and Desi were about the same height. Because her torso was longer, whenever they were filmed sitting on the sofa together, a board was inserted under his cushion so he would not appear shorter than she. As Maury Thompson remembered, "If he did sink down, she'd say 'Where did you go?' " She was a great one for roughhouse tricks and often goosed her favorite men on the set. Once when Desi bent over, she kicked him and hit him in the groin. "He was doubled up in pain and couldn't get up," Thompson said. "She kept saying, 'I didn't mean it. I didn't mean it.' " Her insensibility to the body and its vulnerabilities enhanced her stunts but made her a menace on the set.

Jess came to take on the role of demanding father, as much feared as revered. He kept track of thirteen shows at a time, discussing or editing scripts to be shot two months later, checking the costumes for episodes a month away, and supervising the cutting, editing, and dubbing of shows already filmed. He was the first to read Bob and Madelyn's scripts and call for changes. If he could not persuade someone of the soundness of his judgments, he ultimately and decisively forced him to see he was correct. In the case of the often high-handed Lucy, he simply insisted she treat others with respect, and she was sufficiently dependent on him to knuckle under and make amends to those she knew deserved them.

As strong-willed as she was, she was the first to defer to men, and she worked out a way to seem equally subservient to her producer and to her director, calling Jess "Bossman" and Desi "Mr. President." Desi initially also yielded to Jess and gave him a trophy with a batter inscribed "To the Man Behind the Ball."

Cast and crew, who had been hired for thirteen episodes, signed on for another thirteen as ratings climbed, and then a third; then they renewed for all thirty-nine episodes the following year. Lucy and Desi made a second home for themselves at the studio, setting up a suite with two large dressing rooms, a bathroom, living and dining rooms, and a kitchen where Willie Mae Barker prepared their lunches and Lucy's afternoon peanut butter and jelly sandwich, with milk and snacks for the cast at night. On dress rehearsal nights, Desi or Willie Mae cooked dinner for sixty people who sat around critiquing the show. "Lucy and Desi wanted to create a family," observed one of their employees.

During the week, Papa Freund stalked the set, a flask in his hip pocket, certain his lights were the key to the success of the show. Freund rehearsed his cameras and crew of twelve for two days before each filming, choreographed and marked their every movement on the floor, and cued them to their places by talking into a mike beamed at their headsets. When he was not giving orders, Papa kept to himself, somewhat disdainful of this crew of neophytes—Jess was to him "the old man with the young face."

The young men, in turn, regarded Freund as a notable but eccentric elder statesman. Herb Browar, the stage manager, who distinguished himself by coming up with the idea of turning a soundstage into a theater by renting bleachers to seat an audience, remembered Freund's first words to him as "Herp, I vant a pinter!"

" 'Pinter, Mr. Freund?' I thought he wanted a piece of equipment until he acted out painting," said Browar.

Freund corrected unflattering lighting by adjusting the exposure of his negatives and perfected his close-ups by retaking them after the audience left. Inspired by a few martinis, he thought he could film Lucy more attractively by shooting her close-ups after the show with back lighting. Jess insisted that such shots would not match those of the rest of the show, but Papa was convinced only when Jess inserted them in a special presentation for CBS executives and invited Freund. These close-ups were so mismatched that the audience of professionals was shocked, and Freund never bothered with back lighting again.

Each week Lucy rehearsed thoroughly, learning over the years how to balance a fifteen-pound showgirl headdress, adjust to the weight of the loving cup as it slipped down over her head, and imitate an armchair. She rehearsed enough, but only enough, to know how much she could get out of a prop so that on filming nights she could forget about it, like a tennis player who ignores the racket and concentrates on the ball. During a scene with Vivian, she was supposed to pick up a paper bag from a table, blow it up, and punch it to make it pop. She rehearsed three hours, changing the size and weight of the paper bags and rearranging the stacks until she could produce the maximum noise in the middle of an excited dialogue and seem totally spontaneous. Claudio Guzman, the show's art director, said, "When she did a routine, she wanted to see if somebody else could do it, and then she'd refine it. She would ask me, 'If you choke someone, how do you put your hands on their neck? If you fall, where do you put your feet?' She'd copy where you put your hands or how you fell down. She'd see how to do it."

The prop man knew that if the script called for her to work with a basket, he needed to bring six baskets to fulfill her demands. She would pick each up and get the feel of it to try its comic potential. "This handle is too short," she would say, and pronounce another too long. He, like others, knew that not only was she testing the props, she was testing him as well.

The writers knew her faces, gestures, and physical moves so well, many of which began on "My Favorite Husband," that they indicated them with code words on the script—"Lightbulb" and "Credentials" joined "Spider," "Puddle," and "Small Rabbit."

When she was finally before an audience, it all seemed spontaneous. People began to giggle, then guffaw, as she transcended herself and entered the realm of art, of Chaplin and Keaton. She had an ability to hold the reaction and amplify it, so that people laughed first because she was funny and kept laughing because they had time to think about how funny she had been. "I never found a place of my own, never became truly confident until, in the Lucy character, I began to create something that was truly mine. The potential was there. Lucy released it," she explained. On show nights, she was a force giving life to the inanimate. Props were transformed as she spun them, tossed them, gave them a kick. Candy marched as an army, bread swelled to a battering ram, and pizza leapt, whirled, and fell down on her head, reconstituted into a floor-length veil. Her kind of comedy had not been seen since the two-reelers. She did what Ed Sedgwick, godfather to her child, advised. She let herself go.

She wanted her staff to enjoy their work, provided they did it well. "If Lucy liked you, she loved you. If she didn't, look out," said Bernard Weitzman, who went to work in Desilu's business affairs department. How much she liked people also had much to do with whether they made her laugh.

To honor the wittiest, she asked Herb Browar to set up a large board two by three feet with the names of the key people on the show. Whenever anyone said something she found especially funny, she put up a gold star by his or her name. The one person who did not earn a star, ever, was director Marc Daniels. Coming from live television and theater, he was slow to become comfortable with television filming techniques. More damning in Lucy's eyes was his habit of trying out bits just because they were funny, even if they did not make sense in context, such as someone walking on top of a bed instead of around it. Once in a scene involving a toaster, he and Lucy argued over whether to use real bread. Daniels had her use balsa wood, which flew wildly into the air. She could not gain control of it, no matter what technique she tried. Finally she snarled, "It's *my* bread, bring it in," and did some business with the real toast that proved her point. When Lucy Ricardo was dieting and driven to fight for a scrap of meat under a table with a dog, Marc insisted she do it his way until she was driven to tears. Desi burst on the set ready to attack him for making his wife cry, and Herb Browar and an electrician had to hold Desi back until everyone declared the incident forgotten, which, of course, it never was.

Vivian, however, ultimately won her over, as she had set out to do. At first Lucy did pick on her in subtle and unchallengeable ways. "You like blue suits? So you really like *blue* suits?" she would ask with a pointed tone of incredulity. Although Lucy did want her to look matronly, the legend that Vivian was obligated to weigh twenty pounds more than Lucy was not true, according to those involved with Vivian's contract. But in the first show, when Vivian was as slim as Lucille, who had not yet lost all the extra weight from her pregnancy, she appeared in a top as loose as a maternity outfit. Lucy's testing of Vivian was such that one night Maury Thompson drove Viv home to the Shoreham Apartments and asked, "What will you do with her?" Viv said, "If this show's a hit, it will be the biggest thing in my career. I will learn to love that bitch."

Eventually she did, and Lucy loved her back. Vivian wooed her with jokes, some about her analysis and many of them naughty: "My father made me so ashamed of my body that half the time I tried to hide it under men," Viv said. When the two women disagreed about how to play a scene, Viv capitulated, usually with mock humility: "Well, you do own the studio." Sometimes Lucy then tried it Viv's way. Toughened by trying experiences and forced to rely primarily on themselves, they eventually came to trust each other. Lucy had the upper hand, but they developed a sisterly bond with its blood rages and bone-deep love and bouts of occasional pettiness that seemed to come from nowhere.

While Lucy accepted Bill's gruffness, Vivian could not, and their relationship was at best only correct. Her first mistake, according to Maury, was that she took it upon herself to tell the old trouper how to read a line. As the series wore on, the bickering Fred and Ethel were like lovebirds compared to the indignant Bill and Viv. Soon Bill's only interest in the script was the pages marked for Fred, and he sometimes dozed as the others read. He professed not to understand the excitement over *I Love Lucy*. He never paid attention to the plot, but turned up and acted a scene like the contract player he had been.

"What is so funny about 'Hello, Ethel'?" he once demanded of Desi when everyone around the table cracked up at the line.

"When you say it, Ethel is disguised as the back of a horse!"

"Oh, yeah, that is funny," Frawley admitted in a rare show of enthusiasm.

As much as anyone else, Bob and Madelyn also could displease Lucy. She frequently disliked and berated their scripts. "That's not right! Don't you have better jokes?" she would demand, as if they had been holding their best lines in reserve. Only Desi could appease her: "Hunny, they have never let you dun."

"We dreaded the run-throughs," said Madelyn, who was reduced to tears more than once. "But when she blew up, no one was sorrier than she was. She told us, 'Desi knows how to say the right things and doesn't hurt people's feelings,' and she said she wished she was like that too." A sign of how much she appreciated their brilliance was her plea that they never travel on the same plane, a request Bob considered both complimentary and insensitive. Only in public was her support for them unwavering. She was the rare star who consistently told the press that her gift was that she had learned to execute what her writers created.

Bob and Madelyn were too busy to read the manual they had bought on writing for television and had quickly outgrown it in any case. When they got spooked by the numerical size of their audience, they tacked up a sign in their office that said "It's only a show." They acted out each of Lucy's adventures to see if they were within physical possibilities, going so far as to handcuff themselves to each other to see if such a thing would work. They learned that during the show if the studio audience feared their beloved Lucy was in real peril, rather than laugh, they held their breath in suspense. If a character was cruel to her, the audience would all but hiss. Thus the writers developed certain guidelines: Nobody is mean to Lucy. She must never seem to be in danger. Don't be topical. (A mention of Harry and Bess Truman was an early and rare exception.) Lucy should never knowingly get drunk. No script should contain blue or vulgar material.

They reworked a trove of "My Favorite Husband" plots as *Lucy* premises and amplified stories Lucy told and acted out. On Halloween Betty Garrett and Larry Parks had come to the Arnazes' door with nylon stockings pulled down over their heads. The sight of their misshapen faces nearly caused Lucy to faint with shock, so a few months later Ricky covered his face with a stocking and stopped the show. The story of how the Arnazes mediated an argument between married friends by making fun of their own old silly fights, which caused them to renew those quarrels, was adapted for the Ricardos and the Mertzes. Later Lucy and Marcella Rabwin's attempts to win money for matching evening gowns at the Del Mar track, which cost them far more than buying dresses would have, became an episode in which Lucy and Ethel buy the same dress and cattily rip them off each other while performing a sister act at a fund-raiser for charity.

Bob and Madelyn had a simple work schedule: Write all the time, except for one night off to celebrate or commiserate. On Thanksgiving they broke off at noon to have dinner with Bob's family, then proceeded to Madelyn's mother at six. Madelyn came up with the situations, and Bob supplied the jokes. Their unseen guide was his uncle Bert. "If he didn't know about something, we wouldn't put it in. I didn't let us mention Brooks Brothers, because he would not have known what it was," Carroll said.

Jess, head writer as well as producer, insisted that the premise for each show be believable. Lucy Ricardo did improbable things, but she had to have an understandable reason for doing them, so that the audience could identify with it, even if they had to be coaxed a bit. In a pinch, Ethel would be recruited to say "That is the dumbest thing I ever heard of," which lessened the audience's disbelief by voicing it. If Ricky and Fred were so misguided as to be fooled when their wives disguised themselves as hillbillies, Fred was the first to scoff: "Do you think I wouldn't recognize my own wife?" The audience laughed because he hadn't. *I Love Lucy* was not *Studio One* or *Philco TV Playhouse*, live original theater written for the new medium. It did not dramatize real life or satirize society. It was simply timeless farce set in postwar middle-class America, what Molière might have aimed for had he been working at Desilu.

Most people needed to go to the bathroom, take a break, have a moment to themselves, but not Lucy, who drove her company on. Extrovert, star, and boss, she established the tone of the set. Many of the men, from executives to stagehands, had crushes on her that dated from *DuBarry Was a Lady,* and some affectionately called her "Big Red," knowing full well that she could lose and recover her temper in an instant. The more sensitive ones made sure she saw them before they approached her, because when she felt crowded, she was unnerved by an attack of claustrophobia.

She never wanted them to leave her, however. When cast and crew took a break, she wanted them to stay together in a group to listen to Marco Rizo, the pianist in Ricky's band, play tunes from *Too Many Girls.* As much of a perfectionist as Lucy, as eager to redo things until he had them right, Marco was the only one who puzzled her. "She'd look at me at rehearsals and say 'Don't you ever get tired? You're not a youngster.' " In fact, Marco was six years younger than she.

The set was not an overtly joyous place, but there were moments of prankish fun. Sometimes when Bill Frawley dozed in a corner, his fedora dipped low over his eyes, Desi lit a match and gave him a hotfoot. He even occasionally teased his wife. During one rehearsal, Desi broke up the crew by burping repeatedly. Lucy finally said, "I can't stand this. You have to stop." He burped in reply. Lucy griped, "Oh, Desi," until the crew took up the chorus like schoolboys. That evening after he rehearsed songs for the episode, he burped during the critique. Herb Browar exclaimed, "Desi, that's the first time you've been on key all day." Lucy broke up laughing and ran out to the board to place a gold star by Browar's name.

One key element of the show with which Lucy never made peace was Philip Morris cigarettes. She preferred Chesterfields and was talking in a cloud of their smoke in a corner of the set one day during rehearsals when Ed Feldman, who worked for Biow's advertising agency, saw she was holding the rival brand. He raced from the control booth and pulled her into a corner. Henceforth she carried her Chesterfields in a Philip Morris tin box.

Old friends, especially former contract players needing a job, showed up regularly. Charles Lane and Irving Bacon from *Broadway Bill* in 1934 were cast as a clerk and a justice of the peace, and appeared again in other roles, as did Sam Hearn from *The Next Time I Marry*, Barbara Pepper, her fellow Goldwyn Girl, grown plump and alcoholic, and Viv's husband, Phil Ober. Old friends also provided many names for the show. Mertz had a dual heritage—a Dr. Mertz lived near Madelyn when she was a child in Indianapolis, and the Boy Scouts in Jamestown had a Camp Frank Mertz. Characters called Marion Strong or Norman Van Vlack were dropped in occasionally, and the venerable name of Appleby was also invoked.

Lucy actively intervened in casting only once, according to Mercedes Manzanares, when she gave a Turkish actor named Alberto Morin a role he asked for. Mercedes told her it had already been cast and pretended to ignore her wrath, but nevertheless refused to go on the set unless Jess went along to protect her. Then Mercedes braced herself as Lucy bore down on them. "She said, 'Mercedes, I came to apologize.' For her to say she was sorry! I'll never forget it," the woman recalled.

Desi, who put his band on the payroll, was indifferent to casting except for the episode involving the visit of Ricky Ricardo's mother from Cuba. Desi wanted to be sure that the actress who represented his mother would reflect favorably on Lolita. Mercedes found Mary Emery, a youthful, gentle woman with dark hair who was fluent in Spanish. When the show was filmed, Mercedes sat with Lolita to answer any questions she might have in Spanish, but Lolita was enchanted by her stand-in.

As meticulous as Lucy was about rehearsals, so was she streamlined about everything else in her life. She was so delighted to be free of daily makeup and coiffure and the exhaustive fittings she had known in films that on the set she took to wearing tops and blouses she could get in and out of without mussing her hair. The success of the show gave the Arnazes financial security, but she did not splurge. In late 1953 she attended a charity ball wearing a dress with a tight black bodice and a fluffy pink net skirt—a gown she had purchased in 1938 and had shortened. Later, when the original wore out, she had it copied exactly. Not until the second season of *I Love Lucy* did she acquire her first mink coat, something she was so proud of that she, like Lucy Ricardo, wore it to bed.

A strict production schedule—ten to six every day, except on those nights when they had dress rehearsals or filmed and stayed in town—allowed time off for home life, including motherhood, at night and on weekends. Thrilled with her baby, Lucille nevertheless insisted, particularly to mothers with babies younger than her own, that a woman should not let her children run her life. On workdays little Lucie was cared for by a nurse, with DeDe looking in. Lucy's mother now lived in Canoga Park, a middle-class community just south of Chatsworth. Lolita, who lived in Beverly Hills, found herself jealous of DeDe, who drove herself around the city with ease and was able to spend more time with their granddaughter.

Never diffident, DeDe at fifty-nine fairly bloomed with her daughter's success. As if basking in her child's redheaded glow, she colored her hair auburn and had it styled just before each episode was shot. On nights the show was filmed, she directed who would sit around her and once kicked Milton Berle out of her row when he innocently joined her. She was outspoken, salty, and self-assured with reporters who came to her for stories of Lucy's childhood. The gist of her remembrances was that the girl was much like Lucy Ricardo.

Cleo now worked on the show, sometimes running the switchboard, while her husband, Ken Morgan, handled public relations. The Morgans had briefly lived in South Africa, where Ken found his job insufferable. Although Lucy had declined to send them money to come home, by the time they made their way back, *I Love Lucy* was starting up and she and Desi put them on the payroll. Being family, however, did not exempt them from Lucy's flares of temper. Ken, for example, could not understand Mercedes's distress over the casting incident: "What difference does it make?" he asked. "She yells at me all the time."

Loyal as the Arnazes were to friends and family, as demands mounted with their success, they were prepared to be generous only when they were sure they were not being taken advantage of. To a Cuban relative requesting financial assistance, Desi wired not money but a message: "Drop dead!"

Lucille Ball had always had a reputation for being funny, so no one in Hollywood claimed to be actually surprised by the depth of her ability, only by the magnitude of her overdue success. The revelation of *I Love Lucy* was Desi. When they watched the shows, Jess, Bob, Madelyn, and Marc realized he really was as good a comic actor as Lucy had insisted. To heed her wishes, they conspired in the first episode to make Ricky's club integral to the plot so that his singing could not be cut from the show, as CBS had demanded. But Desi soon effectively relaxed into the role of Lucy's long-suffering straight man. He gave the show a dash of sex and was the only one of her leading men to mute her strength. In her films, she had never been really feminine or vulnerable, but Desi's presence brought out those qualities in her. He also got laughs on his own account, especially for his mispronunciations, which provided any number of comic possibilities. In their enthusiasm for this development, the writers spelled Ricky's dialogue the way he said it—"fis'in' " and "televish-un" and "clop" for fishing, television, and club, but when Desi said those words as spelled, his pronunciation improved and the laughs disappeared.

Possibly because of his ear for music, he knew better than any of them the rhythm of an English sentence and how it would play. Jess attributed some of his comments to his incomplete grasp of English, but often they were based on a sense of Lucy Ricardo's character: "Great line, but not for Loocy." While Lucy studied her lines and went about muttering dialogue to herself, breaking a fifty-four-page script into points of interest, action verbs, and descriptive adjectives, Desi proved to have a photographic memory and knew the script as soon as he read it.

Two innovations in the first season were truly his own. He hated the way television sets abruptly went black during the transitions between a show and its commercials, so he worked with the film editor, Dann Cahn, to integrate them seamlessly so that music bridged the two, as is now standard.

Second, there was the improvement of the laugh track. Radio programs had used recorded laughter to prop up jokes that flopped, and Glen Glenn Sound adapted the technique to television audio mixing. When Desi learned that some of the laughs broadcast on *I Love Lucy* came from a box, he was appalled at what was to his mind a breach of the audience's trust. Persuaded that the track was necessary for the best sound levels, he insisted that no laugh be used that had not come from the actual *I Love Lucy* audience. James G. Stewart of Glen Glenn Sound therefore went through the recordings of "Desilu" laughs, cataloging and arranging them—a twitter here, a giggle there, and the occasional guffaw. Each got a number, starting with L-1, and they were added to the soundtrack first of *I Love Lucy*, then of other Desilu shows. Thus the laughter of DeDe, Lolita, and Bob Carroll's father eternally reverberate through the land of nostalgia television.

I Love Lucy was so successful that such celebrities as Robert Taylor, Marilyn Monroe, and Joe DiMaggio came to see the show. The office manager, Felice Green, was so awed by the Yankee star that she snatched the cushion he had sat on and hung it on her office wall. Others, including Eve Arden, Danny Thomas, and Frank Sinatra, who were going into television themselves, dropped by not just in tribute but to learn how the show was done. Soon Desilu was filming their series as well as Lucy and Desi's own. One time late in January 1952, *I Love Lucy* was shot on a Wednesday so that the facility could be used to make the pilot of Eve Arden's *Our Miss Brooks,* which Desilu produced for CBS. Desi even charged CBS a rental fee for the use of the lights the network had given him for free less than a year before.

Desi was evolving into a resourceful television executive and had managed to assemble an extraordinary television facility of which he was president. Those who marveled over the transformation of the "bongo player" into the impresario of a new medium had not been paying as much attention to him as he had been paying to everything since he arrived in Miami nineteen years before. From Xavier Cugat he had learned to heed the audience and give them what they wanted, from George Abbott he learned to concentrate on detail and express concern for the people who worked for him, and from Bob Hope, during his tenure as musical director of Hope's radio show, Desi learned how to conduct a writers' conference. The fractured compliment Louis B. Mayer had paid Desi—that he was like a race-horse that seemed common until he got to the track—was manifestly true. A month after the *Brooks* filming, Lucy had key people urge Desi to assume the title "executive producer" of *I Love Lucy,* which gave him production credit and indicated, erroneously, that he had authority over Jess, and over her as well. "You never heard her saying much when Desi was around. He'd leave and she'd start talking," Martin Leeds said. As she was star of the show, Lucy was eager that her husband be seen as star of the business.

On weekends she stayed at Chatsworth with her baby and, to relax, took up painting, favoring watercolors because she was too impatient to wait for oils to dry. Desi, supposedly with a male pal or two, headed for his boat. She and Desi were working together, but they had to go separate ways if they were ever to rest. As the first season ended, they had met their goal of being together so successfully that they deliberately scheduled time apart.

14

As THE FIRST victorious season of *I Love Lucy* progressed into the spring of 1952, Lucille Ball was so undone by the energies unleashed in her life that she sought psychiatric help. Even she who preferred chaos to calm realized she had somehow disconnected from herself. Now when she related the minutiae of her life—anecdotes involving the dogs, her baby, some mishap with the car—she rattled off her stories rather than savoring the effect she had on listeners. She became overwrought and sought composure as triumph followed triumph with dizzying speed, outpacing even the march of disasters that had laid siege to her childhood.

Lucy was often in such a state that Harriet was afraid to leave her on her days off, a concern Lucy exploited until her friend Dot fell ill; only then did she send Harriet to look after her. Lucy's psychiatrist assured her that her anxiety and fatigue were due simply to her having had a baby and undertaken a television show all at the same time. She helped Lucy to learn to appear calm, even if she could not achieve genuine inner peace. "She taught me how to rest in a roomful of people, to hold all my emotions in, instead of talking about them," Lucy said, explaining the flat seriousness of manner that seemed to come upon her. "That's why people sometimes complain that I'm staring at them deadpan. I'm trying to be deadpan inside too, so that I won't fly apart."

Lucy was nominated for an Emmy as best comedy performer, and with great hopes she drove with Desi to the Cocoanut Grove in Hollywood on February 18, 1952, for the ceremony. Red Skelton was the winner, however, and she gamely applauded with the rest of the audience until he reached the podium to claim his prize and said, "Ladies and gentlemen, you've given this to the wrong redhead. I don't deserve this. It should go to Lucille Ball." As he tried to present it to her, she waved him away in appreciative tears.

Lucy soon achieved one of the great performances of her career in the "Vitameatavegamin" episode in which she becomes hilariously drunk on the tonic she is promoting on a television commercial, but as she feared, a strain of evil appeared to offset her good fortune. The dreaded House Un-American Activities Committee, which for years had terrorized Hollywood, summoned her to appear in closed session before it. This body relentlessly delved into the purported Communist infiltration of show business and had already destroyed many by merely insinuating they had left-leaning sympathies. HUAC notified her that it discovered she had actually registered to vote as a Communist in 1936, and it wanted her to explain this matter to them. During the first week of April 1952, she left rehearsals of the episode in which she pretends to be the Maharincess of Franistan in an effort to further Ricky's career and confronted her investigators. The committee seemed to accept her explanation that she had registered only to please her late grandfather, particularly since her registration card clearly indicated she had never voted for a party candidate. She returned to the set relieved, and no word was leaked to the press.

After a few weeks, Lucy ended her counseling sessions certain she had conquered her fears. But on a trip to New York to promote the show, she was still in some turmoil, fearing her good luck would end as surely as she had lost the home she had loved in Celeron. She consulted Dr. Norman Vincent Peale, a popular clergyman who had just published *The Power of Positive Thinking*, at his Marble Collegiate Church on lower Fifth Avenue. "She came into my office and put her elbows on the desk and started to cry," Dr. Peale recalled. "She said, 'I've come a long ways and I want to know if it will all fade away. I'm so afraid it will disappear and I'll be back where I was.' Lucy told me about the hard times of her youth, and I told her, 'If it all disappears, you'll create it all again as you are on top of it.' When I told her her success was in herself, she cried a few minutes more."

In May, ten months after the birth of her daughter, as she was looking forward to a brief but needed rest followed by a summer tour that would take her and Desi to the Roxy and the London Palladium and earn them $200,000, Lucy learned she was pregnant again. She had wanted another baby and certainly hoped for a boy, but her life was now more complex than it had been when she and Desi were desperately childless. Each change in her life now ricocheted like a pinball triggering points and penalties. The fact that she would soon swell to double her size would almost certainly jeopardize the professional success she had finally achieved. At MGM, Mayer automatically suspended pregnant actresses, and Lucy had no assurance that her position was secure simply because she and Desi owned the top show in television (an audience of 31 million and rating of 67.3, compared to 54.7 for *Arthur Godfrey's Talent Scouts,* at number two).

In its infancy, television was a highly moralistic medium. Although they were married even in real life, on *I Love Lucy* Lucy and Desi could not share a bed. The couple feared that her obvious pregnancy—proof that Ricky Ricardo had hopped onto her mattress—might be too controversial for television. Herb Browar overheard her grumbling "Goddam it, I'm pregnant again!" even as she longed to be able to give Desi a son.

Fearing they had brought the show to an end and cost everyone his job, Lucy and Desi faced Jess like teenagers with guilty news. When they approached him, he was sitting in his office wondering how they might freshen the standard storyline of Lucy Ricardo's scheming to get into show business. Desi's face indicated that whatever he was going to announce was bad. "We've just been to the doctor. Lucy's going to have a baby," Desi said, implicitly asking if this news was disaster. Jess, to their surprise and relief, was delighted. Lucy Ricardo would have a baby too.

Philip Morris and CBS were less enthusiastic. They suggested that Lucy be filmed standing behind chairs or with her body otherwise blocked from view. They reluctantly agreed to allow Lucy's pregnancy to show only after Alfred Lyons, the chairman of Philip Morris, sent his staff a memo reading: "To whom it may concern: Don't fuck with the Cuban!" To make sure the proprieties were observed, a rabbi, priest, and Protestant minister reviewed each of the seven scripts that dealt with Lucy's condition. They were reportedly mystified when CBS insisted the word "expectant" be substituted for "pregnant."

The public was not informed of the happy news immediately. Instead, Lucy and Desi canceled their personal appearances, using the excuse that they wanted to spend more time with their daughter. After a few weeks of rest in Idaho, they, the writers, and the crew went into high gear a month ahead of schedule to complete as many episodes as they could while Lucy was still able to work. They shot nine "normal" stories and five with extended flashbacks of earlier episodes to allow her time to recuperate after the birth.

The pregnancy was revealed in the episode "Lucy Is Enceinte." The premise was that Ricky was so involved with work that the only way she could get a private word with him was to send him a note in the middle of his nightclub act. Ricky was supposed to be exultantly joyful when he learned he was going to be a father, but when Desi Arnaz stood before the cameras, he was flooded by the real emotions he felt when he learned his wife was pregnant after years of childless marriage, and he started to cry. Trying to save the filming and his dignity, he hid his head behind his wife's shoulder, but Lucy's eyes were welling up also. They tried to rally and deliver what was supposed to be a jubilant rendition of "We're Having a Baby," but as they sang, the audience, including DeDe and Lolita, began weeping too. In the control booth, William Asher, who had succeeded Marc Daniels, wiped his own tears and called for a retake. They managed a merry upbeat version, but it could not compare with the heartfelt original. Largely at Jess's insistence, they broadcast the first take.

All the endearing clichés of pregnancy—the husband's jealousy, the surprise baby shower, discussions over names—inspired episodes during the pregnancy. Mrs. Arnaz craved cream puffs, pickles, and lobster, but Mrs. Ricardo wanted ice cream covered with chocolate sauce and sardines—all in one lump. So she could get the fish down without gagging, the actress called for mashed potatoes and gravy as stand-ins.

Although after thirty-nine episodes she was not yet confident of her own performances, Lucy felt so strongly about how the show should be performed that she tested her new director. Asher had done the pilot of *Our Miss Brooks* as well as episodes of *Racket Squad* and a number of live shows. His first *Lucy* episode was "Job Switching," the classic in which Lucy and Ethel take a job at a chocolate factory and run afoul of its conveyor belt. That went so smoothly that the professional candymaker who worked with Lucy in the routine told Herb Browar that the day of the filming, which included being slapped by Lucy on camera, was the most boring she had ever spent.

On Asher's second show, Lucy took it upon herself to tell guest actors how to react while she played "Glow Worm" on the saxophone. As he recalled, "I told her if she wanted to do it, she should direct." Stung, Lucy ran off to her dressing room in tears. Asher, who had not been given an office, decamped to the men's room and sat on the toilet seat. There he was set upon by Desi, loudly protective of his pregnant wife. Asher told him that he felt lucky to be on the show, but if he was going to be director, he had to be allowed to do his job. Desi, who himself sometimes assumed the director's prerogatives, agreed. Asher then went to Lucy. "I cried. She cried. We hugged each other," he said of the reconciliation.

But Lucy never stopped giving other actors advice. Asher recalled, "Someone would come on the show and give a weird reading. When I'd ask why they had done it that way, they wouldn't answer. I would tell them, 'If it was Lucy, don't say, but don't do it that way again.' "

Throughout her television career, Lucy had two strategies for dealing with directors. She either came on strong or pretended to be ignorant. At readings, no matter how many times they had gone over the script, she would ask Asher to explain each scene to her, so that he began to wonder if she was in fact slow-witted. "It was several seasons before I realized she wanted to make sure whoever she dealt with knew what he was talking about," he said.

Because Lucy regularly did routines that might have made a fool of her, even in rehearsals, she had to know she could trust those with whom she worked. When the others were not around, she perfected stunts like barking like a dog or walking like a chicken with Asher. "After one routine she asked me if I would ask my wife to do these things," said Asher, who was married to the actress Dani Sue Nolan. "I said, 'I'm not married to Lucille Ball.' She quipped, 'You bastard!' because she knew that was no answer."

On each episode, one speech would give her particular trouble, so he would place a cue somewhere on the set to jog her memory. "One night she stopped in the middle of filming and froze. I thought she'd had an attack. She was wide-eyed. She left and went to her dressing room. I ran to her. She said, 'Bill, look at the lamp.' I did. It was an old prop, and stuck on it was a line from thirty shows before."

Lucy felt more secure and shows went more smoothly if she was working with people she trusted. Mary Jane Croft and Doris Singleton were actresses she knew from radio days. Since they were also married to producers whom Desi did not want to offend, he was less apt to proposition them. Both were also ladylike—as was Elvia Allman, who played the forewoman in the candy factory show—and Lucy tended not to quarrel with well-mannered people, who intimidated her. "Lucy would put other actresses in their place," said Dorothy Aldworth, who became a script supervisor. "They surrounded her with people she knew so that wouldn't happen."

As Lucy's pregnancy advanced, Desi began to call her "Thumper" because she was so heavy on her feet. He urged everyone to do what he could to accommodate her, and Asher obliged by playing her part in rehearsals while Lucy looked on. In mid-November 1952, two months before the baby was due, she stopped filming and went home to Chatsworth to rest. Since Lucie was delivered by cesarean, her second baby would be too, and doctors obligingly scheduled the surgery for the Monday when Lucy Ricardo would go to the hospital as well. No one seemed to worry that anything might go amiss in Lucy's real pregnancy, or that the delivery could be any less predictable than winding a clock. The only question was whether she would have a son or daughter. Doctors predicted a boy, as they had when Lucie was on the way. Desi knew this pregnancy was his last chance to have a son, and since there was no guarantee this would be the case, he asked the writers to give Ricky Ricardo a boy. On the morning of January 19, 1953, Lucy lay on the operating table of Cedars of Lebanon Hospital alert despite spinal anesthesia, asking "What is it? What is it?" as the baby was delivered. At 8:15 A.M. the doctor showed her her son. Lucy murmured, "His nose is so turned up he'll drown when it rains. Desi will be so happy," and promptly fell asleep.

Desi heard the news in the waiting room. "Now we have everything!" he shouted, and picked up the phone to tell Jess, who had been on the line for half an hour. For his prescience in agreeing to give the Ricardos a boy, Jess in his excitement shouted that he was the greatest writer in the world. The Associated Press, which had been issuing hourly bulletins on Lucy's condition, sent out the news. Seven minutes later it was broadcast as far away as Japan. To help the press Desi took the Rolleiflex of one of the photographers into the nursery. *"No comprendo,"* he claimed when the staff tried to tell him flash photos were forbidden, but he was too excited to remember which button operated the shutter. That night 44 million Americans (more than one fifth of the population—and 30,000 of whom sent personal congratulations) tuned in to watch as Ricky, Fred, and Ethel raced off to the hospital almost forgetting to take Lucy. At the end of the show, over footage of a new baby, an announcer said, "May their lives together be filled with as much joy and laughter and carefree happiness as they have brought all of us week after week. To Lucy, to Ricky, and to the new baby: love and kisses from Philip Morris and from all America." The show upstaged Dwight D. Eisenhower, hero of D-Day. When he was inaugurated as President of the United States the following day, admittedly not in prime time, only 29 million tuned in to watch.

In Chatsworth, the arrival of the real Desi Jr. turned the household upside down. Lucie's nurse became overprotective of her when Desi Jr. appeared, and they had to let her go and search for a replacement. An electric organ was delivered, one of Desi's larger gifts to commemorate the arrival of his son, and then three of Lucy's cocker spaniels died, one after the other. "It seems like God waited for the children and then took my dogs," she told Hedda Hopper, who came to the house for an interview. Three weeks after the birth she had lost twenty-seven pounds and proudly showed Hedda that her pants were about to fall off. Friends who drove out to see Lucy and the baby brought gifts not just for the children, but for the house as well. Lucy packed away their French lamps and Italian modern sculpture and resisted all suggestions that they upgrade their decor or move to Beverly Hills or Bel Air and live like the stars they had become. She insisted they were people of fixed habits and that the new freeway would enable them to get to the studio in twenty minutes. She said they would stay where they were happy.

The new mother was featured on the covers of most major magazines, including *Look*, *Life*, and *Newsweek*, and that February she and the show won Emmys. *I Love Lucy* was the number-one television program in America, and Philip Morris agreed to sponsor the show for two and a half more years for $8 million, of which $5 million went to the Arnazes and their company. In response to their new deal, Lucy told the press: "This couldn't happen to two nicer kids. I mean our children, of course." Perhaps most exciting of all, Lucy and Desi agreed to do a film for MGM, the studio where each had been rejected the decade before.

Only one thing marred her success. In early May Ed Sedgwick, godfather to both her children, died in his sleep at his home in North Hollywood. "Buster and I got to his house just before Lucille arrived," said Eleanor Keaton. "She walked in and she and Ebba fell apart." Ed's widow, Ebba Havez Sedgwick, born in Sweden, was a filmwriter who was as rotund as her husband. Although she would live for thirty more years, she never regained her own initiative and came to depend on Lucy, who personally cleaned her house, bought her clothes, and supported her in her old age. In the days following Ed's death, Lucy seemed to submerge her own distress in Ebba's and did everything she could to help her, which DeDe resented. The rosary prayer service, conducted before an open coffin, must have pained Lucy, but when Ebba, who was sitting at the front near the casket, dissolved into sobs, Lucy left her place and sat beside her to offer comfort. According to Maury Thompson, DeDe whispered to him, "Look at Lucille kissing her ass. She hates that old broad."

Lucy's own grief was deep and unsentimental. Her view of life was uncompromising, and she had the courage to face it. Ed Sedgwick, who believed in her, knew her perfectly, and guided her as a father would have, no longer existed. Lucy said she believed in God but not in an afterlife, although she said she wished she could: "It would be nice, but 'tain't true, even though it's awful hard to let go of those people you love."

A few weeks later, in early June 1953, just after the last *Lucy* show of the season wrapped, Lucille Ball returned to MGM, driving onto Lot 2 where the Andy Hardy series had been filmed, under a banner proclaiming "We Love Lucy." She and Desi, who was aware that he was slighted in comparison with the buildup given his wife, were about to begin *The Long, Long Trailer*, a romantic comedy about hapless newlyweds who simultaneously tackle marriage and a mobile home. To Lucy's own surprise, she was now acknowledged, at least tacitly, as a bigger star than the greatest names the movies had produced, greater than Ginger Rogers, Katharine Hepburn, Joan Crawford, or even Bette Davis, who had so outshone her at the Minton–Anderson School of Drama.

As Lucy's fortunes had changed, so had those of the studio. Louis B. Mayer had been forced out in 1951, and Dore Schary, who had won his stripes as an RKO executive, had taken over. Despite such classic hits as *Singin' in the Rain* and *Pat and Mike*, the studio was scrambling to cope with the challenge of television. It gave Lucy and Desi a $250,000 contract, payable to Desilu, which was said to be the most expensive deal in MGM history.

More than any other in her life, 1953 was a roller-coaster year in which Lucy inspired the most tender feelings in the American populace and became the target of some of its most concentrated hate. Her pregnancy only added to the sentimental love the public bore her, but then, soon after she and Desi signed television and film contracts making them two of the nation's most triumphant exemplars of capitalism, HUAC, whose questions she thought she had resolved seventeen months before, reopened its investigation of her. She was vacationing in Del Mar at a house they had rented next to the Rabwins when she picked up the phone and was told that the committee wanted to see her again to review her statements. Her popularity and renown had made her a target and caused committee members, who were hungry for headlines, to reopen a case they had closed to their satisfaction, according to even George Murphy, who was prominent among those working to root out Communists. CBS executives in New York had been informed by a HUAC representative that Lucy was under suspicion and relayed the information to Harry Ackerman, who phoned Martin Leeds, whom Desi had put in charge of Desilu production. At the end of this woeful relay, Leeds phoned Lucy and arranged to meet with her the next day to learn how this accusation had all come about and go over what she would tell the committee. Then he alerted MGM that the star of one of its movies was in a bind.

Lucy was terrified. Of all those HUAC had ruined, none was more tragic than her friend Larry Parks. In 1951 he had been called before the committee and admitted that he had joined the Communist party in 1941 as a young man of twenty-seven and left it four years later. Reluctantly and with great regret, he allowed the committee to intimidate him into naming others who were members with him, effectively precluding any sympathy he might have received. Those who did not condemn him for his brief party affiliation shunned him as a traitor to his friends. Not until 1960, when John Huston cast him in *Freud*, did the talented Parks act in films again. Others in the movie business, notably the Hollywood Ten who refused to say whether they were Communists or not, were blacklisted by film executives for years. On Lucy's own show actors had to be cleared by CBS and cross-checked in a publication called *Red Channels*, which purported to list Communist infiltrators, before they could be hired.

Lucy broke off her vacation on the Friday before Labor Day and, with her mother and brother, who were also asked to discuss their 1936 voter registration, went before the Republican congressmen William Wheeler and Donald Jackson in their office on Hollywood Boulevard. As she settled into her chair, she was stunned to see that Jackson was wearing a blue shirt. Professional men in those buttoned-down days of the 1950s wore this color only to appear on television, where blue registered as a flattering white. Lucy took this as an ominous sign that Jackson intended to use his investigation of her to obtain publicity for himself, possibly at the cost of her career.

Lucy recapitulated her testimony as if she had not faced the committee before. In two hours of questioning that was recorded behind closed doors, she said that while the documents the congressmen presented seemed legitimate, there was little she could recall about her registration. She explained that she had never been civic-minded or political at all, but that when her grandfather urged them all to register, around the time of her brother's twenty-first birthday, they complied. "In those days that was not a big, terrible thing to do," she said. "It was almost as terrible to be a Republican in those days."

She also confirmed that her name, misspelled, was listed with those appointed to the State Central Committee of the party by an Emil Freed. She said she had no knowledge of Freed and that her only explanation was that her grandfather must have been involved. Wheeler went on to ask her about her membership in the Committee of the First Amendment, a group with hundreds of prominent members, including Humphrey Bogart, Judy Garland, and four U.S. Senators, formed in 1947 to fight HUAC's assault on the motion picture industry. She recalled nothing of it and commented that it sounded like "one of those long democratic souped-up names." As for a suspicious radio broadcast she had done that year, her memory, which she said was vague, was that the Screen Actors Guild asked her to do a radio broadcast to support Okies living in northern California.

After several hours and twenty-seven pages of testimony, which included Wheeler's acknowledgment that her grandfather changed his registration to the Democratic party in 1940, Wheeler and Jackson said they were clearing her of all suspicion and promised to keep her testimony secret. But somehow they let it leak out.

Over Labor Day weekend she tried to calm herself and prepare for the first show of the 1953–1954 season. The world seemed to be on holiday, as the biggest news was that Californian Florence Chadwick had set a new record for swimming the English Channel. Lucy was settled into her rocking chair at Chatsworth that Sunday evening listening to Walter Winchell's program when she heard him bark out in his teletype delivery, "The top television comedienne has been confronted with her membership in the Communist party!" Winchell was the price God exacted from those to whom He had granted fame. She knew who the top television comedienne was and she knew she was in trouble.

Desi was playing cards in Del Mar, just as he had been in Cuba twenty years before when the revolution started and a phone call brought him bad news. This time Cleo's husband, Ken Morgan, gave him the word. Desi told him to get Howard Strickling, who was in charge of MGM publicity for *The Long, Long Trailer*, and meet him in Chatsworth to figure out a strategy to avoid total ruin.

Desi then phoned Lucy to tell her not to panic, but she began weeping as soon as they hung up. Even though the committee had cleared her, the public might not. When Hedda Hopper phoned, Lucy feigned total ignorance of the charges, and once Desi arrived after his 130-mile drive, Strickling tried to be upbeat and stuttered that Winchell might have meant Imogene Coca. Lucy bristled. "I resent that, Howard. Everyone knows that I'm the top comedienne." As he reviewed the transcript of her testimony, Strickling laughed over the stories about her grandfather and her saying that during the Depression it was considered worse to be a Republican than a Communist. His advice was that they stay mum, especially since Winchell had not mentioned her by name. He and Ken left their house about dawn.

In the days that followed, the atmosphere was foreboding. Neither Philip Morris nor CBS corporate executives sent them any word, apparently withholding their support or condemnation until they could gauge public reaction. Desi asked George Murphy to phone J. Edgar Hoover, head of the FBI, to see if the Bureau had anything against Lucy and if influence could be brought to help her. He then decided to go ahead with that week's show as if nothing had happened. Cast and crew, just back from vacation to start a new season of a hit show, went about their tasks stunned, as if someone they knew had died in a car crash. Ironically, that week's episode was "The Girls Go into Business" with a plot that could be construed as a lighthearted parody of the failure of a capitalistic venture. Lucy and Ethel buy a can't-miss dress shop and promptly make five sales to each other. After a few days of losing money, they delightedly sell out for $3,500, only to learn their buyer has sold the property for $50,000 to a real estate developer.

By Friday, the day of the filming, *The Los Angeles Herald-Express* trumpeted "LUCILLE BALL NAMED RED" with a photo of her registration card doctored so that the cancellation of her membership was erased. The possible fall of so popular a star was obviously a major story, and reporters thronged the front gates of the Motion Picture Center, the new headquarters of Desilu, as well as phoning them at home asking for exclusive information.

When they reached the studio the morning of the filming, Lucy and Desi were forced to sneak in to avoid reporters. Lucy was certain that when she went before the audience she would be booed and jeered. No one on the *I Love Lucy* staff so much as mentioned the situation to her, even when she broke down in tears, but Desi arranged to have a doctor standing by to treat her if she collapsed and hired extra security to protect her from any militant right-wingers who might turn up. He realized that not to have filmed, or to have done the show without an audience, would have indicated guilty fear. He took the added precaution of arranging with CBS to preempt that night's episode of *Racket Squad,* at Desilu's expense, if there was unfavorable reaction so they would be able to go live before the American public to explain the situation as she had explained it twice to HUAC. At three that afternoon Philip Morris sent word it was standing by them. Desi passed that happy news to Lucy, who still expected to be booed by her audience.

A few hours before the show was filmed, Donald Jackson was persuaded to hold a press conference to announce that he wished to end harmful speculation about Lucy. He stated that there was no indication that she was ever a member of the Communist party, and although he added "No case is ever closed," a reporter tipped Desi that he could expect positive headlines the next day.

Instead of a warm-up that evening, Desi gave a serious speech. He told the audience that he thought they might have heard some bad things about Lucy that were not true. "Lucy has never been a Communist. Not now, and never will be," he said. A reporter timed the audience applause as lasting one minute. Desi continued, "I was kicked out of Cuba because of communism. We despise everything about it. Lucy is as American as Barney Baruch and Ike Eisenhower. By the way, we both voted for Eisenhower. So, ladies and gentlemen, don't judge too soon. Read for yourselves. Read her story. Don't believe every piece of bunk you read in the papers." As the audience rose up cheering, someone shouted "We're with you!" and in the wings huddled with the staff, Lucy started to sob.

"And now," Desi concluded, "I want you to meet my favorite wife—my favorite redhead—in fact, that's the only thing red about her, and even that's not legitimate—Lucille Ball!" She ran out to a roar of support and a standing ovation, and made a fighter's gesture of shadow boxing.

She could do no wrong that night. The audience laughed when Lucy Ricardo said hello, and if she did something even faintly amusing, they howled. "It was the most enthusiastic audience we ever had," Bill Asher said. "Those three hundred people represented the country, and they wanted to show they believed in her, but their reaction was so out of proportion we had to broadcast it with canned laughs." At the end of the show, leaning on Desi's arm, Lucy thanked the audience for being so kind, then went to her dressing room and collapsed.

The next day Lucy and Desi, sitting side by side in green deck chairs, hosted a press conference by the pool at their ranch. Wearing pink slacks and a white shirt with her fiery hair tied back with a clashing pink bow, Lucy was in shaky good spirits, unable to conceal her nervousness, and sometimes on the verge of tears. She who hated heat sat in 90-degree temperatures and burning smog, trying to seem expansive. "Anytime you give the American people the truth they're with you," she said, dabbing at her perspiring forehead with her handkerchief, "but in the last couple of days I've realized this is nothing to laugh about."

When Desi repeated his quip of the night before—"The only thing red about this girl is her hair and even that we're not so sure about"— he took control of the headlines. Desi's irreverence captured the public's imagination.

A small committed group was not convinced by the Arnazes' statements, however. The ultraconservative columnist Westbrook Pegler scoffed at Lucy's explanations, and employees of an Indianapolis car dealership launched a write-in campaign to drive her off the air, but most people reading accounts of Lucy's close-knit American family struggling to buck up its eccentric grandpa believed her. The show stayed number one. The definitive sign of her acceptance came when President Eisenhower invited her, Desi, Viv, and Bill to join a roster of performers at the White House for his birthday at the end of November.

Lucy's exoneration marked a change in the political atmosphere of witch hunts. Unlike others who went before the committee, Lucille Ball really was presumed innocent, even though she, unlike most of HUAC's targets, had actually signed documents that told against her. Her case was aired publicly and she was cleared without qualification and did not have to live under a taint of innuendo. She was the greatest star to come under attack. When such performers as Judy Holliday, Harry Belafonte, and Gypsy Rose Lee came under suspicion, networks and producers were quietly informed and the actors were covertly barred from at least some television shows. A few years earlier the committee had publicly prosecuted screenwriters the public had never heard of and they were blacklisted, but when the bullyboys of HUAC took on a much-loved performer, full light on their deeds worked against them. Jack Gould wrote in *The New York Times* that her experience should end the practice of blacklisting those merely suspected of being Communists: "One cannot help but wonder if the fear of boycotts is not largely in the minds of those who subscribe to the use of blacklists and private loyalty files of dubious reliability." He called on broadcasters to treat bit players with the same fairness with which they treated their biggest stars.

For various reasons, the shadow of HUAC began to lift. The press, which in the past had simply reported accusations the committee had leveled, began to question the tactics of the accusers. The following March Edward R. Murrow charged on his CBS broadcast *See It Now* that Senator Joseph McCarthy, the nation's leading Communist witch-hunter, repeatedly crossed "the line between investigating and persecuting." Hearings soon began that led to McCarthy's censure.

In the days following her ordeal, even as support mounted, Lucy physically gave way to the stress to which she had been subjected. She developed sties, suffered from bursitis, and lost twelve pounds. Cleo remembered her as being in shock and devoid of recriminations for anyone, but in her times of stillness Lucy mused on the irony of her reward for the help she had tried to give her family. Her bumbling grandfather threatened to destroy her from beyond the grave, while her audience, strangers she had never seen, were writing in to offer support. She received 2,237 telegrams and letters at her home and studio, of which only 24 were critical. Philip Morris had fewer than 200 letters requesting it to drop *I Love Lucy*. In a poll of 1,200 people about the affair, only 2 respondents disapproved of Lucy. Shortly afterward, Lucy said: "I have discovered that the people whom you have helped in your life cannot help you in return. But somebody else does it for them."

In some moments, she realized how her personal force and power could undermine other people. Long before, probably in Chatsworth, she had found a sparrow with a broken wing, made it a nest of cotton, fed it, and tried to make it well. The next morning it was dead, its claws caught in the fibers of the nest she had made. She had grieved over the sparrow for days, and the memory haunted her now. She wondered if her solicitude had similar effects on people she cared for. "Years ago, knowing it would strengthen me to accept responsibility and take care of my family and friends, I gave too much. I spoiled them so that they expected to get everything for nothing. I weakened them," she told journalist Eleanor Harris. "I stopped it. I hope I'll remember this lesson in raising the kids. I don't want to weaken them. I want them to be strong and independent." She called this insistence on independent self-reliance "the Art of Selfishness." For good measure, to protect herself from any fear of repeating her HUAC experience, she never voted again.

Throughout the trying highs and lows of 1953, Desilu Studios grew enormously. As well as producing *I Love Lucy* and *Our Miss Brooks*, it handled technical film production for shows starring Danny Thomas, Loretta Young, and Ray Bolger. It made hundreds of filmed commercials, including those for Philip Morris in which Lucy and Desi themselves urged the public to smoke the brand. To accommodate all this and further expansion, Desilu settled in at the Motion Picture Center on Cahuenga, a few blocks from their first studio. Behind its pseudo-Spanish walls, they converted four soundstages into theaters for audiences and constructed offices and departments for film cutting and editing, hairdressing, wardrobe, and finance. That year Desilu was evaluated at $10 million, did a gross business of $6 million, and made Desi and Lucy a net profit of $600,000 before taxes. To this was added another $500,000 from *I Love Lucy* merchandise, such as pajamas, dolls, and bedroom sets.

To oversee this growing enterprise, in February 1953 Desi had hired Martin Leeds, the executive who had given him the most trouble at CBS, and made him director and executive vice president in charge of production. Leeds was a serious and seemingly impassive manager, but some employees found him deadly. Desi's secretary Johny Aitchison said, "Martin Leeds worked at offending people. He'd call everyone's offices first thing in the morning to let them know he was watching to see when they came in." He was also a superb tactician in business and had a correspondingly pragmatic view of human nature. Desi's philandering, the fact he and Lucy spent weekends apart and usually hired separate limousines when they went on promotional tours, the news that they kept separate financial accounts and that Lucy knew how much Desi owed her, were all noted by Leeds as signs that the fissures in the marriage were widening. "When you got near that marriage you could smell hell," he stated simply. However, their personal problems concerned him as risks to the business. In December 1953 Leeds convinced them to sign a buy/sell agreement whereby one of them could end their business partnership by offering to buy the other out, leaving the other the option of buying him or her out instead.

Their demanding workdays alternated with strained, exhausted evenings when the sight of each other reminded them of all the work they had done that day. They had grown so adept at producing the show that they shortened the *I Love Lucy* work week to four hectic days. Desi frequently went out on the town, but finding that unsatisfactory too, he began to go on extended fishing trips from Newport Beach with Pepito, Kenny Morgan, Dann Cahn, or Bill Asher. "Lucy didn't want him to go alone with Kenny," said Dann Cahn, who edited *I Love Lucy*. "She used to phone Desi at the dock and say 'You and Kenny get into trouble but as long as you're with Danny I know you're all right.' He wasn't. We got into a lot of trouble."

Meanwhile, Lucy stayed home with the children and her watercolors. She took time to do little homey things. Knowing that Marion Van

Vlack liked to sew, Lucy sent her the blue and white gingham dress she wore in the "Vitameatavegamin" episode, which Marion cut and restyled into doll clothes.

Lucy had learned to accept that she could not change her husband, and she liked to believe she had grown more tolerant. "He'd come to the studio with a hangover, and for that matter, so would I," Bill Asher said. "The sicker he was, the more she'd laugh." As easygoing as she tried to be, she still tried to find someone on whom to fix some of the blame for her husband's behavior. At one point she held Bill Asher responsible. "Lucy thought I was contributing to the problem. We talked about it. I told her Desi didn't need any help."

Desi could not understand why, after all their years together, she was still jealous. "What is she so excited about?" he asked all the men who would listen. "They're only hookers." In fact, he was never involved with any woman for long, as visiting starlets learned. Women on the Desilu payroll, such as the pretty costume designer Elois Jenssen, either stayed out of his way to avoid an awkward incident or brushed him off with a joke. "I'd bawl Desi out in Spanish like I was his mother," said Mercedes Manzanares. "I told him, 'You want to know what I'm like in the hay because you knew my husband' and he'd laugh and go away." The men of Desilu also had a dilemma. They were genuinely fond of Lucy, and to condone Desi's womanizing was to help him betray the woman who was also their boss. Leeds said, "The problem we had with Desi was that we knew she knew, and that hurt."

In the spring of 1954, the Arnazes went out on a tour of ten cities, including Jamestown, to promote *The Long, Long Trailer*. The love people bore Lucy approached adulation, which was never more plain than when a woman appeared in their hotel lobby in New York asking the couple to baptize her baby. *The Long, Long Trailer* proved to be a hit, taking in $4.5 million in 1954 and ranking seventeenth in grosses for the year. None of Lucy's previous films had ever made such a mark, and it now seemed she would be able to resume a movie career after *I Love Lucy* came to an end. According to friends, her idea of true success still centered on the movies.

The film also won a bet Desi and Leeds had made with Benny Thau of MGM. Banking on their popularity, Desi wagered that if *Trailer* did not outperform *Father of the Bride*, MGM's highest grossing film to that point, they would refund $50,000 of their $250,000 contract, but if it did do better, the Arnazes were to earn $300,000, a sum they did receive.

Although Desi was allowed to do little but act in *The Long, Long Trailer*, he did try to give MGM the benefit of his ideas. He thought television techniques would produce a better film in less time and that he could beat the moviemakers at their own game. As a condition of their doing another film for the studio, MGM agreed to let him produce it. The couple chose *Forever Darling*, a story about an angel, played by James Mason, who materializes to save a troubled marriage. Lucy and Desi played a spoiled society girl and her chemist husband who try to renew their romance on a field trip in the wilds.

A constant theme of *I Love Lucy* was never do business with friends, but the Arnazes did business with practically no one else. Lucy's old flame Pandro Berman produced *The Long, Long Trailer*. Vincente Minnelli directed it, and the couple let his little girl Liza live with them for a time. Now Desi hired Al Hall to direct *Forever Darling*. Hall had directed the popular *Here Comes Mr. Jordan*, another angel film, but the Arnazes were clearly in charge on this project, and Lucy felt free to badger her old beau if she thought he drank too much. To make the picture, Desi set up Zanra (Arnaz spelled backward) Productions, with him and Lucy owning 80 percent and the rest distributed to key Desilu people, the couple's mothers and children. He told MGM he could bring the film in for $1 million at the Desilu studios, and MGM agreed to give him the chance.

Elois Jenssen worked on the *Forever* costumes during the television season, one of the strategies Desi used to save thousands of dollars. On the June morning that filming began, Desi claimed they were already three days ahead of schedule. Instead of making "test shots" of clothes, sets, makeup, and lighting, he shot actual scenes to be used in the movie and called them "tests." Dann Cahn, who was accomplished in television editing, edited *Forever Darling* late that summer in the garage of the Arnaz summer house. Lucy interrupted his work each afternoon to take him with a large group to the Del Mar track.

Unfortunately, Desilu's efficiency merely cut corners as production of a color feature required more fine-tuning than a small-screen black-and-white program. *Forever Darling* had the restricted quality of a television show and was panned by critics. New York's Radio City Music Hall rejected the film as below its standards, and a reviewer in *The New York Times* quipped, "It is a switch to see two people save their energies for television and toss off a quickie for the films." *Forever Darling* ended Desilu's hopes of becoming a motion picture producer and forced Lucy to reconsider her dreams of becoming as renowned in movies as she was in television.

As Lucy and Desi Arnaz achieved fame and wealth, Lucy and Ricky Ricardo prospered in the pattern followed by others in postwar America. The young city couple grew in affluence, bought a television set and a washing machine, had a baby, ventured across the country to Hollywood where they saw big stars, and ultimately moved to the suburbs, always with antic complications of Lucy's devising. With and against Fred and Ethel, they hung real sixty-five-pound tunas in their closets, were regularly jailed, and vandalized Grauman's Chinese Theater.

To the audience who loved them from afar, Lucy and Desi themselves remained a golden couple. Americans read headlines about their million-dollar deals and noted the Desilu logo at the end of their favorite shows, such as *Our Miss Brooks* and *Make Room for Danny*. Their life seemed perfect, and it was easy to believe that they had as much fun at home as they gave to everyone else each week. Desi clearly starred in business as Lucy did on the set. They seemed to have all the money, all the love, and all the luck.

In fact, their differing temperaments were more and more a source of conflict. A friend remembered Desi sitting on his porch in Del Mar one afternoon during their vacation marveling at the sight of a spectacular sunset when Lucy joined them.

"What are you doing?" she asked.

"Looking at the sunset."

"What do you want to do that for?" she questioned. "There's a gin game down the road."

Tension, whether passionate or simply the product of irritation, had been part of their lives for so long that Lucy did not consider it a danger signal. But it was the always sensitive issue of her husband's philandering that brought their problems to a head. In December 1954 the scandal magazine *Hollywood Confidential* ran the headline "Does Desi Really Love Lucy?" over a story about his infidelities. It claimed that Desi had spent twenty minutes with a prostitute at the Beverly Hills Hotel the summer after Desi Jr. was born, then passed her on to a "male relative" who accompanied him. "A real man should have as many girls as he has hair on the head," Desi was quoted as saying.

Lucy was curious to read the story herself and flustered her staff by asking someone to bring her a copy, explaining "Christ, I can't go out and buy it *myself!*" She and their employees read *Confidential* furtively in corners of the studio, but Desi took the matter head on. He burst onto the *I Love Lucy* set, brandishing a copy and expressing exasperation and innocent amazement: "Look what those SOBs are saying about me now!"

However tolerant she had become of Desi's affairs, the humiliation of the *Confidential* exposé left her unable to brazen the situation out. Driving to Palm Springs with Mary Jane Croft, she broke down completely. "Lucy was distraught, just distraught," Mary Jane recalled. "She had her pride, and it was hard because she was just mad for Desi."

In public, silence was her defense. She, Desi, and the Martin Leeds were at an industry dinner seated with Danny Kaye, Lily Pons, and Andre Kostelanetz when Kaye suddenly exclaimed, "You made *Confidential!*" Lily Pons wanted to know what *Confidential* was, so Kaye explained, "It's a magazine about fucking." Mortified, Lucy was unable to join the conversation for the rest of the evening.

She was more expressive when she was alone with Desi. Whatever joy remained in their marriage effectively ended with the story in *Hollywood Confidential.* Harriet told her closest friend that in the course of one argument at the height of their fame, possibly during this period, Lucy knocked Desi out cold. She often "shot" him with the lighter shaped like a dueling pistol, but on this particular occasion she actually picked up a hammer and hit him on the head. He fell down unconscious and when he did not respond to her attempts to revive him, Lucy screamed for Harriet. The two women applied ice packs with no noticeable results. Certain that she had killed him, Lucy and Harriet decided that their story would be that he had fallen and hit his head. While they rehearsed it before calling the police, much as Lucy Ricardo and Ethel Mertz might have done if *I Love Lucy* had been set in hell, Desi revived. As he sat holding one of their ice packs, he realized that he would have to explain his appearance when he went to the studio and agreed to go along with their explanation that he had fallen and hit his head.

An occasional punch did not seem out of line to either Lucy or Desi. Once when Herbert Kenwith had dinner at their home, they began quarreling and Desi struck Lucy in the face and split her lip. Harriet then appeared bearing a bottle of wine and conked Desi over the head. While he groaned, Harriet took Lucy to the bathroom to clean her up. "When Lucy reappeared, they acted as if nothing had happened," Kenwith recalled. "I didn't know what to say to any of them. It was like being with the Three Stooges."

Lucy continued to hope that their lives would work out together and even prayed for it, sheepishly ashamed to be calling on God only in time of need. But she no longer believed that staying with Desi was worth the sacrifice of herself. With the *Confidential* article, she felt she stood shamed before "the public," that amorphous mass that began at the outskirts of Hollywood and sent their greetings through the mail. She was forced to confront the details of his escapades and the call girls' appreciative assessment of his lovemaking. Whether the facts of the piece were exactly as reported or not, Lucy knew the gist of it was true and she knew that everyone else did as well.

For his part, Desi continued to deny the allegations. When the matter was resurrected in the course of a libel suit against *Confidential* in August 1957, along with gossip about other stars, Desi told the New York press that the story was "a lot of baloney," adding with justification, "I was the victim today, but tomorrow it will be somebody else."

Like Lucy, Desi took emotional refuge in the Ricardos, whom they both recognized as people nicer than themselves, an ideal they could not attain. In the hours when they were Lucy and Ricky Ricardo she had the marriage she wanted, complete with tricks that her husband thwarted with loving strictness, as had Lillian Appleby so long ago. When Lucy and Desi worked to bring out the most in Lucy and Ricky, they showed their understanding of each other. If Desi suggested a scene she disagreed with, she would try it halfheartedly to prove his idea was lame and he would know immediately what she was doing.

"You god-damned redhead sonofabitch, if you're going to try it, you got to try it but you're going to do it as good as you can do it, and I know what that is!" he would yell in exasperation.

"You sonofabitch. You noticed."

"You're god-damned right I noticed."

Satisfied that they had taken each other's measure, they played the scene full out so that he could tell if he was right, or if she had been, and they could make it perfect.

No matter how much tension she was under in her personal life, Lucy was able to focus on the show and through that transcend everything else, a feat that demonstrated not only her artistry but her will. Lucy later said the last five years of her marriage were a sham redeemed only by her enthusiasm for her work.

Throughout the first half of 1955—a period during which they lived through a kidnap threat against the children, purchased controlling interest in the Motion Picture Center rather than see it sold to Harry Cohn, dealt with Philip Morris dropping its sponsorship of *I Love Lucy* because its surveys indicated that children and older women were its audience, and worried about competition from Jack Webb's *Dragnet*—Lucy and the team managed to produce the series of classic shows where Lucy Ricardo goes to Hollywood. Bill Asher recalled that Lucy was thrilled to have such stars as Rock Hudson, Van Johnson, Richard Widmark, and William Holden, all plugging new movies, appear in these episodes. She was in awe of them, according to Asher, but they were in even greater awe of her.

For his appearance, John Wayne showed up at the run-through a half hour ahead of everyone else, and the cast found him sitting at the conference table when they arrived. New to television, Wayne obediently allowed Lucy to drag or push him to his marks while they rehearsed. Another highlight of the season was the classic "mirror bit," a pantomime from the Marx Brothers' film *Duck Soup*, in which

Lucy tries to make Harpo think he is looking at a mirror when he confronts Lucy Ricardo, who has tried to impersonate him. Humble enough to be insecure, yet confident enough of her stature to be demanding, Lucy would call Harpo aside during breaks so they could practice to perfection. Harpo did his routine intuitively, but so that she could understand it, Lucy had him break it down into such detailed separate movements that Harpo himself became confused. The most acclaimed episode set in Hollywood, where William Holden lights the cigarette of a disguised Lucy and sets her putty nose ablaze, was filmed that winter.

Although neither of the Arnazes was threatened any longer by the fear that the other would leave—they had been together too long and had come through too many difficulties patched if not healed—the growing strain in their marriage was felt at Desilu Studios. Now that Desi had proven himself in business, Lucy did not feel the need to build his ego, but told him that each expansion of the business added to his crushing workload and consequently to his need for drink. When Desi realized he would have to buy the Motion Picture Center rather than risk having Harry Cohn take it over and cancel his leases, Lucy gave him no support. Forgetting they had once before outfoxed Cohn when he held her to her contract, Lucy warned her husband that Cohn was unbeatable. The outcome was scheduled to be decided one Sunday afternoon, and as the hours crept by at Chatsworth, Desi began to agree with her and give up hope when he saw headlights turning into the driveway. It was the owner, Joe Justman, coming to tell Desi that the center was his. Lucy's response to Desi's triumph was "You bought yourself another coffin."

In the early days of their marriage, Desi cut off Lucy's complaints about his being on the road by suggesting she give up her career. Now he broached the subject again by telling her she always had the option of giving up the show. She could simply do a television special or film whenever she wished, or even just stay home, he suggested, while he ran Desilu. They could live quietly with their children, or expand Desilu to compete with the major studios, lest they be driven out of business by them. After their second season, she said she thought they should end the show after two more years. But in May 1955, that time was coming up, and *I Love Lucy* was second only to the upstart *The $64,000 Question*, which edged them out by 1.4 rating points.

"I don't want to quit," she told him, and the subject was closed.

After the kidnapping scare in early 1955, the Arnazes felt unprotected in Chatsworth. The population of the San Fernando Valley had mushroomed in the postwar boom, swelling traffic, ending their feeling of being in the country, and lengthening their already long commute to the studio. They decided to move nearer to the studio and to Beverly Hills, whose police department was so vigilant that it questioned unfamiliar pedestrians walking through residential neighborhoods.

The purchase of their first home had been a shared and treasured milestone, but Desi was now so busy that the job of looking for their new house fell to Lucy alone. Although abstract business matters, such as the contracts she often signed without reading, held little apparent interest for her, she had a knack for getting a good deal, a knack she brought to bear in this search. A realtor drove her to 1001 North Roxbury at the corner of Lexington Road in Beverly Hills and showed her a modern mansion she thought worthy of the Arnaz status. Lucy was unmoved, and when the realtor warned that it wouldn't be on the market long, Lucy said she could not buy anything until Desi saw it. As they returned to the car, Lucy noticed across the street a huge two-story brick-and-shingle colonial, a full-size version of what she had aimed for in renting the bungalow on Ogden Drive for her family, a house that would have fit in on elegant Fairmount Avenue in Jamestown.

The broker protested that it was not grand enough, and in any case was not for sale, but Lucy crossed the street, walked up to the door, and rang the bell. The elderly woman who let her in did not recognize her but said with some amazement that Lucy's arrival was an extraordinary coincidence, for she and her husband were in fact thinking of selling. They had built a guest house for their son in the backyard, but he had just died in an accident, and they could not cope with the memories. Lucy looked at the circular entrance hall and staircase, at the four bedrooms and servants' wing, and offered $75,000 on the spot. They waited for the woman's husband, who asked for $85,000, to which Lucy promptly agreed. Lucy stepped outside and told the waiting broker she had just bought the property at 1000 North Roxbury Drive.

The beauty of their new house in no way assuaged their grief at leaving their first home. Buying and developing that ranchito, much of which Desi did with his own hands, represented a bond that was almost as strong as their love for their children, yet they sadly sold their property to the actress Jane Withers and her husband. Lucy, who was more comfortable spending an afternoon suspended by an overhead wire flying above the set than thinking of moving her rocking chair from its established place at home, contemplated the packing and moving of all her treasured objects with dread and uneasiness.

Desi put his brother-in-law, Fred Ball, in charge of double-checking renovations while they filmed *Forever Darling*, but just as they were ready to move in late spring 1955, a pipe burst, damaging parts of the house and forcing them to postpone the move until new carpeting was installed. Desi was known to have a temper, but his rage at what he saw as an unnecessary calamity was unbridled and stunned those who knew him.

Although thoughts of Chatsworth would always make Lucy melancholy, so that a special softness would come into her voice even in old age whenever she mentioned "our first house and our garden," she did take pleasure in having made it to Beverly Hills, in having the money and status to entitle her to purchase a fine house in what was then the ultimate neighborhood.

Tour buses bearing ogling fans annoyed most of her celebrity neighbors, but Lucy regarded them as a mark of stardom and had fun with them. While their children were young, she and Desi were afraid to install a pool, so she used her neighbor's across the street. One day, hidden in dark glasses and scarf, she was headed there with Herbert Kenwith when a bus driver leaned out his window to inquire if Lucille Ball lived in the house they just left. "Oh, no," said Lucy. "She lives way down the block." The buses were incorporated into *I Love Lucy*, and her own house was used for an exterior when Lucy Ricardo invaded Richard Widmark's trophy room and disguised herself, first as a stuffed animal by tucking cigarettes in the corners of her mouth to simulate tusks, and then in a bearskin rug.

As her home changed, so did the team responsible for *I Love Lucy*. By 1956, five years after the show had begun, the pioneering group she relied on had in some ways let her down. Al Simon and Herb Browar had formed their own production company and produced *I Married Joan*, about a wacky wife with Joan Davis and Jim Backus, for NBC. Lucy missed them and when she was still pregnant with Desi Jr. she went to their new offices and trudged up the staircase to tell them she felt they had made the wrong decision.

Madelyn Pugh and Bob Carroll, Jr., did not marry each other, as Lucy had wished, and when she realized they never would, she refused to speak with either of them for a time. The pair at one point quit the show feeling they were written out and Jess hired the team of Bob Schiller and Bob Weiskopf. Their wit was both affable and mordant, more verbal than physical. Weiskopf had worked with Jess in radio and together they had written for Danny Thomas, George Burns, and Janis Paige. Although they had never watched *I Love Lucy*, Schiller and Weiskopf were happy to have a contract. They were husky, sporty types who shared Desi's interests in boxing, baseball, and sports, so Lucy always thought of them as "Desi's boys" and wondered what the three got up to. When Bob and Madelyn, bored with hiatus, returned to the show, both writing teams worked together in an arrangement that Madelyn likened to a double date.

Karl Freund departed in the spring of 1956, later saying he was tired of coping with the personalities at Desilu and the commercial restrictions of television. Most devastating of all, Jess left on April 15, 1956, at the end of the fifth season, and went to NBC to develop new shows. Although he and Desi could not find a way to work together, they and everyone else, including Bill Frawley, were teary-eyed at the farewell party Lucy and Desi threw for him under a striped tent on Roxbury Drive.

Even the Arnazes loosened their ties to the series. To finance buying control of the Motion Picture Center and other expenses, they sold their rights to *I Love Lucy* to CBS for $4.5 million in October

1956. A year and a half before, Desi had entered the rerun market by leasing the first fifty-two episodes to sponsors for broadcast on Sunday evenings. They had cost $24,000 each to produce; Desi leased them for $30,000. In late 1955 the rerun market showed further potential when Chertok TV sold residual rights to *Private Secretary* with Ann Sothern to CBS for more than $1 million; the old shows were retitled *Susie* and broadcast by independent, nonnetwork stations while *Private Secretary* was still running on CBS.

Desi, Jess, and others involved were apparently mindful of the potential of reruns from the debut of *I Love Lucy*. Except for one magical Christmas episode, they did no holiday shows lest some Thanksgiving episode be rerun in the middle of August and jar the audience. Over the next three decades the 179 episodes they sold CBS grossed $75 million, prompting some to remark that the couple would have had a greater fortune if they had sold Desilu and kept the rerun rights, but at the time, selling syndication rights was the better deal. Lucy was financially conservative, but the Arnazes sought to achieve more than just wealth. Martin Leeds said, "As much as that money, we got the use of the money. The studio could have held it and compounded at 6 percent for thirty-five years without using it, but we bought studios and made products with it instead." The couple also sold CBS *December Bride* for an additional $500,000 and received $1 million for exclusive rights to their own performances for the next ten years. Through such transactions, Desi and Lucy joined the ranks of the small company of performers able to exploit the business opportunities of television. Dick Powell, Danny Thomas, and Ozzie Nelson were also businessmen as well as stars, but none of them created an empire as Desi Arnaz had.

From September 1955 to June 1957, the Desilu television roster included *I Love Lucy, Our Miss Brooks, The Danny Thomas Show, The Lineup, December Bride, The Whirlybirds, The Sheriff of Cochise,* and numerous other shows and pilots. This represented an output of 691 half-hour programs, plus many rejected pilots. Jay Sandrich recalled that during this remarkably creative period, the studio had a family atmosphere in which performers felt free to wander onto one another's sets. Lucy would stop by *December Bride* to see what Spring Byington was doing, Danny Thomas looked in on

Lucy, and everyone checked out Eve Arden on *Our Miss Brooks.*

Lucy did not want to quit working, but she did think about slowing down, about other possible ways of living. She wrote Marion in the middle of the 1950s saying that they were thinking of retiring and buying one of the big lakeside houses outside of Jamestown to spend their summers. But probably the closest she actually came to resting was to allow herself time for a foot operation to repair the injuries she had lived with since *Fancy Pants.*

At the beginning of 1957, the Ricardos and the Mertzes moved to the country. Everyone involved, except their audience, was growing weary. Still, in their sixth season, Lucy achieved the longest laugh of her career. The episode in which it took place had the Ricardos in the egg business and harkened back to her chickens at Chatsworth. When Ricky calculates that the eggs cost them $18 apiece, Lucy and Ethel sneak in store-bought eggs to make it seem their production has improved. Lucy hastily stuffs them into her blouse when Ricky insists they practice the tango they plan to perform at a PTA meeting. He pulls her close to himself in the dramatic movement of the dance and crushes the eggs. As he feels his wife's chest turn to liquid, her expression vividly conveys the feeling of raw eggs running down her body. The audience exploded with laughter, and Lucy kept them going. She had rehearsed the scene with hardboiled eggs but used raw ones to make the filming fresh. Her eyes swelled, her mouth curled, she shimmied, she wiggled, and then when the audience began to recover, she shook her foot to signal that the goo had traveled all the way to her shoe. It was timed at sixty-five seconds. Sandrich said, "The laugh was so big we had to cut it down so we could use it. The amazing thing was that just before the tango, the audience saw a baby chick accidentally crushed by a camera, which had sobered them."

On April 4, 1957, they filmed the last *I Love Lucy* in the half-hour format, "The Ricardos Dedicate a Statue," in which Lucy wrecks the town's memorial to a Revolutionary War soldier. She passes herself off as a stone sculpture for the unveiling until a dog—one of the many animals that loved Lucy—licks her face.

The following season, the Ricardos and the Mertzes made only five one-hour comedy programs, each of which featured guest stars. The first, co-starring Ann Sothern (playing her Susie character) and Cesar Romero, was the story of how Lucy met Ricky Ricardo, and convinced Rudy Vallee to give him a job with his band. Desi got so caught up in the plot that he let it run to seventy-five minutes, and then convinced U.S. Steel to shorten its program, which followed, so the entire episode could be aired. The Lucy-Desi special ran on Wednesday, November 6, 1957, and helped propel *The U.S. Steel Hour* to its highest rating ever.

Instead of lightening their workload, doing the five one-hour shows that season required as much time and effort as a year of half-hour episodes had. Of these, the one that stood out in the minds of all concerned was the program that co-starred Tallulah Bankhead. Lucy had ardently wanted to hire Bette Davis for "The Celebrity Next Door," but Bette hurt herself in a fall, and they got Tallulah, an outrageous personality who made a trademark of her fondness for booze, sex, and self-indulgence. Lucy had mimicked her theatricality and the affectation of her cigarette holder in an early *I Love Lucy* episode, but she was less taken with Bankhead when she showed up at Desilu in person.

Tallulah rehearsed in a haze of alcohol and had not bothered to learn her lines. The cast coped with these liabilities, however, until one climactic incident at a meeting in Desi's office. Exact details of how it came about are remembered differently by everyone involved. Either it was evening or afternoon, either Tallulah was excluded from the meeting and crashed it, or she was invited in the glow of good feeling. Either Tallulah was asked to return someone's sweater, or she tried to bestow her beautiful crocheted one on Lucy, who had praised it, when Vivian made the grievous error of admiring her slacks. Whatever incited the incident, they all remember that Tallulah tore off her clothes, and that despite their shock they noted that her crotch hung down toward her knees. Sandrich said that everyone's second reaction was to look at Madelyn to see how she was coping because she was the only woman in the group who had remained ladylike through the years. Madelyn had placed her hands over her eyes.

Satisfied to have them agog, Tallulah sat down cross-legged. She permitted Desi to drape a dressing gown over her and remained on the floor for the evening. Lucy, for whom rehearsals were almost a religious rite, complete with flagellation for all involved, wanted her fired. Bernard Weitzman, Martin Leeds's young protégé who handled business affairs at the studio, had a way of making people see the sweet reason of a situation. He talked Lucy out of her demand by telling her that Tallulah would never return her fee.

"The night of the show will be a disaster!" Lucy predicted as she stormed off, but that evening she and the others uncharacteristically blew their lines while Tallulah, who was interested in acting only with an audience present, was letter perfect. Afterward, Tallulah scoffed at rumors that there had been any unpleasantness with "those wonderful people," although she said she was blinded by hair spray during one rehearsal. She found Lucy "divine" and added: "Desi? He's brilliant! He *has* a temper, however. But that's because he's fat. It worries him." She was apparently still miffed that Desi had been driven to tell her they were paying her good money and that she should do her best.

Given their hectic schedules, the Arnazes developed a striking ability to compartmentalize their lives. Both Lucy and Desi explained their knack of tackling disparate projects simultaneously by saying that they kept different parts of their lives in different mental "drawers" and that they worked on only one drawer at a time. Lucy said she learned this technique from FDR. Desi sometimes said it came from Lincoln, at other times he attributed it to Napoleon, both of whom were his heroes. If Lucy felt some guilt about not opening wider the drawer marked "Motherhood," her excuse was the challenges they faced. At the time of the Tallulah show Desi made a bid to purchase RKO. Lucy and Desi's former professional home had fallen on hard times. Howard Hughes had owned it for a while, then sold it to General Tire & Rubber Company, which had since wearied of losing money. It offered RKO and its properties in Culver City and Hollywood to Desilu for $6.5 million. The company only had $500,000 in available cash but would be able to recoup much of its outlay by renting out RKO facilities to other television production companies. Desi, advised by Leeds, was prepared to pay General Tire just over $6 million.

Lucy had no part in these preliminary negotiations. In the first ten years of their marriage, she connived constantly to help promote Desi's career, but now that he was about to catapult himself to the rank of a Mayer or a Goldwyn, he had an associate tell her they were on the brink of one of the great acquisitions in Hollywood history. It was left to Ed Holly, the company's tall, serious treasurer, who also handled the couple's personal finances, to explain the deal to Lucy, who was the company vice president. She was rehearsing bits of slapstick with Vivian on the set when he asked to see her in her dressing room. "RKO is *for sale*? Can we afford it?" she wondered aloud, and after he explained that Desilu needed more space to produce its shows, she asked only two questions—first, what Desi thought of the deal, and second, if the RKO employees would lose their jobs. When she heard that Desi was in favor of it and that no one would be fired, she said, "Okay, let's do it" and returned to the set without giving any indication that something significant was afoot.

During the intermission of the fateful Tallulah show, filmed September 27, 1957, Desi went to the phone in his office where Ed Holly and Argyle Nelson, the vice president of production at Desilu who had been an RKO executive when Lucille was a contract player, were waiting for him. They were intent and businesslike, a contrast to the appearance of Desi, who was in costume dressed as an English lord, complete with stockings and plumed hat. He made his offer to General Tire of slightly more than $6 million for the property and had his bid accepted. Fully aware that they now ran the most powerful film studio in Hollywood, the three men jumped and yelled like victorious Indian braves until Desi had to return to the set. Jay Sandrich was standing by Lucy when Desi came up to tell her they owned an empire. "Her reaction was pretty much 'What do you need this for?' " he recalled. "I never understood if Lucy was unhappy with the economics of it, or that Desi would be working so hard. I did have the feeling that here was a man who was proud of his accomplishment, and didn't get much satisfaction from it."

After the filming, as Tallulah accepted praise for her flawless comic performance, Lucy and Desi walked off the set—she in a suit of armor, he in lordly raiment—and went to her dressing room, where Argyle Nelson and Ed Holly were waiting with a bottle of iced champagne. Martin Leeds, who was in New York arranging financing, was the only other executive who knew of their coup before General Tire publicly confirmed the sale.

Twenty-five years before Lucille Ball had stepped onto the RKO lot after having just been fired from Columbia. She remained there seven years until she was let go. Now she owned the place. Filling their glasses with champagne, Desi talked about how they could expand their production facilities, but Lucy wanted them to tell her about the studio's inventory, certain props such as the miniature gorilla used to depict King Kong, and the wardrobe department with dresses her old friend Bernard Newman had designed. They owned not only the studio where they met, where a prideful, sometimes unintelligible young Cuban had driven on the lot with the grandiosity of a mogul, but also the old Selznick studios in Culver City where a rain-soaked Lucy did a brandy-filled audition for *Gone with the Wind*.

Like generous fathers, the men promised that Lucy would have any dressing room she wanted. She, who was to Desilu what Rogers and Hepburn had been to RKO, decided the bungalow she would remodel to her own taste was the one that her friend Ginger Rogers had used when *she* was queen of the studio.

15

THE RKO LOT that Lucy returned to in January 1958 was a forlorn warehouse that all but creaked in the occasional breeze blowing down from the Hollywood hills. As she, Desi, and a few of their key executives walked past the mullioned window behind which successive RKO presidents had briefly ruled, past Lela Rogers's old theater, now a storage room, and on toward the soundstages where they had made *Too Many Girls*, she proclaimed the place "dusty, rusty, falling down, creaky." In the wardrobe department, the muslin figures of Ginger Rogers, Katharine Hepburn, and Irene Dunne were lined up on the shelves like the armor of slain warriors. "Let's air out the soundstages and wait for a brighter day," she told them. "I don't need this tour." Then in the prop room, among airplane models, machetes, and crystal chandeliers, she found a green bombé chest and was so taken with it that she had it sent to her house on Roxbury Drive.

Workmen soon painted "Desilu Studios" in huge black letters on the silver water tower where the RKO trademark lightning bolt had

240

been. Wreckers, carpenters, and plasterers enlarged old cubbyhole offices and built a nursery for Madelyn Pugh's baby. She had married Quinn Martin, who had come to Desilu as a sound cutter and eventually became one of its most important producers.

Lucy buzzed around the lot in her own private golf cart with her name emblazoned on its front. She beeped her horn all the way to the chain-link fence that marked the boundary of Paramount Studios, playfully chasing old friends, such as Nat Perrin, into doorways as she went on her way. For herself she redecorated Ginger Rogers's former bungalow in yellow and white, replacing the tub with a shower, and economically painting Ginger's pink tiles white rather than replacing them. She called for a rose trellis and a carriage light installed beside her entrance.

A few doors away, on the second floor of the Administration Building, Desi took over the president's spacious wood-paneled office with its private dining room and small piano. On the wall he hung his family coat of arms and a framed original page of *The New York Herald Tribune* announcing the death of Lincoln. The proximity of their separate headquarters made it somewhat easier for Jay Sandrich when he had to call them to the *I Love Lucy* set, now on the RKO lot. Neither would move until assured the other was in place. "My job was to get them both coming out the door at the same time," Sandrich said. "So you'd say to Desi 'We're ready' and he'd ask, 'Is Lucy there?' I'd say, 'Yes, she's on her way,' knowing that it took Desi ten minutes to get out the door. Then I would rush to Lucy and say 'Desi is leaving his office right now.' That was really the hardest part. Everybody had to be waiting. One time I got them both there at the same time and Vivian had just gone to the ladies' room." Desi exploded, and later said he was sorry, but even after he had decades of successful shows behind him, Sandrich remembered the sting of Desi's anger.

Lucy sometimes apologized for his behavior, just as he did for hers, but those who worked for Desi knew that despite his flashes of anger, they could depend on his good nature. Once when he was getting his hair colored for filming, he told the stylist, Irma Kusely, he did not have time to take his shirt off because he would be called away at any moment. When the phone rang, he jumped for it and splashed himself with black goo. His lucky golf shirt was ruined and he was desolate, so Irma promised to fix it. The stain resisted all soaps and would not be removed, so she decided to have the shirt rewoven, and cut out the spot in preparation.

She was talking to Lucy with the unmended item under her arm when he arrived and asked if she got the stain out. "Sure did, Des," said Irma, holding the shirt up and showing him a hole the size of a silver dollar. "He went into orbit yelling in Spanish and Lucy doubled over laughing. We explained what we were doing and he started laughing too. His anger was very particular. He'd raise Ned with people who made a mistake that could have been avoided. You could come up behind him and ask a question and he'd give you his undivided attention, then go back to yelling at the person he was talking to in the first place. But when Madame had a beef, she carried it," Irma said.

That summer of 1958 Lucy turned forty-seven and tried to make some accommodation to the passing years. She had changed Lucy Ricardo's hairstyle from combed-back curls to a layered artichoke cut during the filming of "Lucy Hunts Uranium" in the desert with Fred MacMurray, but she felt that more than cosmetic alterations were needed for the character. Lucy Ricardo's dizziness felt too silly for her now, although she did not think she looked awkward portraying her. Lucille Ball was starting to feel matronly. Responsibility was no longer an aspect of her personality, it was the center of her being. The word often used about her was "tough," but she thought of herself as a total realist who had less and less time for nonsense. "I always felt she laughed too hard to mean it," said one longtime associate. Lucy herself was without artifice. "She was like a good male companion and she would show up at the studio in nondescript clothes like something you would buy on impulse at a tourist market and throw out as soon as you got home." As an actress she sometimes thought it would be delightful to be another, more stable character for a change, but Lucy Ricardo she remained.

At the time Desilu took over RKO, Lucy's children were six and five years old, each plump with dark, curly hair like their father. Willie Mae Barker, their housemaid, proved to be more loving and effective than the nurses Lucy hired, so Lucy promoted her to nanny. Motherhood was a less engaging state than she had expected it to be. Although adults listened, or pretended to, when Lucy told them how to live their lives, her children were less malleable. Lucy was no gentler with them than she had been with herself. Preoccupied, unable to disengage from the happenings at the studio or what she planned to do the next day, she had little tolerance for their whims, misbehavior, and childish spats. Her son later said, "Even when we were young, my mother was never really able to turn off from whatever it is that drives her in her work. Ever since I can remember, she has talked about 'getting away,' and when she does, she's great—for about three weeks; then she has to get back to work."

Her disembodied voice would often be heard over the intercom demanding "Be quiet!" or "Go to sleep now!" A ruckus would prompt what Desi Jr. called her motto: "The first who gets hurt gets hit." Desi, in contrast, lavished his children with brief but undivided attention, mostly in the mornings before he left for the studio. Spending more time at home, Lucy often ignored their appeals for attention.

When she realized she was being impatient, she felt pangs of guilt. Becoming a parent at forty was difficult, she admitted: "The hardest thing to learn is patience. If you are sharp and speak in anger, it hurts you inside for a long time, although young children soon forgive and forget."

At the studio Lucy's own position was not unlike that of a favored child. She was the focus of attention, self-centered and sometimes egotistical. It was her cute antics that kept them all employed and formed the basis of an entire production company. Once when Desi saw her trip over a length of cable, he grabbed Bob Weiskopf's arm and said, "Amigo, if anything happens to her, we're all in the shrimp business."

Watching their parents' happy adventures on television, Lucie and Desi Jr. knew the playful couple on the screen was quite different from the one they saw at home. Lucy and Ricky took care not to argue in front of their son, but at home in Beverly Hills, Lucy and Desi separately told their children the other parent was to blame for whatever went wrong in the house. Young Desi often heard fighting and the sounds of physical struggle through his bedroom wall, and even when Lucy tried to control her anger, the children knew that an outburst was eventually coming.

On Lucie's birthday, Lucy gave the child a costume party at Del Mar, but the girl thwarted her mother by locking herself in the bathroom and refusing to join the other children or count the candles on her cake. Marcella Rabwin recalled, "I knew then that she was emotionally affected and I think she locked herself in, not out of shyness particularly, but to frustrate the mother who had put a lot of effort into the party. She was always frustrating her mother and vice versa."

In contrast, Lucy loved her son with such uncritical adoration that Marcella considered it her one great weakness. But even in the fierce light of Lucy's attention, Desi Jr. was no mama's boy. He was more likely to go to DeDe or Willie Mae to tie his shoe or bandage his scrapes. "From the time he was a little kid there was always somebody that he loved that took the edge off his need for her," Marcella explained.

Lucy did love children, which was particularly apparent at Desilu picnics when she romped unself-consciously among gangs of her employees' offspring, but she was formidable and could intimidate them as well. Keith Thibodeaux, who played Little Ricky, lived at the Arnaz house during the season and was Desi Jr.'s closest friend. He recalled that the atmosphere was tense and her reactions unpredictable. Tom Schiller, son of the writer Bob Schiller, remembered visiting the set one time when his father was testing a new Polaroid camera. "Lucille said 'Come here, Tommy,' and sat me on her lap. She scared me. She was loud with a deep gravelly voice and orange hair. She smelled of cigarettes and nail polish. I thought of her as a monster."

Bob Schiller recalled her imploring him at the end of one season "Come to lunch! I have nothing to do." Schiller retorted, "Go home and be a mother to your children!" But she had no model of a mother who stayed home and played with her offspring. Lucy's son and daughter would never want for pencils, as she had, nor would they be so eager for discipline that they would equate it with love.

Lucy still loved to give new mothers the benefit of her advice. Soon after Lorenzo Lamas was born to Arlene Dahl and Fernando Lamas,

Lucy showed Arlene how to diaper him. "She had a special way of folding them so that the baby would break open before the pin did," Arlene said. "I knew how to change diapers, but I did it her way while she was there." Lucy scoffed when Arlene confessed she was unhappy about leaving her baby at home while she went off to the studio. "Don't let children own you. Let them cry it out," Lucy advised. "Tell them you will be back and then come back. The children are only testing you."

For advice on how to deal with Desi, Lucy turned to the stars. With Arlene she attended lectures by the astrologer Carroll Richter twice a week. She was a Leo with Capricorn rising; Desi a Pisces with Cancer ascendant. Arlene said, "I would ask about Capricorns, since Fernando was one, and she would ask about Pisces to get an idea of what Desi was experiencing." As redheads married to Latins, the two women developed a bond, particularly when their husbands went on the town together. Lucy coped best when she had a partner in frustration, when infidelity seemed not just her problem but woman's lot. "Lucy and I would sit home and say 'If we find them, here's what we'll do.' They were two naughty boys and we were their mothers."

Lucy did manage to persuade Desi that they needed counseling and interviewed several candidates, believing each would side with her. Dr. Norman Vincent Peale recalled having dinner in California with them and their children. During the meal, the maid came in to tell Lucy that a Catholic priest was on the phone. "Tell him to call back tomorrow," she quipped. "Tonight is Protestant night!" Desi tried to ingratiate himself with Dr. Peale by offering him his own television series. Later, when they consulted Dr. Smiley Blanton, a psychiatrist and associate of Dr. Peale, Desi hired Blanton's wife to adapt her book *The Miracle of Bernadette* for the first *Westinghouse Desilu Playhouse* he was planning.

At some sessions, Lucy and Desi fought fiercely and then turned on the counselor when he tried to intervene. Desi soon quit altogether, but Lucy continued alone until one therapist asked about her childhood. "I had a happy childhood," she raged, and left forever.

Desi turned forty-one in March 1958. His hair was gray, covered by a dark rinse when he went before the cameras, and he was putting on weight. The greatest thing about becoming an executive rather than a bandleader, he said, was that he no longer had to worry about what would happen to him when he was old and fat. Not surprisingly for a man from the tropics who found his way to Hollywood, at the studio he dressed in open-neck sport shirts, chinos, and shoes with thick rubber soles that gave him height. At meetings with bankers or network executives, he sometimes wore business suits and Cuban heels. Usually a Cuban cigarillo was clamped in his mouth, and alcohol hit him quicker and harder than it had in his youth. Even he recognized that his health was breaking down. When he went for a checkup, Marc Rabwin found his colon was full of diverticula and warned that his condition would only grow worse with pressure and stress, but still Desi did not slow down.

Desi had hired able young executives, many from CBS, but he was still involved with producing shows and pilots, with selling them to the networks, and with obtaining financing from bankers. He was executive producer of the *Lucy* shows and, of course, continued to play Ricky Ricardo and warm up the audience before each filming. Desilu production grew to fill thirty-five soundstages and a back lot of forty acres divided among three locations: Desilu on Gower, Desilu at Culver City (both from RKO), and Desilu on Cahuenga (the Motion Picture Center). In the manner it was spread over the city, Desilu proclaimed that television had conquered the movie capital of the world. By the start of Desilu's first full season of owning RKO, its gross production was worth $30 million.

Desilu produced such shows as *The Whirlybirds*, *The Sheriff of Cochise*, and *The Texan* in the open air on its back lots; and others such as *The Ann Sothern Show* indoors on its soundstages. Series that leased space and services from Desilu included *The Millionaire*, *The Lineup* and *The Life and Legend of Wyatt Earp*.

The centerpiece of all this, at least as far as the Arnazes were concerned, was the *Westinghouse Desilu Playhouse*, which presented the one-hour Lucy shows, alternating with three original programs that varied from Westerns to drama to comedy. Westinghouse had dropped its prestigious but low-rated live *Studio One* in favor of a $12 million five-year contract for the Desilu series. Enormous effort went into making the show succeed, particularly as Desi had promised

Westinghouse that its *Playhouse* advertising would double its sales in a year. In a wild moment, he also pledged that Lucy would appear on the show each week. Schiller and Weiskopf helped him ease out of the commitment by suggesting that she simply comment on the show at the end of each broadcast.

Betty Furness, who had become the nationally renowned Westinghouse refrigerator lady, returned to the lot where she and Lucy had been contract players. "Lucy owned it! I cannot tell you what a thrill it was for me. It was 1958, way before women were sticking their chins out," Betty remembered. "When I told her what a kick I got out of it she said, 'Well, you gotta have the right place to work. This way there's nobody to tell you what set you can use and when you can use it.' She showed no signs of being as excited about what had happened to her as I was."

The new commercials for the *Playhouse* called for Lucy and Desi to wander into Betty's kitchen. Both ad agency and sponsor representatives were there for the filming, and Desi let it be known that neither could speak to him directly. "I thought going through an interpreter was such nonsense," Betty Furness said. "Lucy had none of that, but she let him play the boss and she never said boo about it."

The weekend rest his doctor prescribed took the form of Desi's changing his preoccupations from the studio to the creation of a hotel and golf course in the Palm Springs area. Nine months before the RKO takeover, he had opened the Desi Arnaz West Hills Hotel, with forty-two rooms and a restaurant offering his personal recipes, in Indian Wells. He was busy with this venture during the three-day weekends the Arnaz family spent at the seventeenth fairway of the Thunderbird Golf Club in nearby Rancho Mirage. There they built a sleek 1950s house on land Desi won in a poker game. As Thunderbird allowed no Jews or blacks, Desi joked that his hotel was open to Gentiles or Cubans.

Lucy took little pleasure in these developments. She had three homes, but she wanted one in which she could settle. The building fervor Desi had put into the barbecue, bohio (or straw hut), and nursery wing at Chatsworth was now dispersed into working with architects on projects scattered across Southern California that bored him as soon as they were realized. In Palm Springs, she would go to his favorite bar with L. J. Thibodeaux, whose son played Little Ricky, and be there to greet Desi when he walked in with a girl, or she would take Maury Thompson on a wild and fevered ride in a golf cart, aiming for every rut and bump on the way, to confront Desi with his latest playmate on the links.

They were sleeping in separate beds now but remained at their public best at dinner parties and other social occasions. Lucy would start a story, then push back her chair to act it out with gestures. Her food would get cold, while everyone else finished and waited for dessert, but Desi, who had heard the anecdotes before, laughed like the rest of them. Lucy in turn never interrupted him when he claimed center stage.

She was unsympathetic and vituperative, however, when he involved police in his escapades. The Beverly Hills police regularly brought him to the side door of their house on Roxbury Drive and told her they had picked him up before he could get into more serious trouble.

Despite their growing estrangement, Lucy was still pained that no matter what Desi achieved, the public continued to attribute it to her own purported acumen. Even his trusted *Racing Form* betrayed him. In mid-September 1958, when he bought a Thoroughbred racehorse and foal for $31,000 for the Desilu Stables, the paper ran the news with a front-page photo not of him, but of his wife. Privately she described her intense popularity as "what Desi goes through."

To raise revenue for Desi's business and personal expenses, Desilu went public in December 1958 on the American Stock Exchange at $10 a share. Lucy and Desi each retained 25 percent of the stock, with Martin Leeds having the swing vote and shares going to twenty of their key people. Leeds estimated that after paying gambling debts, Desi ended up realizing $70,000 or $80,000, but Lucy took her $2.5 million, paid $600,000 in capital gains taxes, and put the rest into bonds and gilt-edged securities. In contrast to her husband, her gambling was strictly recreational.

By all accounts, Lucy did not know how to really enjoy her money. She was proud of her possessions, but she did not allow herself to freely luxuriate in the best, always keeping an eye on cost. It was as if she jangled her change, not knowing if she should spend it. She would see clothes she liked in newspaper ads for the moderately priced Broadway Department Stores and have them copied by her dressmaker at Desilu. She left it to the dressmaker to decide what kind of material to use, warning only "Just don't spend too much." Lucy valued simplicity, and thrift was an aspect of this. "I dislike anything excessive. It confuses me. It makes for indecision," she said. "I was happier when I had two dresses, both black, and two coats. Now I have more clothes than I can wear and I give them away by the armloads."

When she needed an outfit in a hurry, her first impulse was to seek out a bargain. She was staying at Hampshire House in New York in February 1959 when Bob Fosse invited her to his new show, *Redhead*. She asked Herbert Kenwith to go shopping with her so that she would not have to go out onto the street alone. He recalled, "When we got into a cab and she said 'Gimbel's,' I asked her if she was buying housewares. We went to the store basement, and she picked out a dress with a short skirt and a red rose pattern. She was long-waisted, the dress was short-waisted, so the skirt fell straight from her bustline. When I told her it was terrible, she got defensive and bought it. Fortunately, she didn't stand up in the audience when her presence was announced."

If she thought she could get long use out of something, she would buy the best quality, but more often than not Lucy could be tacky and cheap. There was at her core an ordinariness so profound that it seemed intertwined with her comic gifts. She recognized that Waterford crystal was preferable to jelly jars, and silk to polyester, but the refinements of couture and caviar and fine art were lost on one who knew the feel of grapes crushing beneath her feet, the sliminess of raw eggs slithering down her body, and the power of stopping a show with the absurdity of her delicate tutu bouncing as she walked like a duck.

One of Desi's programs for the 1958–1959 *Playhouse* was a two-part pseudodocumentary on the gangster Al Capone, which ABC then picked up as *The Untouchables* series. Another crime drama set in the Roaring Twenties, *The Lawless Years*, was already airing on

NBC, but *The Untouchables* was a landmark for flagrant sex and mindless violence on television. The series premiered in October 1959 amid furious controversy that propelled it to the top ten in the 1960–1961 season. Desi designed the show so that it would seem to be factual, even to the point of having Walter Winchell narrate it as if reporting actual case files. Each episode was a bloodbath with two or three lurid slayings and an exposé of public corruption, elements that would later be standard in prime-time television. Critics at the time protested the new low in taste, but Desi answered them by saying the show's details were historically accurate and based on the memoirs of the real-life Elliot Ness, who with his "untouchable" agents had been instrumental in stopping Capone in 1931.

Desi, who obtained rights to the book, at first thought of playing Ness himself, then tried for Van Johnson, who asked for too much money. Finally he settled on classically handsome Robert Stack, who stayed cool and even-tempered as he faced a host of intriguing villains portrayed by such talented newcomers as Peter Falk, Robert Duvall, Ed Asner, and Telly Savalas.

Despite Desilu's special relationship with CBS, it had long been eager to sell to other networks and to establish a reputation for drama as well as comedy. Leeds remembered how overjoyed ABC executives were to finally have a show at the top, but *The Untouchables* did put Desi in the line of several crossfires, including a few coming from Lucy. Desi believed that Walter Winchell had public appeal and created *The Walter Winchell Files* for him in the 1957–1958 season. After that flopped, he signed him for *The Untouchables*. Lucy was appalled that he would give work to someone who had almost destroyed her life and her career by associating her with communism. She was also repelled by the violence of the show and was leery of Barbara Nichols, a buxom but talented blonde actress who appeared on it frequently. Bob Schiller had introduced Nichols to the Desilu group by bringing her to a Directors Guild dinner honoring *I Love Lucy*. Lucy had planned to pair Bob with Vivian, who had just divorced Phil Ober, so when Nichols appeared on his arm, both women were disappointed. Nichols paid little attention to Schiller that evening and concentrated her attentions on those who could help her, including Desi and Madelyn's husband, Quinn Martin, who was producing *The Untouchables*.

Desi found more formidable antagonists in Frank Sinatra and the Order of the Sons of Italy, who claimed he was defaming Italians; his high school pal Sonny Capone, who sued him unsuccessfully for $1 million in damages; and J. Edgar Hoover, director of the Federal Bureau of Investigation. Hoover was known to become incensed if he was displeased by a fictional portrayal of the FBI, so Desi sent him scripts and films to review. Hoover responded by stating that Ness had never been one of his agents and told Desi that the Bureau assumed the name FBI only in 1935, and therefore its name should not be used in the series.

As the 1950s ended, Desi was acknowledged as one of the most important executives in the television industry, but he was increasingly difficult to find when he was needed at the studio. He coped with the pressures of producing *I Love Lucy, Westinghouse Desilu Playhouse*, and *The Untouchables* by playing truant, by drinking bouts, and by spending time with starlets and hookers. "Desilu is a family," the writer Bob Weiskopf quipped, "but Daddy's never home." Desi liked to approve each episode of *The Untouchables*, but he would keep those involved with it, such as Dann Cahn and Quinn Martin, waiting for him in the courtyard outside his office until eight at night. "God knows how many drinks he'd had when he finally came back on the lot," Cahn said. "We would follow him in to show the projections and we'd stay till midnight to get it done."

Martin Leeds took care to bring him papers that he needed to sign before 10:00 A.M., when he had his first drink, and executives found it increasingly prudent to make certain that Lucy as vice president was apprised of company matters and approved of them. Lucy knew that in turning to her executives were indicating they that did not entirely trust Desi to do his job. Other than this tacit recognition, she did not acknowledge that her husband's behavior was getting out of control. The farthest she went was to quibble to intimates such as Vivian about the stupid poker moves Desi made when they played with friends. Her brother, Fred, said, "Everyone else had to keep at arm's length—DeDe, Cleo, and me. The only ones who got close were the business managers."

In fact, Lucy involved herself in business details only after executives insisted. As vice president of Desilu, she co-signed checks for amounts she said were too large to pronounce, set standards for the commissary, relocated the shoeshine stand to a shady area of the lot, and organized the company picnics along the lines of good times she remembered at Celeron. One night she invited two Desilu executives and their wives to dinner on Roxbury Drive. After the meal, Lucy said to the women, "Come in for girl talk. The men have to work."

With executives, she exerted her authority obliquely. Bert Granet and Jerry Thorpe, producer and director of the hour-long *Lucy* shows, once brought a rough cut of the show to Rancho Mirage for Lucy and Desi to approve. A projector was set up in their bedroom and Lucy sat in the corner painting her nails at a lamp table, warning her children to sit still so their heads would not blot out the picture, and hushing the yipping poodles (which had succeeded her cocker spaniels) while listening to the men dispute various points of editing. Without looking up from her manicure, Lucy would speak and the arguments would stop, with every man subsequently insisting that she had expressed exactly what he meant.

In her late forties, Lucy was also feeling a need to nurture young performers. Seeking to pass on what she had learned to the new generation, she decided to renovate Lela Rogers's Little Theater and set up a course of instruction. When the executives discovered it would cost $500,000 to refurbish the structure and to pay scale wages for two dozen young performers, they cautioned against it, but Desi told them that Lucy was the mainstay of the company and that it was important to keep her happy. To justify the expenditure to stockholders, they decided to treat "the Workshop" as a training program for a company of available players needed on Desilu shows. From this came Nick Georgiade, who played one of the "untouchables," Roger Perry and Georgine Darcy of *Harrigan and Son,* and Ken Berry, who became a regular on *The Ann Sothern Show* and later starred in *F-Troop.*

Lucy found such students by passing word to agents and by sitting in on acting classes and rehearsals in Los Angeles and New York. She chose twenty-two to put on a drama, but then decided it would be better to do a musical instead. Partly because she selected more men than women, a decision some interpreted as an attempt to keep girls from Desi and others as the self-protection of an aging actress, she discovered she lacked a comedienne. An actress named Mildred Cook was recommended. Lucy tracked her down in Warren, Ohio, where she was doing summer stock. Mildred thought it was a joke when she heard herself paged over the loudspeaker: "Mildred Cook, Lucille Ball is calling from Los Angeles." A hearty young woman from Texas who had already spent several years in New York auditioning in show business and supporting herself as a bra model, Mildred packed her clothes in a box and flew out to California for an audition and overnight stay in Lucy's guest house. "When a maid asked me for the key to my luggage, I said 'Just cut the string with a butcher knife,' " she recalled. With that remark, Lucy decided this was the person she most wanted to help.

Lucy took Mildred out to dinner and suggested she change her name. Mildred agreed. Lucy suggested Carole because Mildred had the same healthy irreverence that Lombard had. Mildred agreed. Lucy scribbled the name with various spellings on the tablecloth and told her the "A-R" combination was lucky. "You didn't do too badly with Lucille Ball," the new Carole Cook pointed out. "I didn't make it big until I became Lucille Arnaz," Lucy replied. Carole was so amazed when Lucy kept laughing and marveling over her cleverness that she exclaimed, "I'm doing smart-assed quips and you're running a studio!"

Lucy was less involved than Cook and the public assumed, but she made little effort to hide her annoyance that Desi was abrogating his business responsibilities and thought she could find a way to remedy the situation. She asked his secretary, Johny Aitchison, to report to her on Desi's whereabouts and was miffed when he declined out of loyalty to his boss. "I admired her and she respected me, but our relationship was never the same after that," Aitchison said. "I was worried about Desi too and told his driver that I didn't want to know what Desi did, but I did want him to phone me and let me know he was all right."

The Arnazes were able to find little joy in the recognition of their peers when the Friars Club honored them in late November 1958. Milton Berle stood before an audience of 1,200 of the leading figures in show business and admonished, "Desi, I never want to see you get a divorce, because Lucy is smart and a good businesswoman, and if you get a divorce, she'll get the studio and the kids and you'll get Olvera Street." Berle referred to the historic Spanish section of Los Angeles, and like him, most speakers addressed their remarks, both complimentary and comic, to Desi, who for once had top billing and was in a position to give them all work. He had been called "Dizzy" and "Daisy" and "D.C." when he arrived in Hollywood, so when the comedian Parkyakarkus acknowledged "Danny" as one of his best friends, Desi fairly barked with laughter, but then the evening turned tragic. Parkyakarkus, who had been in ill health, collapsed, and after doctors who were present desperately tried to start his heart with pen knives and bare electric wire, the comedian died. With Lucy weeping, Desi sadly went to the microphone and asked, "They say the show must go on. Why?" Milton Berle recalled, "It was one of the saddest moments of my life. Lucy and Desi were shining and wonderful, but there was a curse on the evening."

By May 1959, Lucy was under such stress that she allowed her public façade to collapse in Oklahoma City, where she had agreed to appear at a Kiwanis Club youth rally. Discovering that only 2,000 people turned out in a stadium built to accommodate 15,000, she blamed the organizers and left abruptly, generating national headlines that were even more critical than those she experienced during her personal Red Scare.

Possibly on the advice of their marital counselors, Lucy and Desi decided to go on a six-week vacation to Europe, away from the pressures of business, to see if they could revive their marriage. Rather than travel alone together, as Desi wished, Lucy insisted that the children and Cleo and Kenny accompany them. They sailed on the French liner *Liberté* in mid-May, a week after her debacle in Oklahoma, and the crossing was anything but a romantic idyll. Not only did Lucy's left arm swell painfully in reaction to a vaccination, but she managed to break her toe, and Desi kept wandering belowdecks to make friends. Inside their stateroom, the couple fought horribly. "I wish you were dead!" she screamed at him as Desi slumped in a chair, etching in young Lucie's mind the image of her mother standing over her father with long red nails like claws. The press welcomed them both in England, but in France, where *I Love Lucy* had not aired, he was "Mr. Ball." They visited Maurice Chevalier, who had been a guest on their show, at his home outside Paris. The aging entertainer apparently thought their situation hopeless and told Lucy that while the end of a relationship seemed the most painful thing on earth, remaining together after love ended was worse.

The entire journey was a fearful time for the children, who took their father's drinking for ill health and kept crying "Poor Daddy." In Rome Desi Jr. refused to leave the hotel room when they dressed him up to go sightseeing. "I don't want to go outside. It's all ruined," he said. The adults thought his comments hilarious, but the truth was that the Arnaz marriage and family life were wrecked as well.

Lucy knew they had reached an impasse, but she no more wanted her marriage to end than she had ever wanted to change her decor at her beloved Chatsworth. After their trip, she suggested that they take a complete respite from one another, at least for a time. This would take the form of her fulfilling her lifelong dream of doing a Broadway show in New York. At one point she insisted that Desi have no involvement in whatever show she did, but as she had an exclusive contract to work for Desilu, and as neither she nor Desi desired to generate profits for another employer, it was decided Desilu would finance whatever show she decided on. She began to make frequent trips to New York to discuss projects, among which was *Big Blonde*, based on a short story by Dorothy Parker.

Columnists were speculating over their probable breakup. Some accounts said that lawyers were already dividing their assets, others claimed that they could not break up even if they wanted to because their business commitments were indissolubly intertwined. Lucy dismissed all rumors that they were separating. "We've got through that kind of thing before, and we'll get through it again," she told a journalist. "Maybe it's good for some couples to be separated for a time—maybe it can renew and refresh a relationship." But she gravely admitted that a separation could wreck a marriage as well.

Some reporters tried goading her into admitting that the marriage was over. As she was filming "The Ricardos Go to Japan" with Robert Cummings, she gave an interview dressed in her geisha costume. She had just finished a crying jag over her marriage, but when the reporter said the show worked only because of her talent, she exploded. Her eyes blazed teary red against her white makeup as she fixed her gaze on him and snapped: "That's where you're wrong! Desi did three-camera! Desi built this studio! He never got credit for being the greatest straight man in the business!"

The workshop project only added to her frustrations. It emerged less the child of Lucy's maternal creativity than a voodoo doll manifesting the dark wishes and emotional currents of the dying Arnaz marriage. When she had chosen the members of the ensemble, Lucy had promised almost every one of them that they would be showcased. That proved unworkable, and those she reassigned to assist with directing were frustrated. Lucy would also go to dinner with her favorites among the cast, leaving those who remained behind unhappy. The goal of her workshop was to put on a show to be filmed for the *Westinghouse Desilu Playhouse*. Hearing that the production was not going well, Desi stopped by to help. Lucy could not direct an actor without losing her patience, but Desi knew instantly how things could be improved. "You've got to find the groove of a show," he advised. "You don't have the groove yet." Furious that he could solve technical problems that mystified her, she would watch him work, intently concerned above all that he not make a play for any of the young actresses.

On the night of the dress rehearsal for *The Desilu Revue* they discovered their sixty-minute program, with guest stars including Hedda Hopper and Lassie, was six hours long. At midnight, when they were about to begin the second act, Desi came in wrapped in a blanket and carrying a large drink. This time he was in no condition to help. When he started to offer advice from the orchestra pit, Al Kramer, who was directing, told her, "Get rid of the drunk!"

"You can't talk that way about my husband!" she snarled.

"He's drunk!"

"He owns the studio!"

"We'll never finish if we don't get rid of him." She insisted Kramer apologize, but he resigned instead. They then talked it over and Kramer said he had always found Desi agreeable, except for that one occasion, so Lucy persuaded Desi to leave so that they could wrap up undisturbed.

In September 1959 Desi was arrested in Hollywood and briefly jailed for drunkenness. Newspapers did not reveal that he had just left a house of ill repute, but disclosed the charge and the fact that at the station he had insisted that he be allowed to contact J. Edgar Hoover. When Lucy railed that he had disgraced them, he was indignant that she would not stand behind him as he had stood up for her when she was accused of communism.

"Desi tried to destroy her with his outrageous behavior, and her grief and humiliation at the end of her marriage were profound," Marcella Rabwin recalled. Both were mourning, and although when they were away from each other they were tortured by memories of their happier and luckier times, they took care never to reveal their vulnerability to each other. In late October both were in New York, she to discuss preparations for Broadway, he to sail on holiday to Europe on the *Queen Mary* with Jack Aldworth, associate producer of the *Lucy* shows. Aldworth recalled, "As we were leaving I looked over and there was Big Red on the dock. Perhaps she wanted to make sure he got on the boat." When they were at sea, Desi got a ship-to-shore call from New York, possibly a report from a detective he hired, that deeply upset him. "He knew the end of the marriage was coming close. When he came back to the railing, his tears started. He said, 'I'm fine.' That's the only time I ever saw him sentimental."

Their friends generally agree that Lucy finally gave up any hopes of preserving their marriage when she found him in bed with two hookers at home in Beverly Hills around this time, but in hindsight it is difficult to pick one incident as the concluding one in this convulsive marriage. Later Lucy would often say that it was she who insisted on a divorce, but she told several reporters and one writer who spent extensive time with her that, at the very point when she had made up her mind she could no longer stand her marriage, Desi insisted on the final break. This too was his version of the events.

According to his account, late in November 1959, five months after their European trip, they had a vicious argument in his office, possibly over reports that he was asked to leave a Las Vegas hotel after fighting with another patron and charges that he had assaulted an actor on the Desilu lot. Lucy stalked out of his office and stormed down the hall, stopping just short of the staircase at the water fountain where she bent over to take a drink. Desi came up behind her and said, "I want a divorce."

"She looked up at me, [with] those big blue eyes that can express many emotions, the desire to kill not being the least of them," he wrote in his memoirs. Without answering him, she turned her back and left. That night when he came home she asked if he meant what he had said, and when he told her he did, she was enraged. "Why don't you die then? That would be a better solution, better for the children, better for everybody!" She vowed she would take everything he had. "By the time I get through with you," she threatened, "you'll be as broke as when you got here. You goddam spic . . . you . . . you wetback!"

According to his story, he then went to his dressing room to get a small cardboard box where he had written a man's name and New York address, presumably someone Lucy had been seeing. Meanwhile, Lucy reverted to an old ritual dating from their earliest days in Chatsworth. She found the dueling pistol lighter that signaled a call for truce and ran upstairs with it. She found him in his dressing room holding the box and a cigarette. She aimed at his face and pulled the trigger, but this time as he lit his cigarette with the lighter, he held the box up to her eyes so she could read the name he had written on the bottom. He told her not to make threats against him again and left the house.

Desi, who knew they would be dividing their homes in Beverly Hills, Rancho Mirage, and Del Mar, bought a ranch in Corona with forty acres and a Spanish-style hacienda a few days before Christmas. At the suggestion of Martin Leeds, who was concerned that they keep their dignity and protect their image in the divorce proceedings, they employed the lawyers Art Manella and Milton A. (Mickey) Rudin to apportion their assets fairly, and then they braced themselves for the far more painful matter of telling their children.

When Lucy and Desi sat their children down in their Rancho Mirage house and delivered their news, Desi Jr., age seven, begged: "Can't you take it all back?" That night he phoned his friend Keith Thibodeaux long distance to confide that his parents had broken up.

Lucy and the children lived in Beverly Hills while Desi divided his free time between a hotel and his new ranch. The only thing that held the couple together now was the Westinghouse contract, which called for one final Lucy show. In February 1960 their guests for "Lucy Meets the Mustache" were Ernie Kovacs and Edie Adams. The

Arnazes spoke to each other through intermediaries and, for the first time, Lucy was inflexible when Desi made suggestions on her performance. When she saw that something needed to be done, such as adjusting the light on Edie's face in close-ups, she called for it herself, rather than informing Desi as director. "There was no room for adjustment in her attitude," Irma Kusely said. "I knew they were breaking up."

Lucy also kept finding fault with Edie's hairstyle. At first she disliked her blonde pageboy, and then she rejected Edie's curls because she said they made the woman look too much like her. For the actress, it was trial by hair dryer. For Kovacs, the show proved to be an ordeal of repetition. His own genius lay in offbeat manic free association, but Lucy was meticulous, a stickler for the script, which frustrated him. Kovacs, who couldn't stand to do the same thing twice, deferred to her, saying "This lady knows what she is doing," but later asked Desi how he could live with such a bitch.

The premise of the episode is that Kovacs has hired Little Ricky for his television show instead of Ricky Sr., so Lucy tries to make him reconsider, maneuvering her way into his presence by disguising herself as a mustachioed chauffeur. At its conclusion, Ricky tells Lucy, "From now on, you can help me by not trying to help me. But thanks anyway!" Their final kiss at the end of twenty years of love and partnership, failure and vindication, surpassing love and corrosive hate, was their teariest on the set since Lucy had told Ricky they were having a baby. Desi hid his face in her hair, and Lucy shut her eyes tightly. "You're supposed to say 'cut,' " she said as a tear ran down her cheek. Around them those who had been with them since the first show were crying too.

"I know," he said. "Cut, goddam it!"

Lucy and Ricky, with Fred and Ethel at their side, would go on forever enjoying happy endings, but Lucy and Desi were through. On the morning of March 3, 1960, Lucy arrived at the Santa Monica Superior Court wearing a simple black and white tweed suit and carrying a jeweled black umbrella like a walking stick. She clowned for reporters as usual, until someone asked her how she felt. "Not good," she admitted. "How should I feel?" On the stand her composure vanished. Her chin quivered, and she tried to nod in response to questions until Mickey Rudin asked her to reply audibly. Her grounds were mental cruelty, Desi's "Jekyll and Hyde" behavior, and outbursts of temper in front of the children, as evidenced by his irrational reaction after the pipes burst in their Beverly Hills home. Cleo testified on her behalf, and Rudin submitted a sixty-eight-page agreement dividing their property. She kept the houses in Beverly Hills and Rancho Mirage. He got the one in Del Mar and his ranch in Corona. Each received 25 percent, or 282,800 shares, of Desilu stock. They were granted joint custody of the children, and Desi agreed to pay $450 per month in child support.

In 1944 she had been a radiant divorcée when she knew she had already reconciled with Desi, but this time she was devastated. No small part of her sorrow was knowing that she was disappointing those who had watched them so faithfully through the years. The public did indeed react with the devotion she had come to expect. The studio was deluged with 8,000 letters protesting and pleading against this terrible news. Around the country, nuns led Catholic school children in prayer that Lucy and Desi would reunite. Even sophisticated Desilu employees found themselves grieving over news they thought they were prepared for. "It was like your parents getting a divorce," said Madelyn, whose own marriage was ending.

Bob Schiller decided to try to make some sense of it all by asking Lucy one day in her dressing room, "Why do you think he married you? You were six years older." She retorted, "I knew Latins had a mother complex, but I didn't know he hated his mother!"

That levity was a single bright note in a dirge of emotions that provoked a series of fainting spells. Lucy asked friends to talk to Desi and get them back together, but people were afraid to interfere and risk the anger of either. Some avoided them altogether, even when Lucy looked for someone to accompany her to the doctor. At the time Lucy tried to distract herself with preparations for her Broadway debut, she turned up in Del Mar with her children in tow and wailed to friends, "What will I do in New York while you're all working here?"

Her anxiety after the breakup redoubled her long-standing fear of flying. When Lucy traveled with Irma Kusely, she had her move up front from the nonsmoking section to hold her hand during takeoff.

Desi was coping no better than she was and, to his characteristic bravado and drinking, he now added tears. He had been so shattered after they told their children about the divorce that in Palm Springs he had broken down in front of an audience and muttered drunkenly, "I love you, Lucy, don't do this." The actor John Carroll, who with his wife, Lucille, had been the Arnazes' neighbors in Chatsworth, had been with him that weekend, and tried to help him by joining him on stage to sing "Granada."

Once Desi moved out of the Beverly Hills house, he made the Chateau Marmont, a hotel on Sunset Boulevard that catered to celebrities, his home in town. He threw bachelor parties and impressed bellboys as a friendly man and a big tipper. Since he was determined to renew himself, he checked into a hospital for a ten-day rest cure, which included detoxification from alcohol. He emerged looking fit and saying he had given up drinking.

As Desi worked at relaxing, Lucy threw herself into work. While readying herself for her Broadway debut, she made her first movie in five years, *The Facts of Life*, with Bob Hope, which was shot at Desilu. It was a comedy about adultery, one of the sexless sex farces of the period. It was also daring subject matter for these two personalities, as they must have known since each agreed to do the picture only if the other co-starred. When plans were finalized Lucy quipped, "I don't want it to be the 'Road to Infidelity.' "

On the first day of July 1960, filming a scene in which she was supposed to step into a rowboat, Lucy caught her foot and fell nine feet, gashing her leg, smashing her face, and knocking herself unconscious for several minutes. Her first sight when she came to was the anxious Hope peering down at her. In a reference to his television sponsor she said, "I hope the ambulance is a Chrysler."

Desi rushed from his new ranch to be with her at Cedars of Lebanon. When she was released, her eyes black, her face bruised, and her right leg bandaged, he went with her and the children to Del Mar where she could recuperate by the sea. The press duly reported they were back under the same roof, and columnists said that the reconciliation everyone was praying for could be at hand. Walter Winchell, for one, informed readers that he was trying personally to get them to see reason, "to keep two of my best friends from making what would be—in my opinion—a terrible mistake." But the Arnazes were more like stunned survivors cleaning up after a natural disaster than lovers brought to their senses. They knew they could not bring back what they had lost. "I never tried to get over Desi," Lucy said. "There was a period when I was very ashamed. Very embarrassed. Very depressed by what was going on, as any wife would be. But the fact that we remained friends shows I never tried to put him out of my life." Through the publicist Ken Morgan they tried to end public speculation about their reconciliation. They acknowledged that they cared about each other but reaffirmed their plans to live apart.

Around the time she filed for divorce, Lucy decided that the show she would do on Broadway would be *Wildcat* by N. Richard Nash, who had proven his talents with the greatly successful *Rainmaker* a few years before. Nash envisioned his heroine Wildy Jackson, who went wildcatting in the man's world of the Texas oil fields, as a twenty-seven-year-old girl, but Lucy, at forty-nine, saw the role as perfect for herself. She was the biggest star in show business, so Nash and the director, Michael Kidd, who had previously choreographed *Finian's Rainbow*, *Guys and Dolls*, and *Can-Can* on Broadway, thought they could make it work. Nash did feel Lucy had the temperament of *Wildcat*. "She was fresh, wild, took chances with life and was reckless," he said. If it had been a straight play, the difference in ages between her and the rest of the cast would not have been so pronounced, but she was a generation away from them and had never been truly trained as a dancer or singer.

By September 1960, with the Kennedy-Nixon presidential campaign in full swing, Lucy moved to New York City with DeDe and her children and enrolled Lucie and Desi in Catholic schools. At the start of rehearsals, she said she hoped to be on Broadway for five years, and she leased two apartments on a top floor of the Imperial House, a new luxury high-rise on East Sixty-ninth Street. She knocked down the wall between them so she would have a sunny Hollywood-size sixty-by-thirty-foot living room, with views of both the East and Hudson rivers. She filled the place with French Provincial and contemporary furniture upholstered in yellow and white damasks and brocades, and had five vanloads of personal items, including their television sets, moved from Beverly Hills. The key adjustment she made at the Imperial House came after Willie Mae Barker entered the elevator with Lucie and Desi and was told that Negroes had to use the service elevator. When Lucy learned about the incident, she told her landlord, "If they can't ride in the elevator, I won't ride in the elevator," among other choice words. The house rules were changed.

Although John Charles Daly, the television personality and host of *What's My Line*, also lived on the floor, and his father-in-law, Chief Justice Earl Warren of the Supreme Court, was a frequent visitor, for Carlos Davis, a twelve-year-old neighbor, having Lucille Ball living next door was a far greater thrill. He so identified her with Lucy Ricardo that he called DeDe "Mrs. McGillicuddy," for that was Lucy Ricardo's maiden name. "The grandmother was a delight," he recalled. "She clearly loved the kids. Lucille Ball was always very sweet to me, but she did not seem like the happiest person in the world, and when she came home at night her adrenaline was pumping. Of them all, the feistiest was the girl and the most pleasant was the grandmother. Desi Jr. was moody and played his drums a lot."

Desi Jr., who was eight, noticed that Carlos did not have a father around. "I said he had died a few years before. He said he didn't see much of his either. We went ice skating and bowling. Lucille Ball went ice skating too, but as I recall, she went by herself."

To Lucie and Desi, native California children, New York seemed cloudy and dark, a place of perpetual gloom compared to the clear light of their own Beverly Hills. They were beset both by luxury and lack, uncomfortable arriving in school by limousine, but dumbstruck that their recess playground was a blocked-off street. Lucy feared that something would happen to them in Central Park and refused to let them play there, even when an adult was present.

When Lucy took time to consider the challenges facing her in *Wildcat*, she knew she was in trouble. She was not a singer and did not know how to put over a song. This frequent plot device in *I Love Lucy* held no humor for her now. Cy Coleman and his partner, Carolyn Leigh, who had made their reputation with such songs as "Witchcraft," "Firefly," and "The Best Is Yet to Come," were hired to do the music. Both in their twenties, they were intimidated by the responsibility of writing for Lucy and avoided working on what they knew would have to be a big opening song. Coleman remembered that everything he wrote sounded like warmed-over Ethel Merman until Leigh set him free by asking, "If you were doing it for someone *like* Lucille Ball, what would you write?" He came up with "Hey, Look Me Over," but the exacting team initially rejected its drum-banging and repetitions as too simplistic. As it turned out, that song was the one standard to come out of *Wildcat*.

"We finally met her in the publisher's office. What impressed me was that she was more frightened than I was," Coleman recalled. "After we played the score, the publisher asked us to play 'Hey, Look Me Over.' For the first time she lit up. We went to the spinet in the corner and whenever our eyes met they locked in a frightened stare. At the end of it she said, 'Let's not do that again. My eyes hurt.' We became fast friends after that."

As rehearsals for *Wildcat* proceeded, it became apparent that the one thing Lucy could always rely on—her capacity for hard work— was failing her. The tremendous physical energy the musical demanded undermined what strength remained after the traumas of filing for divorce and the injuries sustained in her serious fall, including scars on her face that healed poorly and required special makeup.

She had hoped to expand her talents, renew her zest for performing, and outdistance the pain of her divorce by learning new things on Broadway, but she was coming to understand that she would have to soldier through the show with the same determination she needed to get through the rest of her life. *Wildcat* was on her shoulders. The chorus, all of whom were much younger, had time offstage to get refreshed, but Lucy was the focus of every scene, often strutting and banging a drum as she sang at the top of her voice.

She had been accustomed to filming half-hour episodes in four days. Now she found she had to slave for hours to get the details right for one scene that she might repeat over and over for the months or years the show would run. In black leotards and a long purple sweater that clashed vividly with her orange hair, she rehearsed seven days a week, morning until midnight, sometimes until she fainted away. While singing remained her weak point, she tried to perfect her abilities. Her vocal coach suggested, to Cy Coleman's horror, that she confine herself to one note while the orchestra played the melody. When she did try real singing, Lucy would sometimes pause to ask Coleman what key she was in. "Knowing she wouldn't know the difference, I would say anything," Coleman recalled. Key of A, E, or Q did not matter, it all came out the same.

One story that made the rounds was that on the Sunday morning she went to record the cast album, she walked into the studio in her mink coat and slumped against the wall grumbling "I have all the money in the goddam world and I have to get up at eight A.M. to make an album."

With the demands of her schedule, she was aware that she was neglecting her children. When she went to Philadelphia to try out the show, Lucie and Desi stayed in school in New York and DeDe brought them to see her on weekends. One night when she had a dinner interview there with Don Ross of the *New York Herald Tribune,* she arranged for DeDe and the children to eat at another table where they could all at least see one another. Lucy had always been able to charm journalists, to win them by playing the Lucy they expected to see, but a brittleness was now emerging. Ross found her "hard-boiled" when she arrived at the restaurant before a performance in a black jacket and pants, with her hair in curlers under a light-blue kerchief. After bestowing her mink coat on the waiter for safekeeping, she sat down and complained, "Goddam it. Why don't they make tables so you can put your legs under them?" The vigilant owner immediately produced another chair, and on this she hoisted her black boots and reclined as she talked. "It is difficult to detect any spiritual qualities in the Ball public personality," the reporter wrote. "But when she looks at Lucie and Desi IV and listens to their gabble her hard public face turns almost soft and misty."

Desi Sr. was on hand for the opening in Philadelphia and agreed with critics who found it lacking. The only song he thought memorable was "Hey, Look Me Over," and he advised Kidd to insert it at the opening, the finale, and two times in between. Desi insisted that Wildy should be defined by the rules of conduct that writers had developed for Lucy Ricardo. Just as Lucy was never disreputable, so Wildy, who was avaricious, should be allowed to connive only because she needed to support her crippled younger sister. The star insisted that she hoped to set Lucy Ricardo aside, and Nash pointed out that no line could be changed without his consent, but Lucy finally acquiesced to Desi's suggestion that she give the audience what they wanted and Nash was ignored. She first tested the idea when an actor came onstage wearing a nightgown and Wee Willie cap, the very outfit that guaranteed a laugh for Bill Frawley. Wildy asked him if he ever heard of someone named Fred Mertz, and the house came down. Lucy then decided Desi was right: From now on she would present not what she had hoped to in defining a new character, but what her fans had paid to see.

She also attempted to develop an esprit, a family feeling, with the cast and chorus and lessen their awe of her. She went to their parties and when they got to the Alvin Theater on Broadway she pronounced the dressing rooms awful and suggested they paint them themselves, much as she had Vivian scrubbing toilets as they prepared the first episode of *I Love Lucy*.

At the New York opening on December 16, 1960, she jumped out on stage lanky in blue jeans and a long red fall, and the opening night crowd was ecstatic. She banged her drum, bamboozled her fellow roustabouts, found romance, and struck oil to applause and appreciation. After the finale, as she took her bows, Desi threw a bouquet of orchids at her feet and later hosted a party that Vivian and Milton Berle attended. As guests admired a tiny electrified pump fashioned like an oil derrick that squirted ink from the center of a flower arrangement, reviews came in that were as bad as everyone feared. Critics were respectful of Lucy's beauty and unique comedic accomplishments, but declared she had landed in a show that betrayed her stature by not hanging together very well. The kindest thing they said about *Wildcat* was it was tame.

Shows were sold out nonetheless, for audiences did not care about the quality of the vehicle, so long as they could be in the presence of Lucille Ball. Michael Kidd recalled that the adulation she received was like nothing he had seen before or ever again. "Hundreds of people lined up at the stage door yelling 'We love Lucy!'"

The love of her fans was her only unalloyed pleasure during this period. Often when she left the theater after a performance, rather than duck out to join waiting friends, she worked her way to her limousine through the waiting crowds drawing energy from their enthusiasm. In the confident knowledge that the public was on her side, she told interviewers she knew the show was not as good as it should have been and said she was disappointed not only in the play, but in the choreography. On stage, if she muffed her lines, she would stop the show, say that she had made a mistake, and start over, thus endearing herself to the audience but breaking a cardinal rule of the theater. One day, when an animal defecated in the middle of a performance, she announced that her contract demanded that she clean up the mess, and did so with a broom and dustpan. She salaamed on entering, and mugged, all the things dramatic purists disdained as "crowd pleasing." On some nights she energized the audience before sending them home by strutting and thumping out an especially rousing encore of "Hey, Look Me Over." When Lucie and Desi Jr. came to see *Wildcat*, she called them up to march around on stage with her.

For all her apparently spontaneous theatrics, Lucy was always keenly aware of every facet of the show, particularly after it opened. Kidd remembered her exiting into the wings one night and telling him that one of the performers was wearing pink shoes when she was supposed to wear white. "I told her she was correct, but asked how she saw that. She simply said, 'I saw.'"

Although Lucy referred to herself as a "sad sack" to such friends as Arlene Dahl, she placed great value on still being considered an attractive woman. At parties in New York, she cultivated the male guests. "Wives learned to smile like wallpaper," according to Nash's wife, Kathy, who was present. Arlene introduced her to men she hoped Lucy would like, and Lucy went out on a series of unsatisfactory dates with agents and business executives who all too clearly valued her celebrity more than her self. Another hindrance to her social life was the need to protect her reputation. When she learned that one man who intrigued her was said to have mob connections, she was more interested than ever, according to a friend, but she quickly gave him up rather than court bad publicity.

One night before *Wildcat* opened, she and the agent Danny Welkes were having dinner at Danny's Hideaway, a dimly lit show business hangout. At another table a men's clothier from Miami Beach named Mickey Hayes was buying dinner for a struggling comedian named Gary Morton to thank him for having fixed him up with a pretty girl. On their way out, Welkes introduced them to Lucy. Morton's looks were of the kind Lucy called "ugly/handsome," a composite of broad rugged features that were wrong individually but balanced one another well, leaving an overall impression of bland roughness not unlike that of Al Hall. As Gary leaned over to shake her hand, the end of his silver tie dropped into her coffee cup. Quickly he poured pepper on the stain. "You fool!" Lucy gasped. "My maid says to use salt on spots!" Gary agreeably tossed salt on the pepper and exited.

The next day Lucy phoned Danny to find out where she could buy a silver tie to replace the one Gary had ruined. She obtained his address and had Saks send him three, presumably one for each seasoning plus a spare. Gary then phoned Danny and Mickey and got Lucy's number to thank her, and soon the two were dating regularly.

Except for the disparity of their achievements, the attraction between the two is not hard to understand. Gary was tall, which was one of Lucy's requirements, and he was lively and streetwise, one of the ubiquitous "swingers" in show business in the early 1960s, a breed whose elite was represented by Frank Sinatra's Rat Pack of Kennedy-era fame. Brash, somewhat crass, Gary was born Morton Goldapper in the Bronx a decade after Lucy. He had an awkward stoop, so that his neck never quite touched his collar, and he obviously wore a toupee, but he was so comfortable with himself and so relished the good things that came his way that women found him appealing. He had tried marriage once briefly.

After World War II, around the time he legally changed his name, Gary Morton began to play the trumpet at resort hotels in the Catskills, but when he recognized his ability to break up his fellow musicians with his jokes, he started doubling as a comedian. Partly because more established performers found him amusing and always ready to play golf, he developed a minor but adequate career as an opening act for Al Hirt and Tony Bennett.

Lucy and Gary double-dated with Paula Stewart, who played Lucy's sister in the musical, and her fiancé, the comedian Jack Carter. At the Silver Moon, an unpretentious Italian restaurant on Second

Avenue ten blocks from Lucy's apartment, where the foursome often went for pizza, Gary was anything but fawning. He made a show of looking her over, dismissing her by saying "So you're the big lady?" and calling "Check, please!" Lucy started laughing at this performance, but when she took out her cigarette, expecting a light, Morton ignored her and talked to Paula and Jack as he pointedly took puffs of his own cigarette. Lucy was taken aback and not quite sure if he was teasing her, but punched him as he slighted her. When Gary went on a scheduled road trip to Ohio, he called or wired her every day and kept the romance alive so well that she soon depended on him to phone after every performance of *Wildcat*.

Gary was an effective but intermittent distraction from the stress of the show and her divorce. She also had the comfort of *The Art of Selfishness*, a book by David Seabury first published two decades before. Its basic theory was that if everyone looked after his own needs, no one else would have to, and life would fall into place. Among Seabury's principles was this one on divorce: "One whole and peaceful parent is twenty times as good for a child as two quarrelling persons." On Sundays she turned to a Practical God at Norman Vincent Peale's Marble Collegiate Church on Twenty-ninth Street and Fifth Avenue. While she usually sat with Mrs. Peale under the Tiffany windows, one day she took a place in the congregation, her face covered by a conspicuous veil. Afterward she stopped by Dr. Peale's study where, as the minister recalled, "I said 'Why the getup? Everybody recognized you, including me in the pulpit.' She raised her chin and shook her head and said she wanted to mix with the people."

A few weeks after the show opened, despite having met Gary, Lucy decided that a bad marriage to Desi with all its fighting had more loving than none at all and was ready to call off the divorce. Lucy and Desi had seen each other every night the week the show opened, going to public places but sitting and talking for hours at quiet tables. Much of it was about *Wildcat*, but for the first time in years they had the pleasure of being together on their best behavior while they worked on a common purpose. Desi telephoned her every evening after he returned to California, timing his calls to reach her between the first and second acts. If he was a minute or two later than she expected, she became obviously agitated until the phone rang.

They came close to reconciling, according to friends, around the time of Desi Jr.'s eighth birthday on January 19. Desi was so on her mind that she bought him a vicuña coat so he could keep warm when he came to visit in the New York winters. He did propose again, and her pride demanded that she keep him waiting for an answer. As she contemplated a future with Desi, one night an elderly couple came backstage after the show bearing something they had found in Hawaii they believed must belong to her—a gold chain with a St. Christopher medal and a wedding ring inscribed "To Desi with Love from Lucy." He had lost them following an argument during their vacation in Hawaii the summer after they bought RKO. When the couple left, she held the ring and started weeping. Remembering not the good times she had had with Desi but their argument on the day he lost the ring in the Pacific waves, and all the other fights before and since, she decided they could never be married to each other again and gave his vicuña coat to an actor in the show. Two weeks later she was so debilitated physically and emotionally that she was forced to drop out of *Wildcat* for several weeks. Guided by *The Art of Selfishness*, she now taped a note to herself on her bathroom mirror that read: "Is this good for Lucy?" and used this question to plan her day, to decide whom she saw and what money she spent. She considered that in this manner she was straightening out her life.

Soon she and Gary Morton were considered "an item," and he was referred to as "Lucille Ball's boyfriend" in various columns. She was in the audience when he opened for Johnny Ray in Miami Beach and went up to the Concord Hotel in "the Borscht Belt" of New York's Catskill Mountains to see him on the bill with Tony Bennett, taking her children along. Lucy immediately realized how he could improve his delivery, but for once she checked her bluntness. She held back her comments for weeks, until she finally told him he was talking so fast he was throwing away laughs. He responded by saying that helpful criticism from her was welcome advice from the queen of comedy.

That one of the most respected and richest people in show business would take up with a second banana amazed those who did not know her well. "What are you going around with that kid for?" Bob Hope asked. Had she looked for a man her equal, she would have needed

Hope himself or the head of a major corporation, someone whose life was as driven and demanding as her own. Gary seemed oblivious of the achievements that so impressed everyone else. He claimed that because he so often worked in clubs on Monday nights, he had never seen *I Love Lucy*. He was a philosophical, optimistic Sagittarius, a sign compatible with Lucy's own. His passions were golf, reading, magic tricks, and hi-fi equipment. Also to his credit, as far as Lucy was concerned, he ignored mounting health reports linking smoking to cancer and heart problems. He did not, as others were doing, suggest she give up cigarettes. Gary was, in her view, his own person. She liked him, but she did not love him, and when he suggested two months after they met that they see each other exclusively, she said she was not ready for that serious a commitment. She was, however, ready for everything else. Instead of staying in on matinee day and having a light lunch, she went out between performances; after evening shows she stayed out until three in the morning. *Wildcat* had become but one of her activities, and not the center of her life, as perfecting *I Love Lucy* had been.

As *Wildcat* creaked on, her profligate expenditure of energy undermined her health. She suffered severe bursitis, which affected her so badly one night that the curtain was delayed thirty minutes so a doctor could administer a painkilling shot. Her singing so strained her vocal cords that they developed nodes, whose removal left her voice forever after gravelly and harsh. After being out sick for most of February, Lucy collapsed on stage in late April and fractured the wrist of the actress who broke her fall, leaving her understudy to finish the show. Over the Easter holidays, she took the children to Jamaica. On her return she told the press she hated the place and that the only thing she enjoyed about it was helping a restaurateur close up his bar for the season.

After Lucy returned to *Wildcat* she revived herself between acts by inhaling from an oxygen tank. In early June, just after her divorce became final, she was so debilitated that she weighed only ninety-five pounds. Dr. Sym Newman, who had treated her in her vaudeville days with Desi, insisted that she leave the show. She agreed on the condition that she return in mid-August. She had starred in 171 performances, but the joke was that without her the show was less likely to turn up at the theater than the audience. Since *Wildcat* receipts depended completely on her presence, the show went on hiatus as well, along with the young performers' paychecks, but it never reopened because the musicians' union insisted its members be paid during the layoff. Desilu, which anticipated revenue not only from the show but from a television special based on it, had to refund $165,000 in tickets, an advance greater than the one they had started with before the poor reviews.

Despondent, Lucy felt she had failed them all. Her life, in terms of what mattered most to her, was a disappointment. She did not want to do any more films, and she felt finished with television, where she knew she could never top the success she had had. She felt so keenly the humiliation of her failed marriage, of being the most famous wronged wife in Hollywood, that she never wanted to live there again. New York was not a possibility as she would not contemplate the thought of another Broadway show. "I was giving up," she recalled. "The farthest I got in my thinking was spending all my time with the kids. I enrolled them in schools in Switzerland and planned to move there."

In the summer of 1961, as her fiftieth birthday approached, Lucy returned to Beverly Hills to prepare her houses there and in Rancho Mirage for sale. Gary came along to keep her company as she set about to cash out of her past life and prepare to move to Europe. "I looked at the houses, at all the stuff I had, and to get rid of it just suddenly seemed impossible," she said.

DeDe considered Lucy's notion of abandoning show business and moving to Switzerland as nonsense. She was also unable to appreciate her middle-age daughter's enduring interest in men. DeDe's first husband had left her widowed in her midtwenties with two children to raise, and her second had proven to be weak and ineffective. By her early forties, when Lucy brought her to California, DeDe had finished with romance. She valued her independence, her ability to lead her own life, and her freedom from taking orders from anyone, except on occasion from Lucy. When someone asked why she had never remarried after Ed died, DeDe sat back in her rocker and said tartly, "You couldn't give me a man if his ass was studded with diamonds and you handed me a gouger to get them out."

Knowing Lucy looked to her for guidance and to men for approval, DeDe came up with a solution that would keep her daughter before the cameras and out of trouble: She advised Lucy to settle down with Gary Morton. "My mother was not one to be crazy about anyone who was hanging around me, but one day she said, 'Gary is a nice man and those kids are going to grow up, and you're going to be alone.' That was all I had to hear," Lucy recalled.

Gary agreed to a prenuptial agreement. She joined him in New York in November, the month she had married Desi there. Wearing the same black and white tweed suit she wore the day she divorced Desi, she went with Gary down to New York's cavernous Municipal Building to obtain their marriage license. Lucy toted up the numbers on the document and let out a happy squeal when she realized their sum was her lucky number, 19. As she told a reporter, "There are other things associated with 19, but they're in a past era." Lucy had been married to Desi for nineteen years.

On November 19, 1961, teary-eyed, she wed Gary at the Marble Collegiate Church while a thousand fans pressed against police barricades outside. "I look forward," she told journalists, "to a nice, quiet life." With that, she ended her marriage to Desi Arnaz.

A week later she began rehearsals for a television special, "The Good Years," with Henry Fonda, Mort Sahl, and Margaret Hamilton, and produced by Leland Hayward, who had rejected her when Pandro Berman had tried to get her into the Broadway version of *Stage Door* years before. Set in America before World War I, it had a kaleidoscopic variety format in which Lucy played a suffragette, Carrie Nation, and a woman charged with disorderly conduct in 1912 for doing the Turkey Trot. She was now back at work with enthusiasm, heckling Fonda when he flubbed lines and sticking out her tongue at those she deemed too serious. She was at all times the center of attention, the egotist, show-off, and pleader for attention. She was back to herself.

16

LUCY BEGAN HER NEW LIFE with Gary in the same house on Roxbury Drive that she had fitfully shared with Desi Arnaz. The new Mr. and Mrs. Morton installed a rock-rimmed pool with a sparkling waterfall reminiscent of Chatsworth. Indoors they added a sunny sunken lanai and an upstairs family room. Although they adopted a few of the French Provincial touches that were popular in those early days of the Kennedy administration, Lucy remained most proud of the cozy practicality of her home. The chairs were upholstered in white vinyl, the carpeting throughout was nylon, most tabletops were Formica, and the flowers were usually artificial. Lucy also wanted what she had already seen and liked, rather than the latest style selected by a decorator. When she was taken with the wallpaper on one of Ann Sothern's sets at Desilu, she simply had the French print of citrus fruit installed in her kitchen. She could not entirely reject her old furniture, or even her bathroom fixtures. She had them carted off to a storage facility, where they would remain until the day they might be again needed.

274

When Lucille arrived in Hollywood, the silent film director Ed Sedgwick said she had the potential to be the greatest comedienne in the country. Almost two decades later, she honored him with a birthday party on the *I Love Lucy* set. Sedgwick's wife, Ebba, sits at his side. (Collection of Mercedes L. Manzanares)

Karl "Papa" Freund, who began his career in German silent films, devised the lighting system that made it possible to film *I Love Lucy*. He rehearsed his camera crew of twelve for two days before each show. (Personality Photos)

The *I Love Lucy* gang in the second season. From left: James Nevin, Mercedes Manzanares, Jess Oppenheimer, Vivian Vance, Desi, Bill Frawley, Lucy, Ed Sedgwick, Bill Asher, Kenny Morgan, Cleo Morgan, Hazel Pierce, and Maury Thompson. (Collection of Mercedes L. Manzanares)

Lucy made her art look simple, even in the Hollywood episodes, but the *I Love Lucy* show was a triumph of her carefully rehearsed antics and the innovative technical accomplishments of her crew. (Neal Peters Collection)

Desi helped Lucy clean up after her classic candymaking episode. (Personality Photos)

The mothers of the stars, DeDe Ball and Lolita Arnaz, watched the filming of every *I Love Lucy* episode. (Personality Photos)

I Love Lucy writers Jess Oppenheimer, Bob Weiskopf, Madelyn Pugh Martin Davis, Bob Schiller, and Bob Carroll, Jr. (Collection of Gregg Oppenheimer)

Makeup man Hal King performed the most famous nose job in television history as Jess Oppenheimer and Karl Freund looked on. (Personality Photos)

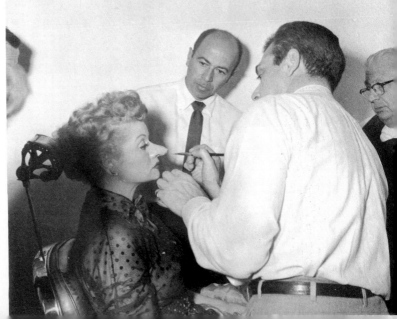

Lucy met the press in the backyard of her home in September 1953 after being cleared of charges that she was a Communist. Desi's secretary Johny Aitchison takes notes behind her. (Archive Photos)

Lucy was twenty years older than the character she played in *Wildcat* and untrained in musical comedy, but she soldiered on with Keith Andes, who played her love interest. (Archive Photos)

Desi threw an opening night party for Lucy's Broadway show, the musical *Wildcat*, despite their divorce. (Neal Peters Collection)

Desi and Lucy tried to convince Desilu stockholders that they remained friends, but she bought him out soon after this annual meeting in August 1962. (Bettmann Archive)

When she applied for a marriage license with Gary Morton, Lucy dressed in the same suit she had worn when she appeared in court to divorce Desi. (Personality Photos)

Lucy's schedule allowed little time for motherhood, but she posed with Lucie and Desi Jr. at her daughter's birthday party in 1962. Desi, who was present, was not part of the family photo. (Bettmann Archive)

Lucy's mistreatment of cast, crew, and other performers on *The Lucy Show* ended her friendship with Herbert Kenwith, who directed it for a time. Lawrence Welk, who guest-starred in one episode, is at right. (Collection of Herbert Kenwith)

Lucy, Gary, and Desi insisted they were comfortable being together.
(Archive Photos)

Backgammon and the friendship of her young fan Michael Stern were two of the
few enjoyments of her last years. (Collection of Michael Stern)

Stung by her poor reviews, Lucy believed that the public did not accept her performance as a bag lady in *Stone Pillow* because seeing her as an old woman reminded them of their own mortality. (Bettmann Archive)

The standing ovation that greeted he and Bob Hope at the Academy Awar in March 1989, a month before her death, reassured Lucy of the public's affection for her. (Personality Photos

Gary expressed himself in the selection of art. Whereas Lucy liked genre scenes along the order of Currier & Ives and Grandma Moses, and had some of the popular Keene paintings of sad-eyed children with sparrow hair, Gary preferred abstracts. The day Martin Leeds acquiesced when Gary insisted he stay longer to meet "my art man from Palm Springs," he thought Gary's selections awful and was on the brink of saying so when Lucy nudged him and murmured, "Leave it alone. Just leave it alone."

However pleased Lucy was with her new husband, she acknowledged to herself and sometimes to others that she was in fact a "career woman"—driven and focused on work—rather than the housewife she sometimes claimed to be. "Luce, for God's sake, lighten up!" Gary would exclaim when she was tense or suddenly turned on someone. Gary was much more easygoing than she, and she felt he was more tolerant of others. He also had sudden comic flights that entertained her. In the middle of an interview with Earl Wilson in Manhattan, he stood up and pretended her back was a piano while singing "Auld Lang Syne." "He's a nut," she explained to Wilson, "so we get along."

She wanted everyone to meet him. She and Desi had seldom been invited out after his drinking worsened, but to her delight, she and Gary were fêted at rounds of parties and quickly became part of the Hollywood social scene. Gary got a kick out of being a curiosity and kidded his wife that he felt like a lamp on display. He bought himself the watches, clothes, and cars he had admired in his less prosperous days and drew attention to his new acquisitions with an unalloyed delight that some found gauche. He showed Herbert Kenwith their redecorated pink and aqua bedroom and the new jeweler's case filled with watches in his dressing room. "I asked him if he sold them," Kenwith remembered. "He said he collected them. It was a measure of his security. He might have had a million dollars' worth of watches in that case." Gary gave Lucy a gold necklace fashioned in a big lion head with a ring of diamonds through its nose. Ostentation had never been her style—when she met Gary her most impressive piece of jewelry was an aquamarine and ruby ring from Desi—but she wore the necklace often. She appreciated that Gary focused on her exclusively. Even his agent, Lloyd Leipzig, found the swinger he had known a changed man. "I marveled over his concern for her. He was completely attentive."

Gary imparted a new style to Lucy's life. Irma Kusely delighted Lucy by observing that she had gone from "olé to oy vay." The housekeeper, Willie Mae Williams (Willie Mae Barker was the nanny), worked to make Gary feel welcome by cooking Jewish food. When the brown and grainy dishes appeared on the table, Lucy asked, "How can you eat that crap? Have some carrots!"

The children, happy to be back home in California and near their father, were polite but not entirely welcoming to Gary, who worked conscientiously to win them over. After weekends with Desi in Corona, where they had horses, they amused themselves on Roxbury Drive by watching their favorite movie over and over on a projector brought from Desilu. It was *The Parent Trap* in which enterprising twins, both played by Hayley Mills, manage to reunite their estranged parents.

Lucy declared herself happy and wanted everyone to know it. Though she did not say so specifically, "everyone" included Desi. She had effectively trumped his adultery by finding another man. Still, she honored her ex-husband's abilities by asking him to direct her guest appearance on Victor Borge's comedy special for *Desilu Playhouse*, filmed in January 1962. Desi was obviously drinking heavily during this period, to the extent that Walter Winchell wrote in his column that the Desilu police force could take care of Fidel Castro with Desi's breath. Yet when Lucy announced a few weeks after her marriage that she was ready to return to a regular television series, she named Desi as her executive producer.

Over the spring of 1962, while plans for her series were worked out, Lucy again teamed up with Bob Hope for the film *Critic's Choice*, based on a play inspired by the lives of the critic Walter Kerr and his wife, the playwright Jean Kerr. During this time Gary was occasionally on the road, fulfilling engagements that often came to him because people wanted to see the man who had married Lucille Ball. Lucy made certain to join him weekends at the Las Vegas Dunes and tried to rearrange the shooting schedule so that she could be with him when he appeared at the Shamrock in Houston.

Warner Brothers, which produced *Critic's Choice*, put its publicity machine into high gear during the making of the film. So many celebrities supposedly wanted to come see Hope and Ball, including Peter and Pat Kennedy Lawford and Lawford's mother, the Duchess of Devonshire, that visiting hours were instituted on the set. Producers gave the president's sister and Walter Winchell bit parts, and when Hope turned fifty-nine in late May, JFK sent him a congratulatory telegram. At the party, Lucy was full of bon mots, probably scripted by press agents: "Bob and I always see eye to eye," she said, "especially at the keyhole of my dressing room." Jack Warner announced that he had known Lucy through five shades of red, a line that Hope appropriated in promoting the movie.

Lucy's great concern centered around her publicity photographs. Her contract called for negatives to be retouched so that facial lines were removed and her cheeks made to look thinner, and for her to review all stills before they were released to the press. Lighting and makeup helped to present her at her most attractive, but she was on the brink of her fifty-first birthday when filming ended. She looked her age, but she went along with one of the plot's creakier devices—that her character was trying to conceive a child and apparently managed to do so.

The film was her fourth with Hope, and because they worked so well together, the public took it for granted that they were personal friends, as were Burns and Benny or Hope and Crosby. Now that Desi would no longer do as her escort, whenever she appeared on television and needed to be paired at the podium with a male star, chiefly at Academy Awards shows, Hope's would be the arm she took. They were the Annette and Frankie of the D-Day generation, and as such they inspired wild cheering. They liked each other enormously and they were delighted with the effect they had together on audiences. "We were friends because we had such success together, and that means a lot," Bob Hope said. "We never had a romance. Nothing after hours. That's how close we were."

As Lucy soldiered through *Critic's Choice*, elements of her new television show began to coalesce. No one involved with the show, including veterans of *I Love Lucy*, expected her to top the success of her first series, which the public still watched in reruns. They simply hoped to achieve some degree of its popularity. It was a given that the audience would accept no substitute for Desi, for Americans were deemed to be as inflexible as the Pope in regard to the indissolubility of this particular marriage. Even though CBS bought the series without asking for a pilot, network executives quietly worried among themselves as to whether Lucy would be accepted on her own. More than any other performer identified with CBS—Red Skelton, Jackie Gleason, or Phil Silvers—Lucille Ball personified the success of the network in entertainment programming. "Everyone said the same phrase 'There will be some loyalty,' " recalled Mike Dann, who was chief of CBS programming at the time, "and they wanted to get Viv and Frawley on with her. We didn't give her her exact time period back. We put her on a half hour earlier."

Desi announced that the new series would be based on Irene Kampen's *Life Without George,* a book about a divorcée's life in the suburbs. But in the afterimage of the audience's collective brain, Lucy would always be Lucy Ricardo, a character no more likely to get a divorce than bare her breasts in Times Square. The only way for her to lose a husband was through death. Thus the main character of what was then called *The Lucille Ball Show* became a scrape-prone widow with a teenage daughter and a seven-year-old son. Because she was on a tight budget, she prudently took in her best friend and her son as boarders. Assuming the name Lucy Carmichael, and sticking to the lucky "A-R" letter combination promised by Carole Lombard's mother, she was to be as jaunty as ever. The first five scripts called for a trampoline, fencing masks, a do-it-yourself plywood kit, a space capsule interior, and a sheep that liked to be sung to.

As co-star, Vivian played the one with the divorce. Tired of being "Ethel" to fans and sick of being typecast as a frump, she became Vivian Bagley, Lucy's contemporary, and dressed in fashionable clothes. In real life, Vivian, like Lucy, had married again. Her husband, John Dodds, was active in publishing and was a decade younger than she. Their home was in Connecticut, but while filming the show, Vivian stayed at Lucy's guest house on Roxbury Drive.

Women without men seemed a dubious notion to the males in the writers' room and executive suite. Lucy and Viv had such a personal bond that some already whispered they might be lesbians, particularly as Viv claimed her husbands had had homosexual pasts. "The

Dyke Show Sans Dicks" was the backstage quip that made the rounds, but probably not in Lucy's hearing.

It was 1962, the year before Betty Friedan energized the woman's movement by publishing *The Feminine Mystique*, and it would be over a decade before television became confident enough to offer the stand-out female buddy comedies *Laverne and Shirley* (Lucy and Ethel as bobby-soxers) and *Kate and Allie* (Lucy and Ethel with raised consciousness). As a major star and media tycoon Lucille Ball herself had too much invested in being the average housewife to want to strike new ground in the depiction of women in television. So, to solve the dilemma of keeping Lucy Carmichael as chaste as the widow Ricardo, while at the same giving her a reassuring interest in men, Dick Martin was hired to play Lucy's friendly neighbor, an airline pilot who traveled too often for serious romance but was often enough on hand to open jars. Don Briggs, a villain in Lucy's 1939 film *Panama Lady*, assumed the role of Viv's beau.

Rehearsals began in July with scripts by Madelyn and the three Bobs. Jess pointed out that he was entitled to a percentage of any show involving the Lucy character, but his arguments were ignored while Desilu commissioned some pilots from him, none of which sold. The only other element of the original *Lucy* missing was Bill Frawley, who had angered Desi by quickly accepting a role as the grandfather on the new television series *My Three Sons* before Desi could tailor a Desilu show to his talents and profit from his popularity. The most notable addition to the ensemble was Gary, who was assigned to do the warm-ups. Some took to calling them "cool-downs" because the audience was so excited at the thought of seeing Lucy in person that they needed to be calmed so they could sit still through her show.

The situation between Gary and Desi was awkward. Gary annoyed Desi, who referred to him as "Barry Norton" when talking to such pals as Schiller and Weiskopf. "Gary was all the things Desi was not. They had different cultures, different styles and approaches. Gary was a buffoon. He could talk about corned beef sandwiches and cars and deals that weren't going to materialize," said Bernard Weitzman, by then a Desilu vice president. In addition, Desi, with alcoholic self-pity, considered Gary to be the man who had usurped his homes and his wife and his children.

Lucy and Desi nevertheless felt it was important to reassure everyone, particularly their children and Desilu stockholders, that they were still good friends. Thus they threw an eleventh birthday party for their daughter, complete with both Lolita and DeDe, who were markedly friendly to each other and everyone else. Lucy and Desi themselves each consistently assured the press that the divorce had only strengthened the bonds of their affection and mutual respect, encouraging the public to view their breakup as just another unlikely jam America's best-loved comedy team had gotten itself into.

In reality, their constant proximity soon proved to be an impossible situation. Desi was drunk most of the time he was on the set of the show. He would slump in a corner, stupefied or sleeping, and Lucy would arrange for a stagehand to trip over his feet to wake him up discreetly. Viv once saw him on a catwalk looking down in tears on the *Lucy* set, lonely and nostalgic. Drinking was also affecting his performance in the executive offices. It was clear that Desilu was in a slide, its magic lost, and Desi could not perform his job. He was usually clear of mind at 9:00 A.M., when he had a drink to brace himself. His vice presidents knew to bring him important matters before 10:30, when he had his first daiquiri. He had tried several times to give up alcohol, but was always defeated by it.

Besides *The Lucy Show* (as the series was renamed a month after its debut), Desilu's only other current production was *The Untouchables*. It had dropped significantly in the ratings, which Desi attributed to toning down its innate violence. In deference to Italians, the show now drew its villains from the Family of Man. Ness battled Dutch Schultz, a Jew, as well as Ma Barker, the WASP, and various Irishmen.

Desilu fell into a deficit after hitting peak sales of $23.4 million in 1960 and was fast approaching the time when it would be the only major television producer operating in the red. In the 1963–1964 season, MCA would have nine and a half hours of prime-time shows, compared to four hours for Screen Gems and only two for Desilu. One galling note was that Quinn Martin, who had produced *The Untouchables,* had left the studio in 1960 when his marriage to Madelyn was ending. He formed QM Productions with backing from ABC and produced *The Fugitive,* the first of his many hit police series, which would include *Cannon, Barnaby Jones,* and *The Streets of San Francisco.*

Desilu's decline was the result not only of Desi's losing his zeal for the business, but of the studio's not keeping pace with a dramatically changing medium. The early 1960s were a time of creative crisis and transition in television. Popular adventure and detective series such as *Combat, 77 Sunset Strip,* and *Hawaiian Eye* were hour-long shows. Since the cost of producing such dramas and buying air time was too great for any one advertiser, they began to co-sponsor. Thus individual advertisers effectively ceded power, and relationships with networks became crucial to studios. Color was being introduced, particularly on NBC, and Desilu and other studios had to begin to make the costly conversion required. Evening network news broadcasts were expanding from fifteen minutes to a half hour in September 1963, but this hardly signaled a quest for quality or profundity. Reaching the greatest number of viewers, not targeting specific age or income groups, was becoming every network's objective. CBS, in particular, believed the way to do this was with such shows as *My Favorite Martian* and *Petticoat Junction.* "Broads, bosoms and fun" was the directive. Newton N. Minow, the chairman of the Federal Communications Commission, made his disapproval known when he decried television as "a vast wasteland."

In situation comedy, the trend was veering toward setting such inane vehicles as *Green Acres* in the sticks, a locale that was not Desilu's forte. It was still the largest TV-producing facility in the world, but it made most of its revenue by renting out its stages. Most successful shows filmed there—such hits as *The Dick Van Dyke Show, Ben Casey, My Three Sons,* and *The Andy Griffith Show*—were made by other companies.

No one knew how to approach Desi about pulling himself together. When Lucy's brother, Fred, told him, "We're concerned that you're not running the studio," Desi retorted, "I'll tell you who's running the studio. You're fired." Finally Ed Holly and other key people advised Lucy to take over Desilu herself by triggering the buy/sell agreement they had signed nine years before.

Holly, who handled Lucy and Desi's personal as well as corporate finances, said, "Desi couldn't fully function. We presented everything to Lucy and she made the decision to offer to buy him out, giving him thirty days to sell or buy her out. It was a very difficult time. She felt uneasy and unsure of her own abilities as businesswoman at first. She depended so much on Mickey Rudin, Art Manella, Argyle Nelson, and myself. Desi wanted to be bought out. I'd sat through sessions with him and his doctors. I was in the position of being Desi's main confidant."

Rudin said, "There came a time in both the personal and professional activities of Lucy and Desi that it made sense for both of them for Desi to end his participation in the affairs of Desilu. That was accomplished without any dispute, acrimony, or bitterness. It was done in a manner which was fair to both of them."

Desi said he wanted out. He acknowledged that if his former wife left Desilu, the company would be crippled. He also said he was tired of the hectic life of a studio executive, which had undermined his health. The company stock was then hovering around $7, down from its high of $20. Lucy bought him out at $10 per share, for a total of $3 million, in early November 1962. After the papers were signed and her check presented, he went to sit in his office one last time, no longer in charge of the company he had built. He surveyed his memorabilia and picked up an octagonal photo holder a few inches high with photos of his children, then departed his office at Desilu forever. It was almost two years before Lucy let anyone else occupy this space.

When Lucille Ball became the first woman to own controlling interest in a major film studio and to be listed as chief officer, she left no doubt that she would leave the running of it to others: "I had been vice president in charge of dusting. Now I get to sweep up." Wearing an aquamarine taffeta housecoat for one of her first interviews as an executive, her clown's hair tucked behind her ears, Lucy was ever the actress. She impersonated herself as president, uttering "Oh!" sagely when informed of developments and "Oh, really," when called upon to be substantive.

However much she delegated, Lucy keenly felt the responsibility of being the one who ultimately had to say yes or no. "I miss someone to rely on to make the big decisions and I miss the hours I used to be able to lock the door and relax. But I don't resent it," she said. "I always felt the responsibility before too, but I never had to do anything about it then. I had been concerned in the past with just my group. Now suddenly my group is the whole place."

She had never had trouble bossing men around, even when she tried to cover her strength with seeming deference, but she was uncomfortable with having men actually report to her. "I could read their minds, unfortunately, wondering 'Who is this female making this decision?' not realizing that maybe I'd consulted six experts first," she said. Gossips speculated that she would install Gary in Desi's old job, but she in fact gave him no role in the company until 1966, when she put him in charge of live television programming at the film studio. However, she did immediately bring back her brother and named him director in charge of real estate investments, chiefly in Arizona. "Lucy made sure I was successful," Fred Ball said. "I worked with her business managers, bought property and developed it. She made money, and I made money too. We discussed that whatever I did was to help my kids."

Aside from having their children with him on weekends, Desi at this time was out of her life. Four months after he left Desilu, and almost two years after his divorce decree, he married Edie Hirsch, an attractive redhead who bore a striking resemblance to Lucy. She and her previous husband, Clement Hirsch, a noted businessman and horsebreeder, had been the Arnazes' neighbors at Del Mar. After Edie's quick Mexican divorce, she and Desi were married in Las Vegas on his forty-sixth birthday with the Rabwins, the Jimmy Durantes, and Van Johnson in attendance. Lucy sent a floral arrangement in the shape of a horseshoe for good luck and seemed too busy with her own life to have many regrets, especially after she learned that Edie had had to drag Desi from the gambling tables on their wedding night.

When Lucy presided over her first annual meeting in August 1963, one hundred stockholders arrived early, many with their children, and lined up for her autograph. She walked into the Desilu Theater in a vivid floral print sheath, read her statement through horn-rimmed spectacles, and could not resist pulling a face when she reported that a rig drilling for some of Los Angeles' ubiquitous oil on the Culver City property had come up dry. She now understood what her executives were talking about when they brought business matters to her attention, but she answered stockholders' anticipated questions from prepared typed notes. At the end of her inaugural meeting, true to form, she compulsively checked the directors' table for stray pencils that she could take home.

She relied on her proven method of compartmentalizing her life. When she was rehearsing, she did not allow herself to think about corporate matters. Her secretary, Wanda Clark, taped reminders of things to be done at home to the steering wheel of her Lincoln Continental ("Pick up bagels for Gary," "Invite Bennys to dinner"), so when she drove off at night, tiny message flags fluttered at her elbow. Still following the principles of *The Art of Selfishness*, Lucy kept a note saying "Be Good to Yourself" affixed to her mirror. Bob Hope, another tycoon, counseled her always to stay on time, because if she was late for one thing, she'd be late for everything that followed. And as she worked on her show, presiding over script conferences as Desi used to do, she found a glass of vodka or scotch helped her to keep herself calm.

She overstepped Jack Donohue, her director, whom she first met when he was a choreographer at MGM. He was tall, good-looking, and had the kind of history Lucy could appreciate. While working as a welder in New York, he got a place in the chorus of *Fifty Million Frenchmen* because he loved to dance. He claimed that it was a night in the dressing room when he jumped up on a chair and said, "What sonofabitch stole my powder puff?" that made him realize he needed a change, and so he went to Hollywood. He and Lucy had the easygoing relationship of old friends, so when she challenged him, he held his ground. "Is there a redheaded woman yelling things against what I said?" he would ask innocently when Lucy forcibly pulled the actors to their marks, demanded more light on her face to fade the deepening lines, or usurped his privilege of yelling "Cut!" Lucy then chuckled subserviently and obeyed him for a time. An unintended parody of their relationship was presented in one particularly successful episode of the show in which he played a symphony conductor driven from his podium by her impossible meddling.

She did not rest secure that anyone, including those she had worked with for years, would do his job. "Pneumonia out here!" she called if she thought she was unlit in a scene. Lou Krugman, who had acted on the *I Love Lucy* show several times, found her greatly changed when he played a mad chemist on *The Lucy Show* early in 1963. "The Lucy I first met was only an actress. Now she would look through the camera and use idiot cards, and it was difficult to do a scene with her when her eyes were looking somewhere else. At one point I hid from her and later I explained I wasn't feeling well. I really wish she and Desi had not gotten the divorce."

Carole Cook, so close a friend that Lucy was matron of honor at her wedding, appeared in many shows. During one rehearsal, attended by a large number of visitors, she made her entrance to hear Lucy bark, "Carole, you lost heart in the middle of that speech. Never do that again!" Carole's eyes welled up with embarrassment at being dressed down in front of strangers, and to cover for it, she threw back her head and retorted with mock defiance, "Someday I'll own all of this!" A few endless seconds passed. "Lucy finally guffawed and then everyone else did too," Carole said. "It could have gone against me as well as for me. I always wanted to ask if she thought of firing me. She'd been a star so long she'd say 'Do this!' Not 'Carole, honey, do this please!' When power and fame come to you," Cook said, "you're no longer sucking up."

Lucy also had to face the problems of aging, both as a woman and as an actress. During *I Love Lucy*, she loved to look outlandish, but now that she was in her early fifties, her signature clown grimaces and eye pops were as rare as her close-ups. The first *Lucy Shows* began with an animation of Viv and Lucy rolling the credits. Later the show opened with a kaleidoscope of Lucy in various disguises ending with her smiling as a serene and befeathered beauty in a heart-shaped frame. She had never seriously considered a face-lift, not only because she feared surgery but because her face healed poorly, as the stitches she required after making *The Facts of Life* proved. Her makeup man, Hal King, who was related to the Max Factor family and a friend from her earliest days in Hollywood, came to the rescue by pulling her facial skin taut with elastic bands and developing a rubbery foundation to erase decades from her increasingly lined countenance.

Between scenes, Lucy might sign contracts, initial labor agreements, or renew a lease to store the railroad train Desilu had acquired as a prop. Sometimes she did these chores in the yellow cocoon of her bungalow with Wanda, Cleo, and Irma in attendance. Then she wanted to play Scrabble or would whip out scratch pads to play word games with people on the set. "Everybody—we're not doing anything. Come here!" she would demand with a glint in her eye. She played Jotto in her head, but others needed paper to keep track. "After a while I refused to play Scrabble with her because when I made a mistake, she would say 'And you're a college graduate!'" Carole Cook remembered.

Vivian was inured to Lucy's excesses, much as Ethel had been to Fred's. Carole recalled, "Viv said to me in front of Lucy, 'Working with her has cost me $100,000 in psychiatric bills.' Lucy thought this was hilarious. The two of them laughed over it. Viv was as bossy as Lucy and DeDe."

DeDe still had her special perch in the grandstand under the control booth on filming nights. She introduced herself to those within earshot as Lucy's mother and was loudly opinionated to those she addressed: "Why do you have your hair that way? It doesn't look as good." "Are you on this show? Thank God!" Carole said, "She was selective about what she said only if she didn't like you."

At around the time Lucy bought Desi out, she also persuaded Gary to give up his career as a comic. He ended on a high note. "Gary managed to put together an act that was funny and he put on a good show at the Copacabana," Jack Carter recalled. "He wanted to show her what he could do and when he did she said, 'Very good, Gary. You're out of the business.'"

The idea of having a husband on the road pleased her no more in this marriage than it had in her first, but now she had the leverage to get what she wanted and no incentive to adjust to behavior she found upsetting. "If he had done something bad, I would have left," Lucy said of Gary years later. After renouncing stand-up comedy, he set about to develop a twelve-acre golf center in the San Fernando Valley and produce offbeat short films. In the second season of *The Lucy Show*, he had a role as Lucy's boyfriend, a golf pro. Always a believer in family, Lucy hired his cousin Sid Gould, a talented comedic character actor, to appear as a waiter and bank teller and any number of stock characters the series called for. Gary's mother, like DeDe, frequently sat in the audience. Understandably, she was amazed to be transported into this new world. One story held that when she learned she was to be Lucille Ball's mother-in-law, she feared she might be the target of kidnapping threats.

Lucy allowed none of the demands placed on her to threaten her being as the collapse of her marriage to Desi had done. Rather than break, she hardened. She became brittle, striking many as a troubled, unhappy woman who could not express emotion. Those who knew her well explained her behavior with one striking image: "She's been forced to put steel around her heart."

As she closed herself off, she began to alienate some of the people she most relied on. Willie Mae Barker had made a wise and loving nanny for Lucie and Desi when they were younger, but she did not know how to manage teenagers growing up in affluent Beverly Hills in the permissive era of the 1960s. Lucy knew it was time for Willie's role to change, but not knowing how to do it tactfully, she decided to drive her off by picking fights. When Herbert Kenwith dropped by Roxbury Drive one day, he and Lucy made pleasantries against a cacophony of breaking dishes, which Lucy seemed not to hear. "Finally she said, 'That's just the kitchen.' I asked her why she wasn't going in to check, but she refused to investigate. Finally Willie walked out. Lucy then followed her and begged her to come back. Willie did, but then she left two days later," he said. "Everyone in that house had to outdo each other and no one ever won." After the air cleared, Lucy and Willie Mae reconciled. When Lucie married, Willie Mae's husband escorted DeDe down the aisle.

Then there was the matter of her writers. Bob Carroll, Jr., and Madelyn called Desi "the Cuban arm" because he knew how to persuade them to rewrite scripts or take on projects that did not interest them. Only later did they realize that his high praise and just appreciation had meant that they had to redo some script from scratch. Lucy, in contrast, treated them as if they were coasting on past efforts rather than struggling to come up with new premises or freshen plots they had used since 1951. In its first season, her show had tied with *Bonanza* for third place in ratings (29.8 share). By early 1964, when Schiller and Weiskopf left to work for Red Skelton, it had dropped to eighth (26.6 share). (Later Schiller and Weiskopf wrote *All in the Family* and *Maude,* the fractious Norman Lear comedies of the 1970s.) A few months later, after Lucy had become particularly angry with them at a story conference, Bob and Madelyn found their belongings boxed up in the hallway and decided they were fired. (They went on to work with Desi on several projects, and in the 1970s did *Alice* starring Linda Lavin, which ran on CBS for eight years.) Milt Josefsberg, who had written for Jack Benny, was named head writer and assembled a team that included Ray Singer, Bob O'Brien, Alan Levitt, Jerry Belson, and Garry Marshall (who later became one of television's most successful producers with *Happy Days, Laverne and Shirley,* and *Mork & Mindy,* among other shows).

Lucy also altered her relationship with Vivian in a way she had not intended. She had come to regard her co-star as a great "show doctor," one who like her had learned from Desi how to add or to subtract from a production to make it work. For her part, Vivian complained about her transcontinental commute and sat out a few episodes while Ann Sothern made guest appearances on the show. Perhaps to compensate in some way for the loss of her faithful writers, Lucy wanted to give Vivian an opportunity to direct, produce, and write for Desilu. In the spring of 1965, she had Bernard Weitzman approach Viv's agent to set up the deal, but after Vivian asked for $500,000 in compensation, Weitzman told Lucy, "Vivian thinks she's you. Either she's your partner or she's out." Lucy decided she had to let Vivian go. "They stayed friends that way," Weitzman said. "We figured that if Lucy could only work with Vivian, how good could she be?" Vivian returned to the show in subsequent seasons as a guest star.

Amid all this change, Lucy clung to Gale Gordon as if to a life raft. He had joined the show after the first season as her comic nemesis, the banker Theodore J. Mooney. Since the days she had hoped to hire him to play Fred Mertz, he had been a featured cast member of *Our Miss Brooks* and *Dennis the Menace,* and had appeared on other shows, including *I Love Lucy.* He excelled in playing blustery, lovably dyspeptic types, but on the set he fit in perfectly with Lucy's way of doing things. "Lucy was the only genius I ever met," he said. "I loved to go to work. We could almost anticipate what the other would do.

With others in the scene there was the tension of not knowing what would happen, but we had a wonderful feeling of relying on each other."

After a few years away from television, Desi, at forty-nine, silver-haired and portly, signed an agreement with CBS to develop shows for the 1967–1968 season. He went back to Desilu and rented the old Selznick studio space at Desilu Culver, but he still seemed to attract trouble. He was in the middle of working on shows that were to star Carol Channing and Rory Calhoun in late August 1966 when he chased some noisy teenage boys away from his beachfront property at Del Mar by firing a gun into the sand at their feet. They called the police, who held Desi a few hours until he was released on bail. Desi claimed he had fired blanks to scare them, but he had emptied the chamber before the police arrived and could not prove it. Lucy tried to help him bolster his story by sending a driver down to Del Mar with a gun loaded with blanks.

Whether Lucy and her ex-husband loved or hated each other at this point is hard to tell. The constant of their relationship was passion, a spectrum of emotions that ran from love to hate, which she expressed in a patronizing pity. "I hope the poor soul gets his life together," she repeatedly told their daughter mournfully. She lamented publicly that Desi threw away everything he had built—"Desi Sr. drank too much, and he couldn't stand success." "Maybe Latins have an instinct for self-destruction"—comments that Desi chose not to respond to lest he risk a public fight.

They did rely on each other for advice, largely because they wanted the other's insight, partly because they liked to trace the edges of their old, triumphant collaboration. Lucy asked Desi's opinion on scripts and writers, and since he found her judgment of people generally sound, if not the way she treated them, he asked what she thought of various performers he might cast in pilots. After Desi sold *The Mothers-in-Law*, a situation comedy written by Madelyn and Bob and starring Eve Arden and Kaye Ballard, to NBC, Lucy took a great interest in Kaye, who was her neighbor in Rancho Mirage. "Before anyone else saw the pilot, even me, she showed it to a group of people at her house, including Milton Berle. I thought it was strange," Kaye Ballard said. "Lucy would try to get me to tell her things about Desi, but I loved Edie too, and I didn't want to tell Lucy what Desi was doing. Edie loved Desi as much as Lucy did, and she suffered as much from him."

Kaye especially remembered enjoying Lucy's parties, where comics such as Burns, Benny, and Hope swapped stories of their early days as Gary chimed in. Lucy seemed amazingly cheap to the open-handed crowd, however, for when the meal was over, the kitchen was closed for the night, prompting Milton Berle to call out, "Hey, rich lady, open the fridge!" For all her wealth, Lucy was amazed by how others in the community spent money. She was as impressed by displays of affluence, by marble and fine leather bindings and antiques with marquetry, as she must have been the night that Harpo took her to Goldwyn's house. She seemed not to consider that those things were as accessible to her as to any other multimillionaire.

Lucy was no more cognizant of her preeminent status in show business than she was of her wealth. Meeting new people who were obviously coming up or someone who just had a hit excited her to the point of wistfulness. "I don't think she knew she was good," said Kaye Ballard. "She was the most famous woman in the world and she wanted to be with whoever at the moment was hot."

She did refuse to be crossed by forces human or bestial. She and Kaye were riding bikes one day when a mad dog, literally foaming at the mouth, ran out of a stand of palm trees and growled menacingly. "You get the hell out of here," Lucy commanded, and frightened the mad dog off. In that moment, Kaye felt she saw the force that made Lucy the Queen of Show Business. But Lucy could also be pensive, especially after a few drinks, which hit her harder as she grew older. While pedaling her bike past the protected walls of Rancho Mirage one day, Lucy suddenly announced, "I'll live two years or twelve." Not for the first time, she spoke with more theatricality than accuracy.

When Lucy took over the studio, in late 1962, the elusive corporate goal had been to produce successful shows again. Don Sharpe attempted to make Desilu a presence in daytime television and developed several pilots, of which *You Don't Say* with Tom Kennedy was the only success. Then, through the Ashley-Famous Agency, Lucy hired Oscar Katz from CBS in the spring of 1964 to be executive vice president, and Herbert F. Solow from NBC daytime programming to assist him. Their task was to get one show on each of the three networks. They sold a pilot for a Western written by Gene Roddenberry titled *April Savage*, but ABC scrapped it before it went on the air. The others were two fantasy shows, each filled with special effects, a tremendous undertaking for an increasingly rundown television studio.

When CBS requested a half-hour adventure show, Solow hired Bruce Geller, a producer of *Rawhide*, to create it. He boiled down an unsold feature script inspired by the popular caper movie *Topkapi* into a half-hour cliffhanger called *Briggs Squad*. After CBS turned it down, Lucy was ready to abandon it, but Weitzman and Solow pressed for Geller's idea. They knew that CBS gave her, as well as other top stars, such as Jackie Gleason and Red Skelton, development funds over and above their salaries, much of which they were free to pocket. Gleason used his to build a lavish home, and Skelton bought the old Chaplin Studios in Hollywood. Lucy could use hers for Desilu. Weitzman said, "We told Lucy that with that $600,000 we could do the pilot, even though CBS says it doesn't want it." Lucy agreed, and they proceeded. CBS told Solow and Katz on a Friday afternoon they would consider it as an hour-long show. By Monday Geller had the second half of the show written. CBS gave the go-ahead, and they shot a pilot at Mount St. Mary's College north of Brentwood and at the Burbank Airport, with CBS sponsorship. Frank Sinatra lent Desilu his private plane for the complicated final scene.

William S. Paley, the chairman of CBS, was taken with *Briggs Squad* and its elaborate plots set in a different locale each week, and later admitted, "I didn't think they would be able to keep up the quality, but we went ahead." Now titled *Mission: Impossible*, the show starred Steven Hill, who was later replaced by Peter Graves. At the insistence of CBS, two guest stars, Martin Landau and Barbara Bain, became regulars. Lucy's funding had made it possible, but she had only one request. She wanted to meet the actress hired for the series. "She didn't want her to read. She just wanted to look at her," Solow recalled. "I don't know if she was concerned that we hired Barbara just because she was married to Marty Landau, but Lucy had her in, saw her, and everything was fine." *Mission: Impossible*, which debuted Saturday, September 17, 1966, was soon the medium's most compelling suspense series. It lasted seven seasons and was revived for two more in the late 1980s.

Lucy took slightly more interest in the other fantasy series Desilu was undertaking. "How are you coming on the one about USO entertainers?" she inquired of Solow when he made his report to the board. He stood in Desi's old dark oak-paneled boardroom temporarily at a loss as to what she meant. "You know," she urged. "*Star Trek.*"

"She mistook UFO for USO. What else would stars have been to her? They had nothing to do with the heavens. Stars to her meant Hollywood," Solow said.

Star Trek was created by Gene Roddenberry, who had written for *Have Gun, Will Travel* and had also created some police dramas. CBS had first option on *Star Trek*, but after interviewing Katz and Roddenberry about it, the network rejected it as a gimmicky concept that was mostly about technology. Meanwhile, CBS went on developing *Lost in Space* about a family adrift in the universe. Katz and Solow next pitched *Star Trek* to NBC, arguing that it had the appeal of various kinds of shows—frontier challenges, the opportunity for big-name guest stars, the magic of time travel and science fiction. When NBC ordered a pilot, Desilu built a papier-mâché planet on its Culver lot and signed Jeffrey Hunter to star.

The quality of the pilot was so high, particularly compared to that of other space shows, that NBC said it could not be considered a typical episode. The network then asked them to try *Star Trek* as an hour-long show. Hunter had other commitments, but a Canadian actor named William Shatner agreed to play Captain James Kirk of the starship *Enterprise*. Rather than waste footage they had already shot, Roddenberry incorporated Hunter's scenes by writing the first episode as a story about Captain Kirk's dealings with a sister ship that met a tragic fate.

Star Trek would have as strange, and ultimately as triumphant, a history as any program in television. It dealt with social issues that were generally avoided as being too controversial for a mass audience. The Cold War was parodied through the maneuvers of the

United Federation, the Romulans, and Klingons. In the Civil Rights era, the show broke racial stereotypes—Asians and blacks were heroes. *Star Trek* nearly established a feminist breakthrough as well. Roddenberry had wanted to put a black woman as second-in-command on the *Enterprise,* but had to settle for her playing the communications officer, Lieutenant Uhura, who shared television's first interracial kiss with Captain Kirk. When the actress who played Uhura, Nichelle Nichols, later considered leaving the show, Martin Luther King, Jr., advised her against it, because her role meant too much to black people. And finally, in a passionate political time, who better than the pointy-eared science officer Mr. Spock, a mixed-race Earthling/Vulcan, to demonstrate the merits of reason? Vulcans had no emotions, and it seemed that Earthmen had nothing else.

Coolly rational in Desilu's own command center, Argyle Nelson and Ed Holly estimated that with their high production values and musical scores, *Star Trek* and *Mission: Impossible* would cost an estimated $225,000 apiece to produce each week. Actual costs were about $180,000, but still short of the weekly revenues of $160,000 per show. Holly was adamantly opposed to them. "I advised Lucy and the board that we'd have to sell the company if we did those pilots. She alone made the decision to go forward with the two series. If it had not been for her, *Mission: Impossible* and certainly *Star Trek* would never have gotten on the air."

Why did she do it? Herb Solow said, "At a board meeting I told her 'If you want Desilu to be a major player in the television business, you've got to do this.' "

Star Trek premiered on September 8, 1966, and ranked fifty-second for the week, an apparent flop just ahead of *Iron Horse.* Those viewers it did have, however, were passionate fans. Because of them, the series managed to stay on the air for three seasons despite continuing lackluster ratings; in syndication, of course, it became a huge success. Six motion pictures were spun off from it, plus *Star Trek: The Next Generation* on television in 1987. So significant a part of the nation's cultural heritage did it become that the Smithsonian Institution honored it with an exhibit in 1992. Lucy was not on hand for the twentieth anniversary celebration in 1986, but Holly recalled Gene

Roddenberry putting his arm around him that evening as if they had been colleagues all along. "Gene," Holly asked him, "who are we kidding?"

Despite her craving for attention, Lucy did not accept accolades she did not feel she deserved. When she discussed being an executive, she talked about how she hated it and how credit should go to others; she never touted what Desilu accomplished under her presidency after Desi left. Part of her humility was admirable—she had little to do with the creation of the shows, and she knew it. Some of it might have been her finely tuned public relations sense that lovable women did not run studios. Solow was pleased that she immediately approved, without asking to see it, when he told her he had had a new Desilu logo designed. He left her office feeling she had trusted him with the image of the studio, but as soon as he was out the door, she turned to the writer Bob O'Brien and asked, "Bobby, what the hell is a logo?"

She was stung when a stockholder questioned whether as an executive she was worth her salary, which she seemed not to know. She liked the prerogatives of stardom (never, never was she to smell fresh paint on her set), but she had no interests in the perquisites of corporate power. Even as president and majority stockholder, she was scrupulous about expenses unless someone else was paying for them. In Atlanta with Irma doing a guest appearance, she ordered a large tray of caviar and exhorted, "Eat up! It's not on Desilu!"

The business details she related to best were basically domestic. When she learned that Desilu maintained an account at a filling station on Cahuenga Boulevard to buy gas for its vehicles and productions, her immediate concern was to know who got the Blue Chip trading stamps. With such stamps she had obtained a small clock that she displayed in her home; supposedly, she wanted Desilu's supply for her own use.

Lucy was never comfortable with the new executives hired after Desi left, and she did not know how to cope with them or her disappointment that more shows did not get on the air. Oscar Katz, who was more experienced in broadcasting than in production, left Desilu after two years. Solow, at Mickey Rudin's insistence, succeeded him as production head. She did not like Herb, a peppy Dartmouth man in his thirties who identified more with the actors than with management. He was rambunctious and creative and talked back to her. She would have fired him if Rudin and Weitzman had not pressured her to let him stay. Lucy liked to let a man feel he was in charge, while at the same time intending that he do exactly what she wanted him to do. This ploy did not work with Solow. "Herb, this is the actress on Stage 12. You never come see me," she would trill into the phone to summon him. They regularly met on Fridays, the day after her show was filmed, in Desi's old office, which she occupied one day a week to handle corporate matters. Rather than sit in Desi's old chair, she leaned against the desk dramatically like a lady executive in an old RKO movie. Her stage makeup was washed away and the tapes that lifted her face were removed, leaving sagging skin lit by firecracker hair under a flower-dotted orange kerchief. She was clearly a tired fifty-four-year-old woman, less well preserved than some of her Jamestown pals. "She would hardly be recognizable," Solow said, remembering those meetings, "but she would be acting like Lucy Ricardo as an executive. I'd say 'Don't do Lucy!' She was happiest on her set, and the nicest she ever was to me was when she wanted me to see her on Stage 12 as the star of her show."

In the third year of her marriage, she asked Herb to involve Gary more actively in studio matters. "I refused. She yelled 'You think my husband is a shit!' I told her that she owned the studio and that I worked for her, but either I did my job my way or I would go," he said.

Solow was entitled contractually to be credited as executive producer of all Desilu programming, but his name was never listed on her show. Instead, Lucy named Gary executive producer and took the higher title executive in charge of production for herself, without informing Solow. "Lucy was afraid to tell me and I heard about it in a roundabout way. To her surprise, I told her that since I had nothing to do with her show, she might as well give it to Gary."

Gary did not have many supporters on the Desilu lot. Mary Jane Croft, a regular on *The Lucy Show*, said, "We used to ask each other why she hadn't married a wealthy businessman who could have taken care of her. But she'd already been married to a hard worker. Gary made her laugh and he was taller. In a strange way she was very insecure. Maybe she thought she couldn't measure up to someone else intellectually."

Gary was cheap. Whereas Desi had given everyone on the crew a bottle of liquor each Christmas, Gary rolled in a keg of beer. Maury Thompson said, "Everybody walked out when Gary said, 'Who wants beer?' but Lucy said, 'I'll have some!' She never drank beer."

Gary himself managed to earn top dollar. He went to Bernard Weitzman and told him that Lucy said he could get a $10,000 weekly raise. "There was nothing we could do," Solow said. "She wouldn't tell us. *He* would tell us and we had to work the budget out."

Perhaps because she knew people compared him unfavorably to Desi, she built Gary up by tearing Desi down: "Desi enjoyed building houses. I prefer living in homes. Gary has made this a home for the first time." Gary was, in fact, held in as low esteem as Desi had been when she married him, and Lucy was a master at defending her husbands. "I didn't want Gary to have to go through what Desi went through," she said. She relied on his ability to ignore others' opinions and expected him to learn enough of the business so that she could find him a role. "I'm all for nepotism," she acknowledged. "I've had my kids and both husbands and a brother-in-law, sister, brother, and everybody working for me when they could cut the mustard, but they had to cut the mustard first."

After the 1966–1967 season, Desilu programs, chiefly *Mission: Impossible, Star Trek*, and her own *Lucy Show*, were nominated for fourteen Emmys, and both *Mission: Impossible* and *Star Trek* were in contention for the prestigious Outstanding Dramatic Series honor. On June 4, 1967, the night of the awards, Lucy was named Best Comedy Actress, her first Emmy since 1953. She was truly thrilled, and broke down in tears as she gave her thanks, saying she thought the only reason she got the first one was that she had had a baby.

Mission won awards for best dramatic series, actress, writing, and sound and film editing. Lucy made no effort to congratulate Herb Solow or any of the other Desilu winners. "We went to my house in Brentwood and celebrated all night, but we never heard a word from Lucy," he said. "We brought life to a dying studio and never heard a word." Maury Thompson, who directed *The Lucy Show*, had also been nominated, but lost. Not knowing what to say, Lucy said nothing, possibly because she had recently fired him.

Solow's team of writers and performers had great esprit among themselves, much as the *I Love Lucy* gang had once had. They often threw parties, but Lucy never put in an appearance, except through the magic of their gag films in which they spliced in clips from her show. She paid attention to *Star Trek* only when she heard that at Gene Roddenberry's birthday party, a nude woman jumped out of a cake. She was incensed and insisted that such vulgarity should never happen at her studio again.

As an executive, she was reluctant to exert her clout with CBS. For the 1967–1968 season, Solow gave Geller a second show, although Lucy was now expressing misgivings about him. She had learned that his father was Abraham Geller, a New York Supreme Court judge who had presided over a trial that awarded $3.5 million to John Henry Faulk, a radio personality who had been blacklisted and discharged from CBS in 1956. Having herself survived HUAC innuendo had not made Lucy brave but rather unwilling to court any more problems. At one of their weekly meetings, she warned Solow that Geller's background might cause the studio problems. Solow ignored her concerns and assigned him to develop an idea by Richard Levinson and William Link that was the genesis of *Mannix*, a detective show starring Mike Connors.

Bernard Weitzman recalled: "CBS was on the border deciding whether to do *Mannix* or one other show. I told her to tell CBS she would be unhappy if our show didn't get on their schedule. She said, 'I can't do that!' I insisted, 'You're the president!,' so she phoned and told someone there, "I love *Mannix*. We've done all we can to make it great.' " CBS took it, and *Mannix* was on the air for eight years.

In 1967 the network took pains to keep Lucy happy, in part because her show was always in the top ten and also because of her enduring personal popularity. Lucy Carmichael, however, was not a very satisfying character. Whereas Lucy Ricardo typically had to cope with a single situation that escalated out of control—charged with bringing a trophy down to Ricky's club, for example, she finds herself careening blindly through the New York subway system with her head stuck in the cup—Lucy Carmichael, after the first season, was just stupidly incompetent. Appointed chief of an all-woman fire department, she loses her keys, gets stuck in a zipper, and delays her fellow firefighters because she forgets she is responsible for driving the truck—familiar gags that amuse only if no one minds that somewhere something's burning.

Whereas Lucy Ricardo always lost herself in the moment—rolling over like a show dog, burping a cheese she disguises as a baby to get past customs—Lucy Carmichael fairly preened when her moment came, all too aware that she had what the audience wanted and was about to give it to them. She was right, for despite its failings, the show was in the top ten. Lucille Ball was betraying her talents and artistic integrity yet still succeeding because the audience loved her so.

To be able to spend more time with Lucie and Desi Jr., she gave them bit parts on the series, usually as extras in crowds of children. They so enjoyed performing that Lucy had turned the garage on Roxbury Drive into a little theater with a platform stage and single light bulb so they could put on plays for the neighbors, who included Sammy Davis, Jr., Jack Benny, and Jimmy Stewart.

When they did appear on the set, Lucy was satisfied that she could teach them and assess their abilities. As a mother, Lucy was more in the mold of the taskmaster Grandma Peterson than she would have liked to believe. Both her children would remember America's funniest woman as a basically serious person and would be unable to recall a time when she simply played with them.

On the set Lucie seemed quite at home, though she was obviously too young for her part as best friend to Lucy's poised and beautiful television daughter Candy Moore. Yet, despite the fact that chubby Desi Jr. was self-conscious and aware of the camera, Lucy felt that her son would be the one to ultimately make it in show business. He spent his spare time at the studio banging his drums to the distraction of the adults, and just before his twelfth birthday, in December 1964, he and his friends Dean Martin, Jr., and Billy Hinsche formed the group Dino, Desi, and Billy and started playing professional engagements. Desi, the youngest, was the most naïve. Once, when the others heard their cue to go on stage, he was at a candy machine trying to buy a snack. As his baby fat began to melt away, he started to get into trouble. Desi Sr. at first took some pride in his son's rambunctiousness, but he also worried. One afternoon he asked Irma to bring him the bottle of Coca-Cola the boy was drinking. "Desi tasted it and went into orbit. It must have had liquor in it. He could see what Desi was up to and probably felt it was his influence," she said. Lucy either did not notice or dismissed her son's drinking as a show-off stunt, a simple childish experiment that would pass.

The summer he was thirteen, Desi Jr. went on the road with his band playing their hit "I'm a Fool." Lucy was thrilled that he was having such early success as a performer, a life she could only aspire to at his age. She ignored the warnings friends gave her about allowing the boy to tour. "That was the only argument I ever had with her," Marcella Rabwin said. "Desi Sr. was on my side. I spent hours pleading with her. She said she trusted her son and he knew how to handle himself and she said that he would be supervised. Desi Jr. was a thirteen-year-old exposed to an adult world of dope and sex and all the things that go along with being on the road. He came back a different person."

When Lucy realized her son was often drunk or high, she had someone stay with him at all times, often locked in the pool house so he could not get drugs, but the boy managed to obtain them anyway. Marcella said, "You can imagine her heartache. She adored this boy so much, he was her weak spot. He could not have loved his mother very much and hurt her the way he did." Desi Jr. was supposed to be in the bleachers on show nights, and she checked for him when she was introduced. "Let me know when little Desi gets here. I'm kinda worried," she told the audience, her hands in her dressing gown. They laughed sympathetically at the typical mother's predicament.

Lucy sometimes privately blamed herself for her son's addictions, but she publicly complained that her son was trying to be like his father and she inveighed against his schools: the nuns had spoiled Desi Jr. in kindergarten, then the military school she had enrolled him in had allowed thirteen-year-old "generals" to bully him, so she pulled him out. When he came home tired and hungry from Beverly Hills High, she declared his fatigue was the reason his grades were bad.

Through it all, Lucy remained herself. After Hedda Hopper died, Gary bought the Silver Cloud Rolls-Royce from the columnist's estate and persuaded Lucy to give up her Lincoln. Usually she and Gary drove to Desilu in their separate Rollses, but one day she had her driver pick her up at the studio, then took the wheel herself and sped at sixty miles per hour through a residential neighborhood. Noticing the chauffeur check the odometer, she warned, "Don't ever let me catch you driving like this!"

She was heartsick when Jack Carter and his wife decided to divorce and was determined to see them reconcile. "I was sitting by the pool one day and there she was. She had driven from the studio in her Rolls. I was touched that she took time for my personal problems," Carter said. In equal measure he was incensed when she testified against him in a custody hearing and warned his fiancée against marrying him.

By the end of 1966, after *Star Trek* and *Mission: Impossible* debuted, Desilu Productions was very much back in the production business, humming with Vulcans, Klingons, and the Impossible Missions Force as well as with such tenants as Batman and Lassie. Longtime members of the Desilu family were professionally revitalized, while those new to the lot rejoiced in being part of something successful *(Mission)* or at least unique *(Star Trek)*.

Enthusiasm ran from the entrance at Gower all the way to the chain-link fence that marked the boundary with Paramount Studios. There, figuratively and literally, a forty-year-old dynamo named Charles G. Bluhdorn was spending an increasing amount of time staring over the fence. Bluhdorn was a Viennese-born college dropout who started his career with a small auto parts company in Grand Rapids. Then, in 1958, at the time Desi was putting his stamp on the old RKO facilities, Bluhdorn combined his plant with a similar operation in Houston and began acquiring diverse businesses ranging from manufacturers of airplane parts to life-saving equipment. He had turned Gulf + Western Industries into a $650 million operation by August 1966, when he added Paramount Pictures to his acquisitions. In those go-go years of conglomeration, it seemed he might as well acquire Desilu too.

Bluhdorn made an initial approach, and Ed Holly and Mickey Rudin approved of the idea. They knew the stumbling block would be Lucy. "She had no choice about selling Desilu," Ed Holly explained. "We'd undertaken operations beyond our ability. It was a question of liquidity, a real desire to be free from that responsibility."

Mickey Rudin said, "There came a time when Lucy's advisers, which included Art Manella and myself, advised her that it would be in her best interests to diversify her financial holdings. It was also a time when it was difficult for an independent producer of television product to make an immediate profit. It was difficult for Lucy to accept that advice, but she did. She did not think of Desilu on the basis of profit or loss—she thought of it as a family enterprise and was reluctant to sell."

She was so hesitant that on a late February day in 1967, twenty-four hours before she was to sign the papers that would put the matter to a stockholder vote, she tried to avoid the entire issue. She flew to Miami, explaining that she had to talk to Jackie Gleason about the possibility of their doing a movie together. Rudin phoned her repeatedly at her hotel, but she would not take his calls, so he followed her to Florida to encourage her. "I haven't even seen this man!" she protested, referring to Bluhdorn. She said that she wanted to look him in the eyes and shake his hand before she entrusted him with her studio, but Rudin persuaded her to settle for a phone call. Bluhdorn took care to win her over with charm by saying in his Viennese accent, "Miss Ball, one of the things I am prepared to like about you is that you care." She wept into the phone and agreed to sell.

The money Gulf + Western paid for the company—$17 million to Desilu stockholders, of which Lucy as majority stockholder received $10 million—was specified in the contract, but she seemed to think that under the deal Desilu would become a subsidiary of Gulf + Western, preserving what she and Desi had built, including the jobs of their employees. The Agreement and Plan of Reorganization stipulated that Desilu would transfer all its assets, properties, and goodwill to a newly created wholly owned entity ("Desilu Subsidiary"), and that the subsidiary would take on a name acceptable to Gulf +

Western. Indeed, after agreement of the sale was announced, *The New York Times* reported, "Mr. Bluhdorn said Desilu Productions would continue as a separate corporate entity and Miss Ball would remain as president of the subsidiary."

Desi too took it for granted that Lucy would still be in charge. Ten days after the proposed sale was revealed to stockholders, Desi announced he was renting space at Desilu Culver to film *The Mothers-in-Law*. He said of his leasing arrangements, "I might as well give the money to Mama."

Lucy sent a simple memo to the staff to announce the sale. Bernard Weitzman and Herb Solow, among others, picked up their interoffice mail to learn they were now working for a man who had started out in auto parts. "I was a little hurt by the way she did it, but I wasn't surprised when she sold Desilu," said Weitzman. "She didn't enjoy being an executive. She was always afraid the bubble would burst and she would lose everything. Mickey told her she wouldn't have to worry about overhead, keeping people working, all of that."

Despite everyone's hopes for its independence, the "Desilu Subsidiary" was soon folded into Paramount, which did not need two commissaries, two carpentry shops, and two payroll departments. Desilu supervisors were demoted and many jobs were lost. "These people would call Lucy, and she'd call me and yell at me for laying off loyal employees," said Ed Holly. "She hired many of them to work on her own show." When he took a closer look at the business, Bluhdorn also panicked. "He would call in the middle of the night and say, 'Vot have you sold me?' I'd tell him he must be looking at the *Star Trek* and *Mission: Impossible* costs, and say 'Your people saw every figure. They knew what they were doing.' " By 1994, in fact, Desilu properties, which included *The Untouchables* and *Star Trek* with its spin-off feature films, syndication, and merchandising rights, had contributed an estimated $1.5 billion to Paramount's income.

Those who analyzed the sale immediately afterward believed that Lucy would make government-insured investments, which would finally give her a sense of security. Lucy was then earning $350,000 as a performer and $75,000 more as president of Desilu. She could now pay off the $3 million bank loan she had taken out in 1962 to buy out Desi and at last be carefree. But she was forlorn. "I cried. I was sad.

I didn't like the idea of giving up Desilu, but running it didn't interest me. Performing does interest me."

After the sale, which was approved in July 1967, she continued to do her show on Stage 12. When she finally met Bluhdorn in person, she decided she did like him. "He travels fast, talks fast and acts on impulse," she said. "I just hope he stays alive." She was perceptive in that remark, for Bluhdorn would die at the relatively young age of fifty-six.

To handle her projects, Lucy formed Lucille Ball Productions, with Gary as vice president, and was prepared to pay rent on Stage 12 and her bungalow until one day her air conditioner went on the blink and Paramount refused to let her have a new one. She phoned Bernard Weitzman, who had joined Universal after Gulf + Western acquired Desilu. "I just realized I no longer own this," she told him. "I want to be with people like myself."

Universal was run by Lew Wasserman and Jules Stein, who had been wooing her because they thought she could help them develop comedy shows. When told of her distress, Wasserman instructed Weitzman to approach Lucy and Mickey Rudin with a blank check: "They're reputable and won't screw us," Stein said. Rudin advised her not to rush into anything, but to test the relationship by simply renting production space for her show. When she moved to the Universal lot, Stein, one of the most powerful men in the industry, was thrilled finally to have the chance to meet her and told her she could furnish her bungalow with anything she wanted from the Universal warehouse. She and Gary picked out Chippendale antiques. "Deals were not the important thing to her," said Weitzman. "She just cared about the feeling of family. She had to be at home."

17

EACH WEEK, in preparation for *The Lucy Show*, Irma pushed a skull-fracture bandage down over Lucy's head and then tugged it back up to her hairline, lifting the star's sagging face. With a bobby pin she poked through the band, extracted hanks of hennaed hair, and wound them into tight pin curls. Finally she crowned these tormented ringlets with a uniquely orange wig. "When Lucy saw how it pulled her face up she said I added years to her career," Irma recalled. But in the process, Lucy's scalp was scratched and scraped and sometimes oozed with blood. She grew so accustomed to the violence done to her head, and was so inured to throbbing pain, that when Irma accidentally stuck a hat pin straight into her skull she had no sense that anything had gone particularly amiss.

Weekly, Lucy yelled and swore and Irma pulled and pierced in a ritual that had Lucy vowing to do Irma's hair one day. In a scene more appropriate to *The Twilight Zone* than *The Lucy Show*, each was friendly after the wig was finally in position, knowing they would

304

enact the drama over and over again without apparent end in a pyrrhic battle against Time. The many people who criticized Lucy for her treatment of her hairdresser did not know that Irma had exacted a price: "Choose between cigarettes and me." Clouds of nicotine dispersed while the hairdresser did her work. "When I was finished she'd say, 'Get out of here so I can smoke!' " Irma recalled. "The makeup man tried to get me to ask her to not smoke when she was with him too, but I said 'Ask her yourself.' "

After these procedures, Lucy emerged from her dressing room increased in stature and power. More than one associate commented that she had the aura of a giant twelve feet tall. "As she walked on the set you wanted to gasp because it was an entirely different person," said Dorothy Aldworth. "She was formidable. Her eyes were so much bigger, outlined and dark, with a great deal of blue eye shadow. This was Lucille Ball the star."

But the camera was crueler than the eyes of her associates. Years of heavy makeup and California sun, plus the passage of time, had so damaged Lucy's white skin that she now had to be photographed through a special lens with a scrim. Thus she was seldom shown in close-ups with other actors, as the shots would not match those taken without the scrim. In person she looked so different from the woman people knew from television that a little girl who saw her at an airport during this period gasped, "Lucy, what happened to your face?" Lucy was silent and unwilling to speak for the rest of the day.

An even more mortifying reminder of her age occurred at an important Hollywood party when one of the guests stated that it was time to program television for a younger audience. "People like Jack Benny and Lucille Ball should be put away," he said, apparently not recognizing the matronly redhead who had failed to introduce herself. Lucy stepped away and found Gary, who walked over to the group and heard similar statements for himself. Later they found out the speaker was the new network president of CBS.

During the mid-1950s, when she was as popular as Eisenhower and almost as well-known, Lucy was philosophical about the success of *I Love Lucy*. "When you're number one," she often said, "there's only one place you can go." But when *The Lucy Show* actually started to lose some of its audience in the mid-1960s, she anxiously tracked her show as it jagged between the top and bottom of the top ten of the Nielsen ratings. ABC's *That Girl*, starring Marlo Thomas, presented a new female character who was refreshingly contemporary and influenced future programming, but it never finished in the top twenty-five. Lucy's predictable program, however, continued to draw a consistently large audience. Her appeal was such that each spring, when she warned the network she would probably not renew her contract for the following year, executives played the game of wooing her back for yet another season. In January 1968, the year she would turn fifty-seven, her show sank from second place to eighth when she was blindsided by the innovative comedy variety show *Rowan and Martin's Laugh-In*, which NBC scheduled opposite her on Monday nights. *Laugh-In* regularly drew higher ratings and became as much of a national institution as *I Love Lucy* had been, throwing off such catch phrases as "You bet your bippy" and "Look that up in your Funk and Wagnall's!" In that disruptive year of the Tet offensive, Haight-Ashbury love-ins, and political assassinations, even Richard Nixon appeared on the show to exhort "Sock it to me!" Whether anyone took note of the irony that Dick Martin had played her boyfriend on *The Lucy Show* in 1962, the *Laugh-In* cast took to bidding Lucy good night as their sign-off. Pretending she was amused, she sniffed, "You think it's funny, don't you?" when she saw the producer George Schlatter, who had managed Ciro's when Desi appeared there. But she was all too aware that more than simply eclipsing her popularity, *Laugh-In* made her look old hat.

Milt Josefsberg, who had written for Bob Hope and Jack Benny, was then her head writer. Around 1964, *The Lucy Show* began to rely on guest stars, such as Danny Kaye, Ann Sothern, and Arthur Godfrey, to introduce freshness to the formula. The idea of a logical premise for each episode was tossed aside like a superfluous vaudeville pie. In October 1967, when Jack Benny made one of his several appearances, Josefsberg came up with a single gag that cost $25,000, the most expensive in television history to that point. The setup was that to persuade Benny to deposit his money at her bank, Lucy, who was otherwise incompetent, designed a special vault guarded by an electronic eye that triggered a guillotine. Past that, a tribe of Indians, a gorilla, and a stream with piranhas and snapping turtles got into the act, which ended with Lucy and Benny engulfed in a pit of quicksand. The laugh track was cranked up high, but in essence Lucy had surrendered to a strategy she had criticized Marc Daniels for suggesting the first year of *I Love Lucy*—she now did anything for a laugh, whether it made sense or not.

One of the better entries of this era starred Dean Martin. She commissioned the script from Bobby O'Brien, who was especially adept at writing for guest stars and had a knack for getting them all into show business situations, which she loved. The script's premise was that Martin's double asks Lucy for a date, and when he has to work late, Dean Martin himself steps in rather than let her be stood up.

"Lucy worried more than I did," O'Brien said. "She sent the script to Dean and crossed her fingers but said, 'We'll never get him.' " At some point, like Lucy Ricardo, she decided to help things along. Desi Jr. had lost a vicuña coat his father had given him, and Lucy decided he must have left it at Dean Martin's house while visiting Dino Jr. She went over, gained entry, and, forgetting all about the coat, went on a quest for the script to see if he had opened or marked it. "She said she went into the bedrooms and Dean's den, but did not find it, so a few days later she confronted him," O'Brien recalled. According to Lucy, Martin retorted, "My dear, you were in my home. I work at my studio. To learn my lines for my part I take the script to the studio." In that manner, she learned he would go on her show.

Lucy of course worked everywhere. When she phoned Bobby O'-Brien to ask him what changes Martin had requested, he learned she was speaking from a wall phone in the ladies' lounge of Ohrbach's Department Store and was juggling a phone and her purse while holding the script against the wall and marking up the revisions.

When they filmed the episode, which aired on Valentine's Day, 1966, she bossed Martin around just as she did the extras. He had carried a golf club to the set to practice his strokes between scenes, and he was swinging it intently from side to side when O'Brien went over to him. Martin looked up and said, "If she touches me one more time, I'm going home."

That episode remained Lucy's favorite of the series, but she gave her best performance with Robert Stack when she played a gun moll.

In that show, Stack was a law officer out to arrest Bruce Gordon, who had been gangster Frank Nitti to Stack's federal agent Ness in *The Untouchables*. Lucy played her role by impersonating Barbara Nichols—dumb, canny, and oozing comic sex. Freed of the Lucy housewife character, her playfulness seemed genuine. Robert Stack said his experience with her was pleasant because he persuaded her that he knew more about playing the Ness character than she did.

Joan Crawford, in contrast, was undone by working with her. Lucy had found her drinking 100-proof vodka through a straw during rehearsals and threatened to fire her, so Crawford asked Herbert Kenwith to accompany her for moral support. Against his advice, Joan told Lucy that they were old friends. Lucy responded by berating and criticizing her in front of the entire set until Crawford was unable to lift her feet in her Charleston scene and fled to her dressing room, where she stretched out on the floor crying. Herbert called in a makeup woman and helped her compose herself. "My God," Crawford said after her successful performance, "and they say *I'm* a bitch."

Among the loyal people who had worked with Lucy over the years, the Crawford incident stood out as much as Bankhead's appearance had. But while they delighted in telling of Bankhead's peccadillos, when they thought of Crawford, they were embarrassed at the callous insensitivity of the Lucy they had loved so well.

The most publicly famous of her *Lucy* segments was one that featured Richard Burton and Elizabeth Taylor. It was Burton who actually suggested that they work together when he met her one night at a party. "Why have you never had us on your show?" he asked. Lucy knew he was in his cups, but she seized her chance and quickly commissioned a script from Bob and Madelyn, the first they had done for her in six years. The plot they devised was that Burton, while disguised as a plumber to elude fans, is roped into fixing Lucy's sink and hands her Elizabeth Taylor's sixty-nine carat diamond ring, which becomes stuck on Lucy's finger. But Taylor is scheduled to show off the jewel at a press conference, so Lucy hides behind a curtain so she can extend her own hand as if it belonged to the actress, just as in 1952 Lucy Ricardo had stood behind a curtain so Ricky could make a television appearance although he was handcuffed to her.

The Burtons arrived in separate limousines for rehearsals the second Monday of May 1970. The actor, who had been on the wagon for two months, had dropped his weight to a slim 160 pounds and was looking forward to doing the show, despite warnings that Lucy could be "wearing." His wife was not in such fighting trim, having just recovered from a bout with maddening chigger bites and deep cuts suffered when she rode a horse barefoot. She also was facing a hemorrhoid operation the Monday after she finished the show.

Even though she had known Elizabeth at MGM, Lucy was formal and called her Miss Taylor or Mrs. Burton. On the first day, while they were all still friends, Lucy remarked on Richard's loss of weight, prompting Elizabeth to claim that sleeping with him was like snuggling up to Mia Farrow. Thereafter Lucy playfully called him "Mia" when she wasn't addressing him as Mr. Burton or "His Highness."

Lucy was counting on the fact that the Burtons were the ultimate celebrities: At the time only Jacqueline Kennedy Onassis had more power than they to draw an audience. At the end of the 1969–1970 season, *Laugh-In* had been number one for two seasons, and Robert Wood, the network president of CBS, was urging his executives to "get the wrinkles out of the face of the network without eroding our popularity." Lucy, still at heart the girl who climbed back on the horse that fell on her in Jamestown, expected the Burtons to attract a huge audience that would surely beat out her competition.

Lucy knew she had to treat Elizabeth carefully, so aside from telling her that she couldn't act, she focused her attention on Burton, who had a bigger part. In rehearsals Lucy saw that he had the same problem that annoyed her in other guests—he did not speak loudly enough. She also found that he ignored directions, mumbled his lines, threw away laughs, and walked out of camera range. Just before dress rehearsal she could stand it no more. She tapped him on his forehead to summon him to her bungalow. "What is it, love?" he inquired, with apparent good cheer. She told him that by her count he was throwing away eleven laughs. Burton then sat on the floor with the two other actors in his scene and read it her way. He felt as if he were leading an insurrection when he barked each word at her, but Lucy was delighted that the three of them finally had perked up: "That's better, Richard, now I can hear, you're making me laugh."

She had them repeat the scene three times until she was sure they had it and then led them to the set.

But once there Burton did not position himself properly, as he would have to when the show was filmed. "You're off your mark," she complained, while kicking his foot toward the correct spot. Burton exploded. "Lady," he said, "this is not the first show we've done. My wife and I will have coffee and we'll be back." The celebrities kept everyone waiting an hour, which made for an expensive recess. Lucy took the absence calmly, according to witnesses, because she knew she had gone too far. By this time Mrs. Burton was calling her "Miss Cunt."

In his journal, Burton commended Gale Gordon as a brilliant straight man, but he could not figure out why anyone would work as hard as the people on this show did, particularly Lucy, who had been laboring on television for nineteen years. As the time of the performance approached, he complained about the long hours (10 A.M. to 5 P.M.) and scribbled darkly: "I loathe her today but now I also pity her. After tonight I shall make a point of never seeing her again . . . [she] can thank her lucky stars that I am not drinking. There is a chance that I might have killed her."

Although *The Lucy Show* was not the Burtons' first television appearance, it was their first situation comedy. Burton may have thought the part something he could walk through, but nevertheless he was elated when he got a big laugh from the crew at dress rehearsals. Elizabeth Taylor was amazed at his deft comedy and asked what was inspiring him. He told her he copied a mannerism from Jack Benny.

The Burtons were in fact delightful in their roles. Elizabeth Taylor was a witty mistress of noblesse oblige when she gamely blew a cleansing breath on her diamond before Lucy's hand shined it on Taylor's ample chest. Burton gave an appealingly ironic performance, especially when he declined Lucy's offer of a stick of gum by explaining that it was one of the few vices he did not have. He tickled the audience and, between scenes, proudly told Lucy that he had already inspired fifteen laughs.

For all that Lucy could be a harridan, the experience of working with her seemed to inspire him. Burton was so impressed by the stage presence his wife demonstrated that night that he was determined that they would do theater together. Lucy, for whom the only thing that counted was a good show, thought that the fact he was toting up his laughs meant that yet another battered star forgave her.

During these years, Lucy had her children under contract. In September 1968, when Lucie and Desi were seventeen and fifteen, Lucy made them regulars on her show, renamed *Here's Lucy*. Their presence gave them a chance to work with the comic possibilities of the generation gap, and the format was adjusted so that Gale Gordon played her brother-in-law and partner in an employment agency. Since Lucy Carmichael/Carter was essentially still a dizzy housewife in the *I Love Lucy* mode, Lucy eventually would be forced to pay Jess Oppenheimer a settlement of $220,000 or be taken to court.

While Lucie kept up with her regular classes at Immaculate Heart High, Desi, his band days over, was tutored on the set. He loved Irene Burke, his teacher, and marveled that she made learning exciting. "He'd have books to read during breaks. They were psychological, how-do-I-live kind of books. He was searching and drinking," Mary Jane Croft observed.

Lucy was still convinced that Desi Jr. was the more talented of her children and that eventually he would be a star, though Lucie was eager to learn and tried unsuccessfully to persuade her mother to experiment. Nonetheless, she counted the lines of each script to make sure the siblings were treated equally. Herbert Kenwith now directed the show, although DeDe had warned him that it would ruin his friendship with her daughter. "Lucy is a bitch," she warned him in Lucy's presence at Lucy's dinner table in Beverly Hills.

"I am not!" said Lucy. "Only when I'm working!"

"But that is when people see you," DeDe chided, and it was in fact while she was working that Lucy's children spent the most time with her as well. Both seemed inured to her dramatics. One day Lucy was rehearsing a scene in a grocery store and an extra pushed a shopping cart into her shins. As if propelled, Lucy fell against a shelf of carefully arranged canned goods and stood screaming as they rained down upon her. Kenwith and Mary Jane Croft ran to her and called for bandages. Reading in separate corners nearby, Lucy's children looked up when the noise started, realized their mother had had some mishap that set everyone in frantic motion, and then calmly bent their heads back down to their magazines.

Her children, raised in affluence, were of the laid-back generation and had little appreciation of her need to work, to protect her image, or to practice and repractice what she had already done a dozen times. Nor could they understand her unwillingness to try, just once, someone else's suggestion or anything that deviated from her proven notions.

Annoyances that began on the set continued at home, while tiffs of the evening were carried the following morning on to the set. Cleo, whom Lucy had persuaded to act as producer, often served as referee. Just as constant togetherness had damaged Lucy's bond with Desi Sr., so too did working and living together fray her relationship with her children. No one had a respite. On a vacation in Snowmass, Colorado, with her family she made a point of cooking for everyone, even on the night that her son, with his heritage of Arnaz recipes from his father, declared he would prepare the meal for guests. Each unwilling to concede, mother and son concocted dueling dinners, each harassing the other as they worked at sink and stove, then urging guests to try their dishes to the exclusion of the other's. "She doesn't think she's being funny," said her son with some affection, "which is why it is so hysterical."

As soon as Lucie turned eighteen, in July 1969, she moved into her own apartment, a move that Lucy took with such ill grace that Desi Jr. decided he was well off to stay at home. A year later, despite her mother's warnings, Lucie married Phil Vandervort, whom she had dated in high school, a union that lasted only a year. In a magazine interview seventeen years later Lucy was still disapproving of her daughter's behavior as an adolescent and ridiculed her: "Lucie met one boy at fifteen, married him at nineteen and never had another date. They were married for a year and then she grew up."

Just as Lolita had sat in the bleachers while Desi did *I Love Lucy,* so did Desi take his place in the audience with his wife, Edie, when his children's episodes were taped. Desi tried unsuccessfully to produce some shows after *The Mothers-in-Law* ended in 1969, but clearly, his time had passed. Although plagued by stomach problems, he was invariably charming when he visited Lucy's set. Dorothy Aldworth said that he seemed to be reminded of the days when he and Lucy put on shows together. "There was a tremendous pull between the two of them, even though she tried not to show it. Lucy was very nice to him, but she found other things to do while he was there or would go to her dressing room. The people who knew him would surround him so she wouldn't have to be face to face with him." Lucy may have been circumspect in his presence, but Desi was often in her mind. "I must give Desi all the credit for this," she said when the show was going especially well. Friends who visited Roxbury Drive were invariably treated to home movies of Chatsworth with a young Desi Arnaz hamming with his kids for the camera. Gary seemed to take it in stride. He continued to do the warm-ups for *The Lucy Show* and introduced Desi on show nights as "My ex-husband-in-law."

Gary was now vice president of Lucille Ball Productions. Although he attended the first reading of scripts at the oval table where Lucy fought for hegemony with her directors, he spent as little time on the set as possible. When he did appear, she was as likely to hug and kiss him effusively as she was to snap in exasperation: "What the fuck are you doing? Have you nothing else to do? Find nails in the flats and hammer them in!"

"We didn't like Gary," Herbert Kenwith said, "but we lost respect for her because of the way she treated him. By the end of the day she was vociferous." Many attributed her diatribes and moodiness to alcohol, but Desi Sr. regarded them as now a part of her nature: "I pity her yet she was stronger than I was. She'd been boiled hard by the hatred of me. She needed the hatred yet."

When Jack Benny appeared on her show in late 1970, she tried to get him to speed up his famous stare and in one scene insisted that the seventy-six-year-old balance on one leg while she tugged on his other. Benny called Kenwith at home, saying "Herb, you must find her a psychiatrist." Herb told him that such a suggestion was not his to make and that he should talk to Gary.

Lucy commended Herb for the way he did stand up to her. "Herbert, this year it's close-ups only from the knees up," she told him, but he insisted that the camera had to come close enough for the audience to recognize her. After his first week on the job, during which she argued with him over everything, she invited him to join her and Gary for dinner at Matteo's, an Italian restaurant popular with the older Hollywood crowd because it offered the darkly battered decor of a New York hangout. "When I walked in, Lucy stood up and said loudly, 'You have cojones!' I asked her what that meant. 'Balls!' she said, still yelling." Referring to their doing *Dream Girl* twenty years earlier, she said. "I think of you as a baby. You used to be so nice. No one else ever stood up to me. Desi was the only one."

Herbert endured until the end of his second season in 1972 and an episode when Ruth McDevitt, an elderly character actress, appeared and kept missing her marks during rehearsal. She was so heavy she could not see them when she looked at the floor, so Lucy kicked her foot in place. Unlike Burton, who stormed off at similar interference, Ruth began to cry. Knowing she was in for criticism, Lucy tried to avoid Herbert, but at lunchtime he went to her dressing room and told her he was quitting. She responded with rage and an appeal to old affection, then hit him in the face. "My eyes welled up, and I didn't want her to think I was crying," said Herbert, "so I hit her back. She fell on the bed, bounced off, and jumped on my back. She said, 'I love you.' I said, 'Lucy, you don't know how to show love. I'm leaving.' The last weeks of the season she was very pleasant to me and everyone else."

In the spring of 1970, Lucy had faced personal dilemmas that were more serious than any matters concerning the show. Desi Jr. had added another problem to drink and drugs. He had discovered not girls, but women. One prevalent story was that, having learned that he was involved with the mother of one of his friends, Lucy had his belongings packed and deposited on the other woman's front lawn on Mother's Day. That incident was kept quiet, but his affair with the talented and troubled Patty Duke, who was six years older and in the middle of a divorce, was taken up by every celebrity gossip magazine.

Their dates at the Luau and various celebrity hot spots were reported in great detail. Infuriated, Lucy threatened to charge Patty, who believed Desi was nineteen, with statutory rape. As for her son, Lucy vowed to throw him out of the house, cut him from her will, and end financial support. She quickly relented, however, and invited Patty over for dinner. Although she might have been willing to tolerate the relationship and ride out the storm, she was agitated over the way they were all being dragged into the tabloid press. "Lucy felt she was in a crisis situation, and her attitude was efficient and cold, with barely a veneer of politeness," Patty later wrote. Lucy renewed her ultimatums and Desi left the show. She wore the boy down until he agreed to accompany her to Hawaii for a family vacation, but when he returned, he started seeing Patty again, and soon they announced they were expecting a baby.

Once this news became public, Lucy got the brunt of the bad publicity. Despite the torment she had endured during her HUAC investigation, she herself called it "the biggest thing that I've had to live through." Although the public continued to revere her, the media no longer stood in awe, particularly upstart tabloids such as *The National Enquirer* and *The Star*, whose headlines charged that she was not standing by her flesh and blood. Unlike their precursor, *Hollywood Confidential*, these were sold not just on newsstands but in supermarkets where they were available to the entire populace. By some reckonings, Desi Jr. had supplanted Jackie Onassis as the magazines' best-selling personality.

Even after her divorce from Desi, Lucy took pains to cultivate the image of a family that was happy and typical. She went so far as to claim that her greatest discipline problem was to have the stamina to unplug all her son's televisions and electronic equipment when she confined him to his room. As the Queen of Comedy, she subscribed to Ozzie-and-Harriet situation comedy ideals. More and more American families were confronting drug problems and teenage sexuality with anguish equal to hers, but this was not the commonality she was attempting to promote.

The child, whom Patty named Sean Duke, was born on February 25, 1971, a month after Desi Jr.'s eighteenth birthday party, which Patty attended but Lucy did not. Desi Sr. and Lucie visited Patty in the hospital and were caught by the reporters camped out for sight of Lucy, but she went to see the baby only later, at Desi and Patty's apartment, wearing a large black veil. She fed, held, and changed the child, but said that since Patty could not prove that only her son could be the father, she felt no more for it than she would for any other adorable child. Protecting the future of her teenage son, in her fashion, was more important to her than any purported grandchild. "I didn't think of it as my grandchild because none of the dates made sense to me," she explained. As the scandal wore down, Desi Jr. protested Lucy's treatment by the press. "My mother has been the kindest, most gentle, most understanding mother any son could ask for," he told Lloyd Shearer in a *Parade* interview that appeared that October. By then Patty had eloped with someone else. Soon Desi fell in love with another talented woman older than himself, Liza Minnelli, whom Lucy said she had loved since she was a little girl. Eventually, Patty announced that the actor John Astin, whom she married, was in fact the father of her son, now renamed Sean Astin.

Around this time a new story was added to the legend of Lucille Ball, a story that people around the country repeated for years with confidence of its truth—namely that Lucy's behavior was so outrageous that she was banned from an airline, either Trans-World or American. There is no record that this was ever the case, only indications that her fear of flying and claustrophobia caused her to try to insulate herself from strangers. She was obnoxious in ways that would have been overlooked had she not been a personage whom admirers at first wanted to please. Executives who were with TWA at the time say the story began after a flight attendant asked her what she would like to drink and, after not getting an answer, asked a second time. Lucy said to her companion, "Tell her I don't speak to the help." She behaved in similar fashion on other airlines. An executive with American Airlines' flight attendants union remembered having her on board: "You couldn't speak to her or hand her anything directly. Those rumors probably started when someone said that she *should* be banned."

Many people would have liked to strike back at Lucy for her high-handedness, but they lacked the stature or courage or were simply too smart to mess with her. The unwitting agent of Nemesis was a skier who accidentally plowed into her while she was standing by a ski trail at Snowmass, a family resort community outside fashionable Aspen. Snowmass was Lucy's place of refuge from pressures and even from herself. In 1970, on the brink of turning sixty, she took up skiing with such enthusiasm that she purchased from architectural plans three condos there, stacked one on top of the other so that her mother, children, and staff could join her. As in the mid-1950s, when she and Desi had built on land outside Palm Springs that was sure to appreciate faster than acreage in the already popular resort, Snowmass promised to be a good investment and the intermediate slope was situated right outside her door. Lucy would not risk more challenging trails. "If anything happens to me," she told her young property manager, Susan Whitney, on more than one occasion, "a lot of people are out of work."

Equally important, the Colorado mountains offered the brisk and comforting air of her Eastern youth. In the fall its aspens turned vivid hues like the maples and oaks of western New York State, and in the winter snow fell as relentlessly as it had when she lived near Lake Erie. Because the area offered no golf course, it had little appeal for Gary, so Lucy appreciated that he let her stay there without him for weeks at a time.

Snowmass also gave her a taste of normal life. Waiting at the beauty salon to have her hair done, she answered the phones and jotted appointments down in the book. She loved the small stores, like the market where the owner provided DeDe with trout from his own catch and where sometimes, when her fans permitted her to move freely, she could make quick domestic purchases. The more homes she acquired—this was her third, after Beverly Hills and Indian Wells—the more determined she was to have them be as identical as possible. Her mountain retreat had French Provincial furniture acquired for the *Wildcat* run in New York, clubby upholstered pieces gathered through the years, and the shag carpeting that she favored in Beverly Hills. In this familiar setting, much as her fans settled themselves before their televisions to be lifted from their own lives by Lucy's antics, Lucille Ball delighted in watching real life through the screen of her picture window. She was enchanted to see children whom she called "little penguins" in colorful parkas slide down the slope laughing and falling and sometimes too scared to push off. At four each afternoon, as darkness closed in, two red lines of ski patrols converged at the foot of the slope, where to her unending pleasure they looked up toward her window and yelled "Hello, Lucy!" before gliding home.

That the worst could befall her here where she was so content was an especially cruel irony. Just after lunch one day in early January 1972, after a Christmas holiday with Gary, DeDe, and Lucie and her husband, Phil Vandervort, Lucy was resting as other skiers went past when a woman came down the trail and plowed into her. With the sound of a great crack in her ears, she felt her right leg fracture in four places, including a butterfly spiral in her thigh. Medics took her down the mountain in a toboggan, but doctors had to delay administering anesthesia and necessary surgery for hours because she had eaten a hamburger just before the accident. She was given painkillers, but her memory of her agony was that she kissed the hands of the young anesthesiologist who was finally able to place the mask over her nose. She awakened to find herself in great pain and enclosed in a plaster cast up to her waist. In claustrophobic panic, she unscrewed the crank of her hospital bed and chipped the plaster down to her calf. Doctors replaced the cast, but she hacked away at the second one as well.

Lying in the hospital, she gave in to despair and self-pity. It seemed that the beautiful legs she loved to show off in her fifties would never look or be the same again and that her career was at an end. But then, after weeks at Aspen Valley Hospital and rest in Palm Springs, she returned to the *Lucy* set on crutches and filmed the next twenty-four episodes in a wheelchair. To while away her hours of sitting, she took up the newly fashionable game of backgammon, rolling, doubling, and sliding her pieces around the board so fast that her companions could not keep up with her. Like show business, it was a game of luck, skill, and the relentless toss of the dice.

18

THE ACCIDENT, as Lucy soon realized, ushered in the diminished last phase of her extraordinary life. She was never the same afterward, physically or psychically. She was aware that four pins held her leg together and that much of her lateral movement was lost. Her confidence now came not from will but from a leg brace.

Before she had felt invincible. In late 1965, at the age of fifty-four, goaded by Mary Martin's performance in *Peter Pan*, she flew upside down suspended from a wire over the audience of the television special "The Wonderful World of Burlesque II." Turning somersaults in midair and flapping the wings of her butterfly costume, she was more concerned with keeping the bow in her hair than with her own safety. Now, two years after she had taken up skiing, she was afraid to walk. "After the break, she had a sense of her own mortality. She realized it was no longer 1933," said one friend. Almost as sobering as the break was the discovery that her bones were brittle, which she attributed to all the cortisone she had taken for bursitis. She was

319

treated for calcium depletion, a not-uncommon condition in older women.

The accident occurred when she was on the brink of fulfilling a longtime wish to play Mame Dennis, the scapegrace Auntie Mame whom Roz Russell had brought to life on the screen and Angela Lansbury had reinterpreted successfully in a Broadway musical now being readied for filming. Mame was in her way as great a female comic character as Lucy Ricardo, and was a role Lucy had coveted since she saw Russell's film in 1958 and thought she detected a few moves borrowed from Lucy Ricardo.

Lucy's previous film, *Yours, Mine and Ours*, made in 1968, had exceeded all expectations and grossed $20 million, of which she received a percentage. *Yours, Mine and Ours* was a family picture, and far more successful financially and critically than her tempered sex comedy pictures of the 1960s. For that reason, she had turned down *Cactus Flower* and the role of a middle-age nurse quietly pining for her boss that had revived the career of Ingrid Bergman in 1969. Lucy believed that playing the elegant, iconoclastic Mame Dennis and giving particular stress to her maternal love for her young nephew would position her to make important films once she ended her television series. Desi, however, to whom she sent the script, did not want her to take it. He regarded his ex-wife as a combination of Chaplin and Lombard, someone who at her best offered enchanting childlike abandon and not the bitchy theatricality the role called for. Her humor was broadside, not oblique; physical, not verbal, as was Mame's. Moreover, *Mame* was a musical, just as the disastrous *Wildcat* had been. Lucy went ahead anyway, prepared to dance, jump, and ride sidesaddle despite her persistent limp. "Mame is a great role," she said when filming began. "What the hell. If you can't make it in Mame, forget it."

Lucy had looked forward to working with the eminent "woman's director" George Cukor, but when her injury delayed the project a year, he dropped out to do *Travels with My Aunt*, and Gene Saks replaced him. As hard on her directors as ever, she credited the choreographer Onna White with what little success she had in the role and announced appreciatively, "Onna's trying to kill me!"

As direct and forceful as Lucy, but lacking her streak of harshness,

Onna was what Lillian Appleby might have been had she become a choreographer. "Lucy was like a little child, meek. She did what I told her," Onna recalled. Lucy knew she presented a challenge to any choreographer. Even at her best she could not be considered a dancer, although she had been a Goldwyn Girl, yet she had some strengths. Almost a year after her accident, Lucy could kick her foot to ear level, and when she sat cross-legged in yoga position she was able to touch her head to the floor. She could outdo Onna there, as she liked to demonstrate. The problem was she had lost her ability to move from side to side. Onna insisted she renounce her leg brace, even after she fell off a step stool when she was rummaging in her closet and hurt herself again. When Lucy hesitated, Onna had it burned.

She prescribed exercises in its stead. The movements were simple, and the mood was upbeat in the mirrored gym in Lucy's backyard. Lucy's legs were still shapely, as she exhibited by exercising in hot pants, the short shorts that had recently become a fad. Lucy's friend, the character actress Mary Wickes, came by to watch. Appropriately enough, she had played Lucy Ricardo's dance instructor in the episode in which her foot became stuck in the barre during ballet practice. Encouraging Lucy to see herself as strong and capable, Mary sat herself in a comfortable chair in the exercise room and did nothing more than slide her feet in time to Onna's commands. The next day she phoned and made Lucy laugh by assuring her she had not hurt herself in these exertions.

When it came to the dances themselves, Onna drilled Lucy in four bars of steps at a time, and if she made a mistake, they started over. "She had no natural flow, but once she got it, she was fine," Onna said. They moved to the set in January 1973, when filming began. Before the outdoor scenes were shot, Onna and Lucy walked across the fields checking for gopher holes that might cause her or the dancers to fall. The gophers stayed a move ahead, so if in the middle of a number Lucy spied a hole she insisted they stop proceedings to stamp it down flat.

She relied on Onna to help her in every facet of production. "They had her sitting around in her red velvet pajama outfit, and she waited so long it got wrinkled. I said, 'Lucy, go get that pressed!' and she did." Only in matters of casting did Lucy resist her counsel. She insisted, despite Onna's pleas, that Madeline Kahn was too young and pretty for the role of the comically dowdy Agnes Gooch and had her replaced. Handsome, dynamic Robert Preston, whose performance in *The Music Man* on Broadway had made him a national star, was chosen to play opposite Lucy, but she considered him too short and had Onna audition Rory Calhoun and George Montgomery. The will of the producer prevailed, so Lucy bought her dapper co-star shoes with lifts. "I'm very sorry, Miss Ball. I have my own shoes with elk soles," he informed her with the cool disdain of a matinee idol who had been splattered with mud. During filming Lucy could not coax him into playing word games or backgammon. Bea Arthur, appearing as Mame's campy friend Vera, also kept to herself, and even the fact that she was the wife of the director was not proof against Lucy. For their duet "Bosom Buddies," Arthur, a female baritone, had to be the soprano.

Among the extras taking part in a scene set in the Palm Court of New York's Plaza Hotel was a face familiar to Lucy, someone she had actually known in the era they were now re-creating. Costumed in a white fur-trimmed suit and hat, Lucy went over to a table and asked the petite older woman her name. She discovered she was Wanda Perry, who had been in *Kid Millions* and was one of her fellow models in *Roberta*. "Oh, no. I don't believe it, after all these years! I'm so happy you're with us!" Lucy exclaimed, and took this find to meet Gene Saks. She may have reminisced about the band of beauties, most of them more promising than she had been, who came out from New York and, unlike her, had disappeared, for she approached Perry again in the afternoon and asked, "How could you be a showgirl? You're so small."

Desi had been right in his assessment. When *Mame* was released in March 1974, Lucy was no happier with it than she was with *Wildcat*. She shone only in one brief scene where she glided down a street on a single skate. *Mame* was a flop, and even she knew she had been photographed in such soft focus that she had been rendered ridiculous. Mae West, at eighty-four a bewigged and practiced Amazon in the war against age, saw the movie at a screening with Herbert Kenwith and decided something must have damaged the film.

"We in the audience are not thinking of fun," wrote the critic Pauline Kael in *The New Yorker*, "we're thinking of age and self-deception." The interviews Lucy gave to promote the film generated equally brutal copy, partly because it was now an era of slamming celebrities rather than puffing them up, partly because Lucy, possibly thinking she was being blithe and to the point like Mame, gave them ammunition. She growled at interviewers, sometimes while sipping Pouilly Fuissé on ice, told them they were dumb to think she was rich, and expressed annoyance that they kept asking her about Desi Jr. The stories and reviews of the film appalled and chastened her. On *The Dick Cavett Show*, she said her proudest accomplishment was that she had never been out of work as an actress. Then her voice broke when she said she had been happy just to have been part of show business. Soon she was explaining to everyone that she had made the film because the producers insisted on delaying the production for her and that she had felt from the beginning that Angela Lansbury should have had the role.

She ended her long-running television series that spring of 1974, having starred in nearly 500 sitcom episodes since the debut of *I Love Lucy*. *Here's Lucy* was no longer among even the top twenty-five shows, and CBS was unwilling to renew it. DeDe, just past eighty, who enjoyed arranging her friends around her special seat in the studio audience and sometimes selected fans to meet Lucy, was furious with her daughter for giving up. The network was relieved, because it knew her time was past, and gave her Monday night time slot to Bea Arthur's *Maude*. "Lucy ended her television era on a sour note," said Mike Dann. "The executives thought she was great in her day, but it was time to move on. She knew it marked the end of her professional career. None of us spent much time with her after that. It happens in a family. You don't go see Grandma."

Over the next several years, she did specials with Jackie Gleason, Dean Martin, and Art Carney, among others, all produced by Lucille Ball Productions, which Gary ran. They also developed five comedy pilots, including *Bungle Abbey*, which would have starred Gale Gordon as the head of a monastery. Lucy directed them all, but none got on the air.

Only the public continued to revere her, and CBS capitalized on this by giving her anniversary tributes and guest spots. The network insisted that Shirley MacLaine have her on her 1976 special to ensure ratings. "There was friction with Shirley, almost to the point of tears," said Cy Coleman, who was brought in to direct their number because he got along with each. When Lucy and Shirley sang "Bouncing Back for More," a song celebrating the tenacity necessary for success, Coleman had to conduct them so they wouldn't fight. "I ruined several takes because I was standing between the cameras swinging my arms and my arms got in the shot," he said.

Lucy knew that the trends in television had passed her by, and now that she had more time to tune in, her consolation was that she deplored the state of current programming. The violence appalled her. One evening she wondered why *Combat* had been edited so badly and then realized she was in fact watching a documentary on Vietnam. "I was criticizing the director, and blood was dripping off my screen!" she said. Lucy did not like *All in the Family* for putting racial epithets back in vogue and considered the perverse *Maude* and *Mary Hartman, Mary Hartman* self-indulgent.

The general emphasis on sex shocked her: "It's bad enough we've let dope into this country and made all the kids sick. Now they're supposed to be sexual geniuses, too, twenty-four hours a day." *The Mary Tyler Moore Show* and $M^*A^*S^*H$ were more to her liking.

Creating a life between guest appearances was now her challenge. When she had her own show, the Mortons were selective about going to parties and generally stayed home at night, as was her preference. Now she went out because Gary wanted to. She organized a social life, scheduling Thursdays and Sundays as the Mortons' nights out. They often went to Matteo's, a hangout for celebrities of Lucy's generation, with Thelma Orloff and her husband. Gary called him "the Senator" and persuaded valets to park his car near the door because he was expecting an urgent call from Washington. At charity functions, Lucy bought tickets to an entire table and invited the same people to every event, so that they could create a protective wall against strangers who wanted to speak with her. When the hubbub or the crowds got to be too much for her, she would turn to Gary and say "spilkus," which meant he had to take her home.

Gary had protected Lucy in her heyday from distractions and from people he thought were importuning her, but now some believed he was cutting her off from her past. Friends such as the Rabwins from Desi's era were seldom around. Lucy's brother now lived in Arizona, where he owned and operated a hotel. Cleo, who had divorced Ken Morgan, had married the *L.A. Times* critic Cecil Smith and, after *The Lucy Show* ended, kept busy with her new family.

Lucy's long-distance friendship with Marion Strong Van Vlack was as strong as ever, a banked fire that flamed with the slightest encouragement. The coming of spring reminded Lucy of her grandmother's fragrant lilacs, so she phoned or wrote Marion in Jamestown to learn if they had blossomed yet. As they grew older, Lucy sent her old pal clocks. "Hi, doll! I'm giving you more time," she scrawled in her bold loopy hand on the cards accompanying them. Lucy's spreading figure made her appreciate caftans, and knowing Marion loved to sew, she sent her a birthday present of a length of synthetic Qiana fabric with instructions and a sketch on how to make them up: "Two lengths, evenly divided, easy to sew. Just cut room in the middle top for your head and neck thusly and stitch for your figure (comfortably)."

When the Mortons went to the opening of the Turnberry Isle Resort outside Miami, Lucy made a new friend in Lillian Winograd Briggs, who had known Gary from his days as a stand-up comedian. The first thing they did together was play backgammon with several other women, and Lucy so pressured Lillian that Lillian burst into tears. "She took me into the bathroom and helped me pull myself together. I look tough," said Lillian, "but I'm not. She was impressed."

Without the outlet of performing, Lucy had reached a point where she vented some of her energy in practical jokes or, as she preferred to think of them, "gags." She eagerly involved Lillian. "I was going to be introduced at the Turnberry dinner and Lucy coached me in how to enter a room with my head high so I would command attention," Lillian said. "We practiced for three days, and when the big night came and my name was announced, she pushed me aside, stepped in, and walked out in my place with everyone looking at her. I entered the way I always did, saying hello to everyone. She laughed about it all night."

The Mortons invited the Briggses to visit them, and while the men went out on the golf course, Lucy and Lillian sat in their bathrobes playing backgammon. One day Lucy exclaimed, "My God! You've got a callus on your foot! You have a husband. You can't let him see that." Lucy sped for her pedicure kit and seated herself on the floor at Lillian's foot removing the imperfection with great expertise. Another time, having declined a hair treatment, Lillian was in the shower when Lucy appeared, stark naked and bearing a bottle of conditioner that she said Elizabeth Arden had developed for show horses. Lillian screamed as Lucy massaged the substance on her scalp, assuring her she used it all the time, and pulled a plastic bag down over her head. They played backgammon for three hours while the cream set.

Despite the associations of Snowmass with her appalling accident, Lucy continued to spend time there. Invariably, when she arrived she would walk around her condo with her property manager, Susan Whitney, and check to see that nothing had been changed, nothing moved from its assigned place. "She could always tell if I'd moved anything an inch," Susan said. "Then she would call her kids and say, 'I've got your picture from when you were five! Here is the photo of you on the horse.' She anguished over her children. She didn't know the right thing to do. She was trying to be a mom. She was as scared and insecure in that area as she was in acting."

The Snowmass tradition was that DeDe cooked dinner, particularly her famous pot roast, in her second-floor condo and then phoned Lucy to say she was on the way. Then she called Frank Gorey, Lucy's faithful aide and driver, on the first floor. He came up and carried the meal to Lucy's, where they all ate. One evening Lucy and Susan Whitney were at backgammon when DeDe phoned, but the preoccupied Lucy continued the game until with a start she realized her mother would be arriving at any moment expecting to find the table set, much as fifty years before she had stepped off the Celeron trolley expecting to see the children's chores completed. "Get the tablecloth! Get the silver!" Lucy cried. "My mom is going to kill me!"

Lucy's waning sense of adventure was rekindled in the Colorado mountains through Susan's resourcefulness. On one occasion, she arranged for Lucy to have an afternoon of dog sledding followed by an authentic Alaskan dinner cooked on a woodstove. The one problem she foresaw, which she deliberately did not reveal until it was too late for Lucy to back out, was that the only available plumbing was an outhouse.

After a long drive Lucy met her host, Stuart Mace, who with his wife, Isabel, owned the dog teams and the log cabin where they would have dinner. In his midfifties when he met Lucy, Mace was an accomplished trainer who had been in charge of military dog sled teams during World War II and was also a talented photographer and woodworker. Lucy was so awed by him that she refused to call him anything more familiar than "Mr. Mace," even before she learned that he had done the stunts and sledding for the star of the *Sergeant Preston of the Yukon* series in the 1950s. She was mortified when this paragon offered her his arm and squired her to the door of the outhouse in preparation for the trip.

Lucy was settled in the first sled behind the lead dog, Big Red, and DeDe was placed on her lap. Cradling her mother in her arms, she told Susan, "I've got my mother where I've always wanted her," and off they hurtled over the white hills.

"My coccyx will never the same!" Lucy yelled, and continued to fret over the outhouse. Each time they stopped in the frosty alpine air to untangle the reins, she asked Susan for more details of the facilities they would encounter at the cabin. Did they have running water? Plumbing? Why not a working bathroom? Finally she asked Susan to see if Mr. Mace would accept a gift of a bathroom. Before dinner she had Susan announce that Lucy was sending fixtures she had in storage. Eating by gaslight in the kitchen, warmed only by the fireplace and the woodstove, she was so relaxed and joyful that DeDe told Susan, "I have not seen her this happy since she was a little girl."

Although Lucy loved to laugh and lived in fear of being bored, she had little patience when things went comically awry. One night at the condo she herself was cooking pasta and thawing meatballs she had brought from Beverly Hills, but when she turned on the faucet to rinse the spaghetti, the pipe was dry. Susan phoned several people and learned the lower village still had water, so she and Frank drove there with buckets and returned bearing what had not sloshed out on the return trip. Lucy was embarrassed that her dinner had not turned out well, even when Susan urged her to think of the coagulated spaghetti as lasagna. The next night Lucy invited her back. "Come to dinner so I can exonerate myself. It's steaks! We're putting out the good stuff!"

Even in Snowmass, Lucy was preoccupied by hair styling. Sure that Susan would be a ringer for Cheryl Tiegs if only she would lighten her hair, Lucy sent her photos of the model ("A Susan Whitney look-alike!") to illustrate her point. At the "exoneration dinner" Susan insisted on wearing her cowboy hat indoors, and when Lucy asked her why, Susan told her: "My cowlick's back, and tonight you put out steak knives."

Many scripts were submitted to Lucy, and Gary read all of them first. He agreed with Desi's insistence that the public wanted to see something of Lucy Ricardo in every character she played, so he turned down the film *Driving Miss Daisy* and the TV movie *The Story Lady*, both of which Jessica Tandy accepted. Lucy remained a prisoner of that other Lucy, her stereotype, but more important to her than her career at this point was companionship at home.

As she reached her midsixties, death was beginning to take people close to her. Harriet died of cancer, and Lucy learned that Vivian was suffering from it as well. As devastating as these losses were, the worst was having to acknowledge that DeDe herself, then in her mideighties, would inevitably die. DeDe wore hot pants when Lucy took them up and she dyed her own hair red, but her eyesight was failing, and after a stroke she could not be left alone in the house Lucy had bought her in Brentwood. "What the hell am I going to do if I lose my mother? How do you handle it?" she demanded of the actress Betty White. She phoned DeDe every day and sent her flowers on her own birthday, August 6, to thank her and to apologize for any pain she might have caused her. When she was in good health, DeDe herself thought Lucy's behavior somewhat excessive. "I hope she dies first because she can't live without me," DeDe told Maury Thompson and others. But on July 22, 1977, DeDe left her, the final and irrevocable abandonment. On DeDe's birthday that September, not knowing what to do with herself, Lucy sent a basket of violets to Betty White's mother.

When Vivian fell seriously ill, Lucy postponed as long as she could visiting her at Tiburon in the Bay Area, where she was spending her last days. Far from unfeeling, she felt too much. Mary Wickes was appearing in a play in nearby San Francisco, and they went to see her together. For ninety minutes, Lucy and Vivian laughed about all they had done, from the first week when they scoured the bathrooms at General Service Studios to the episode of *The Lucy Show* when they tried to repair a shower and became submerged in a tank of water. "We laughed the whole time," said Mary Wickes. "Then we got in the limousine and cried all the way back. We knew we wouldn't see her again." Vivian died in August 1979.

Desi Jr. had married the actress Linda Purl earlier that year, but the marriage soon ended. After a series of unsuccessful television and feature films, his career sputtered and his drug and alcohol problems continued until he entered a treatment program at Scripps Memorial Hospital in La Jolla in 1982. Lucy and the rest of the family participated in the group therapy session for patients' relatives, even as other participants asked for her autograph and proudly wore *I Love Lucy* buttons.

The 1970s, when Lucie Arnaz was developing her own promising career, were the best years of her relationship with her mother. "She had me all to herself," said Lucie. Lucy now expected great things of her daughter, particularly in 1979 when she starred in Marvin Hamlisch's *They're Playing Our Song* on Broadway, but she also feared that fortune hunters would take advantage of her daughter. Challenging one of her beaux, she offered Gary Pudney, a television executive, $3 million if he would leave Lucie alone. He won the mother over by responding "I'll marry her for three million, or not marry her for three million. Whatever you want." Lucie wed the actor Laurence Luckinbill, seventeen years her senior, in June 1980, at a farm in upstate New York, and Lucy wept as Desi serenaded the guests with the *I Love Lucy* theme song.

The Luckinbills gave Lucy and Desi three grandchildren, something new to share, and brought back happy early memories of Lucie and Desi Jr. She and Gary bought an apartment in Manhattan to be near the Luckinbills, but Lucy was not used to little children and had trouble with their noise and unpredictability when she was around them. When she was younger, a lull in activity was her cue to stir things up. Now Lucy was so uncomfortable with the unexpected that she refused to surrender her rotary phones for new touch-tones, much less cope with smudgy fingerprints. "She made a terrible grand-mother," said Marcella.

Lucy did, however, take a maternal interest in a young fan DeDe had introduced to her when she was still doing *Here's Lucy*. Michael Stern, dark-haired and cherubic, was not quite thirteen when he met the star in 1973. Later she saw him standing outside her house in Beverly Hills and invited him in. As she got to know him, she urged him to spend his time constructively. "She kept telling me to get a job," Michael recalled. "When I told her I was too young, she said I could baby-sit." When at last he announced that he was working at the May Company in the Valley, Lucy told him she was going to check on him. She and Mary Wickes drove "over the hill," as Angelenos call the Mulholland Pass, and found him in the linen department. "I want to make sure you're working," she announced as he stood open-mouthed. "I'm here to shop. I don't want to meet your friends." The frugal Mrs. Morton selected $600 worth of merchandise to promote Michael's retailing career.

Shoppers who recognized her were too stunned to speak, except for one little girl who got an autograph. They formed a silent respectful circle and watched as the computer rejected her charge. She had not used the card in twenty-two years, and her account was deemed closed. Michael phoned the credit office to hear "Make sure it's her. Get her driver's license." Michael asked Lucy to produce it, and Lucy, who had not driven since she broke her leg, countered, "DeDe took it with her." Store policy required Michael to put the purchases on hold. When the sheets arrived, Lucy had them washed and then discovered that she had been sent two bottom sheets and no tops. "How dare you!" Lucy phoned to demand of Michael. "Now that I washed them, I can't take them back!" The May Company rectified the mistake.

When Michael was transferred to the shoe department, she had him send over a selection, in heels no higher than two inches in size $7\frac{1}{2}$. Her favorites were from Bruno Magli for around $300 a pair. Out of twenty boxes, she would keep seventeen and tell Michael, "Return these before Gary's sister sees them."

In January 1980, Lucy formally ended her long association with CBS by doing a special, "Lucy Moves to NBC," for the rival network. Then in September 1981, Lucy and Gary signed a two-year contract with Twentieth Century–Fox TV to develop situation comedies and films. From this relationship came the film *All the Right Moves* with Tom Cruise, which credited Gary as executive producer. His schedule was to go to their office in the morning and golf in the afternoon, after which, in a ritual observed by whatever friend was visiting, Gary would call from the club or his car and say "Can I come home now?" Lucy would hurriedly apply lipstick and arrange her hair and jump up to welcome him when he came in the door amid the yipping of poodles.

Games were her mainstay. In 1980, she and Thelma Orloff joined Pips, a Beverly Hills club founded by Thelma's boss, Stan Herman, and Hugh Hefner. Each Monday night, Lucy played in charity tournaments, indulging her passion for backgammon. Activities that would have invited deeper thought did not interest her. Travel and the theater had no appeal, nor did reading, although she did borrow Mary Jane Croft's copy of *Living Well Is the Best Revenge*, a biography of Gerald and Sara Murphy, because she liked the title.

As if in training, Lucy hired coaches to perfect her backgammon strategies. Sometimes she paid people to play with her because friends who did not want to risk her censure over a wrong move refused to take up the game. Irma declined to learn, but once when Lucy was intently concentrating on a game, the hairdresser slid a mirror under her nose so she could see how her face sagged when she bent over the board. Lucy did not care. To pep up the atmosphere, she played while listening to Bobby Darin's hit "Splish Splash" and other songs from his Copa album. So addicted was she to the game that when Thelma, a real estate agent, held an open house in Beverly Hills, Lucy walked over with her backgammon board and set it up in the kitchen so they could play while clients walked through the property. When one visitor asked Lucy if anyone had ever remarked that she looked like Lucille Ball, Lucy admitted that she had indeed heard that comment before.

Lucy was not without a sense of humor about her mania, or about her friends' concern for her. Her teeth, which had caused her cosmetic problems in her early career, plagued her in her old age. The day she had her molars pulled Lillian drove her home, planning to look after her, but Lucy refused to go to bed immediately as the doctor had advised. Through the wadding in her mouth, Lucy mumbled, "I want to play backgammon!" Nothing would do until they sat down for one game. "I thought she rolled double fours," Lillian said, "but when I looked more closely I saw it was her bloody molars. I was nauseous, and she thought the whole thing was hilarious."

Lucy confessed to Lillian that she was fed up with backgammon, but didn't know what else to do with herself. She hated to shop and she said she'd had enough lunches with the girls. Ensconced in her home, she found an antidote in Scrabble. She approached it as seriously as a major leaguer stepping up to bat. Each day she opened her dictionary to learn a new word, its spelling and meaning. When the writer A. Scott Berg went to Roxbury Drive to interview her for his biography of Sam Goldwyn, Lucy discovered that he was an ardent Scrabble enthusiast and she called for her board. "She was a champion-level player," Berg said. "When she laid down the word 'tyg,' I asked 'What's that?' She said, 'It's a many-handled drinking vessel' as if to say 'I thought you knew how to play this game.' "

Lillian recalled, "She didn't like to go out because people didn't want to see the way she looked. Lucy wanted to stay home and not be involved with the public. When she did go out, she spent the day with makeup people. She would do anything short of surgery to look good." But only cosmetic surgery would have minimized the years. Gary asked Irma to urge Lucy to get her neck done, but not to say it was his suggestion. Lucy rejected the idea utterly.

When she prepared to meet strangers, she was able to approximate the Lucy look by wearing big blue-tinted glasses that hid her baggy eyes and simulated the enormous irises that people expected of Lucy Ricardo. But the cosmetology of Hollywood that she had relied on could no longer preserve her; nor could her general unhappiness be disguised. Even in the mornings she sipped "tea" or "special water" that several interviewers said had the faint smell of vodka.

In what seemed like good fortune, in 1985 she was occupied by a project that interested her, the dramatic television film *Stone Pillow* about a homeless woman. "It was difficult to finally bust out and get to work, knowing that I'd probably get hit over the head for it," she said, but she took the drama as a creative challenge, something that would call forth the pathos of *The Big Street*. She came up with a list of traits to develop the character, whom she named Florabelle after her grandmother. Her Florabelle would take pride in her survival, have rudimentary beauty and health routines, and be foxy in her ability to cadge donations from grocers.

Lucy's health broke under the strain of filming ten hours a day in heavy clothing on New York streets in May. She collapsed several times and was hospitalized. "This is it!" she told loved ones, fearing cancer or serious heart problems had struck at last, but her problems were attributed to high blood pressure and her irregular heartbeat. She thought she was putting her whole self into the performance and making a serious attempt at drama, yet for all that she piled on rags and allowed herself to look as old and bedraggled as possible, her hands remained beautifully manicured. When *Stone Pillow* was broadcast on CBS in early December, Lucy's performance was accepted by neither critics nor the public, who still expected Lucy to make them laugh. She was especially devastated by letters that said she had let her fans down. Marcella, who had known her for half a century, said the only times Lucy ever let her see her cry was when Vivian died and when she talked about *Stone Pillow*. Marcella was so concerned that she suggested Lucy consult a psychiatrist, but Lucy replied, "Why? I know what's wrong!" After a few months, she grew tired of her sorrow and discharged her grievances in a frenzy of housework. She temporarily banished the Chinese couple who worked for her and cleaned her house from top to bottom, opening every drawer and arranging every closet shelf, and then went to her son's house and cleaned his. "That was her emotional release. She didn't scream. She got out and cleaned drawers," Marcella said.

In early 1986 Lucy learned Desi had lung cancer. His life outside the limelight had been as challenging as hers but even more frustrating. He and Edie had almost divorced in 1975, but patched up their marriage. Then in 1976 he published his memoir *A Book*, which put him on the late-night talk show circuit. The years had made him hungrier for attention and less generous to others. He claimed full credit for the backstage developments of *I Love Lucy*, while telling a tale both wistful and barbed of his marriage to Lucy and its breakdown. Edie died of cancer in 1985, and while she was still under treatment at Cedars, Desi stayed in Lucy's guest house where, fuddled by drink, he had terrified DeDe and her friends thirty years before. Desi had been impressed by his son's example and also entered Scripps's treatment program, but he had abused his body so long that his health was undermined. He had so depleted his financial capital that he and his mother, whom he had refused to send to a nursing home, were living together in his small house in Del Mar when he learned he had cancer. Lucy was delighted when he sent her flowers, and when she heard her husband was on the phone, Lucy would quip "Which one?"

As Desi's health deteriorated in early autumn, Lucie and her family were with him, but he did not want Lucy to see him in his debilitated state. She went anyway. Lucy, Desi, and their son and daughter were together as a family one last time, and afterward she and the children walked along the beach where they had mugged for Desi's home movie camera years before.

After *Stone Pillow*, Gary insisted that if the public wanted her to make them laugh, she had to return to television and do just that. Aaron Spelling, who began his career as an actor playing a country lout in the *I Love Lucy* episodes featuring Tennessee Ernie Ford, had conquered the medium as producer of *Charlie's Angels, The Love Boat,* and the prime-time soap opera *Dynasty.* When he decided he wanted to turn his talents to comedy, he approached Gary with the suggestion that Lucy return in a new series and persuaded ABC to sign them up for twenty-two shows without asking for a pilot. The failures of *Mame* and *Stone Pillow* convinced Lucy that her audience accepted her only as Lucy Ricardo, madcap ingenue. "People don't want to see me as an old lady because it reminds them of their own mortality," she said. She knew that she was elderly and tried to make a joke of it: "When I go into a store and they offer me a twenty-five-year guarantee, I say, 'You know, I don't give a damn. Give me a five-year guarantee.' " But Gary was so eager to see her get back to her old self that she finally agreed to return to a regular series.

She gathered as many of her old gang as she could and mourned over those who were beyond her reach, particularly Viv. Bob and Madelyn wrote the series and Marc Daniels, who had directed the first season of I Love Lucy, directed. Particularly important to her was that Gale Gordon would be her co-star.

She filmed this show at the very studio where she had begun her career as a Goldwyn Girl. The spot where she had lined up in a bathing suit with the other girls for Sam Goldwyn's inspection was now a parking lot. The bank where she had deposited her first Hollywood paycheck had been demolished, and the grass lawn where she had sat in the sun eating her lunch while making Roman Scandals was now a mini-mall with dry cleaner's and discount gourmet stores. She herself was the star of a series she had hopes for, but fully expected to be a disaster. The show was Life with Lucy, but as she prepared for it, she called it Life with Angst. She hired Michael Stern to work as an assistant, but only part time. "She wouldn't let me quit my other job until she was sure we had a hit," he said.

Others were confident she would outdo Bill Cosby, NBC's juggernaut, whose family comedy, directed by Jay Sandrich, consistently topped the ratings. ABC scheduled her on Saturday night, which NBC dominated with The Golden Girls. That show mined the dark humor of senior citizenship, but Lucy's Lucy Barker was the hippest, healthiest character on the program. Eating tofu, listening to rock music on a Walkman, and living in a jogging suit, she all but cried Mame Dennis's signature line: "Life is a banquet and most poor suckers are starving to death."

She and Gale played in-law grandparents who run a hardware store together, but the old slapstick didn't work. If Lucy stupidly slid a ladder into his nose, the audience worried that his dear face would shatter. If she flailed about in a madly malfunctioning automatic recliner, they feared she might succumb to an attack. Lucy was friskier than her material, but all of it relied on her. When she was about to do some bit of business, like dance steps from the 1920s, the camera telegraphed it by seeming to pull back to catch every gesture.

They shot each episode in four days, and Gary, who was executive producer, golfed on the fifth. Bob Carroll, Jr., insisted on being home in the evenings, so the writers worked eight-hour days, rather than the usual twelve required of a weekly series. Lucy trusted her knowledge of comedy but was insecure about her performance. When she expressed some reservations about a script, Gary said, "Oh, wait a minute. I'd better read it."

Initial reviews were awful and personal and reviled her for attempting to do her old tricks at her age. When a reporter calling from Jamestown reached her in her dressing room and tried to make her discuss the matter of her seventy-five years, she put the phone down and wept. Her assistant Tom Watson got on the line to say that Miss Ball had been called away while Michael Stern took her for a walk outside. "She told me she wanted to find the room where they stored the scenery so she could commit suicide," Michael remembered. "She kept saying over and over, 'Just because I'm seventy-five, it doesn't mean I can't work.' It took twenty minutes to calm her down."

As bad as everything else was the fact that Desi was dying in Del Mar. Everyone on the set knew it and felt it affected her. She kept flubbing a scene calling for her to participate in a Grandparents' Talent Contest. As she recited "Sunrise, Sunset" to music while looking at a photo of Lucy Barker's late husband, the beauty of the song, its recollection of the poignancy of life, touched her. Every time she started her recitation, she broke down in tears.

What confounded those involved was that the studio audience was madly supportive. People were so delighted to see her in person that they screamed when she did so much as sit down. "No one watched the show, but if we'd sold tickets, we'd still be there," said Casey Keller, who worked with Bob and Madelyn. But *Life with Lucy* was out of touch with contemporary taste and ratings were so awful that ABC dropped Lucy's series in mid-November after eight episodes, although it paid for the twenty-two it had agreed to. Gary was informed of the network's decision the night before the last taping, but kept it to himself. They completed the episode, and he told Lucy the bad news in the car when they went home.

The day afterward the cast assembled at the studio to say farewells. Lucy urged the kids who played her grandchildren not to give up on performing. "This is only the beginning for you, you're talented," she advised them. "Start over." She said good-bye with her head high and walked out with Michael. On the steps she broke down. "I've lost all my friends, Michael, but I still have you." Forgetting about being released by Columbia in 1934, she said, "I've never been fired before." A few weeks later they had a second, more organized gathering on a Sunday afternoon at a cast member's home. Marc Daniels's wife, Emily, said, "It was the most down party I had been to, except for the night Adlai Stevenson lost. Lucy was like a zombie, she was so sad." Experiencing an attack of claustrophobia, Lucy at one point left the larger group to go into the bedroom to play backgammon.

She took to her bed for days and rose up on occasion to demand of Gary, "Why did you push this? Look what happened!" Lillian Briggs, who was staying with them, said that Lucy was devastated not only by embarrassment, but because she had put people out of work. Publicly, she assumed all responsibility: "The problem was me. I chose the writers and directors, and I told them what to do."

But Spelling tried to disagree. "It was my fault, because she trusted me and I went along with what she wanted. We thought she should play a real grandmother, but she brought in her own staff. I wish ABC gave it more time, but that wasn't the way things were done."

When Desi died on December 2, 1986, at the age of sixty-nine, she was taping *Password*. Driving home that afternoon with Michael after she learned of his death, she started sobbing. Whatever scenes were playing in her mind—the day she met him in his tattered football jersey at the RKO commissary, the first night they went to bed, the evening she knocked him out cold—all she allowed herself to say through her tears was "He was a great father," over and over again. Of his importance to her, she could say nothing at all.

She was composed and distant at his funeral, which was attended only by those who had been closest to him. The gang of performers who had saluted him at the Friars Club in his heyday had faded from his life long before. Desi had told Carol Campbell, the wife of his doctor, "You watch. Everyone will be at my funeral because no one's calling now." That, like many others, was a bet he would have lost. The sole representative of the television industry was Danny Thomas, who delivered the eulogy, but the most touching tribute came from the parochial school children who stood silently on the sloping grounds around the church in their uniforms looking like blue flowers against the grass. "They didn't think he was an old man," Carol Campbell said. "They heard that Ricky Ricardo had died."

Lucy's recurring cycle of disaster and triumph held to the end. Three weeks after her show bombed, and a few days after Desi's funeral, she went to Washington, D.C., to receive from President Ronald Reagan a Kennedy Center Award, the highest honor America bestows on its performers.

What remained to her was a tedious expanse of days and the deterioration of her health. Her wealth had been estimated at $25 million, but it was little consolation. "Retirement is death itself," she told Marion when they spoke on the phone. "There's a limit to how many drawers you have to straighten."

At a custom-made backgammon table in the corner of the downstairs den, she spent her days watching *Password* and *Oprah* and *Wheel of Fortune* on TV. In the middle of a conversation, she would scream out "Secret ingredient!" and visitors would know she was solving *Wheel of Fortune* puzzles out of the corner of her eye while talking about something else.

Her arena was now her den, as comfortable a room as one might find in the home of any prosperous American. The walls and carpeting were white, with one redbrick wall broken by white shutters. The sturdy chairs and ottomans were done in limes and orange and lemon shades, like the condo in Snowmass and her dressing room. Susan Whitney once asked her if the constant decor ever caused her to wonder where she was. "If I look out the window and there's snow, I'm near Aspen," Lucy quipped. With Frank Sinatra's songs playing in the background, she adjusted temperature and light from a master panel with dimmer switches near the backgammon table. Once, when Lillian was reading in the corner, Lucy convinced her she was losing her sight by slowly and silently turning down the lamp behind her.

On her birthdays, television stations celebrated by running *Lucy* marathons—all the classic *I Love Lucy* episodes: the chocolate factory, the birth of Little Ricky, the grape stomping—one after the other. She would watch faithfully, irate at the choppy editing. "They cut it up!" she would yell. "You don't know why Ethel is standing there! They ruined it!"

At night she moved over to her couch. Shutters opened to reveal a projector at one end of the room and before her a screen descended so that she could view her old performances and reels and reels of outtakes. They never made her laugh. She watched with utter detachment, as if someone else were performing, holding her glass of scotch and drawing deeply on her cigarette. How had she ever done all that? Now she could not even react to it. Her guests of the evening might sometimes laugh, but the expression of the world's greatest comedienne never changed.

She still dyed her hair according to the formula that Irma wrote down on a slip of paper, which became tattered and splotched from so much use. Unfailingly, Lucy followed the treatment with a henna rinse, a natural antidote to the chemicals with which she alchemized her hair. Thelma, always impeccably groomed, insisted she made it too pink and should see a professional, but Lucy would insist she had done it the way she always had and then wonder if perhaps she had left the mixture on too long.

She was no more able to perfect her personal relationships than she was her hair. Lucy would look forward to seeing Lucie and her grandchildren and would tell Michael how excited she was, but when her daughter arrived, Lucy's first words were critical. "You're an hour late!" "Mom, I've got three kids." "I had kids too!" was how their afternoons began.

Thelma tried to referee. "Lucy wanted to organize activities for the children when they were there. She was afraid her grandchildren would be spoiled, but I said Lucie had her own way of raising them. I told Lucie to listen to her mother while she was there and then do it her way at home." Marcella recalled that the tension between the two was so intense that they once actually came to blows.

Lucy was relieved that Desi Jr. had conquered his addictions, but she was less enthusiastic about the New Life Foundation to which he devoted himself soon after he left Scripps. It was a self-help group formed to study the works of Vernon Howard, whose books included *The Mystic Path of Cosmic Power* and *There Is a Way Out!* The foundation had a hundred committed members, including Desi's second wife, Amy, whom he met there. After Desi Jr. became their spokesman, Lucy took Onna White to hear him deliver a lecture entitled "Success Without Stress." After his talk, which dealt with false selves and life's illusions, Lucy turned to Onna and asked in some perplexity: "What the hell is that all about?"

By this time she was ashamed that she looked old and worried about being unattractive to Gary. He annoyed her friends by going out for brunch and spending his days on the golf course when Lucy was desperate for company at home, but the strain of constant togetherness might in fact have done them more harm. While he golfed, she played backgammon in the afternoons, particularly with a writer named Jim Brochu, who made her laugh.

On May 10, 1988, just before dawn, she woke up and went into her mirrored bathroom in the dark. As she sat on the toilet, she suddenly felt a heavy object fall into her lap. When she picked it up, she realized it was her arm and that, like her mother, she had had a stroke. Gary raced her to Cedars-Sinai Medical Center, and she allowed herself to spend a few hours in intensive care. Then, in an apparent reaction to medication, she saw cockroaches crawling over her stomach and shouted, "Get me out of this goddamned place. I want to go home!" They released her. A nurse, Trudi Arcudi, moved in at Roxbury Drive. Over the next three months Lucy worked on her partially paralyzed right side with Onna until she got her motion and her speech back. "We added making vowel sounds to our exercise program," Onna said.

Fan letters still arrived at her office, which remained in operation to handle them, but *Mame*, *Stone Pillow*, and above all her last comedy show were rejected so decisively that Lucy felt the public finally was finished with her. Whether she could have faced performing again or not, she would have liked to have been asked. At a Professional Dancers luncheon honoring Donald O'Connor, she asked Eleanor Keaton if she was working. "Me neither," Lucy said. "I guess no one wants me."

So she was particularly pleased to be invited to appear with Bob Hope at the Oscars in late March 1989 to introduce a salute to young performers. She asked the fashion designer Ret Turner to style her dress, cautioning "Remember, I don't have that thirty-four-inch waist anymore." From six sketches she selected a high-necked, long-sleeved black dress covered with bugle beads and imitation diamonds that was slit straight up the side to her panty line. The morning of her fitting, she showed up at Ret's salon very much a tired and ailing old lady in her zippered robe, accompanied by her treasured poodle, Tinker Bell. "I didn't see any reason to get dressed and undressed," she told him, and hauled on the gown. Its weight surprised her. "Get away from here, Tink," she advised her dog. "If this dress falls on you it will kill you."

The night of the Oscars she worried backstage about whether she looked old and if her eyes were baggy. Bob Hope's publicist, Frank Liberman, told her, "When the lights hit old war-horses like you and Hope, thirty years melt away, the wrinkles smooth, the shoulders straighten, and you get taller." Hope assured her it was true and extended his arm.

She handed her purse to Turner, explaining, "I don't want to go out there with too much junk," and stepped forward. With a gasp, Turner saw that the slit had been cut to her waist. She and Hope went on stage to an ovation so heartfelt and prolonged that she was stunned and teary. The stars and powers of Hollywood greeted her and Hope with the enthusiasm of ordinary fans.

Over the next few weeks she felt sluggish, and then, one morning, protesting despite intense pain, she allowed Gary and Lucie to drive her to the hospital. Doctors performed six-and-a-half-hour emergency open-heart surgery to replace a torn section of her aorta and a weakened valve. As they heard the news, thousands of people phoned the switchboard to ask about her condition, while others—an average of 5,000 fans per day—flooded the hospital with cards.

Supposedly she was making a remarkable recovery. She was thrilled to hear about all the cards and calls and to realize that people loved her after all. On April 26, 1989, just before she was due to go home, she awoke at dawn with a pain in her back. Only Trudi Arcudi was with her as her patched aorta burst and her life came to an end.

Bulletins interrupted morning news programs across America and then flashed around the world. Her obituary ran on the front pages of major newspapers and *The Jamestown Post* as well. Even the temperate *New York Times* proclaimed on its editorial page, "We Love Lucy Too." In New York, Los Angeles, and Chicago, memorial services were held on Monday, May 8, 1989, at eight in the evening, the night when a younger America settled down for *I Love Lucy*. Privately Gary, Desi Jr., and Lucie interred her ashes, as she had requested, at Forest Lawn Memorial Park in the Hollywood hills in a mausoleum wall exactly next to DeDe's. As long as the stone and steel lasted, they would be together.

Lucy Ricardo, of course, achieved eternal life. Filmed, taped, and digitalized, never separated from Ricky, Fred, and Ethel, she is unchanging and incorrigible wherever there are video screens. Like a few great creations, but no great creators, she beats that killer, Time.

NOTES

PAGE

CHAPTER 1

4   *Lucille knew at once:* Gladys Hall Collection, Margaret Herrick Library, Academy of Motion Picture Arts and Sciences (hereinafter cited as Gladys Hall Collection).

4   *Oil was discovered:* William C. Darrah, *Pithole: The Vanished City* (Gettysburg, Pa., privately printed, 1972), 34–45.

5   *nearby Fredonia:* Federal Writers' Project, *New York* (New York: Oxford University Press, 1966), 439.

5   *After settling his wife:* Anna Carpenter Waite, "Some Genealogical History of Lucille D. Ball," manuscript in the collection of the Fenton Historical Society, Jamestown, N.Y. Also, Hazel Ball to author, Feb. 1992, and Alfred Ball to author, Dec. 1991.

6   *On Sunday, August 6, 1911: Jamestown Evening Journal,* Aug. 9, 1911.

6   *"Mister, help me . . .":* Laura Berquist, "Desi and Lucy," *Look,* Dec. 25, 1956; Cleo Morgan Smith to author, Feb. 1991.

7   *"I do remember everything . . .":* *Look,* Sept. 7, 1971, p. 61.

7   *"screen memory":* Sigmund Freud, *A General Introduction to Psychoanalysis* (New York: Washington Square Press, 1964), 211.

7   *Lucille's antipathy to birds:* John Bowlby, *Separation,* vol. 2, *Attachment and Loss* (New York: Basic Books, 1973), 171.

7   *"Although she didn't know . . .":* Eleanor Harris, *The Real Story of Lucille Ball* (New York: Farrar, Straus and Young, 1954), 17; see also Gladys Hall Collection.

8   *Sassafrassa made her existence:* Gladys Hall Collection.

9   *"If when you were a little boy . . .":* Martin Leeds to author, June 1991.

9   *On Lucille's ninth birthday:* Berquist, "Desi and Lucy." In the 1950s and early 1960s, with more ruefulness than anger, Lucille revealed these Dickensian vignettes to successive magazines. Finally, when reading these piteous tales was too painful, Desirée told Lucille that she was exaggerating and had been with the Petersons for no more than a month (*Look,* Sept. 7, 1971). But Lucille's classmates remember that she had been in Jamestown's elementary grades and joined the rest of the family when she was eleven, after about three years with her step-grandparents.

9   *Lucille was told:* Gladys Hall Collection.

11 *Thomas Hunt:* Waite, "Some Genealogical History," and Charles J. Hoadly, ed., *Records of the Colony and Plantation of New Haven* (Hartford: Case, Tiffany and Co., 1857).

11   *"an excellent worker . . .":* W. R. Cutter, *Genealogical and Family History of Western New York* (New York: Lewis Historical Publishing Co., 1912), 94.

11–12   *Fred's authority:* Smith to author, Feb. 1991.

12   *"My stepfather was a dud . . .":* Fred Ball to author, Feb. 1992.

12   *"Lucille's stepfather . . .":* Pauline Lopus to author, Mar. 1991.

12   *"Domesticity was not . . .":* Smith to author, Feb. 1991.

12   *"We were taught . . . differences of opinion":* Fred Ball to author, Feb. 1992.

13   *"I had a crush . . .":* Gladys Hall Collection.

13   *longing for the mother:* Bertram Lewin, *The Psychoanalysis of Elation* (London: Hogarth Press, 1951), 107–8.

13   *"She had almost . . . clung to them":* Lopus to author, Mar. 1991.

14   *"When Lucille arrived . . .":* Ibid.

14   *A projection booth set high up:* George Samuelson, "Celeron Park's Early Outdoor Movies," *Jamestown Post-Journal,* Jan. 6, 1979.

14–15   *Lucille involved the well-behaved Pauline:* Lopus to author, Mar. 1991.

15   *"When Mrs. Appleby would say . . .":* Ibid.

15   *"She was wonderful . . .":* LB to students at Sherwood Oaks Experimental College, 1977.

15   *"Lillian Appleby was like . . .":* LB to *Erie and Chautauqua Annual Quarterly,* 1989.

15   *"Yose-mite" Valley:* LB to Sherwood Oaks Experimental College, 1977.

15   *"Lucille . . . pushed me out":* Cecilia Ditonto Welch to author, Feb. 1991.

15   *"She didn't know . . .":* Ernestine Young Klomp to author, Aug. 1992.

16   *"I'll perform today . . .":* Welch to author, Feb. 1991.

16   *Her piano teacher:* Gladys Hall Collection.

16   *"The kids asked . . .":* Lopus to author, Mar. 1991

16   *When she was twelve:* Marion Strong Van Vlack to author, Dec. 1991.

16   *"My mother found it . . .":* Welch to author, Mar. 1991.

17   *"Lucille would get cross . . .":* Lopus to author, Mar. 1991.

17   *the Home Bureau:* Ibid.

17   *"Lucille's mother was . . .":* Irene DeVita Roselli to author, Dec. 1991.

18   *"I got along better . . .":* Smith to author, Feb 1991.

18   *"Finally she got it . . .":* Lopus to author, Mar. 1991.

18   *Once DeDe cut short:* Private archives.

CHAPTER 2

19–20   *"She had a phone call . . .":* Pauline Lopus to author, Mar. 1991.

20   *"He wasn't well educated . . . as he thought himself":* Ibid.

20   *"Lucille and Johnny . . .":* Irene DeVita Roselli to author, Dec. 1991.

21   *"My folks clamped down . . .":* Lopus to author, Mar. 1991.

21   *"My brother . . . the rest of us":* I. D. Roselli to author, Dec. 1991.

21   *"Lucille used to love . . .":* Frank Roselli to author, Mar. 1991.

22   *"It was shocking . . .":* Cleo Morgan Smith to author, Feb. 1991.

22   *"high-hat" Juliet:* Jim Brochu, *Lucy in the Afternoon* (New York: William Morrow, 1990), 47.

23   *"We were constantly . . .":* Bette Davis, *The Lonely Life* (New York: G.P. Putnam's Sons, 1962), 66.

24 *"The more I was put down . . .":* Eleanor Harris, *The Real Story of Lucille Ball* (New York: Farrar, Straus and Young, 1954), 7.

24 *Lucille mocked the training: New York Post,* Feb. 21, 1970.

24 *In Celeron she had created:* Gladys Hall Collection.

24 *She envied the self-confidence:* Pete Martin, "I Call on Lucy and Desi," *Saturday Evening Post,* May 31, 1958; *New York Post,* Feb. 21, 1970.

24 *"I knew at least . . .":* Davis, *The Lonely Life,* 76.

24 *"All I learned . . .":* Gladys Hall Collection.

25 *brief legal documents: Jamestown Morning Post,* May 15, 1928.

26 *"She wrote on the walls . . .":* Bernice Faulkner to author, Dec. 1991.

27 *"I was the only girl fired . . .":* Harris, *The Real Story of Lucille Ball,* 24.

27 *Flo Ziegfeld's corpulent right-hand man:* LB to reporter, 1952, private archives.

27 She stayed at a boardinghouse: LB to a seminar at the Museum of Broadcasting, New York, Apr. 1984.

28 *"She can reduce . . .":* "Luxury, Inc.," *The New Yorker,* Mar. 31, 1934.

28 *Lucille found Carnegie's:* Johny Aitchison to author, Feb. 1992.

29 *"This is where I was attacked . . .":* Charles Pomerantz to author, Aug. 1991.

29 *More than thirty years:* Brochu, *Lucy in the Afternoon,* 44.

29 *"I was slow and precise . . .":* Marion Strong Van Vlack to author, Dec. 1991.

29–30 *"The more noise . . .":* Ibid.

30 *"My brother bought . . .":* I. D. Roselli to author, Dec. 1991.

30 *she sought out taller boys:* Van Vlack to author, Dec. 1991.

30 *"Johnny thought she had a license . . .":* Ibid.

30 *"She brought the puppy home . . .":* Ibid., Mar. 1991.

30–31 *"I told her she did things . . .":* Ibid.

31 *"I even bounced . . .":* Gladys Hall Collection.

32 *"We bought Golden Glint . . .":* Ibid.

32 *"She was four or five years . . .":* Margaret Blossom to author, June 1992.

32–33 *"They couldn't put that . . .":* Ibid.

33 *"Miss Lucille Ball, as Agnes Lynch . . .": Jamestown Morning Post,* June 25, 1930.

33 *"Miss Ball gave one of the most impressive . . .": The Chautauqua Daily,* June 30, 1930.

33 *"This brought amusement . . .":* Blossom to author, June 1992.

CHAPTER 3

PAGE

34 *"I didn't see Lucille . . .":* Pauline Lopus to author, Mar. 1991.

35 *The two went everywhere:* Jamestown police to journalists, early 1950s, private archives.

35 *"A true friend . . .":* Marion Strong Van Vlack to author, Dec. 1991.

35 *"My mother said . . .":* LB to author, June 1986.

35 *"When something happens . . .":* Ibid.

35 *"Hattie took me . . .":* Ibid.

36 *"When she was in New York . . .":* Fred Ball to author, Feb. 1992.

36 *"I've never been able . . .":* Lopus to author, Mar. 1991.

36 *"She's responsible for a lot . . .":* Van Vlack to author, Mar. 1991.

36 *She enjoyed the designers:* LB to interviewer, private archives.
37 *Cars were parked undisturbed:* Studs Turkel, *Hard Times* (New York: Avon Books, 1970), 438.
37 *"If you want to be a dress model . . .":* *Cosmopolitan,* Mar. 1953.
38 *a raw October morning:* Private archives.
38 *"Bystanders trooped around . . .":* *The New York Times,* Oct. 26, 1930.
38 *"People used to confuse . . .":* Lucille McDonald Carroll to author, Jan. 1993.
38 *"She just remounted . . .":* Van Vlack to author, Mar. 1991.
39 *Johnny and another young man:* *Jamestown Evening Journal,* Feb. 18, 1931, p. 5.
39 *Four days later Louis was gunned:* Ibid., Feb. 23, 1931, p. 5.
39 *"She disarmed you . . .":* Private archives.
39 *"When I was a clumsy kid . . .":* Eleanor Harris, *The Real Story of Lucille Ball* (New York: Farrar, Straus and Young, 1954), 5.
40 *"Lucille told me . . .":* Van Vlack to author, Mar. 1991.
40–41 *". . . he's good-looking":* Ibid.
41 *"We would go to speakeasies . . .":* Ibid.
41 *"running like a streak" . . . "Lucille and I had a spat . . .":* Ibid.
41–42 *"When Lucille found out . . .":* Ibid.
42 *Roger came to be so important:* Private archives.
42 *"I think it's time . . .":* Ibid.
42 *"She was always willing . . .":* Ibid.
43 *"They were desperate . . .":* Joseph McBride, ed., *Filmmakers on Film-making,* vol. 1 (Los Angeles: J. P. Tarcher, 1983), 93.

CHAPTER 4

PAGE

45 *On their arrival:* Gladys Hall Collection.
45 *While some of the other girls:* Kirk Crivello, "Goldwyn Girls," *Film Fan Monthly,* Oct. 1974.
45 *"Now that the talkies . . .":* Charles Chaplin, *My Autobiography* (New York: Simon & Schuster, 1964), 380.
46 *"He noticed me":* *Rolling Stone,* June 23, 1983; see also A. Scott Berg, *Goldwyn* (New York: Alfred A. Knopf, 1989), 252.
46 *"I could tell a lot . . .":* Crivello, "Goldwyn Girls."
46 *After looking over the girls:* Ibid.
47 *"One girl thought . . .":* Nat Perrin to author, Feb. 1992. Although LB liked to say that during the filming of *Roman Scandals,* she deliberately bumped into the other girls to put life into silly proceedings, spoiling a film that was already behind schedule would not have been pardonable, nor would she have had the gall to do it.
47 *Lucille could see how things worked:* Gladys Hall Collection.
47 *"My stick-to-itness came . . .":* LB to author, June 1986.
47 *the harem's beauty salon:* Eddie Cantor to Cecil Smith, *Los Angeles Times,* undated (c. 1977), University of Southern California, Cinema-Television Library and Archives of Performing Arts, clipping collection.
47–48 *That gag and one:* Hedda Hopper Collection, Academy of Motion Picture

Arts and Sciences Library (hereinafter cited as Hedda Hopper Collection), transcript, July 1, 1962. LB told Hopper that her backside bore the scar of an alligator nip from her Goldwyn days; see also *Drama-Logue*, Sept. 25, 1986.

48   *She pestered Perrin:* Kyle Crichton, "Three Loves Has She," *Collier's,* Aug. 16, 1941.

48   *"She was far from unbeautiful . . .":* Perrin to author, Feb. 1992.

48   *She would call her early years:* LB interview, *Hollywood Citizen,* Nov. 28, 1941.

48–49   *"The only way I remember . . .":* Gladys Hall Collection.

49   *Ed Sedgwick:* Interview in *Los Angeles Times,* May 8, 1953.

49   *"I got a note . . .":* George Murphy to author, Dec. 1990.

49–50   *"When she first arrived . . .":* Perrin to author, Feb. 1992.

50   *"a father—with a gleam in his eye":* Gladys Hall Collection.

50   *"We just sat around . . .":* Interview with LB by Lawrence Grobel, *PSA* magazine, Apr. 1976.

51   *she waited outside the studio gates:* Herbert Kenwith to author, Feb. 1994.

52   *When Grey had a hernia:* Lewis Yablonsky, *George Raft* (New York: McGraw-Hill, 1974), 96.

52   *"What are they doing to you? . . .":* LB often gave this story to journalists. It was probably first quoted in *Photoplay,* Mar. 1947. See also Kay Gardella, "Lucille Ball Is Off for Gotham and Hollywood," *New York Sunday News,* Dec. 9, 1984.

52–53   *She doubled for Bennett: Jamestown Post,* June 23, 1934.

53   *The remedy must have worked:* Johny Aitchison to author, Feb. 1992.

54   *Lucille wrote Mildred:* Mildred Lahr to author, Sept. 1992.

54   *Instinctively, she felt:* John Bowlby, *Separation,* vol. 2, *Attachment and Loss* (New York: Basic Books, 1973), 203–4.

54   *Lucille had sufficient cash:* Yablonsky, *George Raft,* 111.

54   *"When I came out . . .":* Fred Ball to author, Feb. 1992.

54   *She and her new friend Ann Sothern:* Gladys Hall Collection.

54   *". . . anything less than the best":* Fred Ball to author, Feb. 1992.

55   *"Her rise in the cinema . . .": Jamestown Post,* June 23, 1934.

55   *She heartily greeted:* Gladys Hall Collection.

56   *"Lucille had a great deal . . .":* Murphy to author, Dec. 1990.

56   *"Ben Silvie . . .":* Ibid.

56   *For the finale, "Ice Cream Fantasy":* A. Scott Berg, *Goldwyn* (New York: Alfred A. Knopf, 1989), 254.

56–57   *"He told us he wasn't . . .":* Perrin to author, Feb. 1992.

57   *"I didn't want to be a showgirl . . .":* LB to author, June 1986.

57   *He routinely bawled out contract players:* Frank Capra, *The Name Above the Title* (New York: Macmillan, 1971), 82.

58   *This racing picture:* Ibid., 405.

58   *"One day at six o'clock . . .":* LB to author, June 1986.

58   *"I don't want . . .":* Ibid.

59   *$75 a week:* RKO production notes, Theater Arts Library, University of California at Los Angeles.

59   *"Don't take the train! . . .":* LB to author, June 1986.

59   *George Raft's limousine:* Yablonsky, *George Raft,* 111.

59 *Six years later:* Eleanor Harris, *The Real Story of Lucille Ball* (New York: Farrar, Straus and Young, 1954), 28.

59 *"We saw palm trees . . . Lucy needed that":* Cleo Morgan Smith to author, Feb. 1991.

CHAPTER 5

PAGE

61 *Lucille, as one of the Parisian:* RKO production notes, Theater Arts Library, University of California at Los Angeles. Gladys Hall Collection.

62 *After Lucille confessed this:* Joseph McBride, *Filmmakers on Filmmaking,* vol. 1 (Los Angeles: J. P. Tarcher, 1983).

62 *"the top comedienne of all time":* James Harvey, *Romantic Comedy in Hollywood* (New York: Alfred A. Knopf, 1987).

63 *"I thought Lucille . . .":* Betty Furness to author, Oct. 1991.

63 *"I've always been a family person . . .":* Eleanor Harris, *The Real Story of Lucille Ball* (New York: Farrar, Straus and Young, 1954), 30.

63 *"She would get so involved . . .":* Al Gerston to author, Mar. 1992.

64 *They went to industry functions:* Clipping in the Academy of Motion Picture Arts and Sciences library, n.d.

64 *As a florist's assistant:* Jay Sandrich to author, Oct. 1991; see also *Los Angeles Times,* Calendar section, Oct. 12, 1986.

64–65 For details on Pandro Berman's career, see RKO press releases and newspaper clippings on Berman from the Academy of Motion Picture Arts and Sciences library and others; also Berman Oral History, American Film Institute.

65 *"Pandro Berman was crazy . . .":* Cleo Morgan Smith to author, Feb. 1991.

65 *"Lucille was one of the guys . . .":* Arnold Stang to author, Dec. 1992.

66 *"She was very talented . . .":* Berman Oral History, American Film Institute.

66 *"Am I ever going . . .":* Margaret Hamilton to Michael Hearn (as reported to author, Oct. 1992).

67 *"I bought the studio!":* Ibid.

67 *"I posed for . . .":* Harris, *The Real Story of Lucille Ball,* 30.

67 *"My mother went . . .":* Ginger Rogers to author, Feb. 1992.

67–68 *RKO executives found:* Ginger Rogers, *Ginger* (New York: HarperCollins, 1991); Douglas Gilbert, "Stage Mothers," *New York World-Telegram,* May 1, 1939.

68 *"She was very bright . . .":* Furness to author, Oct. 1991.

68 *"Lucy picked Lela's brains . . .":* Smith to author, Feb. 1991.

68 *"Lela took a great shine . . . talking about work":* Phyllis Cerf Wagner to author, Sept. 1991.

69 *"Ginger and her mother . . .":* Gladys Hall Collection.

69 *"If I'd behaved myself . . .":* Henry Fonda, *Fonda: My Life* (New York: New American Library, 1981), 101–2.

69 *"Lucille's mother was charming . . .":* Rogers to author, Feb. 1992.

70 *"I remember feeling . . .":* This quotation and information on Fred Hunt's Communist sympathies from a transcript of LB's testimony to the House Un-American Activities Committee, published in *Los Angeles Times,* Sept. 13, 1953.

70   *When Lucille hired cleaning women:* Harris, *The Real Story of Lucille Ball*, 32.

70   *"Don't tell me you don't know about this":* Smith to author, Feb. 1991.

70   *Lucille's grandfather also hosted: Los Angeles Times*, Sept. 13, 1953.

71–72   *In a film shot in the San Fernando:* McBride, *Filmmakers on Filmmaking.*

72   *Executives immediately called:* LB interview with Lawrence Grobel, *PSA* magazine, Apr. 1976.

72–73   *"Lucille was a friend . . .":* Katharine Hepburn to author, Aug. 1992.

73   *Kaufman's agent, Leland Hayward:* Berman Oral History, American Film Institute.

73–74   *Hey Diddle Diddle* production and reviews come from newspaper clippings from *Variety, The New York Times,* and *The Washington Post,* Jan. and Feb. 1937, New York Public Library for the Performing Arts, Lincoln Center, New York City.

CHAPTER 6

77   *"I thought, the hell . . .":* Hepburn quoted on *Hollywood: The Golden Years,* BBC documentary, 1987.

77   *Ginger pointed out:* Rogers quoted on ibid.

77   *The group bonded:* Eve Arden, *Three Phases of Eve* (New York: St. Martin's Press, 1985).

77   *According to the screenwriter:* George Seaton Oral History, American Film Institute.

77   *"The very way she talked . . .":* LB quoted in *The RKO Story,* BBC documentary.

78   *"I'm damned if I know, Kate":* Katharine Hepburn, *Me* (New York: Alfred A. Knopf, 1991).

78   *"I don't think Lucille . . .":* Katharine Hepburn to author, June 1990.

79   *Perhaps in a fit:* Charles Higham, *Lucy* (New York: St. Martin's Press, 1986), 45.

80   *"What the hell are you doing . . .":* Robert Parrish to author, Dec. 20, 1991.

80–81   *"One of the first . . .":* Ibid.

81   *"She was obviously gifted . . .":* Douglas Fairbanks, Jr., to author, Feb. 1992.

81   *She drove there:* Marcella Rabwin to author, July 1991; LB to students at Sherwood Oaks Experimental College, 1977.

82   *"I saw this beautiful girl . . .":* Milton Berle to author, Feb. 1991.

82–83   *"Al Hall was . . . she was an ambitious girl . . .":* Garson Kanin to author, Aug. 1991.

83   *"If you introduced . . .":* Flo Haley to author, Dec. 1992.

84   *Line reading probably: The Los Angeles Times,* May 8, 1953.

84   *"She and I became . . . Lucille just adored her":* Rabwin to author, July 1991.

85   *"She offered to put me . . .":* Fred Ball to author, Feb. 1992.

85   *"When Lucille started to get famous . . .":* Pauline Lopus to author, Mar. 1991.

86   *"I started as a model . . .":* Joseph McBride, *Filmmakers on Filmmaking,* vol. 1 (Los Angeles: J. P. Tarcher, 1983).

86   *In the first Annabel film:* LB interview with Lawrence Grobel, *PSA* magazine, Apr. 1976.

86–87 *At her best:* Frank Nugent, *The New York Times*, Oct. 13, 1938.

87   *"And of course there is Miss Ball . . .":* *The New York Times*, Dec. 1938.

87   *"She was extremely inventive . . .":* Kanin to author, Aug. 1991.

87–88 *"She is one of the more promising . . .":* *The New York Times*, Feb. 10, 1939.

89   *Miffed to hear:* LB to Dick Cavett, March 1974; and LB to Sherman Oaks Experimental College, 1977.

89   *She was Harpo's date:* A. Scott Berg, *Goldwyn* (New York: Alfred A. Knopf, 1989), 252.

89–90 *"I've never found . . .":* Hector Arce, *Groucho* (New York: G.P. Putnam's Sons, 1979), 261.

90   *Zeppo told Lucille:* LB to Sherman Oaks Experimental College, 1977.

90   *"She didn't know . . .":* Haley to author, Dec. 1992.

90   *"Her material was only so-so . . .":* *Variety*, Feb. 16, 1938.

90   *"In pictures, by the time . . .":* Hedda Hopper Collection, transcript, Jan. 1, 1962.

CHAPTER 7

PAGE

92   *Lucille would turn to astrology:* *Vogue*, Mar. 1974, p. 66.

93   *Desi was dark:* Marco Rizo to author, Dec. 1991; Margarita de Mena to author, Aug. 1991; Desi Arnaz, *A Book* (New York: William Morrow, 1976), 143, 238.

94   *"I am sure Grandma . . .":* Arnaz, *A Book*, 11.

94   *Once in a burst of temper:* Ibid, 99.

94   *Cosseted and cherished:* Nancy Chodorow, *The Reproduction of Mothering* (Berkeley: University of California Press, 1978), 196.

96   *"At these moments . . .":* Dorothy Kilgallen, "The Voice of Broadway," *New York Journal-American*, Sept. 2, 1939.

96   *"I was crazy . . .":* George Abbott to author, Apr. 1991.

97   *"Desi was outgoing . . .":* Eddie Bracken to author, Mar. 1991.

97   *Now forty-five:* de Mena to author, Aug. 1991.

99–100 *Pommer, who had seen:* *The New York Times*, Oct. 7, 1940, section VI, p. 3.

100   *"It is Miss Ball . . .":* Ibid., Oct. 11, 1940.

100   *For her role:* *Hollywood Citizen News*, Mar. 24, 1940.

101   *As a teenager:* Barbara L. Bell to author, June 1993.

101   *"You can't tell me what to do!":* Ibid.

101   *Later, when Lucille:* Maureen O'Hara to author, Feb. 1991.

102   *The lady was . . .":* Maury Thompson to author, Feb. 1992.

102   *"We were competitive . . . earlier the next day":* O'Hara to author, Feb. 1991.

102   *"Anyone who wanted to watch us beat . . .":* Ibid.

102   *"two-dollar whore beaten by her pimp":* Arnaz, *A Book*, 108.

102–3 *"It was like Wow! . . .":* O'Hara to author, Feb. 1991.

103   *"They hit it off . . .":* Abbott to author, Apr. 1991.

103   *Lucille always believed:* Kyle Crichton, "Three Loves Has She," *Collier's*, Aug. 16, 1941.

104   *Waking up beside Desi:* Arnaz, *A Book*, 110.

CHAPTER 8

105 *Lucille paid no attention:* Peter Martin, "I Call on Lucy and Desi," *Saturday Evening Post*, May 31, 1958.

106 *The evening after the first:* Desi Arnaz, *A Book* (New York: William Morrow, 1976), 110; Eleanor Harris, "A Pan-American Romance," undated article in the collection of the New York Public Library for the Performing Arts, Lincoln Center, New York City.

106 *On a two-hour trip:* Martin, "I Call on Lucy and Desi."

106 *She loved it:* Arnaz, *A Book*, 111.

106 *"I had more faith . . .":* Eddie Bracken to author, Mar. 1991.

106–7 *On the set:* Harris, "Pan-American Romance."

107 *"Desi came on strong . . .":* Garson Kanin to author, Aug. 1991.

107 *Lee Marcus:* Theater Arts Library, University of California at Los Angeles.

107 *"very down-to-earth . . .":* George Abbott to author, Apr. 1991.

108 *"She didn't move because she might break":* Bracken to author, Mar. 1991.

108 *"Lucy and Desi were so involved . . .":* Frances Langford to author, Sept. 1992.

108 *F. Scott Fitzgerald:* Sheilah Graham, *The Rest of the Story* (New York: Coward-McCann, 1961), 180.

108–9 *"Whatever she wanted . . .":* Cleo Morgan Smith to author, Feb. 1991.

109 *Desi liked Lucille's mother:* Special collections, San Diego State University Library, the Desi Arnaz Autobiographical Materials.

109 *her first serious gift from him:* Harris, "Pan-American Romance."

109 *"Mr. Arnaz is a noisy . . .":* Bosley Crowther, *The New York Times*, Nov. 21, 1940.

110 *"a terpsichorean Rudolph Valentino":* Time, Nov. 11, 1940.

110 *". . . talent as a comedienne":* Variety, Oct. 4, 1940.

110 *"I kept staring at this beautiful . . . giggling and dancing":* Barbara L. Bell to author, June 1993.

110 *"From that day . . .":* Arnaz, *A Book*, 112.

110 *During her visit:* Harris, "Pan-American Romance."

111 *When Lucille rejoined:* Maureen O'Hara to author, Feb. 1991.

111 *"Grab Grandma Peterson . . .":* Marion Strong Van Vlack to author, Dec. 1991.

112 For salaries, see RKO production notes, Theater Arts Library, University of California at Los Angeles.

112 *Lloyd intervened on the set:* Kevin Brownlow, *The Parade's Gone By* (Berkeley: University of California Press, 1968), 42.

112 *Harriet was not impressed:* Bell to author, June 1993.

112 *"looked like a peach all over":* Arnaz, *A Book*, 104.

113 *In later years, he said:* Special collections, San Diego State University Library, the Desi Arnaz Autobiographical Materials.

113 *"DARLING, JUST . . .":* Harris, "Pan-American Romance."

113 *To annoy him:* Arnaz, *A Book*, 113.

114 *"DARLING IT WAS WONDERFUL . . .":* Harris, "Pan-American Romance."

114 *"You Cuban sonofabitch . . .":* Arnaz, *A Book*, 113.

114 *Lucille estimated:* Harris, "Pan-American Romance."

114 *"SWEETHEART IT IS WONDERFUL . . .":* Ibid.

114 *"I was madly in love . . .":* Arnaz, *A Book*, 113.

115   *"I love you very much . . .":* Ibid., 114.
115–16   *Their day began just before dawn: New York Daily News,* Mar. 21, 1950.

CHAPTER 9

117   *The new Mr. and Mrs. Desi Arnaz:* Notes, Gladys Hall Collection.
117   *The next morning:* Desi Arnaz, *A Book* (New York: William Morrow, 1976), 118–19.
117–18   *"I knew Latin men . . .":* McCall's, Sept. 1960.
118   *"Lucille Ball and Desi Arnaz obliged . . .":* Danton Walker column, *New York Daily News,* Dec. 2, 1940.
118   *"When I looked . . .":* Arnaz, *A Book,* 119.
118   *As they traveled:* Johny Aitchison to author, Feb. 1992.
118   *"Who did we marry?":* Gladys Hall Collection.
119   *"He seems like a nice fellow . . .":* Arnaz, *A Book,* 129. In his notes for *A Book* (Special collections, San Diego State University Library, the Desi Arnaz Autobiographical Materials), Desi claimed he met Fred Hunt only after the wedding, but other sources contradict this.
119   *At first the couple:* Gladys Hall Collection.
119   *Her favorite meal: PM* magazine, Aug. 11, 1946.
120   *Friends gave them chickens:* Arnaz, *A Book,* 131.
120   *"No one else ever . . .":* Marcella Rabwin to author, July 1991.
120   *No one was allowed:* Arnaz, *A Book,* 128 and 122; Marva Peterson, "Living with Lucy," undated article, University of Southern California, Cinema-Television Library and Archives of Performing Arts, clipping collection.
121   *In an audience survey:* Audience Research Institute, Mar. 26, 1941.
121   *"I guess I was a few years . . .":* Arnaz, *A Book,* 132–33.
122   *"The procedure is this . . .":* Kyle Crichton, "Three Loves Has She," *Collier's,* Aug. 16, 1941.
122   *tortured character actor:* Audience Research Institute, Feb. and Mar. 1941; *The New York Times,* Aug. 8, 1941; Hedda Hopper Collection, column, May 9, 1941.
123   *Goldwyn offered the role:* A. Scott Berg, *Goldwyn* (New York: Alfred A. Knopf, 1989), 362.
123   *Lucille knew the role:* Jim Brochu, *Lucy in the Afternoon* (New York: William Morrow, 1990), 82.
123–24   *"Although she is known . . . around to noticing her":* Audience Research Institute, Apr. 24, 1941, May 1941.
125   *In the early months:* LB to author, July 1986.
125   *"That's my Desi . . .":* Crichton, "Three Loves Has She."
125   *"Don't make me look like a fool!":* Rabwin to author, July 1991.
125   *On another occasion:* Eleanor Harris, *The Real Story of Lucille Ball* (New York: Farrar, Straus and Young, 1954), 44.
126–27   *"the sickest film ever made": Interview* magazine, Apr. 1978.
127   *"If you are going to play . . .":* Arnaz, *A Book,* 128.
127   *She so excelled: Philadelphia Daily News,* June 6, 1942; *Life,* Oct. 5, 1942.
127–28   *"You're not going . . .":* Brochu, *Lucy in the Afternoon,* 84.
128   *"the dignity of a wax grape . . .": Time,* Sept. 7, 1942.
128   *RKO approached other studios:* Memo, May 1942, Schary Collection, Wisconsin Center for Film and Theater Research, Madison, Wisconsin.

129 *"She would either scream . . . these situations"*: Arnold Stang to author, Dec. 1992.
129 *"Lucille knew I was spending . . ."*: Ibid.

CHAPTER 10

132 *From a vast office:* "Who's Who at MGM 1924–1944," MGM publicity brochure (in collection at University of Southern California); *Life,* Sept. 27, 1943.
132 *The costume designer Irene:* Gladys Hall Collection.
133 *His intense concentration:* Eleanor Harris, *The Real Story of Lucille Ball* (New York: Farrar, Straus and Young, 1954), 112; *Life,* Aug. 9, 1943.
133 *"When she arrived . . ."*: Sydney Guilaroff to author, Mar. 1993.
133 *He dispatched Lucille:* Irma Kusely to author, Aug. 1992.
133 *"They worked hours . . ."*: Ibid.
133 *They chose orange-toned: Life,* Aug. 9, 1943.
133 *In contrast to this:* Gloria DeHaven to author, May 1993.
134 *"I can't sing! . . ."*: The Daily Trojan (USC newspaper), Nov. 6, 1980.
134 Lucille's singing: Virginia O'Brien to author, Feb. 1992.
134–35 Details on Freund's career are from *Film in Review,* Feb. 1963.
135 *"Lucille herself is almost . . ."*: Life, Oct. 5, 1942.
135 *"Lucille Ball hates the color . . ."*: Hedda Hopper Collection, "Looking at Hollywood" column, Jan. 31, 1945.
136 *MGM spent:* Hugh Fordin, *The World of Entertainment* (New York: Doubleday, 1973), 78.
136 *From a corner of the set: Look,* Aug. 7, 1971, p. 56.
136 *He was grateful to land:* Special collections, San Diego State University Library, the Desi Arnaz Autobiographical Materials.
136–37 *"Busher looks very common . . ."*: Desi Arnaz, *A Book* (New York: William Morrow, 1976), 140.
137 *She made candles:* Fan magazine, University of Southern California, Cinema-Television Library and Archive of Performing Arts, clipping collection.
139 *"Lucille conned me into playing . . ."*: Maxine Andrews to author, Feb. 1992.
139 *Lucille's most popular hors d'oeuvre:* O'Brien to author, Feb. 1992.
139 *"It was such a long bad road . . ."*: Marcella Rabwin to author, July 1991.
139 *"The only trouble with the barbecue . . ."*: Ibid.
139 *On many Sundays:* Gladys Hall Collection.
139 *Barrymore had persuaded Gable:* Peter Jay, *MGM: When the Lion Roars* (Atlanta: Turner Publishing, 1991), 98.
140 *Desi stayed home and fumed:* Special collections, San Diego State University Library, the Desi Arnaz Autobiographical Materials.
140 *Made for $1,125,502:* Fordin, *World of Entertainment,* 83.
140–41 *The studio was forced to suspend:* MGM production notes, USC.
141 *he organized a musical:* Private archives.
141 *"My baby, you called . . ."*: Lucy and Desi: A Home Movie, Arluck Entertainment documentary, 1993.
141 *". . . carton of toilet paper."*: Gale Gordon to author, July 1990.
142 *"DeDe always had a platitude . . ."*: Cleo Morgan Smith to author, Feb. 1991.

142   *She went over to Celeron:* Mrs. Zuhr Faulkner to author, Dec. 1991.
142   *she did visit Johnny DeVita:* Joseph and Florence DeVita Conte to author, Dec. 1991.
142   *"She had a frilly blue bed jacket . . .":* Frances D'Angelo to author, Mar. 1991.
143   *Talking to a reporter: Jamestown Post-Journal,* Jan. 19–24, 1944; clipping, 1980.
144   *filed for divorce:* Arnaz, *A Book,* 153.
144   *"I'm just as much . . .":* Louella Parsons columns, Oct. 17, 1944 and Sept. 8, 1944, in Academy of Motion Picture Arts and Sciences library.
144   *"He called . . .":* Marco Rizo to author, Dec. 1991.
144   *"The divorce for her . . .":* Smith to author, Feb. 1991.
145   *"Well, of course they recognized her . . .":* Marion Strong Van Vlack to author, Mar. 1991.
145   *"I tried to open . . .":* Ibid.
145   *They agreed that each:* Harris, *The Real Story of Lucille Ball,* 48–50.
146   *Their stunt amused them:* Arnaz, *A Book,* 154.
146   *"Lucille used to complain . . .":* Janis Carter to author, Apr. 1993.
146   *"Well then, quit . . .":* Arnaz, *A Book,* 174.
147   *Desi now made the fifteen-minute trip:* Ibid.
148   *typed as something other:* Gladys Hall Collection.
149   *"virtual peonage for employees, even life bondage":* Current Biography, *1944,* 215.
149   *Lucille telephoned de Havilland:* Interview with LB by Lawrence Grobel, *PSA* magazine, Apr. 1976; *Los Angeles Times,* Calendar section, Oct. 12, 1986; Olivia de Havilland to author, Apr. 1991.
149   *"Lucille immediately stood up . . .":* Irene Vernon to author, Nov. 1992.
150   *She challenged both MGM:* Berg/Allenberg announcement to Warner Brothers, Oct. 17, 1945; *Los Angeles Times,* June 12, 1946.
150   *Infuriated, she allowed:* Hedda Hopper Collection, transcript, July 1, 1963; *Los Angeles Times,* June 12, 1946.
151   *Lucille believed that Olivia:* Gladys Hall Collection; LB to Grobel, *PSA,* Apr. 1976; *Los Angeles Times,* Calendar section; Oct. 12, 1986; Olivia de Havilland to author, Apr. 1991.
151   *"Lucille called me . . .":* Kurt Frings to author, May 1991.
151   *a final picture for MGM:* Bob Thomas Associated Press story, Oct. 15, 1947.
151   *"We knew she had talent . . .":* Lucille Ryman Carroll to author, May 1991.
151   *"In a matter-of-fact way . . .":* Andrews to author, Feb. 1992.

PAGE   **CHAPTER 11**

152   *When Desi left the army:* Desi Arnaz, *A Book* (New York: William Morrow, 1976), 161.
152   *Desi maintained his pride:* Martin Leeds to author, Feb. 1992.
153   *"Look what I treated myself to!":* Virginia O'Brien to author, Feb. 1992.
153   *"His act was not the best . . .":* George Schlatter to author, Oct. 1992.
153   *He was as promiscuous:* Fred Ball interview in *Lucy and Desi: A Home Movie,* Arluck Productions documentary, 1993.

154 *"He'd miss being able . . ."*: Marco Rizo to author, Dec. 1991.

154 *Zsa Zsa Gabor described him*: Zsa Zsa Gabor and Frank Gerold, *Zsa Zsa Gabor: My Story* (New York: World Publishing, 1960), 175.

154 *"searching the world for his mother"*: Gladys Hall Collection.

155 *"What are you doing . . ."*: Zsa Zsa Gabor to author, Oct. 1991.

155 *Desi professed a tropical sense*: Special collections, San Diego State University Library, the Desi Arnaz Autobiographical Materials.

155 *"I'm convinced that the reason . . ."*: Arnaz, *A Book*, 175.

155 *He described their reunions*: Ibid., 187.

155 *"You've got two children . . ."*: Sheilah Graham, *The Rest of the Story* (New York: Coward-McCann, 1961), 182.

156 *"She wanted to hurry up . . ."*: Barbara L. Bell to author, June 1993.

156 *"I want Desi's baby"*: Cleo Morgan Smith to author, Feb. 1991.

156 *"She was yelling . . ."*: Herbert Kenwith to author, May 1993.

157 *"You did something marvelous . . ."*: Ibid.

157 *On opening night*: Ibid.

157 *I have seen other productions . . ."*: Elmer Rice, *Minority Report* (New York: Simon & Schuster, 1963), 411.

157 *she was a seasoned trouper*: Hedda Hopper Collection; *New York Herald Tribune*, June 22, 1947.

157 *engagement was cut short*: *Los Angeles Times*, Jan. 11, 1948.

157 *"She has efficiency . . ."*: *Los Angeles Times*, Jan. 6, 1948.

158 *Kurt Frings had an agent*: Kurt Frings to author, May 1991; Leeds to author, June 1993; *Variety*, Dec. 27, 1950; *New York Herald Tribune*, July 31, 1953; *New York Journal-American Pictorial TView*, Oct. 6, 1957; *New York Times*, Nov. 23, 1952.

160 *"I wasn't afraid of her . . ."*: Madelyn Pugh Davis to author, July 1990.

160 *"It began to work . . ."*: Ibid.

160 *A consequence of this*: Gregg Oppenheimer to author, Feb. 1994; Bob Carroll, Jr., to author, Feb. 1994; *New York Herald Tribune* TV magazine, May 9, 1954.

161 *"She was skittish . . ."*: Davis to author, July 1990.

161 *"Grow it back . . ."*: Carroll, Jr., to author, July 1991.

161 *Until then*: *Los Angeles Times*, Calendar section, Oct. 12, 1986; Gladys Hall Collection.

161–62 *"My first impression of Lucille . . ."*: Gale Gordon to author, July 1990.

162 *"It was 'Lucille Ball, . . ."*: Hal Humphrey column, *Los Angeles Mirror*, Jan. 24, 1951.

162 *Buster Keaton and Ed Sedgwick*: Frings to author, May 1991.

163 *On another weekend*: Eleanor Harris, *The Real Story of Lucille Ball* (New York: Farrar, Straus and Young, 1954), 115.

163 *"Lucille was semihyper"*: Eleanor Keaton to author, May 1991.

163 *"I evaded telling her . . ."*: Ibid.

164 *Sedgwick and Keaton shared an office*: Ibid.

165 *"Lucille's ambitions weren't about . . ."*: Janis Carter to author, Apr. 1993.

165 *"We both had a pet hate . . ."*: Ibid.

165 *"Lucille was more devoted . . ."*: Eddie Albert to author, June 1991.

166 *"When the gag bag was opened . . ."*: *Independent Film Journal*, Sept. 23, 1950.

166 *"If there were ever any doubts . . ."*: *Variety*, Sept. 20, 1950.

166 *She described naps as "deadening"*: "Keep Beautiful," by Lucille Ball,

undated article, University of Southern California, Cinema-Television Library and Archives of Performing Arts, clipping collection.

166 *Desi was with her:* Arnaz, *A Book,* 187–89.

167 *To prove that Holliday:* Garson Kanin, *Hollywood* (New York: Viking, 1967), 372–74.

168 *In cities with even one television:* Eric Barnow, *Tube of Plenty* (New York: Oxford University Press, 1975), 113–14.

168 *She appeared on:* Programs listed in the Library of Congress.

168 *"I didn't know she had been . . .":* Ralph Levy quoted in Bart Andrews, *The "I Love Lucy" Book* (New York: Doubleday, 1985), 20.

169 *The first project they considered: New York Times,* July 18, 1950; Hedda Hopper Collection, May 29, 1950, and Sept. 12, 1950.

169 *"He finally came in at one in the morning . . .":* Maxine Andrews to author, Feb. 1992.

170 *"She didn't know what to do . . .":* Lucille Ryman Carroll to author, May 1991.

170 *Lucille and Desi intently staring:* O'Brien to author, Feb. 1992.

CHAPTER 12

171 *"I was terribly depressed . . .":* Marcella Rabwin to author, July 1991.

172 *their sixth anniversary: Los Angeles Times,* Dec. 2, 1946.

172 *So conscientious were they:* Lucille Ryman Carroll to author, May 1991.

172 *Desi admitted to his wife:* Desi Arnaz, *A Book* (New York: William Morrow, 1976), 191.

172 *While she did not go so far:* The Reverend John D. Murray to author, Nov. 1992.

173 *"Before he hit the floor . . .":* Rabwin to author, July 1991.

173 *closed a fallopian tube:* LB to author, July 1986.

173 *The doctor sent her home:* Arnaz, *A Book,* 192; LB to author, July 1986; LB to students at Sherwood Oaks Experimental College, 1977.

173 *"I think they were real friends":* Eleanor Harris, *The Real Story of Lucille Ball* (New York: Farrar, Straus and Young, 1954), 114.

174 *His first step for Lucille: Business Week,* Oct. 5, 1957.

174 *Buster Keaton worked with Lucille: Look,* Sept. 7, 1971, p. 56; Joseph McBride, ed., *Filmmakers on Filmmaking,* vol. 1 (Los Angeles: J. P. Tarcher, 1983), 86.

175 *"I saw Pepito . . .":* Eddie Albert to author, June 1991.

175 *In Chicago, their hotel room: New York Times,* June 3, 1950.

175 *tenth anniversary party: New York Times,* June 11, 1953.

175 Lucille had morning sickness: Marion Strong Van Vlack to author, March 1991.

175 *"The manager had that redhead's . . .":* Barbara L. Bell to author, June 1993.

175 *Upon their return to Chatsworth: American Weekly Magazine,* May 17, 1953, p. 6; Harris, *The Real Story of Lucille Ball,* 63.

176 *". . . against the wall afterward!":* Betty Garrett to author, Sept. 1992.

177 *She was, to her great joy:* Ibid.

177 *"Congratulations, Mr. Arnaz . . .":* Arnaz, *A Book,* 198.

177 *"Moola over the Mountain": Variety,* Dec. 13, 1950.

177 *"Honey, go ahead . . .": Look,* Dec. 25, 1956.

178 *The network's original plan: Variety,* Feb. 7, 1951.

178 *They called this situation comedy:* Screen Writers Guild registration, Mar. 2, 1951.

178–79 *Lucille was six months pregnant:* Ralph Levy to author, June 1991.

179 *"That son of a bitch . . .":* Martin Leeds to author, Feb. 1991.

179–80 *"That was a lot of time . . .":* Barney McNulty to author, July 1992.

180 *"Wait until you see Lucille . . .":* Frances Langford to author, Sept. 1992.

180 *The vice president of CBS network programming:* Leeds to author, Feb. 1992 (*New York Daily News,* Mar. 14, 1954, is source for prices).

180 *his part would grow smaller:* Ed Sullivan, *New York Daily News,* Mar. 14, 1954.

181 *Television shows were being filmed: Hollywood Reporter,* Nov. 1950; *Variety,* May 9, 1951.

181 *Although Edwards's crew filmed:* CBS press materials provided by Gregg Oppenheimer; *Variety,* Jan. 31, 1951.

182 *they gave the couple ownership:* Leeds to author, Feb. 1992.

182 *Desi estimated:* Arnaz, *A Book,* 203.

182 *"I liked her the very first . . .":* Al Simon to author, June 1991.

183 *"We expected the lighting . . .":* Ibid.

183 *"When Marlene pulled out . . .":* Dorothy Aldworth to author, Nov. 1991.

184 *He told her Jess Oppenheimer:* Bart Andrews, *The "I Love Lucy" Book* (New York: Doubleday, 1985), 52.

185 *Oppenheimer surely believed: Writers Guild of America West News,* June 1976, pp. 13–14.

185 *The filming of* I Love Lucy: Marva Peterson, "Living with Lucy," undated article, University of Southern California, Cinema-Television Library and Archive of Performing Arts, clipping collection.

185 *The only real change: American Weekly,* May 24, 1953.

185–86 *"I was thrilled" . . . "My sisters . . .":* Maxine Andrews to author, Feb. 1992.

186 *"Go outside and talk to my husband!":* Joseph and Florence DeVita Conte to author, Dec. 1991.

186–87 Details on the birth of Lucie Arnaz are from Arnaz, *A Book,* 238; Jim Brochu, *Lucy in the Afternoon* (New York: William Morrow, 1990), 103–4; *The American Weekly,* May 24, 1953, p. 15; Leeds to author, Feb. 1992.

187 *"Norman didn't know what . . .":* Van Vlack to author, Mar. 1991.

CHAPTER 13

PAGE

189 *Emboldened by his quarrelsome:* Bart Andrews, *The "I Love Lucy" Book* (New York: Doubleday, 1985), 38.

190 *She had lived with the specter:* Confidential interview.

190 *After some deliberation, Desi approved:* Andrews, *The "I Love Lucy" Book,* 43.

190–91 *During the run-through:* First reading anecdotes and dialogue from Maury Thompson to author, Feb. 1992.

191 *Lucille's nervous energy:* Vivian Vance to Bob Thomas, *New York World-Telegram,* Sept. 1, 1962.

193   *Not trusting:* Andrews, *The "I Love Lucy" Book*, 63.

193   *It was weeks before Lucy:* Ibid., 69.

193   *nearly 14 million:* American Research Bureau ratings in CBS files, Feb. 1952.

194–95   *Even Ricky's vituperative eruptions:* Mercedes Manzanares to author, May 1991.

195   *As strong-willed as she was:* Herb Browar to author, June 1991.

196   *"Lucy and Desi wanted to create . . .":* Browar to author, June 1991.

196   *Freund's first words:* Ibid.

196   *Freund corrected unflattering lighting: International Press Bulletin*, Jan.–Mar. 1965, pp. 18–30; Jess Oppenheimer in "Lucille Ball: First Lady of Comedy," Museum of Broadcasting booklet, 1984, p. 32.

197   *"During a scene with Vivian":* Eleanor Harris, *The Real Story of Lucille Ball* (New York: Farrar, Straus and Young, 1954), 10.

197   *"When she did a routine . . .":* Claudio Guzman to author, July 1991.

197   *"This handle is too short":* Thompson to author, Feb. 1992.

197   *"I never found a place . . .":* Gladys Hall Collection.

198   *She did what Ed Sedgwick:* Hal Humphrey column, *Los Angeles Mirror*, Dec. 31, 1951.

198   *"If Lucy liked you . . .":* Bernard Weitzman to author, May 1991.

198   *"It's my bread, bring it in":* Joseph McBride, ed., *Filmmakers on Filmmaking*, vol. 1 (Los Angeles: J. P. Tarcher, 1983), 87.

198   *"You like blue suits? . . .":* Thompson to author, Feb. 1992.

198–99   *the legend that Vivian:* Martin Leeds to author, June 1993; Philip Welzman to author, July 1991.

199   *"My father made me so ashamed . . .":* Bob Schiller to author, June 1991.

199–200   *"We dreaded the run-throughs . . .":* Madelyn Pugh Davis to author, July 1990.

200   *When they got spooked:* Hal Humphrey column, *Los Angeles Times*, May 6, 1953.

201   *"If he didn't know . . .":* Bob Carroll, Jr., to author, July 1991.

201–02   *"She'd look at me . . .":* Marco Rizo to author, Dec. 1991.

202   *"Desi, that's the first . . .":* Browar to author, June 1991.

202   *Mertz had a dual heritage: Jamestown Post*, June 6, 1934.

203   *". . . I'll never forget it.":* Manzanares to author, May 1991.

203   *Mary Emery:* Ibid.

203   *her first mink coat:* Harris, *The Real Story of Lucille Ball*, 102, 8, and 9.

203   *Thrilled with her baby:* Arlene Dahl to author, Oct. 1992.

203   *On workdays little Lucie:* Margarita deMena to author, Aug. 1991.

204   *"What difference does it . . .":* Manzanares to author, May 1991.

204   *To a Cuban relative:* deMena to author, Aug. 1991.

205   *While Lucy studied her lines: Cosmopolitan*, Nov. 1962.

205   *He hated the way television:* Ed Holly to author, Feb. 1992; Dann Cahn to author, May 1991.

205   *When Desi learned that some of the laughs:* James G. Stewart Oral History, American Film Institute.

205–6   *going into television themselves:* Emily Daniels to author, June 1991.

206   *"You never heard her saying much . . .":* Leeds to author, June 1991.

CHAPTER 14

207 *Lucy was in such a state:* Barbara L. Bell to author, June 1993.

207–8 *"She taught me how to . . .":* Eleanor Harris, *The Real Story of Lucille Ball* (New York: Farrar, Straus and Young, 1954), 53.

209 *"She came into my office . . .":* Norman Vincent Peale to author, Apr. 1991.

209 *"Goddam it, I'm pregnant again!":* Herb Browar to author, June 1991.

209 *Lucy and Desi faced Jess: Newsweek,* Jan. 19, 1953; *Look,* Apr. 21, 1953.

210 *"To whom it may concern . . .":* Desi Arnaz, *A Book* (New York: William Morrow, 1976), 235.

210–11 *Mrs. Arnaz craved cream puffs:* LB to a seminar at the Museum of Broadcasting, New York, Apr. 1984.

211 *the professional candymaker:* Browar to author, June 1991.

211 *"I told her if . . . We hugged each other":* William Asher to author, Mar. 1992.

211 *"Someone would come on the show . . .":* Ibid.

211 *"It was several seasons . . .":* Ibid.

212 *"After one routine . . .":* Ibid.

212 *"One night she stopped . . .":* Ibid.

212 *"Lucy would put other actresses . . .":* Dorothy Aldworth to author, Nov. 1991.

213 *he asked the writers:* Arnaz, *A Book,* 238.

213 *To help the press:* Harris, *The Real Story of Lucille Ball,* 78.

213 *Lucie's nurse became overprotective:* Hy Goldberg, "The I Love Lucy Story," *New York Sunday Mirror Magazine,* Apr. 26, 1953.

213 *"It seems like God . . .":* Hedda Hopper Collection.

214 *Friends who drove out:* Marva Peterson, "Living with Lucy," undated article, University of Southern California, Cinema-Television Library and Archive of Performing Arts, clipping collection.

214 *"This couldn't happen . . .":* Time, Mar. 2, 1953.

214 *"Buster and I . . .":* Eleanor Keaton to author, May 1991.

214 *"Look at Lucille . . .":* Thompson to author, Feb. 1992.

215 *"It would be nice . . .":* Harris, *The Real Story of Lucille Ball,* 117.

215–16 *Her popularity and renown:* George Murphy to author, Dec. 1990.

216 *CBS executives in New York:* Martin Leeds to author, June 1992.

216 *Lucy broke off her vacation:* Joseph McBride, ed., *Filmmakers on Film-making,* vol. 1 (Los Angeles: J. P. Tarcher, 1983), 86.

217 *"In those days . . .":* Transcript of testimony, *Los Angeles Times,* Sept. 13, 1953.

217 *Over Labor Day weekend:* Bart Andrews, *The "I Love Lucy" Book* (New York: Doubleday, 1985), 125.

217–18 *Desi was playing cards:* Arnaz, *A Book,* 240–41.

218 *"I resent that, Howard . . .":* Ibid., 242.

218 *Neither Philip Morris . . .* Asher to author, Mar. 1992.

218 *Desi asked George Murphy:* Murphy to author, Dec. 1990.

219 *When they reached:* Andrews, *The "I Love Lucy" Book,* 127; Asher to author, Mar. 1992.

219 *"Lucy has never been a Communist . . .":* Andrews, *The "I Love Lucy" Book,* 129.

220 *"It was the most enthusiastic . . .":* Asher to author, Mar. 1992.

220 *"Anytime you give . . .":* *Los Angeles Times,* Sept. 13, 1953.

220   *A small committed group: New York Times,* Oct. 7, 1953.

221   *Unlike others who went before:* Jack Gould, "The Case of Lucille Ball," *New York Times,* Sept. 20, 1953.

222   *"I have discovered . . .":* Harris, *The Real Story of Lucille Ball,* 115.

222   *"Years ago . . .":* Ibid., 53 and 104.

222–23   *That year Desilu was evaluated:* Ibid., 12–13.

223   *"Martin Leeds worked . . .":* Johny Aitchison to author, Feb. 1992.

223   *"When you got near . . .":* Leeds to author, Feb. 1992.

223   *"Lucy didn't want him to go . . .":* Dann Cahn to author, May 1991.

224   *blue and white gingham dress:* Marion Strong Van Vlack to author, Mar. 1991.

224   *"He'd come to the studio . . . didn't need any help":* Asher to author, Mar. 1992.

224   *stayed out of his way:* Elois Jenssen to author, May 1991.

224   *"I'd bawl Desi out in Spanish . . .":* Mercedes Manzanares to author, Feb. 1992.

224   *"The problem we had . . .":* Leeds to author, June 1992.

224   *The love people bore:* Hal Humphrey column, *Los Angeles Mirror,* Mar. 5, 1955.

225   *The film also won:* Special collections, San Diego State University Library, the Desi Arnaz Autobiographical Materials.

226   *"It is a switch . . .": New York Times,* Feb. 10, 1956.

227   *"Christ, I can't . . .":* Aitchison to author, Feb. 1992.

227   *"Lucy was distraught . . .":* Mary Jane Croft to author, July 1991.

227   *She, Desi, and the Martin Leeds:* Leeds to author, June 1991.

227   *Lucy knocked Desi out cold:* Bell to author, June 1993.

228   *"When Lucy reappeared . . .":* Herbert Kenwith to author, Nov. 1993.

228   *Lucy continued to hope:* Harris, *The Real Story of Lucille Ball,* 117.

228   *"I was the victim today . . .": New York Post* and *New York Times,* Aug. 14, 1957.

229   *"You god-damned redhead . . .":* Special collections, San Diego State University Library, the Desi Arnaz Autobiographical Materials.

229   *kidnap threat: Los Angeles Times,* Calendar section, Oct. 12, 1986.

229   *John Wayne:* LB to a seminar at the Museum of Broadcasting, New York, Apr. 1984.

230   *Lucy would call Harpo aside:* Asher to author, Mar. 1992.

230   *Lucy's response to Desi's triumph:* Special collections, San Diego State University Library, the Desi Arnaz Autobiographical Materials.

231   *"I don't want to quit . . .":* Arnaz, *A Book,* 282.

231–32   Lucy's Beverly Hills house-hunting is from Jim Brochu, *Lucy in the Afternoon* (New York: William Morrow, 1990), 34–35.

232   *his rage at what he saw: New York Daily News,* May 5, 1960; Irma Kusely to author, Feb. 1992.

232   *". . . way down the block":* Kenwith to author, May 1993.

233   *Madelyn Pugh and Bob Carroll, Jr.:* Madelyn Pugh Davis to author, July 1990, and Bob Carroll, Jr., to author, July 1991.

233   *When Bob and Madelyn:* Davis to author, July 1990.

233   *Karl Freund departed: Films in Review,* Feb. 1963.

233–34   *To finance buying control:* Andrews, *The "I Love Lucy" Book,* 156; *Business Week,* Oct. 5, 1957.

234   *"As much as that money . . .":* Martin Leeds to author, Feb. 1992.

234 *The couple also sold CBS:* Arnaz, *A Book,* 284.

235 *She wrote Marion:* Van Vlack to author, Apr. 1991.

235 *"The laugh was so big . . .":* Jay Sandrich to author, Oct. 1991.

236 *one climactic incident:* Sandrich to author, Oct. 1991; Davis to author, July 1990; Thompson to author, Feb. 1992.

237 *"The night of the show . . .":* Bernard Weitzman to author, May 1991; Sandrich to author, Oct. 1991; Thompson to author, Feb. 1992.

237 *". . . It worries him.":* Andrews, *The "I Love Lucy" Book,* 199.

237 *Desi, advised by Leeds:* Leeds to author, Feb. 1992.

238 *It was left to:* Ed Holly to author, Feb. 1992; LB quoted on *Hollywood: The Golden Years,* BBC documentary, 1987.

238 *"Her reaction was pretty much . . .":* Sandrich to author, Oct. 1991.

CHAPTER 15

PAGE

240 *"dusty, musty . . .":* LB quoted on *Hollywood: The Golden Years,* BBC documentary, 1987.

241 *Lucy buzzed around:* Nat Perrin to author, Feb. 1992; LB to author, June 1986; Dann Cahn to author, Feb. 1992.

241 *"My job was to get them . . .":* Jay Sandrich to author, Oct. 1991.

242 *"He went into orbit . . .":* Irma Kusely to author, Apr. 1991.

242 *As an actress:* James G. Stewart Oral History, American Film Institute.

242 *Willie Mae Barker:* Marion Strong Van Vlack to author, Dec. 1991.

243 *"Even when we were young . . .":* Desi Arnaz, Jr., as told to Joseph N. Bell, "My Mother, Lucille Ball," *Good Housekeeping,* Mar. 1971.

243 *Her disembodied voice:* Desi Arnaz, Jr., interview with *People,* Mar. 1978; Margarita deMena to author, July 1991.

243 *"The hardest thing to learn . . .":* "Lucille and Desi Start Bride School," *New York Herald Tribune,* Feb. 9, 1956.

243 *"Amigo, if anything happens . . .":* Bob Weiskopf to author, June 1991.

243 *Watching their parents':* Desi Arnaz, Jr., quoted in Suzanne Somers, *Wednesday's Children* (New York: G. P. Putnam's Sons, 1992), 85; Arnaz Jr., "My Mother, Lucille Ball."

244 *"I knew then that . . .":* Marcella Rabwin to author, July 1991.

244 *no mama's boy:* Desi Arnaz, Jr., on *Lucy and Desi: A Home Movie,* Arluck Productions documentary, 1993.

244 *"From the time he was . . .":* Rabwin to author, July 1991.

244 *He recalled that the atmosphere:* Keith Thibodeaux in "Remembering Lucy," *People,* Aug. 14, 1989, p. 70.

244 *"Lucille said 'Come here,* Tommy,' . . .":* Tom Schiller to author, Oct. 1992.

244 *"Come to lunch! . . .":* Bob Schiller to author, June 1991.

245 *"She had a special way . . .":* Arlene Dahl to author, Oct. 1992.

245 *"I would ask . . . their mothers":* Ibid.

245 *Lucy did manage to persuade:* Johny Aitchison to author, Feb. 1992.

245 *"Tell him to call . . .":* Norman Vincent Peale to author, Apr. 1991.

245 *At some sessions:* Jim Brochu, *Lucy in the Afternoon* (New York: William Morrow, 1990), 169.

246 *Even he recognized that his health:* Desi Arnaz, *A Book* (New York: William Morrow, 1976), 287.

247 *"Lucy owned it! . . .":* Betty Furness to author, Oct. 1991.

247 *"I thought going through . . .":* Ibid.

248 *In Palm Springs, she would go: People,* Feb. 18, 1991; Maury Thompson to author, Feb. 1992.

248 *Lucy would start a story:* Dahl to author, Oct. 1992.

248 *Beverly Hills police:* Lillian Briggs to author, Mar. 1993.

248 *"what Desi goes through":* LB to author, June 1986.

248 *To raise revenue:* Martin Leeds to author, Feb. 1992; Desilu Prospectus, 1958.

249 *"Just don't spend too much . . . armloads":* Gladys Hall Collection.

249 *"When we got into a cab . . .":* Herbert Kenwith to author, May 1993.

251 *Hoover responded by stating:* J. Edgar Hoover to Desi Arnaz, Jan. 5, 1959, FBI files, U.S. Department of Justice, Washington, D.C.

251 *"Desilu is a family . . ."* Weiskopf to author, June 1991.

251 *"God knows how many drinks . . .":* Dann Cahn to author, Feb. 1992.

251 *Martin Leeds took care:* Leeds to author, Feb. 1992.

251 *executives found it increasingly prudent:* Ed Holly to author, Feb. 1992.

251 *"Everyone else had to keep . . .":* Fred Ball to author, Feb. 1992.

252 *the arguments would stop: New York Times Magazine,* Apr. 20, 1958.

253 *"When a maid asked me . . .":* Carole Cook to author, Feb. 1992.

253 *"You didn't do too badly . . . running a studio":* Ibid.

253 *"I admired her . . .":* Aitchison to author, Feb. 1992.

253–54 *Friars Club:* Recording of the Friars Club dinner; Milton Berle to author, Feb. 1991. Parkyakarkus, whose real name was Harry Einstein, passed his talent to his son Albert Brooks, who became a respected actor and director. In the movie *Defending Your Life,* which Brooks wrote and directed, the hero's father is a comedian who dies onstage.

254 *Oklahoma City:* Clippings at New York Public Library for the Performing Arts, Lincoln Center, New York City.

254 *"I wish you were dead": Lucy and Desi: A Home Movie.*

255 *The entire journey:* Hedda Hopper Collection.

255 *"I don't want . . .":* Arnaz Jr., *People,* Mar. 1978.

255 *Some accounts said that lawyers: New York Post,* Sept. 14, 1959.

255 *"We've got through . . .": Cosmopolitan,* Jan. 1960.

256 *"That's where you're wrong . . .":* Cook to author, Feb. 1992.

256 *"You've got to find . . .":* Roger Perry to author, Sept. 1992.

256 *Al Kramer, who was directing:* Al Kramer to author, Feb. 1992.

256 *In September 1959 Desi was arrested: Los Angeles Times,* Sept. 20, 1959; *Washington Evening Star,* Nov. 11, 1959; FBI files; Special collections, San Diego State University Library, the Desi Arnaz Autobiographical Materials.

257 *"Desi tried to destroy . . .":* Rabwin to author, July 1991.

257 *"As we were leaving . . .":* Jack Aldworth to author, Nov. 1991.

257 *Later Lucy would often say:* Gladys Hall Collection.

257 *a vicious argument:* Arnaz, *A Book,* 316.

257–58 *"She looked up . . . you wetback":* Ibid., 316–17.

258 *She aimed at his face:* Ibid., 317.

258 *When Lucy and Desi sat their children:* Bart Andrews, *The "I Love Lucy" Book* (New York: Doubleday, 1985), 214.

259 *"There was no room . . .":* Kusely to author, Apr. 1991.

259 *Lucy also kept finding fault:* Edie Adams to author, Oct. 1991; Special

collections, San Diego State University Library, the Desi Arnaz Autobiographical Materials.

260 *"It was like your parents . . .":* Madelyn Pugh Davis to author, July 1990.

260 *"Why do you think he married you? . . .":* Bob Schiller to author, June 1991.

260 *When Lucy traveled:* Kusely to author, Apr. 1991.

261 *He had been so shattered:* Lucille Ryman Carroll to author, May 1991.

261 *Once Desi moved out:* Raymond Sarlot, *Life at the Marmont* (Santa Monica, Cal.: Roundtable Publications, 1987); *New York Sunday News,* July 10, 1960.

261 *"I don't want it . . .":* Bob Hope and Bob Thomas, *The Road to Hollywood* (New York: Doubleday, 1977), 87.

261–62 *"to keep two of my best . . .":* Walter Winchell column, *New York Mirror,* May 19, 1960.

262 *"I never tried to get over Desi . . .":* LB to author, June 1986.

262 *"She was fresh, wild . . .":* N. Richard Nash to author, Apr. 1992.

263 *"If they can't ride . . .":* Dorothy Kilgallen, "The Voice of Broadway," *New York Journal-American,* Sept. 9, 1960.

263 *"The grandmother was . . .":* Carlos Davis to author, June 1992.

263 *"I said he had died . . .":* Ibid.

263 *To Lucie and Desi:* Lucie Arnaz to Pete Hamill, *New York Daily News,* Feb. 23, 1979.

264 *"If you were doing it . . .":* Cy Coleman to author, Feb. 1992.

264 *"We finally met her . . .":* Ibid.

265 *"Knowing she wouldn't know . . .":* Ibid.

265 *Ross found her "hard-boiled":* New York Herald Tribune, Dec. 11, 1960.

266 *She went to their parties:* Michael Kidd to author, Apr. 1991.

266 *"Hundreds of people . . .":* Ibid.

267 *"I told her she was correct . . .":* Ibid.

267–68 *dinner at Danny's Hideaway:* Danny Welkes to author and Mickey Hayes to author, Jan. 1994; Gladys Hall Collection. In later years, Lucy and Gary said that Paula Stewart introduced them, despite evidence to the contrary.

269 *Lucy was taken aback:* Jack Carter to author, Apr. 1991.

269 *"One whole and peaceful . . .":* David Seabury, *The Art of Selfishness* (New York: Julian Messner, 1937), 212.

269 *". . . to mix with the people":* Peale to author, Apr. 1991.

270 *They came close: New York Journal-American,* Jan. 1961; Kenwith to author, May 1993.

270 *Desi was so on her mind: Cosmopolitan,* Jan. 1960; Brochu, *Lucy in the Afternoon,* 173–74; Clifford David to author, Aug. 1992.

270 *She held back her comments:* Earl Wilson column, *New York Post,* Dec. 1961.

270 *"What are you going around . . .":* Bob Hope to author, June 1991.

271 *Over the Easter holidays:* Clipping at New York Public Library for the Performing Arts, Lincoln Center, New York City.

272 *"I was giving up . . .":* LB to author, June 1986.

272 *"I looked at the houses . . .":* Ibid.

272 *"You couldn't give me . . .":* Susan Whitney to author, Nov. 1993.

273 *DeDe came up with a solution:* Ibid.

273 *"My mother was not one . . .":* LB to author, June 1986.

273 *"There are other things . . .": New York Mirror,* Nov. 15, 1961.

273 *On November 19, 1961: New York Daily News*, Nov. 20, 1961; *New York Mirror*, Nov. 20, 1961.

CHAPTER 16

PAGE

275 *"my art man . . . leave it alone"*: Martin Leeds to author, June 1991.
275 *"career woman"*: LB interview with Margaret McManus, *The New York Times*, Jan. 8, 1962.
275 *"Luce, for God's sake, lighten up!"*: Jack Carter to author, Apr. 1991.
275 *interview with Earl Wilson*: Earl Wilson columns, Nov. 1962, clippings in New York Public Library of the Performing Arts, Lincoln Center, New York City.
275 *Gary got a kick*: Gladys Hall Collection.
275 *"I asked him if . . ."*: Herbert Kenwith to author, May 1993.
276 *"I marveled over his concern . . ."*: Lloyd Leipzig to author, Dec. 1992.
276 *"How can you eat . . ."*: Carter to author, Apr. 1991.
276 *Walter Winchell wrote*: Walter Winchell column, Apr. 1962, Academy of Motion Picture Arts and Sciences Library.
277 *Jack Warner announced*: Warner Archive, University of Southern California, Cinema-Television Library and Archives of Performing Arts.
277 *"We were friends . . ."*: Bob Hope to author, June 1991.
278 *"Everyone said the same phrase . . ."*: Mike Dann to author, Oct. 1992.
279 *"Gary was all things Desi . . ."*: Bernard Weitzman to author, July 1991. Special collections, San Diego State University Library, the Desi Arnaz Autobiographical Materials.
279 *Desi, with alcoholic self-pity*: Special collections, San Diego State University Library, the Desi Arnaz Autobiographical Materials.
280 *peak sales of $23.4 million: Wall Street Journal*, July 19, 1961.
280 *only two for Desilu: New York Herald Tribune*, Sept. 15, 1963.
281 *"Broads, bosoms and fun": New York Herald Tribune*, Jan. 19. 1964.
281 *Newton N. Minow*: Eric Barnow, *Tube of Plenty* (New York: Oxford University Press, 1990), 300.
281 *"We're concerned that . . ."*: Bob Schiller and Bob Weiskopf to author, June 1991; Weitzman to author, Feb. 1992; and others. Fred Ball denies he tried to tell Desi what to do.
281 *"Desi couldn't fully function . . ."*: Ed Holly to author, Feb. 1992.
282 *"There came a time . . ."*: Mickey Rudin to author, June 1991.
282 *Desi said he wanted out*: Special collections, San Diego State University Library, the Desi Arnaz Autobiographical Materials; Johny Aitchison to author, Feb. 1992.
282 *"I had been vice president . . ."*: LB to Kay Gardella, *New York Daily News*, Nov. 27, 1962.
282–83 *"I miss someone to rely on . . .": Christian Science Monitor*, Feb. 27, 1963.
283 *"I could read . . .": Look*, Sept. 7, 1971.
283 *"Lucy made sure . . ."*: Fred Ball to author, Feb. 1992.
283 *When Lucy presided*: Associated Press story, Sept. 28, 1963; Holly to author, Feb. 1992.
284 *compartmentalizing her life*: Wanda Clark to author, Feb. 1992; Bob Carroll, Jr., to author, July 1991; Jack and Dorothy Aldworth to author, Nov. 1991.

284 *"Is there a redheaded woman . . .":* Carter to author, April 1991.

285 *"The Lucy I first met . . .":* Lou Krugman to author, Feb. 1992.

285 *"Carole, you lost heart . . .":* Cook to author, Feb. 1992.

285–86 *Between scenes:* Gale Gordon to author, July 1990.

286 *"After a while . . . Lucy and DeDe":* Cook to author, Feb. 1992.

286 *"She was selective . . .":* Ibid.

286 *"Gary managed to put . . .":* Carter to author, Apr. 1991.

286 *"If he had done something . . .":* Michael Stern to author, July 1991.

286 *After renouncing stand-up: New York Daily News,* Nov. 27, 1962.

287 *"She's been forced . . .":* Leeds to author, June 1991.

287 *"Finally, she said . . ."* Kenwith to author, May 1993.

288 *"Vivian thinks she's you . . .":* Weitzman to author, July 1991.

288 *"Lucy was the only genius . . .":* Gordon to author, July 1990.

289 *firing a gun:* Aitchison to author, Feb. 1992; and others.

289 *The constant of their relationship:* LB to Charles Higham, *The New York Times,* Feb. 18, 1973; *Look,* Sept. 7, 1971; Lucie Arnaz to Joan Rivers, *The Joan Rivers Show,* Jan. 15, 1990.

289 *"Before anyone else . . .":* Kaye Ballard to author, June 1992.

290 *"I don't think she knew . . .":* Ibid.

290 *"You get the hell . . . two years or twelve":* Ibid.

291 *"We told Lucy . . .":* Weitzman to author, May 1991.

291 *they shot a pilot:* Herbert F. Solow to author, June 1991; *Time,* Mar. 1, 1968.

291 *"I didn't think . . .":* William Paley to author, July 1986.

291 *"She didn't want her to read . . .":* Solow to author, June 1991.

292 *"How are you coming . . . Hollywood":* Ibid.

293 *"I advised Lucy . . .":* Holly to author, Feb. 1992.

293 *"At a board meeting . . .":* Solow to author, Sept. 1993.

293–94 *Lucy was not on hand:* Holly to author, Feb. 1992.

294 *Solow was pleased:* Solow to author, June 1991.

294 *"Bobby, what the hell . . .":* Bobby O'Brien to author, Mar. 1993.

294 *"Eat up! It's not on Desilu!":* Irma Kusely to author, April 1991.

294 *Blue Chip trading stamps:* Solow to author, June 1991; Weitzman to author, May 1991; Kenwith to author, May 1993.

295 *"Herb, this is the actress . . . give it to Gary":* Solow to author, June 1991 and Sept. 1993.

295–96 *"We used to ask each other . . .":* Mary Jane Croft to author, July 1991.

296 *"Everybody walked out . . .":* Maury Thompson to author, Feb. 1992.

296 *He went to Bernard Weitzman:* Weitzman to author, May 1991.

296 *"There was nothing . . .":* Solow to author, June 1991.

296 *"Desi enjoyed building houses . . .":* LB interview in *TV Guide,* Mar. 30, 1968.

296 *"I didn't want Gary . . .":* LB to author, June 1986.

296 *"We went to my house . . .":* Solow to author, June 1991.

296–97 *"We brought life . . .":* Solow to author, Feb. 1992.

297 *They often threw parties:* Solow to author, June 1991.

297 *"CBS was on the border . . .":* Weitzman to author, May 1991.

298 *Both her children would remember: "Lucy and Desi: A Home Movie,"* Arluck Productions documentary, 1993.

298 *Yet, despite the fact that chubby Desi Jr:* Marcella Rabwin to author, July 1991.

299   *"Desi tasted it . . .":* Kusely to author, Apr. 1991.
299   *"That was the only argument . . .":* Rabwin to author, July 1991.
299   *When Lucy realized her son:* Thelma Orloff to author, Jan. 1991.
299   *"You can imagine her heartbreak . . .":* Rabwin to author, July 1991.
299   *Desi Jr. was supposed: TV Guide,* Mar. 30, 1968.
299   *Lucy sometimes privately:* Charles Higham interview, *The New York Times,* Feb. 18, 1973.
300   *"Don't ever let me . . .":* Frank Gorey to author, Feb. 1991.
300   *"I was sitting by the pool . . .":* Carter to author, Apr. 1991.
301   *"She had no choice . . .":* Holly to author, Feb. 1992.
301   *"There came a time . . .":* Rudin to author, June 1991.
301   *"Miss Ball, one of the things . . .": TV Guide,* July 15, 1967.
301   *The money Gulf + Western paid:* Agreement and Plan of Reorganization, June 19, 1967, p. 1, Clauses 1.1 and 8.2.
302   *"Mr. Bluhdorn said Desilu Productions . . .": The New York Times,* Feb. 15, 1967.
302   *Ten days after the proposed: The New York Times,* Feb. 25, 1967.
302   *"I was a little hurt . . .":* Weitzman to author, May 1991.
302   *"These people would call Lucy . . .":* Holly to author, Feb. 1992.
302–3 *"I cried. I was sad . . .":* LB to author, June 1986.
303   *"He travels fast . . .": TV Guide,* July 15, 1967.
303   *"I just realized . . .":* Weitzman to author, May 1991.
303   *Wasserman instructed Weitzman:* Weitzman to author, May 1991 and Sept. 1993.

PAGE   **CHAPTER 17**

304   *"When Lucy saw how . . .":* Irma Kusely to author, Feb. 1992.
305   *"Choose between cigarettes . . .":* Ibid.
305   *"As she walked on the set . . .":* Dorothy Aldworth to author, Nov. 1991.
305   *In person she looked:* Mel Shavelson to author, Feb. 1992.
305   *"People like Jack Benny . . .":* LB to American Film Institute, Jan. 18, 1973.
306   *"You think it's funny, don't you?":* George Schlatter to author, Oct. 1992.
306   *"Lucy worried more . . .":* Bobby O'Brien to author, Mar. 1993.
307   *"If she touches me . . .":* Ibid.
308   *Robert Stack said:* Robert Stack to author, May 1991.
308   *Herbert called in a makeup woman:* Herbert Kenwith to author, May 1993.
308   *It was Burton who actually:* Bob Carroll, Jr., to author, July 1991.
309   *"get the wrinkles . . .":* Sally Bedell, *Up the Tube* (New York: Viking Press, 1981), 36.
309–11 The account of the Taylor-Burton episode is drawn from Maury Thompson to author, Feb. 1992; Kenwith to author, May 1992; Melvyn Bragg, *Richard Burton: A Life* (New York: Little, Brown, 1988), 331–33; interview with LB by Lawrence Grobel, *PSA* magazine, Apr. 1976; Milt Josefsberg, *The Jack Benny Show* (New Rochelle: Arlington House, 1977), 55.
311   *pay Jess Oppenheimer:* Gregg Oppenheimer to author, Sept. 1993.
311   *Desi, his band days over:* Desi Arnaz, Jr., as told to Joseph N. Bell, "My Mother, Lucille Ball," *Good Housekeeping,* Mar. 1971.

311 *"He'd have books . . .":* Mary Jane Croft to author, July 1991.
311 *Herbert Kenwith now directed:* Kenwith to author, May 1993.
312 *"She doesn't think she's being funny . . .":* Arnaz Jr., "My Mother, Lucille Ball."
312 *As soon as Lucie:* Ibid.
312 *"Lucie met one boy . . .":* LB to author, June 1986.
313 *"There was a tremendous pull . . .":* Dorothy Aldworth to author, Nov. 1991.
313 *"What the fuck . . .":* Kenwith to author, Nov. 1993.
313 *"I pity her yet . . .":* Special collections, San Diego State University Library, the Desi Arnaz Autobiographical Materials.
313 *"Herb, you must find . . .":* Kenwith to author, May 1993.
313 *"Herbert, this year it's close-ups . . .":* Ibid.
314 *"When I walked in . . .":* Ibid.
314 *"My eyes welled up . . .":* Ibid.
315 *"Lucy felt she was in a crisis . . .":* Patty Duke and Kenneth Turan, *Call Me Anna* (New York: Bantam Books, 1987), 210.
315 *Despite the torment: Parade,* Oct. 17, 1971; LB interview with Lawrence Grobel, *PSA* magazine, Apr. 1976.
315 *The child, whom Patty named:* Kenwith to author, May 1993; Duke and Turan, *Call Me Anna,* 209–11; *McCall's,* June 1973; *Parade,* Oct. 17, 1971.
316 *Executives who were with TWA:* Spokesman for International Federation of Flight Attendants (TWA), Oct. 1991.
316 *"You couldn't speak to her . . .":* Spokesman for Association of Professional Flight Attendants (American Airlines), Oct. 1993.
317 *"If anything happens to me . . .":* Susan Whitney to author, Nov. 1993.
317 *no golf course: Look,* Sept. 7, 1971.
318 *Just after lunch one day: Los Angeles Times,* Jan. 8, 1972; *Vogue,* Mar. 1974; LB to Charles Higham, *The New York Times,* Feb. 18, 1973.

CHAPTER 18

PAGE

320 *Lucy believed that playing:* Bernard Weitzman to author, July 1991.
320 *He regarded his ex-wife:* Special collections, San Diego State University Library, the Desi Arnaz Autobiographical Materials.
320 *"Mame is a great . . .": Daily Trojan,* Sept. 28, 1973.
320 *"Onna's trying to kill me!":* Susan Whitney to author, Jan. 1994.
321 *"Lucy was like a little . . .":* Onna White to author, Feb. 1992.
321 *"She had no natural flow . . .":* Ibid.
321 *"They had her sitting around . . .":* Ibid.
322 *Among the extras: Film Fan Monthly,* Oct. 1974.
323 *"We in the audience . . ."* Pauline Kael, "The Current Cinema," *The New Yorker,* Mar. 11, 1974.
323 *She growled at interviewers: People,* Mar. 18, 1974.
323 *her proudest accomplishment:* LB on *The Dick Cavett Show,* Apr. 1974.
323 *DeDe, just past eighty:* LB to a seminar at Museum of Broadcasting, New York, Apr. 1984.
323 *"Lucy ended her television . . .":* Mike Dann to author, Oct. 1992.
324 *"There was friction . . .":* Cy Coleman to author, Feb. 1992.

324 *trends in television: Look,* Sept. 7, 1971; *The New York Times,* Nov. 28, 1976; *People,* Mar. 18, 1974.

324 *She organized a social life:* Thelma Orloff to author, Jan. 1991.

325 *The coming of spring:* Marion Strong Van Vlack to author, Mar. 1991.

325 *"She took me . . .":* Lillian Briggs to author, Mar. 1993.

325 *"I was going . . .":* Ibid.

326 *"My God! . . .":* Ibid.

326 *"She could always tell . . .":* Whitney to author, Nov. 1993.

326 *"Get the tablecloth . . .":* Ibid., Dec. 1993.

327 *"I have not seen her . . .":* Ibid.

328 *"My cowlick's back . . .":* Ibid.

328 *"I hope she dies first . . .":* Maury Thompson to author, Feb. 1992.

328 *On DeDe's birthday: People,* Sept. 14, 1989.

329 *"We laughed . . .":* Mary Wickes to author, June 1991.

329 *Lucy and the rest: People,* May 11, 1992.

329 *"She had me . . .":* Lucie Arnaz, "Mothers and Daughters," *McCall's,* May 1991, p. 28.

329 *"I'll marry her . . .":* Gary Pudney to author, Feb. 1992.

329 *She and Gary bought:* LB to author, June 1986.

330 *"She made a terrible grandmother":* Marcella Rabwin to author, July 1991.

330 *Lucy did, however, take a maternal interest:* Michael Stern to author, July 1991.

331 *Irma declined to learn:* Irma Kusely to author, Apr. 1991.

331 *Lucy walked over:* Stern to author, July 1991.

332 *"I thought she rolled . . .":* Briggs to author, Mar. 1993.

332 *"She was a champion-level . . .":* A. Scott Berg to author, July 1992.

332 *"She didn't like to go out . . .":* Briggs to author, Mar. 1993.

332 *Gary asked Irma to urge:* Kusely to author, Apr. 1991.

332–33 *"It was difficult . . .":* Sidney C. Schaer, *Newsday,* Oct. 29, 1985.

333 *"That was her emotional . . .":* Rabwin to author, July 1991.

334 *Desi stayed in Lucy's guest house:* LB to author, June 1986.

334 *Desi had been impressed:* Dr. Charles and Carol Campbell to author, Nov. 1992; Frank Gorey to author, Jan. 1994.

334 *"People don't want to see . . .":* LB to Museum of Broadcasting, Apr. 1984.

334 *"When I go into a store . . .":* LB to author, June 1986.

335 *"She wouldn't let me quit . . .":* Stern to author, July 1991.

336 *"She told me she wanted . . .":* Ibid.

336 *"No one watched the show . . .":* Casey Keller to author, Apr. 1991.

337 *"I've lost all my friends . . .":* Stern to author, Feb. 1992.

337 *"It was the most down . . .":* Emily Daniels to author, June 1991.

337 *"It was my fault . . .":* Aaron Spelling to author, July 1991.

337–38 *"You watch. Everyone will be . . .":* Carol Campbell to author, Nov. 1992.

338 *"They didn't think . . .":* Ibid.

338 *"Retirement is death . . .":* Van Vlack to author, Mar. 1991.

338 *"If I look out the window . . .":* Whitney to author, Jan. 1994.

338–39 *"They cut it . . .":* Stern to author, Feb. 1993.

339 *At night she moved:* Gary Pudney to author, Feb. 1992.

339 *Lucy would look forward:* Stern to author, July 1991.

339 *"Lucy wanted to organize . . .":* Orloff to author, Jan. 1991.

339 *Marcella recalled:* Rabwin to author, July 1991.

340 *"After his talk . . .":* White to author, Feb. 1992.
340 *On May 10, 1988:* Jim Brochu, *Lucy in the Afternoon* (New York: William Morrow, 1990), 17, 25.
340 *"We added making vowel sounds . . .":* White to author, Feb. 1992.
340 *At a Professional Dancers luncheon:* Eleanor Keaton to author, May 1991.
341 *"Remember, I don't . . . it will kill you":* Ret Turner to author, Aug. 1992.
341 *"When the lights . . .":* Frank Liberman to author, June 1991.

BIBLIOGRAPHY

BOOKS AND ARTICLES

Adamson, Joe. *Groucho, Harpo, Chico and Sometimes Zeppo*. New York: Simon & Schuster, 1973.

American Institute of Public Opinion & Scholarly Resources, Inc. *Gallup Looks at the Movies, 1940–50*. (Microfilm, 1979.)

Andrews, Bart. *The "I Love Lucy" Book*. New York: Doubleday, 1985.

Arnaz, Desi. *A Book*. New York: William Morrow, 1976.

Barnow, Erik. *Tube of Plenty*. New York: Oxford University Press, 1975.

Bedell, Sally. *Up the Tube*. New York: Viking Press, 1981.

Berg, A. Scott. *Goldwyn: A Biography*. New York: Alfred A. Knopf, 1989.

Blesh, Rudi. *Keaton*. New York: Macmillan, 1966.

Bowlby, John. *Attachment*. Vol. 1, *Attachment and Loss*. New York: Basic Books, 1969.

———. *Separation*. Vol. 2, *Attachment and Loss*. New York: Basic Books, 1973.

———. *Loss*. Vol. 3, *Attachment and Loss*. New York: Basic Books, 1980.

Bragg, Melvyn. *Richard Burton: A Life*. New York: Little, Brown, 1988.

Breslin, Jimmy. *Damon Runyon*. New York: Ticknor & Fields, 1991.

Brochu, Jim. *Lucy in the Afternoon*. New York: William Morrow, 1990.

Brooks, Tim, and Earle Marsh. *The Complete Directory to Prime Time Network TV Shows*. New York: Ballantine Books, 1992.

Brownlow, Kevin. *The Parade's Gone By*. Berkeley: University of California Press, 1968.

Capra, Frank. *The Name Above the Title*. New York: Macmillan, 1971.

Cermak, Timmen. *A Primer on Adult Children of Alcoholics*. Deerfield Beach, Fla.: Health Communications, Inc., 1989.

Chaplin, Charles. *My Autobiography*. New York: Simon & Schuster, 1964.

Chase, W. Parker. *The Wonder City*. New York: New York Bound, 1983.

Chierichetti, David. *Hollywood Costume Design*. New York: Harmony Books, 1976.

Chodorow, Nancy. *The Reproduction of Mothering*. Berkeley: University of California Press, 1978.

Croce, Arlene. *The Fred Astaire and Ginger Rogers Dance Book*. New York: Outerbridge & Lazard, 1972.

Crichton, Kyle. "Goldwyn Girls." *Film Fan Monthly* (October 1974): 12–22.

371

———. "Three Loves Has She." *Collier's* (August 16, 1941).

Curcio, Vincent. *Suicide Blonde*. New York: William Morrow, 1989.

Cutter, W. R. *Genealogical and Family History of Western New York*. New York: Lewis Historical Publishing Co., 1912.

Darrah, William C. *Pithole: The Vanished City*. Gettysburg, Pa.: privately published, 1972.

Davis, Bette. *The Lonely Life*. New York: G. P. Putnam's Sons, 1962.

Drury, Aubrey. *California: An Intimate Guide*. New York: Harper & Bros., 1935, 1947.

Duke, Patty, and Kenneth Turan. *Call Me Anna*. New York: Bantam Books, 1987.

Federal Writers Project. *Florida*. New York: Oxford University Press, 1939.

———. *Los Angeles*. New York: Hastings House, 1951.

———. *New York*. New York: Oxford University Press, 1966.

———. *Planning Your Vacation in Florida: Miami and Dade County*. Northport, N.Y.: Bacon, Percy & Daggett, 1941.

Fonda, Henry. *Fonda: My Life*. New York: New American Library, 1981.

Fordin, Hugh. *The World of Entertainment*. New York: Doubleday, 1975.

Freud, Sigmund. *A General Introduction to Psychoanalysis*. New York: Washington Square Press, 1964.

Gabor, Zsa Zsa, and Gerold Frank. *Zsa Zsa Gabor: My Story*. New York: World Publishing, 1960.

Graham, Sheilah. *The Rest of the Story*. New York: Coward McCann, 1961.

Grobel, Lawrence. "Interview: Lucille Ball." *PSA magazine* (April 1976): 32–39.

Harris, Eleanor. *The Real Story of Lucille Ball*. New York: Farrar, Straus and Young, 1954.

Harvey, James. *Romantic Comedy in Hollywood*. New York: Alfred A. Knopf, 1987.

Hay, Peter. *MGM: When the Lion Roars*. Atlanta: Turner Publishing, 1991.

Heimann, Jim. *Out with the Stars*. New York: Abbeville Press, 1985.

Hepburn, Katharine. *Me*. New York: Alfred A. Knopf, 1991.

Hoadly, Charles J., ed. *Records of the Colony and Plantation of New Haven*. Hartford: Case, Tiffany and Co., 1857.

Jewell, Richard B., with Vernon Harbin. *The RKO Years*. New Rochelle, N.Y.: Arlington House, 1982.

Jones, Gerald. *Honey, I'm Home. Sitcoms: Selling the American Dream*. New York: Grove Weidenfeld, 1992.

Josefsberg, Milt. *The Jack Benny Show*. New Rochelle, N.Y.: Arlington House, 1977.

Kanin, Garson. *Hollywood*. New York: Viking, 1967.

Kay, Karyn, and Gerald Peary. "Dance Girl Dance." *The Velvet Light Trap* (Fall 1973): 26–31.

Knight, Arthur. *The Liveliest Art*. New York: New American Library, 1957.

Lasky, Betty. *RKO: The Biggest Little Major*. Englewood Cliffs, N.J.: Prentice-Hall, 1984.

Lewin, Bertram. *The Psychoanalysis of Elation*. London: Hogarth Press, 1951.

Luft, Herbert G. "Karl Freund." *Films in Review* (February 1963): 93–108.

McBride, Joseph, ed. *Filmmakers on Filmmaking*, vol. 1. Los Angeles: J. P. Tarcher, 1983.

Museum of Broadcasting, *Lucille Ball: First Lady of Comedy*. New York: Museum of Broadcasting, 1984.

Rogers, Ginger. *Ginger*. New York: HarperCollins, 1991.

Sarlot, Raymond. *Life at the Marmont*. Santa Monica, Calif.: Roundtable Publications, 1987.

Seabury, David. *The Art of Selfishness*. New York: Julian Messner, 1937.

Sklar, Robert. *Movie-Made America: A Social History of American Movies*. New York: Random House, 1975.

Smith, Sally Bedell. *In All His Glory: The Life of William S. Paley*. New York: Simon & Schuster, 1990.

Somers, Suzanne. *Wednesday's Children*. New York: G. P. Putnam's Sons, 1992.

Turkel, Studs. *Hard Times*. New York: Avon Books, 1970.

Verrill, A. Hyatt. *Cuba of Today*. New York: Dodd, Mead, 1931.

————. *Cuba Past and Present*. New York: Dodd, Mead, 1920.

Winnicott, D.W. "The Capacity to Be Alone." *International Journal of Psycho-Analysis* 39 (Sept.–Oct. 1958): 416–20.

Woon, Basil. *When It's Cocktail Time in Cuba*. New York: Horace Liveright, 1928.

Yablonsky, Lewis. *George Raft*. New York: McGraw-Hill, 1974.

TELEVISION DOCUMENTARIES

Hollywood: The Golden Years. BBC Television Productions in Association with RKO Pictures, 1987.

Lucy and Desi: A Home Movie. Arluck Entertainment, 1993.

MGM: When the Lion Roars. Turner Pictures, 1992.

LASER DISK

"I Love Lucy." The Voyager Co., 1991.

UNPUBLISHED MANUSCRIPTS

Butler, Albert, and Josephine Butler. "Encyclopedia of Social Dance." 1975. New York Public Library for the Performing Arts, Lincoln Center, New York City.

"Genealogy of the Hunt Family of Jamestown." n.d. Fenton Historical Society, Jamestown, N.Y.

Waite, Anna Carpenter. "Some Genealogical History of Lucille D. Ball." August 1990. Fenton Historical Society, Jamestown, N.Y.

TELEVISION APPEARANCES OF LUCILLE BALL

"The Bob Hope Show," Sept. 14, 1950, Oct. 18, 1956, Feb. 15, 1961. NBC.
"Bob Hope in Who Makes the World Laugh," Part 2, Apr. 4, 1984. NBC.
"Bob Hope's 30th Anniversary TV Special," Jan. 18, 1981. NBC.
"Bob Hope's All Star Comedy Tribute to Vaudeville," Mar. 25, 1977. NBC.
Bob Hope Special: "Bob Hope's Road to Hollywood," Mar. 2, 1983. NBC.
Bob Hope Special: "World of Comedy," Oct. 29, 1976. NBC.
Bob Hope Special: "Happy Birthday, Bob," May 29, 1978. NBC.
Bob Hope Special: "Happy Birthday, Bob," May 23, 1983. NBC.
Bob Hope Special: "Unrehearsed Antics of the Stars," Sept. 28, 1984. NBC.
"Carol + 2," Jan. 15, 1967. CBS.
"CBS Salutes Lucy—The First 25 Years," Nov. 28, 1976.
"CBS: On the Air," Mar. 26, 1978.
"Cher and Other Fantasies," Apr. 3, 1977. NBC.
"Circus of the Stars," Dec. 5, 1977. CBS.
"Danny Thomas Special: The Wonderful World of Burlesque II," Dec. 8, 1965. NBC.
Dinah Shore Special: "Like Hep," Apr. 13, 1969. NBC.
The Ed Wynn Show, Dec. 24, 1949. CBS.
"Everything You Ever Wanted to Know About Jack Benny But Were Afraid to Ask,"
    Mar. 10, 1971. NBC.
"From Hollywood with Love: The Ann-Margret Special," Dec. 6, 1969. CBS.
"Gene Kelly . . . An American in Pasadena," Mar. 13, 1978. CBS.
"General Electric's All-Star Anniversary," Sept. 29, 1978. ABC.
"Happy Anniversary and Goodbye," Nov. 10, 1974. CBS.
"Have Girls—Will Travel," Oct. 16, 1964. NBC.
"Hedda Hopper's Hollywood," Jan. 10, 1960. NBC.
I Love Lucy, Oct. 15, 1951–Sept. 24, 1961. CBS.
"The Jack Benny Special," Mar. 20, 1968. NBC.
"Jack Benny's 20th Anniversary TV Special," Nov. 16, 1970. NBC.
"Jack Benny's Birthday Special," Feb. 17, 1969. NBC.
Life with Lucy, Sept. 20, 1986–Nov. 15, 1986. ABC.
"The Lucille Ball Comedy Hour," Jan. 22, 1967. CBS.
"A Lucille Ball Special Starring Lucille Ball and Dean Martin," Mar. 1, 1975. CBS.
"A Lucille Ball Special Starring Lucille Ball and Jackie Gleason," Dec. 3, 1975. CBS.
"A Lucille Ball Special: What Now Catherine Curtis?" Mar. 30, 1976. CBS.
"The Lucille Ball Special," Nov. 21, 1977. CBS.
"Lucy Comes to Nashville," Nov. 19, 1978. CBS.

"Lucy in London," Oct. 24, 1966. CBS.
"Lucy Moves to NBC," Feb. 8, 1980. NBC.
The Lucy Show, Oct. 1, 1961–Sept. 2, 1974. CBS.
"The Milton Berle Special," Nov. 1, 1959. NBC.
"Mary Tyler Moore Hour," Mar. 4, 1979. CBS.
"The Music Mart," Feb. 8, 1980. NBC.
"A Salute to Stan Laurel," Nov. 23, 1965. CBS.
"A Salute to Television's 25th Anniversary," Sept. 10, 1972. ABC.
"Shirley MacLaine: Gypsy in My Soul," Jan. 20, 1976. CBS.
"Show Business Salute to Milton Berle," Dec. 4, 1973. NBC.
"Show of the Year for Cerebral Palsy," June 10, 1950. NBC.
"Sinatra—The First 40 Years," Jan. 30, 1980. NBC.
"Steve and Eydie . . . On Stage," Sept. 16, 1973. NBC.
"The Steve Lawrence Show," Sept. 13, 1965. CBS.
"Super Comedy Bowl 1," Jan. 10, 1971. CBS.
"Swing Out, Sweet Land," Apr. 8, 1971. NBC.
"A Tribute to 'Mr. Television' Milton Berle," Mar. 26, 1978. NBC.
"Twelve Star Salute" (salute to the Federation of Jewish Philanthropies), Dec. 9, 1961. ABC.
Westinghouse Lucille Ball–Desi Arnaz Show, Nov. 6, 1957–Apr. 1, 1960. CBS.

FILMOGRAPHY

Broadway Thru a Keyhole. United Artists, 1933.
Blood Money. United Artists, 1933.
Roman Scandals. United Artists, 1933.
Moulin Rouge. United Artists, 1934.
Nana. United Artists, 1934.
Bottoms Up. Fox, 1934.
Hold That Girl. Fox, 1934.
Bulldog Drummond Strikes Back. United Artists, 1934.
The Affairs of Cellini. United Artists, 1934.
Kid Millions. United Artists, 1934.
Broadway Bill. Columbia, 1934.
Jealousy. Columbia, 1934.
Men of the Night. Columbia, 1934.
The Fugitive Lady. Columbia, 1934.
Carnival. Columbia, 1935.
Roberta. RKO, 1935.
Old Man Rhythm. RKO, 1935.
Top Hat. RKO, 1935.
I Dream Too Much. RKO, 1935.
Chatterbox. RKO, 1936.
Follow the Fleet. RKO, 1936.
Bunker Bean. RKO, 1936.
That Girl from Paris. RKO, 1936.
Don't Tell the Wife. RKO, 1937.
Stage Door. RKO, 1937.
Joy of Living. RKO, 1938.
Go Chase Yourself. RKO, 1938.
Having Wonderful Time. RKO, 1938.
The Affairs of Annabel. RKO, 1938.
Room Service. RKO, 1938.
The Next Time I Marry. RKO, 1938.
Annabel Takes a Tour. RKO, 1938.
Beauty for the Asking. RKO, 1939.
Twelve Crowded Hours. RKO, 1939.
Panama Lady. RKO, 1939.
Five Came Back. RKO, 1939.
That's Right—You're Wrong. RKO, 1939.
The Marines Fly High. RKO, 1940.

You Can't Fool Your Wife. RKO, 1940.
Dance Girl Dance. RKO, 1940.
Too Many Girls. RKO, 1940.
A Girl, a Guy, and a Gob. RKO, 1941.
Look Who's Laughing. RKO, 1941.
Valley of the Sun. RKO, 1942.
The Big Street. RKO, 1942.
Seven Days' Leave. RKO, 1942.
DuBarry Was a Lady. MGM, 1943.
Best Foot Forward. MGM, 1943.
Thousands Cheer. MGM, 1943.
Meet the People. MGM, 1944.
Without Love. MGM, 1945.
Abbott and Costello in Hollywood. MGM, 1945.
Ziegfeld Follies. MGM, 1946.
The Dark Corner. Twentieth Century–Fox, 1946.
Lover Come Back. Universal, 1946.
Easy to Wed. MGM, 1946.
Two Smart People. MGM, 1946.
Lured. United Artists, 1947.
Her Husband's Affairs. Columbia, 1947.
Sorrowful Jones. Paramount, 1949.
Easy Living. RKO, 1949.
Miss Grant Takes Richmond. Columbia, 1949.
A Woman of Distinction. Columbia, 1950.
Fancy Pants. Paramount, 1950.
The Fuller Brush Girl. Columbia, 1950.
The Magic Carpet. Columbia, 1951.
The Long, Long Trailer. MGM, 1954.
Forever Darling. MGM, 1956.
The Facts of Life. United Artists, 1960.
Critic's Choice. Warner Brothers, 1963.
A Guide for the Married Man. Twentieth Century–Fox, 1967.
Yours, Mine and Ours. United Artists, 1968.
Mame. Warner Brothers, 1974.

INDEX

Berle, Milton, 253–54, 266, 289
    Lucille's dates with, 82
    as "Mr. Television," 167–68
Berlin, Irving, 67
Berman, Pandro S., 61, 64–66, 76,
        103
    and Lucille's career, 71, 73, 74, 75,
        273
    Lucille's relationship with, 65–66, 82
    move to MGM by, 99
    as producer, 64–65, 225
Bernie, Ben, 44
Bernstein, Leonard, 167
Berry, Ken, 252
Best Foot Forward, 140, 148
"B films," 85, 99, 107, 124
Big Street, The, 35, 126–28, 129, 135,
        161
Biow, Milton, 180
bit parts, 51, 52–53, 55–56, 58, 65–67
    and dialect, 61, 64
    and slapstick, 47, 71, 73
blacklists:
    and blue shirts, 216
    and persecution, 221
"Blackouts," 136
Blanton, Smiley, 245
Blazing Beulah from Butte, 169
Blood Money, 51
Blossom, Margaret, 32–33
Bluhdorn, Charles G., 300–1
Bogart, Humphrey, 217
Bolero, 52
Bolger, Ray, 121, 222
Bonanza, 287
Book, A (Arnaz), 333
Boors Nest, 164
Borge, Victor, 276
Born Yesterday, 167
Bottoms Up, 53
"Bouncing Back for More," 324
Bow, Clara, 38, 45
Bowery, The, 51
Bowman, Lee, 80, 159
Bracken, Connie, 103
Bracken, Eddie, 97, 98, 103, 106,
        109
Breakfast for Vanora, 68
"Breakup," 25–26
Brice, Fanny, 148, 160
Briggs, Don, 279
Briggs, Lillian Winograd, 325–26, 332, 337,
        338
Briggs Squad, 291

Broadway Bill, 58, 202
Broadway thru a Keyhole, 51
Brochu, Jim, 29, 340
Broderick, Helen, 82
Browar, Herb, 198, 202, 233
Bungle Abbey, 323
Bunker Bean, 70
Burke, Irene, 311
Burns, George, 83–84, 177, 233, 290
Burns, Mel, 72
Burton, Richard, 308–10, 314
Buzzell, Eddie, 150
Byington, Spring, 234

Cabot, Bruce, 173
Caesar, Sid, 178
Cagney, James, 125
Cahn, Dann, 205, 223, 225, 251
Calhoun, Rory, 289, 322
Calloway, Cab, 30
Campbell, Carol, 337, 338
Cantor, Eddie, 47, 141
    and *Kid Millions*, 54, 56
    and *Roman Scandals*, 43, 50, 51
Capers, 33
Capone, Al, 249–50
Capone, Sonny, 95, 251
Capra, Frank, 57, 58, 87
Carey, Ernestine Gilbreth, 173
Carlson, Richard, 103, 119, 145
Carnegie, Hattie, 27–28, 33, 34, 36–38
Carney, Art, 323
Carnival, 63
Carroll, Bob, Jr., 289, 308, 335
    and Desilu Productions, 174
    fired by Lucille, 287–88
    and *I Love Lucy*, 178, 180, 185, 195,
        199–201, 233
    and "My Favorite Husband," 159–61
    and rewrites, 287
    and spin-off shows, 279
Carroll, Earl, 26–27
Carroll, John, 261
Carroll, Lucille McDonald, 38
Carroll, Lucille Ryman, 151, 164, 169, 172
Carson, Jack, 111
Carson, Johnny, 178
Carter, Jack, 268, 286, 300
Carter, Janis, 146, 165
Catholic Legion of Decency, 46
CBS, 305, 309
    and Desilu, 250
    Desi's agreement with, 289
    and developed funds, 291

Morris, Chester, 88
Morton, Gary, 290, 317, 340
    audience warm-ups by, 279, 313
    background of, 268
    and Desilu, 295–96
    as executive producer, 331, 335–36
    final act at Copa of, 286
    golf center developed by, 286
    and live TV programming, 283
    Lucille protected by, 325
    Lucille's choice of, 295–96
    Lucille's treatment of, 313
    marriage to Lucille, 273
    mother of, 286–87
    relationship with Lucille, 268–69,
        270–71
    scripts read by, 328, 336
    and social life, 275–76, 324
    and top dollar, 296
    as vice president, 303, 313
Mothers-in-Law, The, 289, 302, 312
Motion Picture Center, 222, 229, 230, 233,
    246
Motion Picture Production Code, 46
Moulin Rouge, 52
movies:
    cinematographers for, 134–35
    cuff shooting for, 76–77, 79
    cutting corners in, 225–26
    with dialogue, 163
    earnings of, 140
    filming methods of, 50, 134, 322
    home, 138, 186
    innovations in, 123
    moving cameras for, 134
    and personality, 87
    salaries in, 112, 114, 150–51, 164
    screen tests for, 42, 107
    silent films, 45, 76, 84
    studio control in, 85, 169
    talkies, 60
    vs. television, 168, 225–26
    and true success, 224
Moviola, for editing, 193
Mr. and Mrs. Cugat (Rorick), 158
Mr. Pinkie, 122
Multicam, 181
Mulvey, Jim, 43
Murphy, George, 49, 56, 111, 137, 216,
    218
Murphy, Gerald, 331
Murphy, Sara, 331
Murray, Ken, 136
Murrow, Edward R., 221

"My Favorite Husband," 159–62, 168, 169,
    183, 200

Nana, 53
Nash, Kathy, 267
Nash, N. Richard, 262, 266
Navy Comes Through, The, 129
Nazimova, Alla, 100
NBC, 178, 331
Nelson, Argyle, 238, 282, 293
Nelson, Harriet Hilliard, 67, 159
Nelson, Ozzie, 128, 159, 234
Ness, Elliot, 250, 251
New Life Foundation, 339–40
Newman, Bernard, 63–64, 86, 239
Newman, Sym, 271
New York City:
    apartments in, 262–63, 329
    clothing industry in, 36
    drama school in, 22–24
    Lucille as homesick in, 23–24, 36–37, 38
    social life in, 39, 40–41, 42
    Wildcat in, 262–63, 265
New York Times, The, 86–88, 109
Next Time I Marry, The, 87, 202
Nichols, Anne, 73, 74
Nichols, Barbara, 250, 308
Nichols, Nichelle, 293
Nixon, Richard M., 306
Nolan, Dani Sue, 212
Normand, Mabel, 49, 84
Nugent, Frank, 86–87

Oakie, Jack, 87, 119
Ober, Phil, 190, 202, 250
O'Brien, Bob, 288, 294, 307
O'Brien, Edmond, 111, 112, 121
O'Brien, John P., 116
O'Brien, Virginia, 135, 139, 148, 153, 170
O'Connor, Donald, 340
O'Hara, Maureen, 99–100, 102, 110, 111,
    112
O'Hara, Scarlett, tests for role of, 81
Olivier, Laurence, 40
Onassis, Jacqueline Kennedy, 309
O'Neill, Arthur, 40–41
Oppenheimer, Jess, 160, 174
    as father figure, 195
    and *I Love Lucy,* 178, 180, 182, 184–85,
        195, 206, 233
    and Lucille's pregnancy, 209, 210, 213
    and Lucy character, 279, 311
Order of the Sons of Italy, 251
Orloff, Thelma, 324, 339